Julie Fielder's father worked on the door at West Runton Pavilion during the 1970s, and before she was 13, Julie had watched several popular bands from the small private balcony at the back of the hall. She met some of the stars and developed a life-long love of music. Nowadays, discussions with other local music fans often turn to the glory days of West Runton Pavilion and another popular venue, the Royal Links Pavilion, Cromer. A desire to record the memories and uncover the facts led Julie to embark on a period of extensive research. This book is the result. As one of her contacts observed: 'It's about time somebody did it!'

This book is dedicated to the thousands of music fans who went to either venue over the years, to the hundreds of artists who provided the entertainment, and to the owners and staff who made it all possible.

WHAT FLO SAID

*The Story of West Runton Pavilion
and The Royal Links Pavilion, Cromer*

JULIE FIELDER

BOOKS

Edition Books
PO Box 500, Happisburgh
Norwich
Norfolk
NR12 0WX

www.edition-mag.co.uk

Published in Great Britain

A catalogue record for this book is
available from the British Library

ISBN-13 978-0-9554129-0-5
ISBN-10 0-9554129-0-0

Set in Bembo by
Edition Design
Happisburgh, Norfolk

Printed in Great Britain by
Biddles Ltd

Contents

Acknowledgements

Special thanks to:

My husband, Steven, for his patience, encouragement and understanding.
Our sons Jake, Bruce and Freddie – may they be inspired to follow their dreams.
My parents Jean and John Mason.
Maureen and Martin Chapman – special friends.

Thanks are also due to:

Frank Boswall, Rod and Margaret Blow, and Nigel Hindley, without whose support this would not have been contemplated.

Terry Bunting for his knowledge and advice.
Elaine and Neil Morrell for proof reading.
Steve Bullimore at The Lighthouse Inn in Walcott.
Phil Stewart at Edition Books.

Keiron Pim at the *Eastern Daily Press* in Norwich.
Richard Batson and staff at the *North Norfolk News* in Cromer.
Rosemary Dixon at Archant Archives.
North Norfolk Radio and Radio Norfolk.

Everyone who has submitted articles, reviews, photos, press cuttings and memories, or has taken the time and trouble to contact me.

Lynn at RBM Concerts for her help (www.raymond-froggatt.com)

Raymond Froggatt, together with Hartley Cain, his guitarist, appeared at both venues more times than any other touring band – a total of 40 times between 1969 and 1979. 'Froggie' still mentions the venues with fondness when he plays in Norfolk. It is fitting, therefore, that he should introduce this book and I would like to thank him for allowing me to use his eloquent contribution in this way.

Foreword

After 40 years in the music industry, it's bound to be difficult for me to single out certain days.

If God were to grant me one week of my life that I could re-live, at the end of my time on earth, two days would be re-lived in Norfolk: one day at Cromer Links and the other at West Runton Pavilion. Two venues, I am sure, which appear on God's own personal rock and roll map.

Our band was young then and the East Anglian people we found there were the first people we had known outside of our own area. My young band and me found a love there that remains to this day: a perfect memory of wonderful times.

Our generation was as young as new grass then, and music was our mutual dream of hope and future. Cromer Links and West Runton Pavilion were perfect springboards for us all to grow from.

We all grew, and our band travelled all over the world. My guitar player and me are still living that dream. We paused a few times in Cromer and West Runton. Still we carry the cheers and care of the young people we shared our youth with. Their voices ring in our ears to this day.

Those rooms are silent now, but the walls of time hold the sounds of a generation who now have children of their own. We are proud to have been part of two venues where young people met, listened to music, fell in love, and grew into gold.

My beloved Norfolk, find the joy you gave to me.

Raymond Froggatt

Raymond Froggatt
December 2005, Telford

Preface

During the course of my research for this book I have contacted over 200 people from all corners of Norfolk and other parts of the UK, from Denmark, the United States and even Australia. I have listened to demo recordings by local bands, old vinyl albums of long-forgotten stars, and bootleg cassettes of top groups recorded in handbags. I have driven nearly 2,000 miles, made countless phone calls, sent hundreds of e-mails, looked at scores of photos, studied numerous old newspapers, spent many hours on the internet, and done not a lot of hoovering!

I wouldn't have had it any other way.

This book has been a journey and I would like to thank everyone who has accompanied me on it. It would have been a very short trip without you.

Wherever possible, I have endeavoured to verify information given to me with a second independent source. Where this has proved difficult, articles have been included as submitted by the contributors, in good faith, and I apologise for any inaccuracies therein. No items have been included with the intention of causing embarrassment or upset and if this has occurred I am deeply sorry.

I have attempted to obtain permission to use all stories and photographs in the book and acknowledgements are included wherever possible. I apologise for any omissions or errors, which should be notified to the publisher and will be corrected on any subsequent print runs.

I have tried to contact everyone I have been told about to get their stories, and to include all of them in the book, wherever possible. Inevitably, there are people I have been unable to speak to before the book went to print and I am sorry if they are disappointed.

The views expressed in the book are not necessarily my own.

If you have stories to tell about the venues, you can post them on my website: www.whatflosaid.co.uk

Julie Fielder

July 2006, Wood Dalling, Norfolk

1

From Kings To Campers

In 1888, at the top of the hill overlooking Cromer and the sea, the grandest hotel in North Norfolk was built. The five-storey Royal Links Hotel boasted 150 bedrooms and stood in its own magnificent seven-acre grounds. Legend has it that a 'coach-and-four' could be driven through its enormous front doors, should the need ever arise. History does not record whether this claim was ever proven. However, there would have been no shortage of stage-coaches calling, bringing local and national dignitaries to stay at this fine hotel, since Cromer was traditionally the exclusive coastal resort for many of the country's leading figures during the summer, and the Royal Links was the hotel of choice.

Several members of the Royal family stayed there over the years including, in the early days, Queen Victoria, and later her great-grandson George VI. Winston Churchill was another guest, and Sir Arthur Conan Doyle is said to have found inspiration for his famous work *The Hound of the Baskervilles* whilst staying at the Royal Links Hotel during a golfing holiday. It appears that one evening a friend of his told him the tale of the huge, menacing phantom dog 'Black Shuck', who was rumoured to prowl along the nearby coastal paths. However, Sir Arthur chose to set his next mystery on the misty Devon moors rather than in the jolly seaside town where he had first heard of the hound from hell.

In 1926 a ballroom for the hotel was built at the foot of the hill. At the time, the hotel was owned by a German, who designed the dance hall himself in the architectural style of a Rhine schloss, meaning a type of castle. It was a timber-framed building made with massive wooden trusses and, although it did not look much from the outside, inside it had elegant balconies and a fully sprung maple floor.

During the 1920s and 1930s the building was used for dining and dancing typical of the period. It was very exclusive and expensive. It is said that it would have taken an ordinary Cromer resident over six months to save enough to be able to afford to attend one of the public social evenings held in the dance hall. These constraints would not have applied to the likes of George VI and Winston Churchill, who frequented the establishment whilst staying at the hotel. In 1947 the interior of the dance hall was painted with seven murals depicting Arabian and Venetian scenes.

The hotel was used as a barracks during the Second World War and, after the Army moved out, the building was completely renovated. One evening in late January 1949 there was a celebration for the completion of the work. At around 11.00pm a fire started; it is thought in a room full of paint tins which had been used by the workmen. A local weekly newspaper, the *North Norfolk News*, reported on 2 February 1949 that 9 fire brigades and around 50 men worked for over 12 hours to get the blaze under control. The report declared, 'This was the biggest fire at Cromer within living memory.' The hotel was left in ruins, with only the outer shell remaining.

The hotel was never rebuilt and, after a time, the grounds were adapted as a caravan site. A bungalow was built on the site of the old hotel using some of the original foundations and remaining walls, which were solid and about two feet thick. The licence was transferred to the dance hall which became known as the Royal Links Pavilion. Mr Alfred James Letch was licensee for a short time, then in 1950 Leonard George Goldsmith was recorded as the owner and licensee.

Mr Goldsmith and his wife built up the caravan site and hosted dances in the Pavilion for the holiday-makers throughout the 1950s. One of the bands which played during one or two summer seasons was the AJ Band led by Arthur Jones. In addition to Arthur on drums, the band consisted of Alan French (piano accordion/ tenor sax), Fred (vocals), Ray Gee (double bass), Derek Page (acoustic guitar) and Ollie Scott (piano). The music was all ballroom – quicksteps, waltzes and foxtrots – and included popular numbers such as 'Sin to Tell a Lie' and 'What'll I Do?' Alan French recalls that the dances finished at about 11.45pm and, as he lived just outside Norwich, he would usually get stopped by the police in Aylsham at about one in the morning on his way home.

Co-incidentally, also during the 1950s, another Derek Page – nick-named 'Vic' – played in a band at the Links Pavilion. He was a piano player in the Paul Chris Band and also played with Gerald Amis, a band-leader from Cromer. This second Derek Page explains that he had been in the RAF based at Swanton Morley, near Dereham, and always seemed to have the weekends off, so he was able to go and play at the Links on a Saturday evening. He says that, at the time, Mrs Goldsmith also owned the East Cliff Hotel in Cromer, as well as running the Pavilion and caravan site with her daughter. When the Goldsmiths went away for two or three months, Derek's wife was asked to look after the East Cliff Hotel and take the bookings. This proved to be very convenient for Derek as he could play in the band at the Pavilion and then go home to the East Cliff, instead of making the long trek back to Swanton Morley.

The Pavilion changed hands around 1959 with Mr and Mrs Ernest Fred Carter, of EF Carter and Co of Maidstone, becoming licensees. In 1962 they sold the business to John Fletcher Dodd from Great Yarmouth and, a short while later, Mr Dodd sold it to three brothers named Farmer from Birmingham, who traded as a limited company. The owner and licensee in 1963 is recorded as one Alfred John Farmer.

In June 1964 it was announced in the *North Norfolk News* that 'one of East Anglia's most picturesque caravan sites, the Royal Links at Cromer' had been bought by Mr Edward Burt Stanley Blow, who had formerly managed the Runton Mill site. The Cromer site covered seven acres, comprising the grounds of the old Links hotel, and could accommodate 96 vans. Mr Blow's son Nigel, now known as Nigel Hindley, remembers:

The caravan site itself was a big business but the people who had been running it had got it into a mess. Father was an accountant but he wanted a caravan site, and with his accountant's eye he could see the potential, so he bought it.

The deal included the Royal Links Pavilion, which had also seen better days and was virtually boarded up. Nigel, together with his younger brother Rod, went to Cromer to work for their father, and Nigel remembers the family talking about what to do next. They said, 'The Pavilion's sitting there, what are we going to do with it?'

Their decision would change the lives of thousands of Norfolk teenagers forever.

2

Dance Band Days

Almost thirty years earlier, a few miles along the coast at West Runton, another pavilion was beginning life as the North Norfolk Sports Club, owned by Mr Harold Abbs. Speaking to the *North Norfolk News* in February 1987 Mrs Esme Mills, who used to live nearby, said, 'I remember being down there not long before the War started and the police came along and said there was no blackout and therefore it would have to close even though war hadn't been declared.' This early sports pavilion is said to have had a shooting gallery, and tennis courts marked out on the floor.

The Village Inn, which joined the sports pavilion, was built originally as a coach house for Runton House, and had become a public house in 1927. During the War, the pavilion began hosting dances and the venue became known as the North Norfolk Pavilion, West Runton. Harry and Doris Short ran the Village Inn and the Pavilion from about 1943. Their son, Brian Short, recalls that the music in the early days of the dance hall was provided by a collection of military bands:

These were greatly enjoyed by the troops: the Welsh regiments from Runton, the Scots from nearby Beeston, and the Air Force units from all over Norfolk (including Douglas Bader's lot from Coltishall). The first celebrity big band was Henry Hall and his Palm Court Orchestra in 1947. They were listened to every Sunday night on the radio.

Brian adds, 'We boys used to play Pooh sticks – floating objects in the stream which ran under the Pavilion!'

The North Norfolk Pavilion at West Runton was the first dance hall in the country to operate a free coach service to and from the dances, starting in 1947 with a single coach from Wells. This was later extended to include other towns and villages such as Fakenham, North Walsham and Holt. It was an important and valued service to dancers living in a rural area with little public transport or, in many cases, no access to a car.

Gwen and Jim Rickets managed the Pavilion and Village Inn when Mr and Mrs Short left, until about 1953. They continued to book the London bands including Joe Loss, Ted Heath and Edmundo Ros. Norman Potter, Gwen's brother, lived with his parents on the Kelling hospital estate in the house nearest to the present

5

railway station. At the time there was a railway bridge and Norman remembers that cars returning towards Holt after a night at the Pavilion would often forget to turn left and go straight into the side of the bridge instead!

Local man Jim Baldwin went on holiday with his parents to West Runton a couple of times in the late 1940s or early 1950s. They stayed with a Mrs or Miss Porter who was a friend of his aunt. Although not related, Jim was told to call her Granny Porter:

I remember that Granny Porter went ballroom dancing at the Pavilion and was quite well known for her expertise in this graceful hobby. She continued her dancing at the Pavilion when she was into her 80s and I think that she only stopped when the ballroom dancing stopped.

Bill Jervis recalls that his late wife, Nancy, lived opposite the Village Inn in the house behind the newsagents. She had described to him how, when she was a young girl, she would sit in their upper sitting room and peer out of the window, to watch older girls arrive and walk past the pub entrance to the dance hall entrance round the side at the back of the Village Inn. Some would be dressed in evening dresses. Bill observes, 'Romance and glamour, Hollywood sunsets etc were all the rage then and Nancy could not wait to be part of the scene.' Territorials on their annual visits caused some annoyance and fighting after the War, but apart from that Nancy could recall no trouble.

Many soldiers and airmen from away met local girls at West Runton and married them, and Bill Jervis was one of them.

1952 was the year I first visited the Pavilion. RAF personnel from RAF West Beckham were very much in evidence then in the pub too, where there was a very long bar in those days. A special camp bus would ferry us back to West Beckham after the Saturday night dances. Coming back from leave in Lancaster just after Christmas, 1952, I missed the last bus from Sheringham Railway Station to RAF West Beckham but managed to catch the last one going in the opposite direction.

I alighted at West Runton and went into the Pavilion, knowing I'd be able to get a lift from there. I had a dance and I saw a beautiful girl standing on one side of the ballroom. I asked her to dance, arranged to meet her again and, back at camp, told my room-mate that I had just met the girl I was going to marry. Nancy and I were engaged six weeks later. We married in West Runton Church on 1 September 1954 and the reception was held in the Pavilion.

When the War ended, a demobilisation camp was set up at Weybourne and soldiers from there used to visit the Pavilion dances. Laurie Kendall's father was demobbed from the forces at Weybourne and they settled in the area. Laurie recalls that the dances at Runton were 'the place to go on a Saturday night.' He and his friends would get a bus from Sheringham but would often walk back on summer evenings. He remembers seeing the resident six-piece band as well as Sid Phillips, and Harry Gold with his Pieces of Eight.

Local man Joe Tuck was a drummer and founded the Al Collins Band. He heard Muriel Ward sing one night and asked her to join him. They played for the troops at Stiffkey, then, after a few months, they had a trial booking at the Pavilion. They were appointed as the resident band and continued there for almost 30 years. Muriel sang with the band for five years under her stage name 'Carole', which Joe had chosen for her because he thought it was a nice name.

In an interview with the *North Norfolk News* in February 1987, Joe said of the time:

The atmosphere was absolutely first-class. If I saw somebody smoking on the dance floor I would stop the music and ask them to stop ... the owner wouldn't tolerate any misbehaviour. There was never any serious trouble.

Harold Abbs, who owned the Pavilion, took over the running of it in 1953. A poster, which has been kept by Muriel Ward, announced that the first special Saturday dance was to commence at the North Norfolk Pavilion, West Runton, on Saturday 20 June at 8.00pm. There was to be non-stop dancing, jive sessions and competitions featuring Frankie Dey with his Rhythmic Rhythm on the Hammond Organ, and Al Collins and the Pavilion Orchestra with Carole. Admission was three shillings and sixpence, and late buses had been arranged to Cromer, Sheringham and Holt.

Jean Towers went to Runton around this time. She would go on the local bus from Sheringham and get the West Runton Pavilion coach back, every Saturday. She says:

It was usually two shillings and sixpence but increased to three shillings and sixpence when there was a big name on the bill. We would have to queue to get in and it was always packed. The Army came from Weybourne and there were many nationalities from elsewhere: the Dutch from Langham, and Australians, Americans and Canadians would be there too.

Jean remembers seeing the Billy Duncan Band, and also Ken Mackintosh and Oscar Rayburn.

By March 1954 the venue had taken on its more familiar title of 'West Runton Pavilion'. Another of Muriel Ward's posters advertised the appearance of 'Europe's greatest girl trumpet star Gracie Cole with her All Star Girls Orchestra featuring Margaret Mason, Mary Lou, Dorothy Burgess and male singing star Dennis Peters.'

The Pavilion Orchestra was also there with Carole, ensuring dancing from 8.00pm to midnight. Admission was now five shillings at the door and an additional coach had been organised to leave Fakenham Post Office calling at Melton Constable, Briston and Holt.

In May 1954 the admission price had increased to six shillings and Britain's radio and recording stars Norman Burns and his Band, with Kerri Simms and Johnny Green, were to play. The evening also featured the Nearing Shearing Quintet and, of course, the Pavilion Orchestra with Carole.

On Whit Monday there was a Carnival Dance until 1.00am when the guest was Chick Mayes, trumpet star from Nat Temple's Band. A buffet was provided and the MC was John Stockdale.

'Music for dancing, for listening, for pleasure' was promised in July 1954 with an appearance by top London band the Ronnie Scott Orchestra, featuring Patti Lane, Art Baxter, Lennie Bush, Tony Crombie, Jimmie Deuchar, Victor Feldman, Bennie Green, Derek Humble, Pete King, Ken Wray and the Victor Feldman Trio. Later that month 'Johnnie Gray and his Band of the Day with Irene Miller' appeared. A bus service was now running from North Walsham, calling at Trunch, Mundesley, Trimingham and Overstrand.

Local man Stanley Jennings was a talented pianist who played with the Al Collins Band from about 1954. He had learnt classical music, then turned to jazz. His widow, Doreen, says, 'He had the world at his fingertips and could play any tune you asked him to.' In later years, Stanley played with the Trevor Copeman Band and made solo appearances in prestigious hotels and high class establishments such as the Savoy in Norwich. Previously, Stanley had had his own trio in Kings Lynn. He played with Irish singer Ruby Murray and with the Dankworth Seven.

Johnny Dankworth had formed the Dankworth Seven in 1950 as a vehicle for his writing activities and a showcase for several young jazz soloists. In 1953 he formed the Dankworth Big Band. Cleo Laine joined and they toured dance halls throughout England, marrying a few years later.

Sheila Gaskins (was Attoe) saw Cleo Laine and Johnny Dankworth at West Runton Pavilion. Sheila lived in Briston and when she started work, aged 15, she sometimes walked to the Vicarage Corner in Briston to catch the bus to West Runton Pavilion. She says she didn't go often, however, because her parents weren't keen and she wasn't much of a dancer!

The resident six-piece Pavilion Orchestra was regularly joined by guest artists from Cyril Stapleton's BBC Show Band. The Show Band would be broadcast on the radio on Saturday mornings, then members of the band would travel up to Norfolk to appear at the Pavilion on the Saturday evening.

Gerry Bircham remembers:

I used go to West Runton Sports Club on a Saturday night regular, when I got out of the

Air Force. They used to send down Bill McGuffie, the pianist, and Stan Roderick, from the Show Band in London. They used to join the local band there and it was terrific, very exciting. All the boys used to go on their motorbikes and there was never no trouble like you get nowadays. If you were lucky, you would take a girl on the back of your motorbike with you! The popular drink then was Red Barrel.

There was one of these special appearances by Bill McGuffie in July 1954, when he was billed as 'Britain's number one pianist'. Top trumpet star Stan Roderick and George Chisholm, leading trombonist, were also there. Resident singer, Muriel Ward, recalls that George Chisholm was in the habit of leaving his trombone on his seat and on one occasion she accidentally sat on it! Fortunately, it was undamaged and the show continued.

On Friday 27 August 1954 the *Norfolk Chronicle* contained the headline, 'One man draws the largest crowds to West Runton.' The piece continued:

An unassuming and modest man, Mr McGuffie says he enjoys playing away from London for a change and that he likes West Runton very much. Born in Glasgow, he is aged 26 and has been playing the piano for 20 years.

This fantastic pianist has a finger missing on his right hand. It appears that in his young days he was playing Cowboys and Indians with his brother and got the finger trapped in a door and had to have it amputated. When hearing him play, however, one would imagine he had twenty fingers rather than one missing.

With Bill McGuffie at the Pavilion last Saturday were Stan Roderick, lead trumpet player with the BBC Show Band and Derek Collins, the saxophone and clarinet stylist, who has often been featured in broadcasts with Frank Baron and his Sextet. These three joined Joe Tuck (drummer) and Leslie Smith (bass) of the resident orchestra and delighted the large attendance with their renderings.

Bill McGuffie's brilliant piano technique was a highlight of the evening, and for most of the time he was playing, a group of admirers were clustered round the piano watching his extraordinarily nimble fingers flying up and down the keyboard as he extemporised in fine fashion. The expert trumpet-playing of Stan Roderick was evidently much appreciated, while no less adept on both saxophone and clarinet was Derek Collins.

What do the local musicians feel at playing with these stars? 'It is a highly exciting experience,' said Joe Tuck yesterday, 'and we feel it a great privilege to play with such fine musicians.'

Muriel Ward recalls that Bill McGuffie's favourite song was 'It's Just a Little Street Where Old Friends Meet' but, unfortunately, it wasn't very well known. She says Bill was so pleased when he found out Muriel could sing it that he gave her a signed photograph on which he wrote, 'Nice to have worked with you and thanks again for knowing "It's Just a Little Street".'

Other songs Muriel sang included 'Sunny Side of the Street', 'That Old Feeling', 'You'll Never Know' and 'You Made Me Love You.' She worked most Wednesdays and Saturdays and says the most she earned in an evening was £12!

Also in August 1954 Reggie Goff appeared with his Sextet, which included Pete Harris, George Harrington, Jack Penn, Chiz Bishop and Ronnie Fallon. Reggie Goff was billed as, 'Your favourite deep-voiced singer, star of radio and records.' Later that month Freddie Randall came to West Runton Pavilion with his All Stars. A bus service was now available from Wells, calling at Stiffkey, Blakeney and Cley.

Bill McGuffie returned in September, as did Norman Burns, featuring the Nearing Shearing Band – which had now reduced to a quartet – with David Francis and Kerri Simms. On Friday 17 September the Royal Air Forces Association held a dance with the Pavilion Augmented Dance Orchestra, and at the end of the month the venue welcomed Johnny Hawkins and his band.

Attractions during October included the Orchette Royale from Nottingham and Johnnie Holton from the Lyceum Theatre, London, with his Hammond Organ.

On Friday 5 November a Guy Fawkes Old Time Ball was held featuring Bert Galey and his Orchestra hosted by David and Eileen Jacobs, costing four shillings and sixpence.

The Christmas Eve dance that year saw the Pavilion Augmented Dance Orchestra providing the entertainment with Jackie Garde on the trumpet and saxophonist Stan Coleman. A special dance was held on Monday 27 December featuring Al Collins and his Dance Band, with Neville Turner and his Hammond Organ. On Friday 31 December revellers were encouraged to 'Greet the new year in with a dance and a smile,' enjoying balloons and prizes with the Pavilion Melody Makers under the direction of Joe Tuck, all for five shillings. A new bus was organised from Aylsham Market Place, stopping at Blickling Hall, Itteringham and Matlaske.

The dances continued throughout the 1950s. The usual attendance, particularly during the summer for dancing to the resident Pavilion Orchestra, was around 300 but rose as high as 700 for a special night with well-known musicians.

Bill Blackiston recalls how West Runton Pavilion holds very special memories for him:

I was a regular soldier. Periodically I came to Weybourne AA Camp to train regular and TA units to fire 3.7 inch AA guns. In April 1957 I went to a Saturday dance at West Runton. During the evening another officer and I split up two girls dancing – my choice later became my wife in 1959. We went several times to the 'hops' and saw many famous bands – Ivy Benson, Carl Bainton, Joe Loss, and I suspect there were others, but my memory is not so good! Anne always remembered how we met – she and her sister sharing a 'gin and Italian' together and then meeting me! Unhappily, she died five years ago, but we had many years of a great marriage.

Ivy Benson led a renowned all-girl band for over 40 years and Joe Loss played the violin with various dance orchestras before forming his own, which catered to the dancing public by playing whatever music was popular at the time.

Gerald Clarke went to the Pavilion at around the same time as Bill Blackiston and remembers:

There would be a regular seven- or eight-piece band on a Saturday night and the place would be packed. The car park would be overflowing with cars and coaches. Occasionally they would still get big star names.

Unfortunately, Gerald found it too expensive to go to Victor Sylvester but he saw Ted Heath a couple of times and Sid Phillips. He remembers the barmen wore black waistcoats and black ties. The public had to be smartly dressed too, or they wouldn't be allowed in. Ties were kept near the entrance and loaned for the evening to any man who arrived at the dance without one.

Ray Spinks says he got to know West Runton Pavilion in his teens after moving to Aldborough.

The small coastal village of West Runton became the place to go on a Saturday night. That was in the days when the resident band was Al Collins and the cost of admission was half a crown, or 12½ pence in today's currency. However, when a nationally known band appeared this went up to seven shillings and sixpence, or 37 pence. These occasions were rare, however, and the only two I remember were the appearances of Victor Sylvester and his ballroom orchestra and Sid Phillips with his band.

In those days there was much competition for dance partners, with large numbers of service personnel attending from the many bases in the area such as RAF Trimingham and West Beckham, together with the Army from Weybourne and Stiffkey Camp, not to mention the Americans from USAF Sculthorpe. Sometimes this competition led to heated exchanges between the local lads and the servicemen. The Military Police were often in attendance to help sort things out, but there would be just two members of the Norfolk Constabulary on duty at turning-out time.

In March 1958 a 'Dance Diesel' train was organised from Norwich to take people to see the Sid Phillips Band at West Runton Pavilion. It left Thorpe Station at 7.35pm, calling at Wroxham and North Walsham. It took half an hour and had room for 300 people. Recordings of Sid Phillips' music were played during the journey. Buses met the return train at Norwich at 12.39am. The total cost for the dance and train trip was seven shillings and sixpence.

Carole Savage used to attend the ballroom dances doing the cha cha, rock and roll and the stomp. She remembers they used to catch the bus from North Walsham to the Pavilion each Saturday and the boys came from the surrounding RAF camps and towns. Her first courting was done in the coaches as the drivers used to leave them unlocked! She says:

The local boys didn't tend to go ballroom dancing so lots of the girls married RAF chaps and left the area. My friend Christine Wiseman (now Locke) used to be travel-sick. We often had to clean her up – and the bus – before we went into the dance. She would spend the whole night smelling of sick but she still managed to meet her future husband there!

Carole recalls there was a mirror ball in the centre of the Pavilion ceiling and the building itself reminded her of 'a big old barn'. She says the favoured drink was John Collins, which was a long drink made with bitter lemon and gin.

Ashley Purdy occasionally went to West Runton Pavilion in the late 1950s–early 1960s to see jazz bands. He would catch a mini-bus from Cawston, which went through Reepham and possibly Aylsham. He remembers seeing Terry Lightfoot's Jazzmen with Kenny Ball on the trumpet in 1958, which would have been just before Kenny formed his own band, Kenny Ball's Jazzmen. That band went on to have great worldwide success with many hits including 'Midnight in Moscow' and 'When I'm Sixty-Four' during the heyday of the traditional jazz boom of the 1960s. Terry Lightfoot was a clarinet and saxophone player, as well as a vocalist.

Also in 1958, at West Runton Pavilion, Ashley saw Mick Mulligan's Jazz Band featuring George Melly, a jazz and blues singer. Ashley describes George Melly at the time as being 'pencil slim dressed all in black'. In 1960 he saw Bob Wallis' Storyville Jazzmen.

Mike Redway, a popular singer of the time, sometimes guested with the resident band. Mike remembers on one occasion he had driven up from London to appear at West Runton, and as he arrived he received a message to go to his wife at Leeds where she was with his new-born son! Needless to say, he did not appear on stage that evening. Mike has enjoyed success as a solo performer and as part of the Mike Sammes Singers. He appeared on many recordings by other famous artists including the Beatles. Amongst his solo recordings was the 1973 hit 'Good Morning'.

In August 1962 the local newspaper advertised that West Runton Pavilion had 'car parking for 400 cars' and a 'large new maple dance floor'. One of the regular dancers, Mrs Fox, remembers what she called the 'marvellous sprung floor' which was renowned for miles around. She saw Duke Ellington there.

Also in the advert, the Pavilion was said to have 'ample sitting-out space' and an 'eleven-piece resident dance orchestra first formed 15 years ago'. The musical policy of 'dance-music, first and foremost' was said to be supported by featuring 'during each session a band within the band which plays current popular Dixieland and traditional numbers in first class manner.'

At this time Danny Barwood was the manager of the dance hall and host of the adjoining Village Inn public house. Later in the sixties Marie Brindle and her husband ran the Village Inn for about eight years until Harold Abbs, the proprietor, died.

Marie remembers that they served food and snacks in the Village Inn, but there were also two bars and a buffet in the Pavilion. On one occasion, when Acker Bilk was appearing at the Pavilion with his Paramount Jazz Band, he arrived a bit early for the show. Marie says:

He came into the bar first and wanted something to eat. I went into the kitchen and got cheese, butter and fresh bread which we'd bought from the local bakery that morning. He scoffed the lot and said it was the best meal he'd ever had!

She describes Acker Bilk as 'a delightful man' and had an LP of his which he signed for her. Like Bill McGuffie, Acker Bilk had attained musical success despite what nowadays might be described as being 'digitally challenged', because he had lost half a finger in a sledging accident. The loss of two front teeth in a fight at school was, similarly, no deterrent, and he was a popular and accomplished clarinet player. He had topped the charts on both sides of the Atlantic with his 1961 recording 'Stranger on the Shore', which was the theme to a BBC children's television series of the same name.

However, as the decade wore on, the charts were becoming more dominated by pop music, which would be reflected later in the changing entertainment offered at West Runton Pavilion. Unfortunately for its fans, the days of the dance band were numbered, and one enterprising Norfolk family was about to catch on.

3

Top Pop Stars

Back at their kitchen table in Cromer, the Blow family were discussing their new acquisition. Nigel says:

We sat round the table and said, 'What are we going to do with the Pavilion?' It hadn't been part of Father's business plan and the people he bought it from had pretty much got the shutters up at the windows. I said, 'Well it's a ballroom, we must run dances.'

It was agreed that the Royal Links Pavilion would not be run exclusively for the caravan site but would host regular dances and other functions open to the public. Nigel recalls, 'Father always said he could remember dancing there back in the 1930s, never dreaming at that time that he would end up owning it one day.' In the *North Norfolk News* of June 1964, Mr Blow was reported as saying he had 'a very real interest in it.'

Nigel continues:

We didn't know anything about running dances so we had to find out. We just dived in at the deep end. We had led fairly sheltered lives, though, and we were very anxious not to get into a situation we couldn't control. That first summer old Alfie Howard used to come up, the Cromer town crier, and he used to help MC the nights. We'd have the knobbly knee competitions, and the breweries used to give all of these promotional things: key rings, glasses, clocks and all that sort of thing, but they were dead strict tempo dances, ' steam bands' as we used to call them. Once a night on a Wednesday.

Then on the Saturday night, in that first year, we would have a steam band and a pop group, and they'd do an hour apiece. The idea being, quite wrongly because it failed, that we would keep everybody happy. In fact we kept nobody happy because the youngsters didn't want to dance to the steam band and the older generation wouldn't come in because of the noise of the pop group. It was chalk and cheese. They stood each side of the dance floor eyeing each other up. We fell between two stools.

A leaflet of the time for the Royal Links Caravan Park gave full details of the venue:

The famous Royal Links Pavilion Ballroom with maple sprung floor. Rock, rhythm and blues dances; modern ballroom dances. Intimate lounge bar. Free House. Venue of the annual Cromer Lifeboat Dance and the annual Cromer Carnival Dance. The Pavilion presents an ideal opportunity of meeting and making friends.

The Ronnie Mack Quartet featured heavily in the line-up that summer as the resident steam band, and the pop groups appearing with them included local favourites the Highwaymen, who played popular chart songs of the time which was predominantly rock and roll. The early line-up was Alan Cannell (lead guitar), Bobby Secker – who later joined another local band, Memphis Index – on bass guitar, Graham Fulcher (vocals/rhythm guitar) and Hilson Hatley on drums. They won first prize of £50 in a Beat Contest. By January 1965, Graham Fulcher had left and Keith Artis had joined as singer, with Tony Powell, who would later join East Coast Rock, on rhythm guitar. The Highwaymen (or Ye Highwaymen as they were sometimes known) supported many famous stars over the years including Gene Vincent, Van Morrison, Heinz and John Leyton. They recorded a single and later on played at the famous Two Eyes Club in Soho, London.

Another local band, the Planets, played a few dates at Cromer Links in the summer of 1964. In about 1958, Tony Wright ('Beano') – later to feature in Berry and the Treetops – had started drumming at Roger Reynolds' house in Briston with a band they named the Wildcats. John Jarvis, who would later sing with Iron Tonic and its various incarnations, joined around 1960 as singer. Then, in about 1962, part of the Vikings from Aylsham joined with part of the Wildcats to form Barry Lee and the Planets. This new band consisted of Michael Dyball (rhythm guitar), Tony Dyball (lead guitar), Roger Reynolds (bass guitar), Barry Lee (vocals) and Angus Jarvis (drums).

The *North Norfolk News* of Friday 6 November 1964 reported that the band had written thirty of their own numbers, including 'So Much in Love', which they were hoping would gain them a recording contract. Two months later, the same paper announced that the Planets had signed a seven-year recording contract with the Capable Management Agency, which also handled the Rockin' Berries, a band who would soon provide the breakthrough for the Links.

The Planets were managed by Hilary Mitchell, an 18 year old from High Kelling, who worked at the Cromer office of Eastern Counties Newspapers Ltd. The report continued, 'Barry explained that their ambition is to reach the number one spot in the charts despite the observation made by Angus that his ambition was to become a millionaire.'

Angus recalls that they played a few dates at the Links, then went professional playing clubs up north. Simon Williams has kept a publicity photograph signed by Roger Reynolds captioned 'Barry Lee and the Planets – One of the Country's Top Entertaining Acts.' Under the words 'the Planets' Roger Reynolds has written

'… were nearly stars!' In 1965 they won a Beat Competition, organised by local newspaper the *Eastern Daily Press*, with prize money of £150. On this occasion, Ye Highwaymen came second, and Ricky Lee and the Hucklebucks were third. When they started to concentrate on the cabaret side of their act, the Planets changed their name to the Barry Lee Show and would, during the mid-1970s, make many television appearances as comedy/impression act the Brother Lees.

During a quiet autumn at the Links, the Blows reached a decision. Nigel recalls, 'It was 1964 and we thought, well, the future has got to be pop so we'll go pop, so that's what we did. We quickly realised the way forward was the pop bands.'

Amongst the first bands to appear at Cromer Links under the new format were Paul Raven and the Pack (later to find fame, or should that be infamy, under the name of Gary Glitter), Gene Vincent's backing group the Dyaks, and the Herd – just prior to recruiting singer/guitarist Peter Frampton to their line-up. The Symbols appeared on the television show *Ready Steady Go* singing 'One Fine Girl' the day after they came to the Links and prior to embarking on a tour of the United States with another popular group, the Animals. The brewery promotions continued on Wednesdays during the summer of 1965 and the annual Cromer Carnival Dance was held at the Links.

The Rockin' Berries were performing at Great Yarmouth during the summer season and were big stars at the time. They had formed in the late 1950s in Birmingham, and chose the name because they played a lot of Chuck Berry songs. They had released a single 'He's in Town' in November 1964 which had reached number three in the UK charts, and their follow-up 'Poor Man's Son' had entered the top 10 in May 1965. The line-up was Brian 'Chuck' Botfield (lead guitar), Geoff Turton (vocals/guitar), Clive Lea (lead vocals) and Terry Bond (drums). Bass-player Ray Austin was replaced mid-1965 by Bobby Thompson. Clive Lea was also an impressionist, which led to the band's popularity as a cabaret act.

Nigel explains how his brother Rod got them involved:

The Rockin' Berries came up to do a stint at Cromer Carnival; they were going to crown the Carnival Queen and all that sort of thing. Rod got talking to them and we did a deal, to book them for the end of the summer season. So they were going to finish the summer season at Yarmouth and then come and do a night for us. I have to admit, I was anxious because this was a very expensive act compared with what we had been paying out. So I was anxious that we weren't going to be able to make ends meet, but we did. It went very well. After that, really, there was no holding us. We just got bigger and bigger and bigger.

Unfortunately for the family, Rod and Nigel's father died in 1965. As Nigel says, 'Suddenly, we were dropped in at the deep end. I was 23 and Rod was 20, but we decided to try and make a go of it. It was a lot to take on; the caravan site itself

17

was a big business.' Their mother, Alice Jane Blow, took over as resident proprietor. The family was able to carry on because, as Nigel explains, 'A lot of people would come and help us. We had a tremendous pool of casual labour, they all used to help out.'

During the first summer the Blows had taken over the Links, Roger Bunting worked there whilst on college vacation. He remembers Alfie, the town crier, sitting by the bar and it all being very sedate at first. The next summer, he recalls, they were doing heavy promotion. They delivered posters in a blue A55 pick-up and Roger remembers hand painting the sign which read, 'Come Dancing at the Royal Links', which they attached to the side.

Nigel reveals that the pick-up, which belonged to his father, sometimes had a mattress in the back, 'The passion wagon, so I was told,' he laughs.

Steve Bullimore ('Bully') was another helper. He says:

I would have been 10 when I first got involved in the summer holidays, 1965. I lived on a council estate in Cromer. Most of the families had several children, no TV, so we'd be on the street all day. There was a gang of about 10 of us, we didn't do anything really bad, but we scrumped apples, that sort of thing. One of the families was a bit rough and, even at that age, I could sense they were going to get into trouble. I remember the parents' evening, when I was in my last year at junior school, getting ready to go to the secondary modern. Although I was doing all right at school, as such, it was pointed out that it would be better if I was in different company.

I remember going up to the Links and asking if there was anything I could do. I collected milk bottles off the caravan park, walked this dog – well he took me for a walk – and I swept the floor of the dance hall the next day after the dances. I used to get probably two or three dustbinfuls of rubbish. One Saturday night they asked if I could pop in and wash some glasses. They were actual glasses to begin with: pint mugs, half-pint mugs, and dumpy tumblers made of safety glass which shattered like a windscreen. Rum-and-black and vodka-and-lime were the drinks. Anyway, that's how I got involved really. My parents weren't over-keen to start with. I remember when I was that age I was working until 10 o'clock, then someone else used to take over, bearing in mind it was open until quarter to 12. If a big group came, my parents used to let me stay to see the group. I went and helped when the Rockin' Berries came.

The first summer I worked there, I never thought anything about money. I used to get a bottle of Pepsi and a straw, a bag of crisps perhaps, never thought anything of it. Then, just before I was due to go back to school, I got a message, could I go to the office. They'd bought me a transistor radio for all the work I'd done. In them days, it was really something. I was so proud. That was how it was it them days; you didn't think about the work, you were just pleased to be part of it.

I used to go on the poster runs with Rod and Margaret on a Monday or Tuesday. We used to drive miles. We used to go in a café, have a cup of coffee or a burger, and they used to treat me to all that. That's what my wages were, I wasn't fussed about the money.

Rod and his girlfriend, Margaret Crowe, who he would later marry, spent all day every Monday putting up a hundred posters around North Norfolk. They would visit all the cafés and restaurants and then, at night time, they would go to the bars and the hotels.

Another promotional aid was the weekly advertisement in the *North Norfolk News*. Nigel was the script-writer and would think up humorous comments, often linked to the groups which were appearing.

An advert in December 1964 for the Loose Ends ran:

This group, from Brighton, will be supported by the Maniax, while the intelligentsia, until 11.45pm, will be supporting the bars.

A year later, the advert for the Sons of Fred went as follows:

Once upon a time, many years ago, when knights got rusty when it rained, there was a big R & B man called by the distinguished title of Fred. Now you can hear and spring to his offspring. Admission 5/-, you can pay 7/6 if you like.

Sometimes the advert would involve a dialogue:

'You there.' 'Me sir?' 'Yes. Where, might I ask, will you be between 8 and 11.45pm on Saturday?'

The correct answer, of course, was Cromer Links; and if there was any doubt, one advert asked, 'Are you Regular? If not, then it's time you were.'

Many adverts urged, 'Don't be late, see you at eight.'

Another one contained the word 'TOM' in capitals, which was unconnected to the group being advertised. The small-print asked the question for the readers:

'What's that stand for?' 'Two old men.' 'What about them?' 'Well, there's these two old men sitting in deck-chairs, and one says to the other...' 'Shush, you can't tell that, just do your job for once, nice and simple, and tell the folks who we've got.'

On one occasion, admission was advertised as '2/6 per half person', or put another way in a different advert, '5/- per head, 2/6 per foot!' Another helpfully explained that five shillings was the cost of a gallon of petrol.

Following the success of the Rockin' Berries, other popular acts were booked. Johnny Kidd and the Pirates appeared on Christmas Eve 1965. Nigel says, 'I didn't realise how many hits he'd had, he was amazing: tremendous performer.' Johnny Kidd wore pirate gear with high boots and a patch over his eye. The Swinging Blue Jeans, who had sung their single 'The Hippy Hippy Shake' on the first ever show of the television programme *Top of the Pops* in 1963, came to the Links in March 1966.

A local band, Peter Jay and the Jaywalkers, also impressed Nigel:

Peter Jay was a tremendous showman. He had two bass drums and he had a light bulb in every single one of his drums. The impression was that, as he hit a drum, the light flashed on. The arrangement was, when he came to do his big drum solo towards the end of the act, we'd put all the lights down. The great show was the drum solo but also all these flashing lights. I remember the second time we had them, something broke when they were setting up and Peter Jay and I went up to the workshop to conjure something to repair it, which we managed.

On 7 May 1966, Billy Fury was booked to appear. He had had several hits earlier in the decade including 'Half-way to Paradise', 'Last Night was Made for Love', 'It's Only Make Believe' and 'I'd Never Find Another You'. Nigel recalls:

We had Billy Fury one night. He'd been a big star but was on the wane, but we thought, oh well we'll book him. There were all these clauses in his contract about his personal safety when he was on stage. We thought, maybe a couple of years ago but not today. Anyway, he was a real showman and the moment he got on stage and kicked off, the girls just went mad. They went berserk. All these girls who came in week in, week out: Billy Fury comes on they started screaming. I couldn't believe it. They all went charging down the front.

There was this one group of lads from Aylsham: epitome of Norfolk lads, all big and brawny, in their blue suits with their red faces. They were as good as gold. They would stand at the back of the ballroom, drink their pints of mild and enjoy the evening, and then they'd go. So I said to this big bunch of lads from Aylsham, 'Right lads, down the front, keep the girls off the stage, 30 bob a head.' So off they went down the front. At the end of the evening their ties were all over the place and their faces were even redder and they said, 'Cor, that was a hard-earned 30 bob!'

By and large, though, the kids were fantastic in those days, never any trouble. Good as gold, week in, week out.

Roger Bunting remembers there was a bit of rivalry between the fishermen from Cromer and the ones from Sheringham, so Nigel got them on board as bouncers. Dick West was a fisherman who was recruited to the Links staff. Margaret describes him as 'a big chap' and Nigel remembers, 'If anyone was getting out of line he just used to get them in a huge great big bear hug and say, "Calm down".'

Rod recalls:

Dick and I had this sort of double act on the bouncing, which was quite amusing. We very rarely hit anybody, unless it got really bad. He used to try and talk them out of it. We always tried to avoid the fights, if we could. What we used to do was, the two of us developed the ejection system, because most of them were only little lads. We used to get hold of them by the seat of the pants and the scruff of the neck, and march them to the swing doors at the top of the first flight of steps. We used to push them through the doors, we'd got hold of them well and truly. Then, as the doors came back, we would pull them back, so the doors would swing back and might hit them in the face. Then we'd let them go, down the steps, and nine times out of ten that's all we had to do. We tried to avoid trouble if we could.

However, Nigel remembers one night when there was a bit of trouble:

It was rare but, of course, those are the nights that get talked about. I can picture it as if it was now. There was a crowd of lads who were causing bother and the scrap spilled outside. There were two flights of steps, one was inside and one was outside. I was going down the steps, Rod was just coming across the car park and just about to come up the bottom steps and three lads came after him. I yelled to Rod because there wasn't time to do anything, it was that quick. I yelled to him, 'Behind you!' Rod turned round and without a word of a lie he laid out the three of them, and he only hit each one once!

Sometimes Rod wasn't always as successful, as he explains:

It went the other way as well, because you always remember these ones. There was one time we'd had to eject one or two lads. We used to ban them for a month, a cooling-off period. The dance had finished, everyone was off on their way home, milling around outside as they used to. I stood outside with two policemen, one each side of me, talking to them. One of these lads we'd ejected came up to me, I was literally standing between these two policemen, and he said to me, 'Am I banned?' I said, 'Yes. I think it would be a good idea for a while,' and he just took a swing at me as I stood between the policemen. He had a ring on, he hit me well and truly, his ring went through my lip and it was a fairly bloodied affair. One of the policemen said, 'Do you want us to book him, Rod?' They did, he got an ABH or something.

These nights were, fortunately, very rare. Bouncers were employed but virtually had nothing to do. All the pubs were quiet on a Saturday night because everyone went to the Links, including the police, who were in support of the venue. As Margaret explains, 'The police knew everyone was there, all in one place. They were all in the one spot so the police were totally on our side. They had the night off!'

Nigel recalls that, later on, policeman Ronald Mayes ('Ginger') used to come up to the caravan site at any time of the day, during the normal working week, and sit and have a cup of tea with them. Nigel says, 'I'm sure it was to casually see what was going on. He was a classic copper: brilliant bloke.'

Ginger remembers being outside the doors at the Links each Saturday night. He says there were over 800 youngsters and he knew them by name, he knew their parents and he knew where they lived. Because of this, one man could control them.

The *North Norfolk News* reported in August 1966 that two elderly residents had objected to an application by Nigel Blow for four extensions of hours. The application, to which the police had no objections, was granted subject to the condition that admission to new arrivals was refused after 10.45pm. This was stipulated to prevent people from coming out of public houses and getting extra drinking time by being admitted to the Links. Nigel was reported as saying that, since June 1964 when he had taken over the hall, nobody had been prosecuted for drunkenness, disorderly conduct or under-age drinking. He explained that the police were on duty at the dances in uniform and plain clothes, and had never objected to any of the extensions.

One winter's night there was a pre-organised fight at the Links involving rival mods and rockers. It had been well-publicised so the staff and the police knew it was going to happen. Rod Blow takes up the story:

We used to have these big carbon dioxide cylinders pumping the dry ice, which is still done the same today. They weigh about a hundredweight. We found out that if you went outside when it was really cold and turned the gas cylinders upside down and opened the valve, you had the carbon dioxide come out like a jet of gas and it would stand out in the night air. Totally harmless but looks very impressive. If you hit people in the face with it, it momentarily freezes their eyelashes, no harm at all but gives you a slight edge.

So it was all planned and we had the gas cylinders all lined up ready. The fight kicked off outside, there was a fair number involved so off we went out with these gas cylinders. One of the locals saw us and said, 'Yeah, give us one of them, I'll swing the bugger!' because he thought we were going to hit them with it! Anyway, we cleared it in no time. Dick West was picking them up, one under each arm, and carrying them into the ballroom, laying them on the floor, and the police came and booked them. That was the only time something like that happened. Any other trouble would have been an isolated little scuffle.

Nigel recalls:

There was an Irish chap, Brendan, came and stayed in Sheringham. He worked as a bouncer: God he was strong. He was working for a road crew at the time, doing some road works in Cromer. You know these nine gallon firkins of beer, well in those days I could just pick one up with two hands and, as long as I held it tight to me, I could just carry it. He used to pick them up with one hand.

Rod confirms, 'We had people like that and everyone knew it, so there was very little confrontation.'

Nigel remembers a group of two or three lads from Leicester, who were down on holiday:

They spoke to me at the end of one Saturday night and they said, 'How do you do it?' and I said, 'Do what?' They said, 'No trouble, no bottle fights, no knife fights, nothing.' Apparently, where they went in Leicester it was trouble every Saturday. I said, what I truly believe to be the case, 'The youngsters here come here week in, week out, it's their place, they're not going to have any trouble. If you started trouble, you'd have them sort you out, long before I could get anywhere near you.' I used to describe it, as I truly believed it to be, like one big organised party. That's what it was like. If ever we had a problem, they'd help us sort it out. It was their place.

Another weapon in the Blows' armoury against trouble was Rinty the Dog. He was an ex-police dog and one of the first jobs Bully (Steve Bullimore) had to tackle when he started working there was to take Rinty for a walk. Bully comments, 'I was the only person he never bit! I think he got kicked out of the police for being too ferocious. He was a brilliant character though.'

Rinty lived in the dance hall but was put in the office on dance nights. Nigel recalls:

The funny thing about the dog was, if you introduced him to a member of staff, he was good as gold, no problem. But if you brought him out on a Saturday night he'd tear you limb from limb. One night these lads wouldn't leave. The lights went on and the bar stopped serving. I went and got Rinty on his lead and he sat and looked at these lads. One of them waved his arm towards the dog and said something like, 'That thing doesn't scare me!' Well, like a shot, Rinty had hold of his arm. The lad was shouting, 'Get him off!' As soon as Rinty let go, the lads ran out, no problem.

Bully remembers:

Rinty bit a lot of people. He never ever bit me but I can remember him biting a lot of people, including a policeman. We used to stake Rinty out on the lawn at the side of the Pavilion in the summer time. He used to bark a lot and the neighbours complained. The police came round to check we had a dog licence.

As if to confirm the dog's sense of humour, Rod adds, wryly, 'He even bit me once!'

4

Silver Linings And Grey Clouds

Following the trend set by West Runton Pavilion many years earlier, the Links organised free coaches to and from the venue. They covered many towns including Wells, North Walsham, Fakenham and Holt. It was a successful enterprise because as soon as the doors opened the coaches would pull up, and within a short while of opening the place would be full. So the punters were there from the start, instead of waiting until the pubs closed.

As owner Rod Blow says:

It was a win-win situation because the kids were chuffed they'd got free transport backwards and forwards, and we'd got the kids in. One thing I remember about the coaches was it was always the girls that organised it. We started off with one coach and they would come to us and say, 'If we got enough, would you run another one?' The break-even number was about 25 people. Within a couple of weeks it would be full and then they'd want us to put another one on.

Some nights there would be as many as 11 coaches at the Links. Dunthornes ran one from Wells, via Blakeney and Holt; Black Cat coaches ran from North Walsham; and there was one from Roys of Wroxham via RAF Coltishall. In 1969 a coach was advertised as leaving from Bintree and arriving at Cromer via Bawdeswell, Norwich Old Cattle Market and back through Horsford, Hevingham and Aylsham. Music fans were advised to look out for a 'Red and Grey Carley Coach.' On New Year's Eve 1971, British Rail arranged for a train to leave Cromer at 12.29am for North Walsham, Wroxham and Norwich.

Although the idea of free buses and trains had been tried and tested, one innovation which North Norfolk was just starting to embrace was the discotheque. An article in the *North Norfolk News* of 2 December 1966 explained the 'phenomenon':

Since Mr Nigel Blow took over the running of the Royal Links Pavilion, Cromer, in June 1964, many top-name groups have appeared there but their high fees and the fact that few groups can reproduce their 'record' sounds on stage, have helped to popularise the discotheque record sessions.

There are two disc jockeys, brothers Nick and Tim Bartlett. Electronic equipment relays the music throughout the hall and enlarged slides of LP covers are flashed on to the wall as the discs are played.

The main feature, however, is the dancing – teenagers are encouraged to mount the stage and perform their own particular dance, with routines and lighting worked out beforehand and there is the additional attraction of miming to a record.

The article concluded prophetically, 'It seems likely that the idea will catch on.'

The dance craze was encouraged on New Year's Eve 1966 when Sonny Childe came to the Links with the TNTs. Links helper Bully (Steve Bullimore) remembers:

They got people up on stage dancing. There were some radiators at the back of the stage. Bearing in mind it was an old place, they were those big metal radiators like they had in schools. They were a gold colour and people were actually dancing on the radiators.

First billed as 'That coloured American from Brooklyn NY', Sonny Childe appeared a few times at the Links with various large backing bands. One of his visits was rather dramatic, as Bully recalls, 'He put his hand through the dressing room pane of glass. He had all his arm bandaged up but he still appeared on stage and played the piano.'

Ian Foster, another of the Links helpers, remembers Sonny Childe as being 'a very humble man.' His brand of soul music was well-liked at the Links, and other popular soul bands – such as the Pyramids and Sugar Simone – were frequently booked. One advert promised that Watson T Brown would 'drive the girls crazy for his fantastic good looks and raving soul show.'

Local music fan and Links regular Jan Petty later moved to Brixton, where she went to the Ram Jam Club and was the only white person there, but she says she had heard of the bands which played there because of seeing them at the Links.

After the success of Billy Fury, and despite their 'high fees', many famous names had followed. Mike Berry came to the Links in June 1966, having had a hit in 1963 with 'Don't You Think It's Time?'; the Fortunes appeared in the wake of three hit singles: 'Here It Comes Again', 'You've Got Your Troubles' and 'This Golden Ring'; and popular instrumental group the Tornados played there in May 1966, although they had trouble leaving. After the concert the band's organist, David Watts, was driving their mini-bus when it left the road and crashed through the fence of one of the bungalows on the Overstrand Road. He was unhurt, but had to leave the vehicle suspended dangerously over the drop into the sunken garden. Local man Tony Cox remembers coming along the following morning and helping to pull the mini-bus out.

26

Notwithstanding their apparent inability to drive, the Tornados had had a massive world-wide hit and UK number one with Telstar in 1962, which was named after the communications satellite which had been launched around that time. Although he did not appear live with the band, Heinz Burt had played bass on the single. He had his own top 20 single the following year with 'Just Like Eddie' and appeared at the Links in 1966 with his band Heinz and the Wildboys. Owner Nigel Hindley (was Blow) remembers that Heinz had dyed blond hair, almost white, which was fairly novel in those days. Links regular Bernie Galasky recalls the performance:

The band were playing and one of them was playing a guitar with no strings on it. He carried on for quite a while, no-one seemed to notice, then he threw it away!

Rod and Nigel were able to book well-known bands through their association with various London agents. One of the most important of these, Robert Stigwood – who had promoted the Beatles after they had been found by Brian Epstein, and was later to find fame and fortune in Hollywood – looked after the Who.

By the time they appeared at the Links in February 1967, the Who had had numerous hits including 'I Can't Explain', 'My Generation' and 'Substitute'. Their latest single 'Happy Jack' had just entered the charts. Put in context, they were one of the top three bands at the time, along with the Beatles and the Rolling Stones. No wonder the advert in that week's *North Norfolk News* declared:

The Royal Links Pavilion, Cromer, proudly presents the greatest show ever staged in Norfolk, the most fantastic night in the history of pop, the night you will remember for the rest of your lives, it's the Who.

The usual admission was five shillings (25p) for two groups and the free buses, but at twelve shillings and sixpence (62½p), this was one of the few high-priced nights and, as Nigel puts it, 'It was a lot of money for the youngsters to find.'

Rod agrees:

The average wage was about £3 a week. If you were earning that, twelve and six was a huge chunk. In today's money it would be about £75 a ticket. There aren't many places you would go to now that would charge that. The big nights at arenas hadn't been invented then. This was a local venue for local people.

Rod's wife Margaret Blow (was Crowe) says, 'I was on a hairdressing apprenticeship at the time and I was earning 15 shillings a week. A lot of my friends were at the shoe factory on £4 a week.'

The reason for the high admission charge is explained by Rod:

The Who were £600 for 40 minutes and, because they were only doing 40 minutes, we had to have two other groups; so we had a local group from Beccles who were £25, then we had a London professional group which would be £100. We roughly said it cost us about £1,000 to open the doors that night.

Lead singer Roger Daltery was the first to arrive out of the Who. Rod says:

He came in, long before anybody else arrived. I think he was on his own, may have had his driver with him. He went into the changing room and he was ever-so pleasant, got his television set up and all he was worried about was watching The Monkees *– their Saturday teatime show. So he had a bottle of vodka and watched* The Monkees *at about six in the evening.*

Margaret used to take the money at the door. She felt very apprehensive as Rod drove her to the venue:

My heart was in my mouth when Rod came to pick me up. We drove up the Overstrand Road about an hour before we were due to open, and they were queued up right to the bottom of the Overstrand Road into Cromer. I said to Rod, 'My God, I'm on my own on the door, don't you open those doors and let them all at me at once, will you?' He said, 'No, we'll put a couple of bouncers on the door and they'll come in half-a-dozen at a time.' So I sat there with my little drawer, surrounded by cardboard boxes on the floor, and all the 10 shilling notes and pound notes went into the cardboard boxes.

As far as Nigel remembers, there was no licensing limit on numbers. He says the maximum was 'as many as we could get in!' The night the Who appeared, everyone wanted to get in, it was like a tube train at rush hour. Rod laughs, 'We were trying to push them out of the emergency doors at the back so we could get them in at the front, because they were still queued up along the Overstrand Road to come in!'

The hall was packed because, as barman Norman Clowes points out, 'When the big bands were on, everybody left the bars and went onto the dance floor and you couldn't move.' People were standing on chairs and on tables. Jackie Griffin (now Regis) was attending for the first time. Richard Hewitt watched the whole show from the balcony and says he was 'completely deaf when it was over!'

Photographs taken on the night show that those near the stage were only feet away from the stars. As Nigel remarks, 'The groups were on the stage and the kids were right up against it. There was no barrier between them, apart from the Aylsham boys!'

Bouncer Frank Kinsley had to stand at the front of the stage to try and stop the girls from climbing up. He says, 'The sweat was rolling off me, and the girls were going mad.' One of the staff, David Pegg ('Gaffer') used to stand on the right-hand stage steps and he held a guitar for Pete Townshend.

Along with their hit singles, Nigel remembers that one of the tracks the Who played during the 40 minute set was 'Boris the Spider', penned by bass player John Entwistle. Drummer Keith Moon completed the line-up.

Although not used when they played at the Links, music fan Terry Bunting recalls that cabinets containing eight 12 inch diameter speakers had been designed specifically for the Who by Jim Marshall, founder of Marshall Amplification. The band liked the idea but the roadies hated them because they were too big to carry about. So Jim Marshall had sawn them in half, which is how the 'Marshall Stack' came about. Back at the Links, helper Bully (Steve Bullimore) kept part of the Marshall name-plate which had fallen off one of the Who's amplifiers, and added it to his growing collection of publicity photos and autographs.

Once the show was over, the Who headed off in their limousine. Bouncer Frank Kinsley remembers that one of the band was so stoned that he had to be thrown into the back of it. Their destination was Northrepps Cottage which in those days, before it became the Country Club, was a restaurant run by George Hoy. At their manager's request, Nigel had called George and asked if he would keep the restaurant open for the Who and a party totalling about 12 people, so that they could have a meal. George had readily agreed but the following day he rang Nigel and said angrily, 'Don't you ever do that again.' When Nigel asked why, George replied, 'Twelve of them. Do you know what they had? One f***ing glass of milk!' Nigel said, 'Don't blame me, George,' but he did, so it never happened again.

On the strength of the venue's success with the Who, Rod remembers Robert Stigwood phoning them and saying, 'I've got a chance of getting the Beach Boys, they'll cost you £1,000 for forty minutes.' This was almost twice the fee charged for the Who. The family talked and talked about it. Nigel explains:

We had to gamble on the number of people who were going to come through the door, to guess at what the break-even number was going to be, in order to be able to work out what the admission price would have to be. When we had the big names we were prepared to not make a profit on the night, so long as we didn't run at a loss. We would make it up the following few weeks, so when we had the next big name we would be OK.

In spite of this, Rod reckons:

We would have made a big loss because we physically could not have got enough people in to cover it. It's not the sort of thing where you could relay it outside, and the place was only so big. We would have had to have charged the youngsters a pound a head to come in, and it had never been done. I still think we did the right thing.

However, Margaret says, 'I think not having the Beach Boys was the biggest regret.'

One big star they did book was Jeff Beck, ex the Yardbirds, who was billed as 'the greatest guitarist in this country'. He had been on *Top of the Pops* the Thursday before with 'Hi-Ho Silver Lining', but this did not guarantee his acceptance with the Links crowd, as Nigel remembers:

He marked a change in the style of music. Before Jeff Beck, we used to have a lot of soul groups and R & B, which were just fabulous: Motown-style acts you had to dance to, couldn't not dance. Then Jeff Beck came along and the volume was deafening. And this was after the Who! The acts used to come on stage at Cromer with a 50 watt amplifier. Jeff Beck started and it was deafening. There was feedback and the guitars were all screaming everywhere.

We did have a good audience that night because he was a big star, but the place just stopped dead. Everyone just stared at the stage. He carried on, and then it started. They just rained on him: beer glasses, beer bottles, ashtrays, the lot. The wall behind the stage was brickwork, painted with a mural, and these glass tankards and bottles were hitting this and smashing and going everywhere. Their manager came up and said, 'Tell them to stop,' and I said, 'You turn the bloody volume down boy, and they'll stop.' And he did, and they did.

It was more usual, however, for complaints about the noise to come from the neighbours rather than the crowd, which was a concern when the licence came up for renewal. The official closing time for the venue was 10.30pm, but the bar extension until 11.45pm had to be applied for. The extensions could be granted to run for 12 months but could be limited to one month if there had been problems. The argument put forward by the Blow brothers was that the Pavilion had been there for many years, much longer than the modern bungalows that surrounded it. However, in later years, as the bands became louder, they did do a lot of work sound-proofing the building. Links helper Bully remembers one of their early efforts:

They always had problems from the neighbours with the noise. I remember one week we boarded up all the windows in the toilets and cloakrooms to try and keep the sound down. It was an old building, so we jammed cardboard and paper stuff in all the cracks round the window frames and door frames to help absorb the sound. I believe someone came down one Saturday night and monitored it inside and walked round outside. It might even have got brought up in the Houses of Parliament.

Jeff Beck's band included vocalist Rod Stewart who, together with Beck's bassist Ron Wood, would find success with the Faces. Rod then found even more fame as a solo star, while Ron joined the Rolling Stones as a guitarist. As Nigel observes, 'There were a lot of people who are still in the game and are big stars now that were with other groups at the time, working their way up the ladder.' Neil Christian and the Crusaders was another band with a hidden star, for the line-up which played at the Links in October 1966 contained a certain Ritchie Blackmore on guitar, who would later find world-wide success with seventies rock bands Deep Purple and Rainbow.

Marc Bolan is said to have appeared at the Links with John's Children, although no date has been confirmed. He joined the band in February 1967 and had left by May, forming Tyrannosaurus Rex the following year. Several people, including Links regular Tony Cox and owners Nigel and Rod Blow, remember him playing there and another regular, Jan Petty, says, 'They were completely out of their tree. They played one song which they said was written by their friend who was a heroin addict.'

A young and little-known singer and musician called David Bowie appeared at the Links in November 1966 – unfortunately remembered by Pam Gale (was Wells), who got his autograph, as being 'a bit arrogant' – and Long John Baldry's band, Bluesology, included a little piano player called Reg Dwight. Reg later found success as Elton John, taking his new surname from Long John Baldry and his first name from the Bluesology saxophonist, Elton Dean. Long John Baldry had a UK number one in November 1967 with 'Let the Heartaches Begin', just after his second appearance at the Links. He is remembered by Nigel as being quite a character:

We usually paid the acts cash on the night less 10 per cent for the agent. I was told, 'For Christ's sake do not give Long John Baldry any money because he'll be straight into the bar.' He came after me and I said I'd been told not to give him any money and he said, 'You've got to give us some,' so I gave him a little and he got a bottle of vodka.

Unfortunately, Long John Baldry ended up the worse for wear. He was staying in the hotel on Cromer sea front and Margaret and Rod Blow put him in the back of their little mini pick-up and took him over to the hotel.

Margaret remembers trying to get him settled:

I pushed him up three flights of stairs, literally his bum on my shoulder because he was really tall, hence the name. I got to the bottom of the three flights of stairs, turned round, and he was right behind me again!

Rod says, 'He finished up running across the main Cromer road, down the hill and went into the sea in his suit and his shoes. He ruined them.' The shoes, which he had been very proud of, were brand new, very expensive leather brogues. However, Margaret says, 'I was more heartbroken about my shoulder I'd carried him up the stairs on!'

The incident made an impression on schoolboy helper Bully (Steve Bullimore), who observes, 'In those days, a suit like that, for a man of his height, would have to have been tailor-made. He ruined it.'

In addition to walking Rinty the dog, Bully had gradually taken on other responsibilities at the Links:

I used to sort the empty bottles out, because in those days they were returnable. There were big wicker baskets behind the bars and all the bottles used to go in there, and the beer bottles used to go in the crates. I was then given keys to the place. My job was to unlock in the mornings. Rinty used to try and eat the postman most days: he hated people in uniforms. I used to get Nigel up about half-past seven in the mornings, tap on his bedroom window in the bungalow. This was school holidays, weekends, all the time.

When I was still at school I used to be involved in ordering the beer and making sure the bars were stocked up. The beers we used to sell in the early days were Tartan Bitter, Double Diamond, Worthington E and Watneys Red Barrel. I believe when I first started there was no draught lager, it used to be bottles of Harp lager off the cold tray. Then they had Carlsberg put in which was strong Danish lager.

In the summer we had the lounge bar open during the week, 7.00pm till 11.00pm. I remember Sue Tomlinson, from North Walsham, worked behind the bar. I wasn't old enough to serve but I used to clear the tables, wash the glasses and change the barrels for her. We had a really busy night one August and we went to the old 'Jack and Jill' till, you used to push the keys down, and we'd taken £99-something. I gave her some change out of my pocket and she rung it up to make it up to £100.

Other staff at that time included Mick Lines behind the bar, Dave Watts on the door and the Pegg brothers Christopher ('Tiffer') and David ('Gaffer') collecting glasses. Brian Bennett was doing an apprenticeship at Chevertons the printers, based at Bond Street, Cromer, which is where the Links posters were produced. He helped out at the Links and was in charge of stocking the bars, amongst other jobs. He shared Nigel's concern one night when the main act was late for a gig.

Alan Price had been booked to appear in July 1966, the usual publicity photos had been sent prior to the date to help with the promotion but, on the night, there was no sign of the star. Nigel recalls:

The group had turned up, the gear had turned up and it was all set up on stage, but Alan Price hadn't turned up. It was about nine o'clock and it was almost time for him to go on. Brian came rushing in and said, 'He's here, he's here,' and I thought, thank goodness for that.

We'd had some publicity photos of him sitting in the back of a Ford Transit with windows all down the side. We went down the steps and Brian said, 'That's him, that's him, sitting there.' Alan Price was an arrogant sod, not nice at all. He just said, in his broad Geordie accent, 'I didn't think anyone would recognise me in a dump like this.' I have to hand it to Brian, beautiful bit of repartee, he said, 'Well, if you're going to wear the same tatty suit you've got on your publicity photographs, you've got to expect it, haven't you?'

Alan Price went on stage and he did his first number. Nothing. I was very surprised because he is a superb live performer. He did his next number. Nothing. I thought there'd have been a bit of response from the crowd. Finally he said, over the microphone, in his Geordie accent, 'How about a bit of applause for me an' the boys up here, 'cos we're working our f***ing bollocks off for you.' I thought, oh no, there's going to be a riot. The girls sniffed and went to the back of the hall, the boys all clapped and came down the front, and it was OK after that. I think he came close to being lynched, but he was very good.

Everyone was shocked when, a year after the Alan Price gig, Brian Bennett died in a car accident a few weeks before his 21st birthday. It was in the early hours of Saturday 29 July 1967. He had a little grey mini-van and had taken some friends, including Gaffer, back to Sheringham. He was heading back alone towards Cromer and hit a concrete lamppost at the junction of Runton Road and Shipden Avenue. No other vehicles were involved.

Brian was an only child who lived at Southrepps with his father, who was a mobile barber originating from London, and his mother, known as 'Bubbles', who was a Norfolk woman. Nigel remembers, 'They were ever such nice gentle people, which was a thing that characterised Brian: he couldn't have had an enemy in his life. He was very nice lad, bubbly, effervescent and a very good chap.'

At the Links that night there was a period of silence as a mark of respect.

The front page of the *North Norfolk News* of Friday 4 August 1967 carried details of the accident:

Cromer firemen had to be called to cut him from the wreckage of the van. The lamp standard was demolished and the engine torn out of the vehicle.

Mr William Edwards, of 18 Shipden Avenue, who came out when he heard the crash, said the van was separated from the engine by several feet. 'It was like a nightmare,' he said.

Understandably, having lost their only son, Brian's parents were distraught. 'His death absolutely destroyed his parents,' says Nigel, 'they could not come to terms with it at all.'

Brian is buried in the churchyard at St James' Church, Southrepps. A floral tribute at the funeral from 'Everyone at the FAB Links' contained a roll-call of staff: 'Watty, Gaffer, Mickey, Tiffer, Culley, Flo, Chestney and Bully.'

5

A Time Of Transition

Jim Baldwin was working at Cox and Wyman, the Fakenham printers, in the early 1960s. He recalls:

For a couple of Christmases they held their staff 'bash' at West Runton Pavilion, which was the first time that I actually went inside. The house band was led by drummer Denton (Joe) Tuck and I think that Wally Colman was the sax player: I knew them both. At that time I was also working in Fakenham's first rock and roll group, the Electrons, and because two of us worked for Cox and Wyman, we managed to get the interval spot. So I believe that we were the first pop group to play at the Pavilion.

This combination of dance band and pop music would continue later in the sixties at West Runton. John Jarvis, a local singer, explains how it worked:

They would have the dance band on the shell stage, doing the 'Gay Gordons' and the 'Oke Cokey', then the pop group would be on a platform. They would each play for three-quarters of an hour, about two turns each. There was something for all the family.

Tony Wright ('Beano'), who had been going to the Pavilion with his older brother since the beginning of the decade, confirms the set-up:

For several years there would be a dance band and a pop group, which was a nice mixture: the dance band for the older ones, and the pop group for the youngsters.

Beano played there with Berry and the Treetops, a band formed in the sixties by David Waller. The name for the group was derived from the lead guitarist, Berry Bambridge, and the fact that lead singer David Waller was a timber merchant. The early line-up also included Barry Butcher (bass), Ronnie Broughton (rhythm guitar) and George Neave (drums). Mick Miller became bass player when Barry left and Pete North drummed for them for about a year. Pete takes up the story:

In the early days, I played West Runton when they had two stages. We used to play on the smaller one. I was very young then, late teens, and this was one of the first rock bands I had played with. I never even had a decent kit at that time. We played the village hall circuit then, and it was a great experience for me.

When Pete left, Beano became the drummer and David Moore took up rhythm guitar. The famous Norwich band leader and showman Chic Applin looked after the band for many years. They played locally and did numerous summer seasons at the holiday camps until they disbanded in 1974.

David Waller still has some of their set-lists:

Set-list one:

Move It; Don't Be Cruel; Whole Lotta Shakin'; All Shook Up; Young Ones; Do You Wanna Dance/Dancin' Shoes; Apache; FBI; Everyday; Dreams; Someone Loves You; Bad Moon Rising; Hound Dog; Blue Suede Shoes.

Set-list two:

Walk in the Room; Teenager in Love; Oh Carol; Bye-Bye Love; Mary Lou; Then I Kissed Her; Fingle Blunt; Save the Last Dance; Dream Lover; Diana; Kelly; I Think of You; Twist; Ob-La-Di; Armarillo.

Set-list three:

Jailhouse Rock; Blue Suede Shoes; Crocodile Rock; Happy Birthday, Sweet 16; Let's Work Together; Teddy Bear; Half-Way to Paradise; Donna; Apache; Hard Days' Night; Johnny B Goode; Sea Cruise; Make Believe; Wonder of You; Rave On; Summertime Blues; Just 17; Hi-Ho, Silver Lining.

Frank Kinsley, who had worked at the Links, became a bouncer at West Runton Pavilion. He remembers, 'It was a good laugh.' Berry and the Tree Tops were known to him because he was a tree-feller and the boys at the Hevingham wood-yards wanted the timber. David Waller was known as 'Drummer' in those days, although Frank called him 'Flash' because his shoes were always shiny! While everyone else knew the guitarist as Berry, Frank had a special name for him, too. He says:

I used to call him 'Belly'! I remember at one time 'Belly' was on stage at Runton, singing at the front. This boy had given him a load of mouth at different places where they'd played. Runton had a low stage, two or three feet high, so 'Belly' leaned forward and hit the boy in the mouth, and the boy flew back about 30 feet. Someone asked why he'd done that and 'Belly' replied, 'I didn't like him.' The boy was no further trouble to 'Belly'!

Another pop band which appeared frequently at the Pavilion in the late sixties, Iron Tonic, was similarly bothered by trouble.

John Chandler, their drummer, recalls:

In the early days in the sixties we played at West Runton Pavilion quite a bit. It was all a bit wild at times because the audience used to get carried away. There was a group of people called 'Satan's Slaves' who used to come down and they were always looking for trouble.

Bass player Trevor Leeder adds, 'Satan's Slaves were actually nice lads, a bit rowdy, but always OK with the band.'

John Jarvis, Iron Tonic's singer, continues:

We had the following of a motorcycle gang called Satan's Slaves. The band was on the shell stage, this massive fight broke out, and we got the blame. One boy got took to hospital and had to have stitches in his head. Joe Tuck [who arranged bookings for the dance hall] didn't want us back but, because we were popular, the manager said we could come back but he would put us under a different name. He told us to look in the local paper to see what we were called. We were billed as 'The East Coast Rock and Pop Combo.' I had to make the sign for the drum and I could only fit 'East Coast Rock' onto it, so that's what we became.

Tony Powell, former member of popular local band the Highwaymen, joined as rhythm guitarist.

East Coast Rock practised in the Church Room at Hindringham every Monday and Thursday evening. Steve Aldred used to go along to watch and, thus inspired, formed his own band, Storm, in 1972 with 'Noddy' Phillip Beckham and Steve 'Peanut' Dye. He says they couldn't play any instruments when they started. They made good progress, however, and had their first booking in October 1972 with 'Noddy' on drums and vocals, 'Peanut' on guitar and vocals and Steve on bass. They played at West Runton Pavilion several times during the following year. Steve remembers the seashell stage and the cut-out palm trees.

Storm played most sorts of popular music to please the youngsters, then a dance band came on for the older generation. Steve says that there were plenty of other places for bands to play in those days too, and they appeared at lots of local dances in village halls. In 1974 Storm became Wild Honey but kept the same line-up. They appeared at Runton that year but disbanded on New Year's Eve 1975.

For John Chandler, known to many as 'Notchie', appearing at West Runton Pavilion was a dream come true:

When I left school I worked at Gasches [a restaurant in Weybourne]. When we finished work on a Saturday night I used to jump on the back of one of the lad's motorbikes and we used to go down to Runton to the dance. We used to get there about 11 o'clock and get the last hour of dancing. Mind you, we must have stunk because we'd been working in the kitchen, but we didn't think about things like that. I was always mad keen on music and I remember looking at the stage and seeing the bands there and thinking to myself, I'll play on there one of these days when I'm a bit older, and lo and behold, a couple of years later I did. That was always a dream fulfilled.

When his band, East Coast Rock, changed their name in 1973 before going professional, John remembers they broke the crowd record at the Pavilion on their farewell night. He describes it as 'a terrific night' and John Jarvis agrees:

I remember the last night we did at Runton, just before we went professional. When we had finished playing they turned the spotlight on us from the balcony. They announced we were going professional and everyone on the dance floor cheered and stamped for 15 minutes. We had a quarter-of-an-hour standing ovation.

Reverting to a four-piece line-up, the new band was called 'Fascinatin' Rhythm', after the song of the same name, and they were managed by Edward Tartt. The *North Norfolk News* reported in June 1973 that they had a varied repertoire ranging from pop to country and western – including rock and roll numbers – spiced with a touch of comedy. The piece continued:

One of the group's most popular arrangements is a superb medley of Beach Boys' and Beatles' numbers found by many of their listeners to be very close to the original sound. But far from sticking to familiar material – despite the fact that it has given them a great reputation – Fascinatin' Rhythm are looking to new songs and music written specially for them.

Trevor Leeder remembers the band going into the woods in Norwich to have publicity photographs taken wearing garish checked jackets. They got changed in turn and made their way through the woods to where the photographer was waiting. Trevor was the second one to come out and someone walking in the woods stared at him in amazement said to his companion, 'Look! There's another one!'

Fascinatin' Rhythm appeared at West Runton in October 1973 after a successful summer season on the coast and just prior to their appearance on the *New Faces* television programme, a 1970s version of *The X Factor*. They were the first local act to appear on the show. The judges that night were Clement Freud (a liberal MP who had appeared in adverts feeding his bloodhound Henry on *Minced Morsels*), Jean Morton (who featured in the children's television programme *Tingha and Tucker* with a puppet called Willy Wombat) and Tony Hatch. The latter was to blame for writing the theme tunes to *Crossroads* and later *Neighbours* although, to be fair, he had also composed many successful records including Petula Clark's 'Downtown' and the Foundations' 'Call Me'. It was before this panel of early-day Simon Cowells that Fascinatin' Rhythm were to test their talent.

John Jarvis describes the event:

In those days, we toured the northern clubs. We used to do 20 minutes ordinary music, 20 minutes comedy and 20 minutes rock and roll. We went on New Faces the week after Showaddywaddy had been on. We wanted to do the harmony like them but the TV company wanted us to do the impression act because it was a bit different. I wouldn't say we were good, we used to get away with it; we were really better at the singing. We had a rehearsal on Monday and the show was to be recorded on the Tuesday, and we still didn't know which impressions we could do because they had to get permission to do them from the people concerned – Harold Wilson and so on. We ended up with our five minute routine and we came last. Clement Freud said we would do well in clubs for short-sighted people!

Unfortunately, John's memory of their Christmas Eve appearance at West Runton Pavilion in 1973 is not quite so vivid because he got very drunk during the day. He fell onto the floor of the van on the way to the venue and had to be helped to get ready and helped out onto the stage. He can't remember a thing about the night – what he sung or anything. He says he never did it again although many people said that was the best they had ever heard him sing.

Similarly, guitarist Mike Green comments, 'We had some great times there – although I can't remember much about them!' The whole band agreed that West Runton Pavilion was a wonderful place to play.

Fascinatin' Rhythm supported the Equals there in April 1974 and John Jarvis watched them from the balcony and recorded them. Unfortunately, John and his groups never managed to break into the big time. He told a local newspaper a few years ago:

I think we never got anywhere because we had too good a home life. If you look at the successful stars, most of them came from a poverty background. But we were too well looked after. I think, had the Beatles came from Norwich, we would have all been 'discovered' back in the sixties. You always hear about music starting in Liverpool but we were doing the same thing around here at the same time. The only thing to come out of Norfolk in the sixties in terms of hit records was the Singing Postman.

When John left Fascinatin' Rhythm in October 1974 they changed their name to Star. Local newspaper, the *Journal*, reported: 'The group has always drawn packed audiences when it has played at West Runton Pavilion and so chose to make its debut there as Star with Peter Collins.'

Peter Collins was a singer from Norwich, his backing group had been called Style, and he had been the resident singer with the Chic Applin Band at the Norwood Rooms in Norwich. The article continued, 'His appeal is to all age groups, with a style and presentation giving each performance a friendly and exciting atmosphere.' The new band proved so popular that they played Christmas Eve, Boxing Day and New Year's Eve at West Runton Pavilion at the end of 1974.

Emblem were another pop band who played there, doing a couple of 45-minute cabaret slots in the interval, around which the resident band played quicksteps and dance music. In about 1967, drummer Richard Hewitt had joined Ian Lord (rhythm guitar/lead vocals), David Laws (bass) and John Hubbard (lead guitar) in Emblem. They played many times on the smaller stage at West Runton Pavilion while the dance band played in the seashell bandstand. One of the last gigs they did at the venue was in 1973.

By this time, however, the manager at Runton was reluctantly realising that the two-band format was no longer working. Tony Wright noticed it too, 'The youngsters got bored while the dance bands were on, and the older generation didn't like the pop music. Eventually the older ones started to drift away.'

Jim Baldwin agrees:

In the years that followed, pop groups took over the main entertainment nights at West Runton Pavilion. I seem to remember that I went elsewhere if I had a Saturday night off. In later years, my wife and I used to take the free bus from Fakenham to the Cromer Links, but the magic of the 1960s had gone by then and it was a new generation of 'punters'.

As a complete contrast, for about a year in the early 1970s, West Runton Pavilion hosted bingo nights. John Mason recalls joining the team:

Scanning through the Eastern Daily Press *in the early 1970s I came across an advert for staff to run the new bingo sessions due to start shortly at the West Runton Pavilion. This was something new to me but, having decided to give it a go, I acquired an interview with the general manager, Jim Habershoen, who offered me a part-time job straight away with no questions about past experience, references or anything.*

When the bingo started two professional callers were employed. I started as a card checker. After a few weeks one caller was sacked for cracking rude jokes, the other left after giving me a 'crash course' on being a bingo caller.

I used to feel like a celebrity as I walked down the aisle between the tables from the back of the hall towards the stage: I'd get this big round of applause. They all belonged to the 'West Runton Bingo Club' and the same people would be there week after week. One woman would have four bingo cards and be doing her knitting at the same time. Another elderly lady, who insisted on sitting at the back of the hall, would be working only one card and complain that I was going too quickly. If she got a call, I had usually gone on to the next number by then so she missed out.

There were quite good cash prizes and a star prize of a huge joint of meat referred to as the 'West Runton Joint'. They all took their bingo very seriously. I used to go into 'auto-pilot' when calling out the numbers and when someone shouted 'house' I would often forget which had been the last number called. It didn't look very professional if you had to ask someone what it was, but the last number called had to be on the winning card.

I remember the machine was a bit temperamental. On one occasion we were half-way through a game and all the balls came out at once. They were like ping-pong balls and they went all over the floor. One of the checkers helped me pick them up and we put them back into the machine. I was worried we hadn't got them all, but it was my decision whether to carry on and hope all the balls were there, or to start the game again. I didn't think starting again would be very popular so I took a chance and continued. Luckily, we did have all the balls so there was no problem.

When the lever was pulled to let the balls drop down, there were always four balls that got stuck and required pushing down with a finger. The unit had a metal top and on one session, as I pushed my finger through the hole, I touched the 240 volt micro-switch underneath. I swore to myself, but still had the microphone open so everyone heard me. There was a huge gasp of disapproval and I looked up to see seventy-plus pairs of eyes glaring at me in horror from around the hall.

When it came to the last night, it had been decided not to tell people in advance. It was the second half of the evening and I walked in to my usual round of applause towards the front of the hall. I spotted a young girl who came to the dances but I knew hadn't been to the bingo before. I stopped and had a quick chat with her and she told me she had been a member since the club started, but this was the first night she had been in to play. I then took up my place on the stage. There were a few games of bingo and then it came to the jackpot, which had accumulated to £180 over several weeks. Before it started, I announced that this would be the last night of bingo and, if the jackpot did not go in the set number of calls, we would play on to a full house for a reduced jackpot of £50. That was about one-and-a-half weeks' average wage in those days.

It went to a full house and when I looked up I couldn't believe it, the young girl – who had never been before – had won the £50 jackpot. The sound of disapproval from the regulars was obvious around the hall, and especially from a table at the middle left-hand side. Later I was in the pub next door with Joe Tuck, who was manager of the Pavilion at the time. Suddenly the door burst open and I was confronted by five elderly ladies, hardened regular bingo players, who accused me of fixing it so the young girl won the jackpot and could share it with me! They got quite aggressive and wouldn't listen to me. Joe Tuck, meanwhile, was curled up with laughter at the sight of me being harassed by these elderly women. Eventually they went away, but it was obvious I had a lot to learn about being a bingo caller. Maybe it was some higher being preparing me for my next challenge at the Pavilion – that of doorman.

When the bingo finished, Joe Tuck, obviously impressed with his handling of the irate bingo punters, approached John Mason with an offer. John recalls:

Joe's ballroom dance band was losing its popularity at the Pavilion but was still in demand around the Fens area. In order to enable him to play elsewhere on Saturday nights with his band, his request was for me to be on hand at the Pavilion gigs to keep order, man the door, and go on stage to announce any forthcoming attractions.

Keeping the dance hall punters under control did not prove too much of a problem: at that time it consisted mainly of two or three men having a drink-driven fight over a woman. Weighing in at over 16 stones at that time, I may have looked the part but I think that is where it ended. The best advice I got was on my first night from a big, long-serving policeman, who called in for his regular pint up the stairs in the little private balcony. He told me, 'When you are called upon to sort out a fracas in the hall, don't rush in, let them tire themselves out a bit, then go in and throw out the one who is getting the worst of it.'

Dick Woodley started as a barman at West Runton Pavilion in about 1972 and worked there for 11½ years. He says he had a solitary job during the day so it was nice to get out in the evenings and talk to people. The first night he started was a police dance night when he was co-opted to do the bar. The first manager he worked with was Jim Habershoen, who disappeared one night with the takings and was never heard of again. John Mason remembers Jim's departure, 'He threw a big party, locked everybody in, and let them have as much beer as they wanted!'

The next manager was Charlie Blowers who, Dick says, was much older, staid and straight-laced. There was no drinking allowed behind the bar. His wife, Margery, made friends easily and his daughter, Deborah, was in her early teens. They lived in the little house on the edge of the car park and Charlie tried to keep his daughter out of the Pavilion. Drink was sold in proper glasses at first, and Dick remembers one night the glass-collector fell over onto the tray of glasses he was carrying. He was badly cut and they wrapped him in tea towels. Margery felt faint so she was allowed to have a brandy. Others behind the bar felt faint too, so they had to have one as well. In the end the staff finished two bottles!

Mrs Abbs still owned the complex, following the death of her husband. She lived in two rooms at the top of the big house. Dick Woodley remembers she used to sit at her window and count the cars that came into the car park. She would then work out how much money should have been taken on the door and explanations were required if she didn't think it was as much as it should have been.

John Mason recalls:

Mrs Abbs had to be reported to every night before the hall opened for business. She would go into the buffet and make sure the butter was thinned down to make it go further.

In 1973, Mrs Abbs put the whole three acre site up for sale, which included the Village Inn, the Pavilion, the large house she lived in and the car park. On 8 August 1973 the *North Norfolk News* announced that a firm of property developers, F C Boswall of Hertford, had acquired the site for a sum in excess of £100,000. Having earlier built an estate at Ollands Park, Reepham, and completed a large development of luxury flats at Albany Court, Cromer, they had spotted the potential of the site and their intentions for the area were clear.

Fortunately for the youth of North Norfolk, the planning authorities had other ideas. Mr Boswall was going to find himself with a large plot of land he wasn't allowed to develop, and a large dance hall he would have to fill!

6

Fab Links Organisation

Over at Cromer Links, Rod Blow had been finding it increasingly difficult working with his mother, and in 1967 he and his girlfriend, Margaret, left. However, there was to be one memorable night before their departure in which Rod played a key role. He recalls:

There was a coloured girl, very black, I can't remember her name. She was in a minor lead group, not a big name or anything like that because you couldn't have big names every week. They told us that her act was a bit risqué – which it was in those days – and if the mood was right she would do a strip-tease at the end, but it would be very tasteful. We were all up for a laugh. We had these ultra violet lights, 'black' lights as we called them; most places had them going. I did the stage bit in those days and we used them quite a lot to get the effect. They told me what to do and, sure enough, I must have got the signal she was going to do it.

She was quite a good singer, a good act. She started to strip off with these 'black' lights until she was down to her white bra and pants which stood out, because she was really black. The finale was to switch the off the black lights, just as she whipped her top off, and she disappeared off the stage. The dressing room was literally three steps down and she was gone. It was really effective and I know it caused a laugh and a lot of applause. It was done really well and it went down well.

Until they left, Margaret had been in charge of the door and Rod had run the dance hall side, dealing with the actual groups themselves and carrying out any compering that had to be done. He can be seen on some of the photos of the Who, standing at the side of the stage. He says, 'The turnover was awesome,' although as helper Bully (Steve Bullimore) points out:

At the end of the night they used to count out this whole cardboard box full of 10 shilling notes they'd taken, but then they had to pay the band. So you knew they didn't really see that money. They used to pay all the coaches their money, that all used to come out of the takings. Any money left, Nigel would put in this brown briefcase at the end of the night, about half-past 12, and drive up in his Land Rover to the bungalow where he lived and put it in the safe in the office. Later a safe was put in the dance hall.

As well as securing the takings, Rod's brother Nigel was in overall charge of the two bars. As Nigel says, 'We were open one night a week, and we used to shift more stuff than all the rest of the pubs in Cromer put together.' Norwich Brewery used to send two drays into Cromer on a Monday, one was for the Links and the other was for the rest of the pubs. He continues, 'When Coca Cola was delivered, the lorry used to come and the Links would have the lot.'

Nigel remembers one particular night behind the bar:

There used to be a cartoon in one of the papers at the time about Calamity Jane, this very big-breasted girl, and she'd got a couple of scoops on the top of the bar which they rested in! Well, there was this local girl Frances, she was a bit like that, a big girl! One Saturday night I was behind the bar, serving drinks hand over fist. Because of the noise of the band you used to have to have a knack of serving a customer, looking at that customer and at the same time you were eyeing up the people on either side, working out who was next. You would serve that customer and go straight to the next one. I popped up and Frances was up at the bar counter, leaning on the bar, and it was her turn to be served. I got up and looked straight at her. She was about to shout her order and the lad next to her shouted his order. Frances just elbowed him and said, 'My man, I do believe I was next!'

Norman Clowes was barman in the main bar at the Links for about 10 years. He saw lots of bands and has many fond memories of the bands and the great crowd that used to attend. He recalls:

I started with Fred Bloomfield and Mick Lines. I had been wanting to go to the Links but my mum wouldn't let me. The first time I was allowed I was about 13. There was a band from New Zealand coming who had been on [the science television programme] Tomorrow's World *because they had microphones on their guitars. Chris Pegg was collecting glasses and I asked him if there was any chance of a job. He spoke to Nigel who said I could start the next week. I then went home and told my parents I was going to the Links and they starting moaning. When I said I was going to work there, that was OK, so that's how I got in. I started collecting glasses, then I was asked if I wanted to work behind the bar. I was serving alcohol long before I was allowed to drink it. I ran the main bar. Alan Youngs was on the other bar, near the stage.*

Nigel remembers some of the other staff:

We used to have what we called the ladies' cloakroom, which is where the girls used to go to hang their coats. They used to pay thruppence to hang their coat up for the night. The attendant who looked after that was a huge, great big chap called 'Happy', because his disposition was he was happy! He used to drive the dustcart, but what his name was, I can't remember. He did that for ages. We had another lad who did the gents' cloakroom.

46

Paul Knights ran the small bar at the Links for quite some time. He was son of an old North Norfolk estate agency family, Ronald Knights. He was very public school, typical estate agent of the day, suited and booted. He was the most unlikely person to work at the Links, but he loved it. George Hagon collected the glasses; he was a comedian!

Paddy Archer, Dave Watts and Ali Farrow worked on the door. Ali remembers, 'The Links had a bit of a reputation for being rough, but any fights tended to be just one-on-one fist fights.' Patrick 'Pud' Robinson later joined the team. Ali says, 'Pud was a good mate, you were OK if he was on your side.' Pud was obviously very good at his job of keeping order, because one punter remembered him as being 'threatening just sitting in a chair!' but asked not to be named!

Ali continues, 'There was a chap called Fred, who was a car park attendant. People used to try and park in front of the steps but it was staff only, so Fred used to move them on.' Ali was fanatical about minis and had a black one with yellow stripes. He made sure that he never parked it near the steps, in order to avoid the wrath of Fred.

Nigel comments, 'Dave Watts was a nice chap, good as gold. He was one of our helpers, by that I mean not just on the Saturday night, but during the week as well. He used to muck in.'

Helper Bully (Steve Bullimore) reels off other names, 'David Gowan, Kay Farrow, Ryan and Willy Wallace from Overstrand.' David Pegg ('Gaffer') helped with the Wednesday discos along with another member of staff who was to play an important part in the Links history, Ian Foster.

Nigel takes up Ian's story:

A lot of the youngsters used to like to come and help out and work for us. There was one whose name is Ian Foster. He was a smashing lad and, for some reason, he had the nickname 'Flo'. In those days the word 'Fab' was the in thing. We had a little advertising campaign going about the Fab Links – everyone goes to the Fab Links. Then we thought, Fab Links Organisation, F-L-O, and that's where it came from. 'Flo' came up with the pot-bellied rock monster character. So the FLO character evolved and then it stuck.

We used to advertise every week in the North Norfolk News. *When we started using FLO, every week we had the same picture of him, but there was always a little speech balloon, 'FLO says...', and I used to invent those. Some weeks it was a bit of a struggle, but every week I came up with a 'FLO says' and people used to look for them. It would be a big display ad on the back of the paper and each week everyone would turn to the back page to see what FLO said.*

An advert on 23 June 1967 warned, 'Watch out for FLO!' and on the 30 June and 7 July it was promised, 'FLO is coming'. He made his first appearance on 15 July 1967 and was to stay for almost five years.

Ian Foster remembers designing the general 'Top Pop Stars' posters as well. He says, 'They used to print the posters at Beccles, silk screen by hand. You would get seven or eight for £1, which was a lot of money in those days.'

Newspaper advertising was necessary to inform those who lived outside the poster area of who was on at the Links that Saturday because, although many people would attend each week regardless of who was on, there were one or two other venues putting on big acts and vying for the youngsters' custom.

One of these, the Cromer Olympia, or Rollerdrome, as it was more commonly known, had been running as a music venue for as long as the Blows had owned the Links, but the Rollerdrome's pop acts usually appeared on Sunday nights. So although youngsters could, if they wanted, go to both venues at the weekend, lack of money may have meant they had to choose between the two. This was especially true when big acts were booked, because the admission charge would be increased.

In the earlier part of the century, the Olympia site had simply been a large, open-air lawn with a stage at one end. The audience had sat in deck-chairs watching the artists perform. It was eventually enclosed with a roof, and a floor was laid. The venue had been run as a cinema in the 1930s then, when roller-skating became popular after the War, Norman Troller and his wife, Hilda, had hired it from Rusts in 1947 and used it as a rollerdrome. During the 1960s there would be bingo during the week – usually on a Tuesday – and skating on Wednesday evenings, Saturday mornings, Saturday evenings and Sunday afternoons. During the summer season they would stage wrestling weekday evenings. Then they started having discos on Friday evenings and bands on Sunday evenings. Adverts called it 'The Teenage Rendezvous' and urged patrons to 'Rock – Roll – Twist – Jive'.

Norman Troller ran buses for the Rollerdrome dances on Sunday evenings from North Walsham, Holt and Wells. John Chandler used to collect money on the bus and Norman used to let him in for free. John did a few supports there with his band, Page Nine, which included Mike Green, Dave Fuller and John Battrick. Norman sponsored them and bought their equipment.

Another local band, Ricky Lee and the Hucklebucks, supported the Animals at the Rollerdrome in June 1964. Billed as plain 'Hucklebucks' when they played with John Mayall's Bluesbreakers at the Links in December 1967, they appeared at both venues several times with Mick Starling on guitar.

Barry Lee and the Planets played at various village halls in Norfolk and then got a booking with Norman Troller at the Rollerdrome. According to the Planets' bass player, Roger Reynolds, this was the ambition of every local band: it was like getting to the London Palladium. They played at the Rollerdrome several times, later appearing as the Barry Lee Show.

Jan Petty saw several groups at the Rollerdrome including the Animals and, in September 1966, Chris Farlowe and the Thunderbirds – two months after their number one hit 'Out of Time'. The Barron Knights appeared in August 1966 when they had their hit 'Call up the Groups', a pastiche of other chart bands. Other notable acts were Lulu and the Luvvers (August 1964), Manfred Mann (September 1964), Billy J Kramer (June 1966), Dave Dee, Dozy, Beaky, Mick and Titch (August 1966), David Essex (February 1967) and Deep Purple (July 1967).

John Jarvis remembers the venue well:

Gene Vincent was there in 1964. Norman Troller would book people six months ahead and by the time they came there they would often have a hit record but they usually honoured their contracts. The Animals played there when 'House of the Rising Sun' was in the charts and Cilla Black came along when she was doing quite well with 'Anyone Who Had a Heart'. Apparently, she wasn't too pleased to be playing there by that time.

Terry Pardon used to go to the Rollerdrome and remembers that 'Cilla Black had the hump!' He also saw the Tremeloes and the Searchers there.

It was said of Norman Troller, 'He was a clever businessman but in a nice way.' He lost out in the end because of the venue he was trying to promote: it wasn't big enough to hold sufficient people to make much money and was just a plain rollerdrome, which didn't have the atmosphere of the Links.

Rod Blow, from the Links, comments:

Norman Troller was a rough and ready character but I gather he was well-liked and straight, and when things went wrong he'd put them right. I never heard a bad word about him, although we'd probably never shook hands or anything like that – it was all part of the job. We were on the Saturday night and he was on the Sunday and we finished up getting the bigger crowds. We won out in the end because we were bigger and we got the bigger groups. We had the room, the atmosphere, the parking, the coaches: the whole package won out. We didn't start out to do that, it just evolved that way.

Norman stopped having the groups but kept on with the roller-skating until 1974. The building was demolished 10 years later.

Another potentially more dangerous rival to the Links opened its doors on Saturday 29 April 1967 with a concert by the Move. This was the Wellington in Dereham. Free buses ran from Norwich and Thetford, via Watton and Wymondham. Trevor Leeder remembers:

The Wellington was under the cinema. There was usually a fight. While the bands changed over they used to send the kids upstairs to watch cartoons to calm them down!

It seems that the Wellington had a big name every two or three weeks. Those appearing included Cat Stevens, Wayne Fontana, Manfred Mann, Amen Corner, Jimmy James, Jeff Beck, Marmalade, and Pink Floyd with Syd Barrett – when 'See Emily Play' was at number six in the charts. The Nice, who were PP Arnold's backing group, contained Keith Emerson on keyboards, who would later form Emerson, Lake and Palmer. The Nice were supported by Deep Purple, and this was all before the end of 1967! Cream played at the venue on 10 June 1967 with Eric Clapton (guitar), Jack Bruce (bass) and Ginger Baker (drums).

Music fan Terry Bunting observes, 'All of Cream's albums went at least gold, sales-wise – and they played at Dereham! Mind you, they'd played Hoveton Village Hall eight months earlier!'

Jimi Hendrix, arguably the most influential musician of the twentieth century, played at Dereham Wellington on the 7 October 1967. Beck, Clapton and Hendrix in the space of six months was, probably, not something the venue could sustain and it closed a short time later.

Terry came up with another reason for its demise, based on his reading of old editions of the music publication *Melody Maker*:

Someone had written a letter saying, 'We must stop people playing at the Wellington in Dereham.' What happened was that the girls in Dereham were going to see the bands and eyeing them up and the local boys from Dereham were getting really jealous. So the local hard nuts used to try and beat the bands up. At the Nice gig the fans tried to get into the dressing room after the band. There was a roadie up against the door holding it shut. The door gave way and he went under it. They trampled on him and he nearly died. They said the bands should boycott the place because of all the trouble.

Fortunately, this was not the case at the Links. The venue weathered this early competition and after Rod Blow's departure his brother, Nigel, was still able to book the popular bands. The Equals came twice to the Links, having become the first multi-racial pop band to top the UK charts in 1968 with 'Baby Come Back'. Their guitarist, Eddy Grant, would go on to have other hits as a solo artist in the early 1980s. American band the Electric Prunes showcased their two UK singles, 'Get Me to the World on Time' and 'I Had Too Much to Dream Last Night', at the Links in 1967, around the time that 'Baby Now That I've Found You' was number one for the Foundations. They came to the Links the following year when their latest single, 'Build Me Up Buttercup', had just been released.

Soul Survivors became Love Affair in 1967, and shortly after they came to the Links they had a UK number one with 'Everlasting Love'. The band later admitted on television that session musicians had played on the recording and Steve Ellis, the singer, was the only member of Love Affair who appeared on the record. That could well explain why John Wells remembers that Love Affair were good when they came to the Links, but nothing like the single they had released!

They returned to the venue in 1970 then disbanded. In 1972, Steve Ellis came back to the Links with his band Ellis – which included keyboard player Zoot Money – and later in the decade he joined heavy rockers Widowmaker.

The Tremeloes had topped the charts in May 1967 with 'Silence is Golden', justifying their split the previous year from Brian Poole. Their other singles in 1967 included 'Here Comes My Baby' and 'Even the Bad Times are Good'. Nigel was impressed when they turned up to play at the Links in the winter of 1967 despite appalling weather. He says:

We lost money on the Tremeloes, one of the few groups we lost money on but it was not their fault. On the Saturday we had a tremendous fall of snow – an absolute blizzard – and I thought, the act's never going to get through. I thought, never mind, we won't have to pay them, the kids won't make it either, we'll just have to get through the night. The Tremeloes had an accident in their car, they still made it, and virtually no-one turned up. They were really nice guys and so professional on stage, didn't care, just went on and enjoyed it. Their thing was close harmonies and they were in the middle of doing one of their numbers, can't remember which one it was, and suddenly the P.A. system failed. They didn't miss a beat, they suddenly cut into an instrumental number and I thought, that's polished. They finished that number, sorted out the P.A., and carried on. They were superb. Of all the acts we ever had, to my mind they were the epitome of a professional pop group.

According to the Links adverts, Alan Blakeley of the Tremeloes had a brother who was drummer with the Epics, who appeared at the venue several times. On one occasion they were supported by local band Sleepy Talk, who comprised Keith Lamb (vocals), John Sell (drums), Phil Baldwin (guitar) and Alan Fish (bass). They had also supported Pink Floyd at the Wellington in Dereham.

Despite Nigel's concerns, it was very rare for a band not to turn up. Marmalade were due to come to the Links in March 1969, when 'Ob-la-di, Ob-la-da' – which had been number one – was still in the charts. Nigel says, 'We did just wonder whether they would turn up, but they did, they honoured the contract, they were ever such nice chaps.'

Marmalade were massive stars and filled the Links each time they appeared. Their connection with the venue had started in 1966, when they had appeared twice as the Gaylords. The following year they had become Marmalade – probably to everyone's immense relief – and returned to the venue supporting Jeff Beck. The second support that night had been local band Feel for Soul, who appeared at the Links several times during 1967. Terry Bunting describes the fortunes of the various band members after Feel for Soul split up:

The bass player was Boz Burrell from, I think, Kings Lynn: he went on to great fame and fortune with King Crimson then Bad Company. The keyboard player went to Mud. He played on some of their records and at their gigs even though Mud never officially had a keyboard player. The drummer went off with somebody else really big. Ronnie, the guitarist, stayed local and became a highly respected blues guitarist.

One act who didn't turn up at the Links had also been booked to appear at the Gala Ballroom, Norwich, earlier in the evening, with the cost being split between the two venues. Nigel explains:

We didn't get them for half price each, but they would have been too costly if we'd had them on our own. I remember there was one – I think it was Edwin Starr – he was booked into the Gala. We had gone to a lot of trouble to make all the arrangements: booking, contracts, and so on, but he never turned up. They had a bit of a blood-bath, I believe, at the Gala. The manager rang me on the evening to see if he'd turned up at ours first, because he was supposed to go to the Gala first then come to Cromer. He never turned up at either. The man was absolutely spitting tacks and so was I. The kids were not pleased either, because there had been a lot of advance publicity for this guy, he was a big star. We were so cross we went down to London to see the agent.

Sometimes Nigel was not particularly impressed with some of the stars who did turn up:

We had a three girl act, coloured girls – a bit of a name, but not a mega name. I think it was the Sharrons or possibly the Flirtations, I can't be completely certain. They were booked to do a 40 minute spot. Anyway, the support group did the warm-up, then these girls came on to do their 40 minutes. I was watching from where we played the records. They were doing their act and were going down fine, and after 20 minutes they said, 'Thanks ever so much, goodnight', and walked off. I thought, wait a minute.

I went straight across the stage, up into their dressing room and said, 'You're down for 40 minutes, you've only done 20.'

They said, 'We weren't going down very well so we came off.'

I said, 'You were,' which they were. They were absolutely fine. I thought they were very good and they had no justifiable reason for coming off. I was cross, because you don't book any act for 20 minutes, so I said, 'Well if you've only done half the time, I'm only paying you half the money.' They were not amused. They didn't go back on, they said they'd sue me and we'd never open again!

Another star, who played a full set but did not endear himself to Nigel, was vocalist, guitarist, keyboardist and harmonica player John Mayall. Nigel says:

God, he was arrogant.   He wanted the audience to be silent. He said, 'I want absolute silence. We've got to get things absolutely teamed up.' I thought, just get on with it.

John Mayall's Bluesbreakers saw many great musicians come and go. One of them, Eric Clapton, had – by the time of Mayall's first Links appearance in December 1967 – formed Cream. Mick Taylor (guitar/vocals) would later leave for the Rolling Stones, and Andy Fraser (bass) went to Free. His replacement for the April 1968 appearance, Tony Reeves, later formed Greenslade and Curved Air. Saxophonist Dick Heckstall-Smith joined Bluesbreakers from the Graham Bond Organisation, with drummer Jon Hiseman.

Similarly to Bluesbreakers, the Graham Bond Organisation nurtured young talent. Previous members Jack Bruce and Ginger Baker had formed Cream with Eric Clapton by the time Graham Bond came to the Links in the summer of 1967. Bond had helped develop the British R & B movement by mixing in elements of jazz. He introduced the Mellotron – an early-day keyboard or synthesiser which played tapes of other instruments – to British audiences, and was one of the first to use the Hammond organ.

In May 1969 another big name, the Move, appeared at the Links, three months after their single 'Blackberry Way' had topped the charts. Norman Clowes reckons they probably had the most equipment of any of the bands he saw there. Nigel gives his impression of vocalist/guitarist Roy Wood:

Little Roy Wood, lots of hair, but further round than he is up! He had this classic look, very ferocious with all his long hair, but timid as anything. Nice chap. You couldn't tell until you met them, what they were like.

John Wells attended the Move concert and took several slides of the band, which also comprised Carl Wayne (vocals), Bev Bevan (drums) and Rick Price (bass). Roy Wood and Bev Bevan would later form ELO before Roy Wood left to start Wizzard. Roy Wood was advertised to play at West Runton Pavilion as a solo artist in 1978 but it is not certain whether the concert went ahead.

When they appeared at the Links, the Move were supported by popular local band Eyes of Blond. Trevor Jay was sound and lighting engineer and roadie for Eyes of Blond from August 1970 until they broke up in February 1971. He remembers that the band had their own fan club. The line-up when Trevor became involved was Phil Dimitri – real name Holmes – (lead guitar/vocals/bazookie/banjo), Phil Wade (rhythm/six-string guitar/12 string guitar/saxophone/vocals) and Neil Applegate (bass guitar/vocals). Harry Rix had just come from another local band, Skinn, formerly known as Rubber Band, to replace Paul Watts on drums.

Eyes of Blond mostly played covers by bands including the Byrds, the Rolling Stones and the Doobie Brothers, but had written some original songs. They were managed by Phil Beavis of Norwich Artistes and were described on a publicity poster as 'Musicians Extraordinary in the land of harmonious pop'. They had appeared at the Links many times since 1966 supporting artists such as Sonny Childe and the TNTs, and the Graham Bond Organisation. Later, they were themselves supported by other local bands including Barries Magazine, Spencer's People, Kiss and Wildfire.

Barries Magazine were also a four-piece with ambitious publicity material. A flyer from the time declared they were:

One of the Region's better groups ... the ideal group for any 'cold' venue, where the audience needs warming up. This group are guaranteed to go down well with all types of people and are always proving this.

Hailing from Bury St Edmunds, they apparently planned to undertake recording, radio spots and a European tour.

The Alex Wilson Set, who had played second support to the Who, were another local band who were able to mingle with the stars and gain experience playing to a large crowd. In 1968 they joined with the brass section of another local band, Toby Jug, to become Kiss – not to be confused with the American rock band of the same name which formed five years later.

Derek Driver sang with the Alex Wilson Set from 1966 but 'retired' when they became Kiss. Later, he would sing with the Trevor Copeman Band who would become the resident band at the Links for a short time in 1972.

Managed by Tony Baker, Kiss comprised Terry Seeley (vocals), John Tuttle (saxophone/vocals), Dave Knowles (bass/vocals), Dave 'Duke' Smith-Howell (lead guitar/vocals), Jimmy Jewell (drums) and Bryan Turner (flute). When local band Skinn broke up in 1970, their organist joined Kiss. Kiss were advertised as 'progressive soul', having begun as a soul band then developing into Moody Blues and King Crimson type material. Kiss appeared frequently at the Links as both main act and support. Elsewhere they supported the Who, Status Quo and the Beach Boys, amongst others. They played a Christmas season in Montreux Casino on Lake Geneva in Switzerland. The building later burnt down, inspiring the classic Deep Purple song 'Smoke on the Water'.

Nigel was disappointed when Kiss went their separate ways in 1971. He says:

They were my favourite local group. I thought they were really very good indeed. Kiss launched themselves and turned fully pro but they didn't last very long. They couldn't quite make it, but if ever anyone deserved to, they did, because they were very good musicians; very polished, nice lads.

Soon after the demise of Kiss, John Tuttle appeared at the Links with his new band Barabas.

Nigel explains why he thinks some local bands failed to make it:

There was a big gulf between the semi-pro groups that had daytime jobs and just played at the weekends, and the pro groups. It's the same when you're in business for yourself. A lot of people will get to be in business for themselves by moonlighting first of all. When they make that leap they're suddenly in another world. That's how it was with these groups. You would sometimes get the fully pro groups who were possibly not quite as good as the support groups, because they'd gone fully pro and couldn't hang on.

Often some of the main acts at the Links also seemed on the point of success but would find fame very elusive. One of these, who Kiss supported, were Ferris Wheel, a soul-rock outfit comprising Diana Ferris, Bernie Holland, Dennis Elliot and Linda Lewis. They toured extensively and released a few records but disbanded in 1970. As with Eddy Grant, Linda Lewis would later find solo success in 1975 with her top 20 hit 'It's in His Kiss', and would appear at West Runton Pavilion in November 1977.

George Young and Harry Vanda also found success after their band split up. The Easybeats had had a top 20 hit in the UK in 1966 with 'Friday on My Mind', but six months after their Links appearance in June 1969, the band broke up. However, George Young and Harry Vanda went on to produce the first seven albums for George's younger brothers, Malcolm and Angus, and their successful rock band, AC/DC.

John Wells had his camera with him at the Links to capture the performance of Ferris Wheel and also the Alan Bown Set in January 1968. Robert Palmer, probably their most famous member, did not join them until the following year. John Anthony Helliwell, saxophonist with the Alan Bown Set, would join Supertramp at the end of 1973, just before they recorded their successful third album, *Crime of the Century*. John Helliwell's saxophone solos would become a trademark of Supertramp and, during live performances, he also played keyboards.

One band called Ten Years After had just started out when they came to the Links. Less than two years later they would play four numbers on day three at the legendary American music festival, Woodstock. Joe Barber recalls:

Ten Years After played at the Marquee Club in London where all the best bands used to start. They did jazz-style blues rock and played fast guitar licks but people didn't get it. They were nearly as big as Led Zeppelin.

When they appeared at the Links in early 1968, Desmond Dekker and the Aces were advertised as a 'Ten-piece soul act of 007 fame'. Their latest single was called 'Sabotage' and they would reach number one in the UK singles chart the following year with 'Israelites'.

The 6 November 1968, when girl-trio the Paper Dolls played at the Links, left a lasting impression on Nigel for a couple of reasons:

It was that night I realised the power of make up! I remember I was in the ballroom, opening up. This couple came in and, to be polite, the particular girl was, I thought, fairly plain. I asked if I could help her and she told me she was one of the Paper Dolls and I thought, bloody hell! They came on stage, totally glamorous and I didn't believe it! They were professional, came in, did the job.

Nigel concluded by saying, 'They were very polished,' although whether he was referring to the act or the make-up wasn't clear!

The second reason for Nigel's memorable night is explained by Bully (Steve Bullimore):

The Paper Dolls sang a song to Nigel and he was very embarrassed! There were stairs from the balconies going down to the stage and when the Paper Dolls played they'd blocked off the top end of one of the balconies and made a little dressing room. Over the other side they set up a disco spot. Nigel used to do the discos in those days and introduce the bands. The Paper Dolls had a single out called 'Something Here in My Heart (Keeps Telling Me No)'. Nigel was standing up there and she turned and sung it to him, it really embarrassed him.

Another act which was to leave a lasting impression on Nigel, and would appear at the Links more times than any other, was booked for the first time in May 1969. The advertisement for Raymond Froggatt informed the punters that he had written Dave Clark's hit 'Red Balloon' and Cliff Richard's new single 'Big Ship'.

Nigel takes up the story:

I booked Froggie and I thought he was absolutely brilliant. I thought, I've got to have him again. Booked him again, and the attendance went down, and I thought, I don't care, I like him. Booked him again, the attendance went down again, and you'd think after that – two repeats, reducing attendance – I'd stop; but I thought, no, I'll book him again – just for me, and the attendance went up. And it went up and up, and he could do no wrong. We got to the stage where we booked him once every six weeks. The contract used to be for one 45 minute spot; he never got off the stage in under an hour-and-a-half. He is ever such a nice guy, and he absolutely revelled in it. He came in one night and said, 'This place is just fantastic, tremendous atmosphere. I spend six weeks bumming round the country treated like a tramp, I come here and it's just fantastic. The only other place I go down well is my home town of Birmingham.'

As well as Froggie on guitar and vocals, the band at that time included Louis Clark (bass), Len Ablethorpe (drums) and Hartley Cain (known as 'H') on various guitars including steel and 12 string. 'H' says that the band had only been going a couple of years before they went to the Links and it became a major part of their lives. Their association with the venue continued into the 1970s. Links regular Trevor Alford remembers:

One night we were at the Links and they asked us all to cheer as loudly as we could because the Raymond Froggatt Band were going to record a live record there. I think it was 'Sooner or Later'.

One advertisement, penned by Nigel, declared Raymond Froggatt was 'Back again in response to Astronomic Public Demand, this Uniquely Brilliant Artiste. HASN'T THE LORD BLESSED US.'

Norman Clowes agrees with Nigel, 'Froggie was a fantastic success. I don't know why, it wasn't really Links sort of music, but it was always a good night when he played.'

7

Roosters, Turkeys, Chickens And Crows

The start of the new decade saw no let-up in the standard of bands offered at the Links. Badfinger came when their single 'Come and Get It', written by Paul McCartney, was in the charts, as did the Mixtures with their 'Pushbike Song' and Sweet with their new single 'Funny Funny'. 'That Same Old Feeling' was still doing well for Polly Browne and Pickettywitch when they appeared, billed as 'Hughie Green's discovery' from the television talent show *Opportunity Knocks*. John Wells was there with his camera again, but that wasn't all he was looking at!

John explains, 'I was going out with a girl from near Sheringham, who I thought a lot of, when I went to the Links with some friends. I saw a girl that "knocked me out". We dated and eventually married.' He and Tricia are still together. He says, 'If ever we fall out, I just remember those early days at the Links, and remember why we are together!' John's sister, Pam, met her husband there as well.

Other bands included Matthew's Southern Comfort, who came to the Links a year after their single 'Woodstock' topped the charts, and Hot Chocolate, whose single 'I Believe (in Love)' had just been released when they made their first appearance there. Links owner, Nigel Hindley (was Blow), explains, 'We were thought of as being one of the top venues outside London by the agencies and we used to get written up fairly regularly in the *New Musical Express*.' He continues:

We always used to go down to the Pavilion at about half-six to get ready. Even though we didn't open till eight, things had got to be done. One night there were two or three car-loads of people outside and I thought, oh, the group's early. When I spoke to them, it turned out they were from north London somewhere and they'd heard about the place and decided to come and have a look. At the end of the evening they said that they'd had an absolutely fantastic time, better than they used to get down in London, and they'd be back. And they were! They came for several weeks.

German keyboard player Manfred Mann had achieved much commercial success by the time he brought his band to the Links in the summer of 1970. They had had their first UK top 10 hit '5-4-3-2-1' in early 1964 which had been followed by a dozen more including three number ones: 'Do Wah Diddy Diddy', 'Pretty Flamingo' and 'Mighty Quinn'. Nigel says he was surprised when he met Manfred

Mann to find out he was a German although, in retrospect, he says the name should have given him a clue!

Andy Fairweather-Low was another dark horse. He came to the Links with his new band, Fair Weather, but played hits recorded by his previous band, Amen Corner, including their number one from February 1969 '(If Paradise is) Half as Nice'. Nigel recalls they also played 'Bend Me, Shape Me':

I remember being quite surprised because it's quite a powerful number when you hear it yet he's such a timid chap when you meet him. I didn't realise, but he's broad Welsh. He was in the dressing room and I went through to see him – we always used to go through and have a word. He was sitting there and he's very nice and terribly polite. I had a talk to him and he said, with his little Welsh voice, very softly spoken, 'Was that all right for you?'

Local band Murphy supported Fair Weather at the Links and shared a dressing room with them. Murphy had evolved from an earlier band, Ricky Lee and the Hucklebucks. The guitarist with both bands, Mick Starling, describes Andy Fairweather-Low as 'a lovely chap'.

One main act who weren't particularly well known, but who received widespread critical acclaim for their second album, *Medusa*, were Trapeze. This was their first album as a three-piece consisting of Dave Holland (drums), Mel Galley (guitar/vocals) and Glenn Hughes (bass/vocals), and was released around the time of their first visit to the Links. Although the band later enjoyed a great following in the States, Glenn Hughes would leave them in June 1973 to join Deep Purple.

Van de Graff Generator appeared at the Links in the summer of 1971 and Bully (Steve Bullimore) says, 'When they played there, they were on record as being the loudest band in the world.' The band had been formed in 1967 by three students at Manchester University and was named after the American physicist and his invention, which was an electrostatic accelerator or, put more simply, a silver dome that made all your hair stand on end when you touched it in school science lessons!

One intriguing advertisement which cannot go unmentioned was that placed in August 1971 for Danta, which was apparently an 'afro rock' band with 'genuine fire eater'. That one must have been a nightmare for the fire officer!

Links regular Terry Bunting remembers that Siege Band – who were advertised as 'three man heavy' and 'mind-blowing trio' – had the unusual line-up of keyboards, bass and drums. They played the Fakenham School dance in Melton Constable school hall and headlined at the Links three times in 1970. On their first visit they were supported by local band Mister Toad. Mister Toad's guitarist, Chris Mortimer, remembers playing at the Links several times supporting Slade, Status Quo and Rare Bird, amongst others. Slade and Status Quo music was included in their set-list, as well as numbers by Deep Purple, Black Sabbath, Jimi Hendrix and Cream. Chris recalls, 'At the Links they liked it the louder the better.' Mister Toad also included Stephen Kerrison (bass), David Loomb (tenor sax), Alex Blyth (vocals) and Roger Mayes (drums).

Another local band, Wildfire, supported the Seige Band on their other two visits to the venue. Wildfire had formed in 1970 with Brian Kerrison (drums), Bob Walker (lead guitar) and Mervyn 'Coe' Hambling (rhythm guitar) from Aylsham, and Mel Chamberlain (bass) from Wymondham.

Brian and Bob remember some of the songs Wildfire covered, which included:

Jimi Hendrix:	Fire, Manic Depression, Can You See Me, Purple Haze, Red House, Stone Free, 51st Anniversary
The Who:	Pictures of Lily, Can't Explain
Cream:	Crossroads, Sunshine of Your Love
Led Zeppelin:	Whole Lotta Love, Communication Breakdown

The following year Brian left and Chris Hague joined, but Wildfire split up a short time later. Bob then formed the Hoss Band with Brian and Mel, bringing in Richard Gotterson on vocals. They would headline the Links in 1974.

Colin Kerrison remembers:

My first time at the Links was when my brother's band, Wildfire, played there. I had my first pint that night (Watney's special mild). We all looked forward to Saturday nights because you knew you would meet up with all your mates from around the area and a good time would be had by all. The free buses were especially useful in the early days before we had our own transport.

Colin has a photo taken at the Links bar in 1972 featuring Karen Oakes (later Wells), 'Wurzel' (Andrew Wells), 'Plant' (Julian Hudson) and 'Olix' (Martin Skoyles). He has another of his 'very good pal, the late Tim Sapsford, living it up on stage with Crow.'

Crow were another popular local band. They first came to the Links in a support role to Raymond Froggatt in July 1971, but headlined many times during the subsequent three years before becoming the Buster James Band. Terry Bunting remembers, 'Roger James always used to have a mike stand which was done in red and white, like a barber's pole.' As well as Roger 'Buster' James on vocals, Crow's original line-up comprised Clive 'Buzz' Hunt (guitar), Chris 'Don' Warnes (bass) and Paul 'Cass' Callaby (drums).

The equipment used by the band in 1972 was:

Paul – Drums:
Ludwig. 28 inch bass drum, 13 inch small tom, 16 inch floor tom. Light grey oyster colour, recovered at one time by Paul to gold sparkle.

Buzz – Guitar:
Gibson Les Paul (black). Amplifier: Selmer 'treble and bass' 50 watt. Speaker cabinet: Selmer (model unknown).

Chris – Bass:
Fender Precision (sunburst). Amplifier: unknown. Speaker cabinet: unknown.

Roger – Vocals:
Microphone: Shure 'Unidyne B'.

This list was provided by Paul, but his memory of the gigs is not too clear. 'The only thing I can remember is the episode where Don (Chris Warnes) climbed up onto the PA stack during a performance and couldn't get back down again!' he says.

The venue holds special memories for lead singer Roger James:

As far as the band went, the Links was such a special place; something about it was special, it didn't matter who was playing there. West Runton Pavilion never had the atmosphere. We did our first few gigs at the Links with the very early Crow as support act to named bands, then we were headlining. After Crow split we continued with Buster James at both the Links and later at West Runton. By this time we were touring all over the place but the Links was one of the stomping grounds to start with. It had a good atmosphere and loads of character. It's difficult to put into words, it just brings a smile to the face.

When we were a support band at the Links, we used the dressing room downstairs; the top band used the dressing room upstairs. We preferred the support band's dressing room so even when we were headlining, we still went in there.

People in my band now often say they never thought they'd play with me; you don't realise you mean that much to them. A lot of bands started playing because of us, they'd seen us and wanted to play.

It was around this time that Links helper Bully (Steve Bullimore) was due to leave school. Nigel takes up the story:

Bully was a school boy when he came and worked for us. We thought the world of him. The time came for him to leave school and he wanted to come and work for us full-time. His parents were anxious that we could not offer him any kind of formal apprenticeship or trade. I was delighted he wanted to work for us, but I shared his parents' concern that I couldn't guarantee his future. He didn't care, that was what he wanted to do.

It seemed Bully never wanted to go home. He says:

I remember one year we were painting the place out in this dark bluey colour, which was all the rage at the time. Bear in mind I was only young, I had a push-bike. We were painting on the Friday night because we had to get it done so it was dry on the Saturday. My mum came up at midnight, ringing the bell on my bike, to ask if I was going to come home. I was only probably about 11 or 12, but I used to love being there. They used to treat me really, really well.

Bully's whole family gradually became employed at the Links, as he explains:

My mum first got involved when I was doing the washing up. I had to finish at ten o'clock and I think she used to come and take over from me and wash the glasses. Then I was promoted to carrying the glasses from the kitchen, where we washed them, and taking them out of the back door, round the outside, up the steps and putting them behind the bar. By the time I was carrying the glasses, I was there until the finish and my mum would wash them all evening.

I used to carry the pint mugs on my fingers. I could probably carry about 15 or 20 like that. We never used to dry them up because they were washed in hot water and they dried when you took them outside. When it was a really busy night in the winter there would be steam coming out of the eaves of the roof, where the hot air was meeting the cold. The first time I saw it I thought it was a fire, I went running in and told them!

I think at one point my dad used to collect the glasses with about three lads, then my older sister Janice used to do the door for a while, till she moved away.

Bully's younger sister, Rachel, went as well. She says:

I started going to the Links at the age of about 11, around 1968. Mum and Dad both worked there so I went along too. I would go home at the end of the evening with Mum when the bands were packing up and they would often speak to us. They were all very approachable and friendly. It was a great place.

Bully remembers how the venue was staffed:

Originally there used to be two bars and I think two or three people worked on each one. Before they started serving food, a chap would come from Norwich and have a van outside selling burgers and hot dogs. There used to be a ladies' cloakroom and a gents' cloakroom and you used to put your coat in for sixpence and get a raffle ticket and collect your coat at the end. A chap called Dreamy worked there.

Julie Bunting (was Jarvis) went to the Links regularly. She remembers the cloakroom:

You would pay to put your coat in. It would go on a peg with about 10 others. By nine o'clock the cloakroom attendants couldn't walk down the corridor because it was too full. You would leave your bag as well, then you would have nowhere to put the cloakroom ticket they gave you.

Julie remembers each group of people had their own place where they used to stand every week. She was part of the Aylsham crowd and says they always used to stand outside the girls toilets!

Bully continues:

There used to be someone in the kiosk to take the money, and there used to be someone on the door to stamp their hand. If you were quick enough, you could copy the stamp onto somebody else's hand, so they started using letters, which wouldn't come out right because they would be back-to-front. They had five different stamps they used.

Once, when Bully was walking Rinty the dog, he found a little green purse which someone had dropped. Inside, all cut out in cork, were copies of all the different rubber stamps which someone had spent a lot of time making. The scam would have involved sending somebody in to find out what the stamp was for the night, then using the corresponding counterfeit one to get any number of people in. With decimalisation in February 1971, they would be avoiding admission charges ranging from 35p for the first Thin Lizzy visit to 60p for Status Quo.

The first time Status Quo were advertised at the Links was in early 1971 and several appearances followed. They were known in the charts with records such as 'Pictures of Matchstick Men', 'Down the Dustpipe', 'In My Chair' and 'Gerundula'. Roger James' current keyboard player says he saw Quo there and they 'blew him away'.

Julie Bunting has been a fan of Status Quo since she first saw them at the Industrial Rooms in Norwich, backing another band. She caught the drumstick thrown out to the crowd by John Coghlan, then her and two friends went backstage and met the whole band. She saw them each time they played at the Links. At a recent signing of the autobiography *XS All Areas*, written by guitarists/vocalists Rick Parfitt and Francis Rossi, she took the drumstick along to show them – 35 years later!

In the book, Rick Parfitt mentions playing at the Links to about 400 people and being paid what, to him, seemed an enormous amount of money at the time.

Links owner Nigel says:

I was worried about Status Quo when we had them because they were a lot of money, but the queue was right down the road. I thought, thank God for that. We had them several times and the two main characters are really nice guys. Rossi really used to take the pee out of Parfitt. They were really best mates. They were totally down to earth, no side to them, nice guys. They have such fun on stage, and they're like that off stage as well.

Bully joined in the fun on one occasion:

Status Quo were staying in one of the caravans at the Links. After the show, I went back to the caravan and they had some girls in there. We all went skinny-dipping down the beach!

Terry Bunting remembers, 'The first band I ever went to see at the Links was Quo, but they called off. Then they played there a few weeks later and I remember Mike Rossi (as Francis was known then) saying he was really sorry they'd cancelled.'

The cancellation had been regrettable but unavoidable; Alan Lancaster, the bass player, had a poisoned arm. A telegram had been sent to the venue and the band Christie, who had had hits in 1970 with 'San Bernadino' and the number one single 'Yellow River', had come in at short notice. Terry thinks that Christie had a Cromer connection, one of them was from Cromer or had married someone from Cromer, which may have been why they were able to step in quickly.

Status Quo had issued an apology in the *North Norfolk News* for their non-appearance, assuring fans they would be there in the very near future. When they did fulfil the engagement a few weeks later, the band were very apologetic being, as Nigel puts it, 'decent lads' or as Frank Kinsley remarks, 'good blokes!'

Cancellations were, fortunately, quite rare, although the week after Status Quo's non-appearance, the Pretty Things also called off at short notice due to illness.

One of the next bands Terry Bunting saw at the venue was Thin Lizzy, on recommendation of a friend. He says:

I remember Chris Cordy, the singer in my band, saying to me I had to go and see this band from Ireland, Thin Lizzy. He said, 'They will blow your mind.' I must have seen them the second time they came to the Links. I stood right down the front. Phil Lynott had a see-through plexi-glass bass, Eric Bell played a sunburst Fender Stratocaster, and they were fantastic. They played 'If Six was Nine' by Jimi Hendrix, a few original tunes and they did 'I Put a Spell on You', which was absolutely stunning for a three-piece outfit.

I met Phil Lynott after the gig and shook his hand because Chris sort of knew him and wanted to book them. We tried to book them for Fakenham School Dance for £90! Phil Lynott is the thinnest man I have ever met, he was like a stick.

Thin Lizzy's visit to the Links in June 1971 was billed as being 'Back by public demand' after they had played there the previous month. At this time they were appearing in small clubs and touring the circuit as a trio with Brian Downey on drums. Roger James was doing a similar thing with Crow and remembers, 'We played regularly with Thin Lizzy. We bumped into them all over the country.'

Local band Spencer's People – who had previously supported Badfinger, Trapeze, Status Quo and Manfred Mann at the Links – supported Thin Lizzy there which, as bass player Alfie Hall explains, was a great experience:

The Links was great because it gave the youngsters of that era something to aim for. It gave the local bands like ours a chance to play in front of a big crowd. All the groups appreciated it. When we supported Thin Lizzy it was good for us to see how good they were, gave us a goal to work for. We played support to them in Norwich at St Andrews Hall. We also played at the Orford Cellar, but there was nothing to touch the Links in this area at that time.

The band Spencer's People were named after lead singer, Tony Spencer. The line-up also included Harry Collins (lead guitar) and Kenny Philpot (keyboards) – who would both go on to play in another local band called Winner – and Brian 'Ringo' Ward on drums. They played topical pop/rock music of the time including 'Time is Tight' by Booker T and Stevie Wonder's 'Superstition'. Brian remembers on one occasion they were supporting Hot Chocolate and the crowd wanted Spencer's People to do an encore, which meant Hot Chocolate were late playing! Another night, Brian played with the band after consuming a bottle of brandy at Fakenham racecourse earlier in the day. At the end of the set he got up and walked straight through the drum kit, which went all over the stage. Despite the mess, everyone said he played better drunk than sober!

Norman Clowes remembers a similar situation with one of the main bands: 'When Chicken Shack played, Stan Webb drank nearly a whole bottle of Southern Comfort before he went anywhere near the stage.'

In spite of this, Terry Bunting insists, 'Chicken Shack played the blues brilliantly; they were one of my favourite bands at the Links.'

One of Chicken Shack's previous members, pianist/vocalist Christine Perfect, had left in 1969, later becoming Christine McVie and joining Fleetwood Mac. The trio of Stan Webb (guitar/vocals), Paul Hancox (drums) and John Glascock (bass) played on their first few bookings at the Links, then Bob Daisley came in as bass player when John left, to later join Jethro Tull.

The personnel of Jethro Tull seemed to change often and Mick Abrahams, who had left in 1968, came to the Links in March 1972 with his eponymous new band. Another ex-Jethro Tull star, Glen Cornick, appeared in December with his new band, Wild Turkey, promoting their album *Battle Hymn*. They returned to the venue two weeks later to see in the New Year, but it was old favourite, Raymond

Froggatt, who played again on Christmas Eve.

In the Raymond Froggatt Band, Len Ablethorpe remained on drums with Hartley Cain on various guitars, but the line-up now included Jim Phillips on guitar and Steve Smith, who had replaced Louis Clark, on bass. Kevin Dorey has a publicity leaflet from around the time which declares that Raymond Froggatt 'is happiest when on the road with his band entertaining their loyal fans.'

When they returned to the venue the following May, the *Eastern Daily Press* reported:

This Saturday that great performer, Raymond Froggatt, pays a return visit to Norfolk and the Links. Froggie has always received a rapturous welcome when in Norwich, and he seems to go down just as well on the coast. Perhaps it's because we in Norfolk recognise true talent when we see it.

1972 saw the return of Margaret and Rod Blow to the Links, and one of the first things they had to deal with was a bomb scare which took place during a Slade concert.

Slade, from Wolverhampton, had first played at the venue in 1969 when they had been billed as 'formerly Ambrose Slade, taking London by storm.' Since then they had achieved chart success in August 1971 with 'Get Down and Get With It' and a string of number ones had followed, starting with 'Coz I Luv You' in November 1971.

Bully (Steve Bullimore) takes up the story:

I was taking the glasses up the steps and Nigel stood at the top with a police officer. Slade were actually playing on stage and the Sergeant was telling Nigel about the bomb scare. Nigel asked me what we could do. I was only a boy, but he called me his right hand man. I said to the policeman, 'If you do stop the band playing and you have to empty the place, if I were you I'd tell them you'll let them back in and the band can play again, but let them go over the 12 o'clock cut-off, or whatever it was, so they can finish playing.' Slade were really big then, by that time.

Nigel remembers the policeman saying to him, 'We've had a report of a bomb in here, it probably is a hoax, but you've got to empty the place. You'll have to tell them.' Nigel had replied, 'No, you tell them.' The policeman then went up on stage and interrupted the group. The crowd was shouting, 'Get off!'

Meanwhile, Nigel had instructed Bully to unlock three of the double doors leading to the outside to let people out. Bully grabbed the bunch of keys from the office and pushed his way through the crowd to unlock the first door. When he got there, he found that the keys for that door were on a different key-ring, so he had to go back through the crowd to the office to get the other set of keys.

Back on stage, Rod remembers:

Noddy Holder kept the group together and said, 'This is serious, I think we ought to do what the police have asked us to do.' So we put all the lights up and he talked the kids out. The band didn't leave the stage until the whole place was clear.

Margaret agrees, 'Slade were very good at that bomb scare. They stood on stage and he talked every one of those kids out of there.'

Bully had managed to unlock all the doors and he remembers that, 'When the people had left, the floor was covered in glass – some broken, some not – plus loads of different odd shoes and other bits and bobs.'

It was Tim Joyce's first night at the Links and he remembers all the crushed glass on the steps as the Pavilion was evacuated.

Julie Bunting (was Jarvis) says, 'It was really frightening. I wanted to get away from the place once I got outside, but everyone was crowded outside and I couldn't get through.'

Steve Aldred noticed, 'After the bomb scare, it seemed as though a lot more people went back in than had come out!'

Slade, comprising Neville 'Noddy' Holder (vocals/guitar), Dave Hill (guitar), Jimmy Lea (bass) and Don Powell (drums), resumed their place on stage. Ian Wilson remembers Noddy Holder offering the first £50 note Ian had ever seen as a reward to anyone who found out who was responsible for the bomb scare. Tim Joyce says that when everyone had come back in 'Noddy Holder reckoned the bomb was up his arse!'

As Margaret, Rod and Nigel all confirmed, the band were foul-mouthed and very proud of it, but they were good entertainment! Although it is difficult to include precise attendance figures – because reports and memories vary – it is thought that the attendance for Slade was slightly more than for the Who.

The bomb scare turned out to be a hoax and the suspicion was that it had been started by someone who was trying to get a venue going in Sheringham, although this was never confirmed (so presumably Noddy kept his £50).

On the following Monday, Bully made sure that all the keys were all on the same key-ring. Not long after the incident, panic bars were fitted to the inside of the external doors so people could get out from inside. Bully remembers, 'They worked like an oven switch, so if someone opened these doors, the light came on and a bell rang.'

Another of Bully's jobs was checking the emergency lights. He says:

In those days they were 250 watt light bulbs hanging down, connected to either car or lorry batteries, and one of my jobs was to make sure they were charged up and connected up with these crocodile clips. You'd never get away with it today!

The next challenge for the venue was the miners' strike during February 1972, when the three-day week was introduced along with pre-advertised rotas for power cuts, which saw householders shivering in rooms dimly lit by candles for hours on end. It was business as usual at the Links, however, because Nigel arranged to hire a generator.

Bully remembers:

A woman towed a generator on the back of an open tractor from Cley. It was winter time and she had cloth potato sacks tied round her legs and body. She was frozen by the time she got to Cromer. I think Nigel paid £25 to hire the generator for the night.

The venue continued to open throughout the crisis and after it, and more big names appeared.

Stone the Crows came in February 1972 featuring Maggie Bell and Les Harvey, Alex Harvey's younger brother, on lead guitar. Les was tragically electrocuted on stage during a sound-check before a gig at Swansea University three months later.

Quiver, who would later become Sutherland Brothers and Quiver, came to the Links four times between May 1972 and March 1973. Their current releases 'Green Tree' and 'Gone in the Morning' were mentioned in one of the adverts. Quiver's bass player, Bruce Thomas, went on to become part of Elvis Costello and the Attractions.

In June 1972 Atomic Rooster headlined at the Links. They had formed in 1969 with Vincent Crane (organ) and Carl Palmer (drums) – who had both been in a band called the Crazy World of Arthur Brown – and Nick Graham (bass). When Carl Palmer had left for Emerson, Lake and Palmer he had been replaced by Paul Hammond, with John DuCann joining as guitarist/vocalist. When they came to the Links, these two latest additions had left to be replaced by Steve Bolton on guitar and drummer Ric Parnell, son of the orchestra leader Jack Parnell.

Terry Bunting remembers seeing the band:

I used to go to the Links a lot of the time with Jacko, who was my mate from school. You came in the door and the bar was right opposite. Atomic Rooster worked really hard that night and Ric Parnell was dripping in sweat; he'd only have been in his early twenties. He had his shirt off and a towel round his neck and Jacko said to me, 'Look at that poor bastard, he's just been playing his guts out on stage and now he's in the queue for a beer,' and he stood in the queue to get a drink, behind the fans. My mate Derek went to the loo and, much to his amusement, Vincent Crane was taking a leak beside him!

The main acts had a little tiny dressing room at the top of the steps and they wouldn't very often stay in there, so they'd be wandering about the hall or they'd be at the bar. They mingled with you, that was what it was like in those days. It was a different time. The stars never got hassle.

Nigel concurs:

The groups were very accessible in those days because, when they weren't on stage, they would be wandering around the ballroom. These acts were all bumming round the country in these beat up Ford Transits and sometimes on a Saturday night we'd put them up in a caravan for the night and they would potter off the next day.

It was certainly not the kind of lifestyle to encourage conceitedness.

'Everybody drove an old transit,' confirms barman Norman Clowes. 'If they turned up in a big truck it was a real event.'

8

Glitter And Gold

Unfortunately, a short time after Rod Blow returned to help run the Links, his brother Nigel bowed to the pressure of not having had a Saturday night, a Christmas Eve or a New Year's Eve off in eight years, and he left.

According to glass-collector Christopher Pegg ('Tiffer'), the venue was briefly in the care of the grand-nephew of the Antarctic explorer Oates but he was, like his famous ancestor, 'gone for some time'. Keith Allison was then employed as entertainments manager, with the task of creating a new image and livening the place up. He was reported in the local paper as saying, 'We aim to make it an entertainments centre rather than just a dance hall.'

Rod Blow oversaw the refurbishments and the work was finished in early June 1972 at a cost of over £5,000. The alterations allowed the venue to offer entertainment on additional nights of the week. The pop events continued on Saturdays, but dance nights were introduced on Fridays and an old-time music hall evening was offered on Wednesdays in order to widen the appeal of the venue to all age-groups.

The balconies and four of the seven original murals were retained but new features were added. The mural at the back of the stage was replaced by a mirror and the stage itself was equipped with a new PA and disco. A series of 40 'drops', made of coloured plastic tubing, were hung from the ceiling. According to the local paper, each one looked like a cross between a weeping willow and the top of a palm tree. Ultra violet lights would be shone on them and the heat from the dancers would rise and make them turn slowly, creating an effect described by one observer as 'like a moving ceiling of light'.

There was another startling change, too. The familiar cave-man character of 'FLO' was replaced by a new advert showing a shining sun with a flying fish leaping from the sea. A large and colourful version of the new design was reproduced at the west end of the hall, where an old church-style window had been filled in.

The old lounge bar at the front of the building and the hamburger bar in the hall itself had both been completely refitted so that the venue could offer a wider variety of cooked foods, advertised as being 'served by trained hostesses'.

Links helper Bully (Steve Bullimore) says, 'I remember them building where the grand piano used to be. They opened it up and put a hamburger, chicken and scampi-in-a-basket area. Roger Pryce worked behind the chicken bar.' Despite these new facilities, however, Bully says, 'The fish and chip shop in Suffield Park used to do a good trade on a Saturday night.'

The Norwich City football team came to the Links on Friday 23 June to sign copies of their new record 'The Canaries', which had been released to celebrate their promotion to the top league, known at the time as Division One but now called the Premiership.

Dance bands arranged for Friday nights included Geoff Stinton, the Nortones and the Trevor Copeman Band, who became residents during the summer. By September 1972 the Friday dance bands had been replaced by a free disco and late bar.

While the surface of the Links had been updated, the underlying difficulties remained. Rod says, regretfully, 'There were family problems and it was as bad as it ever was and it wasn't going to change. So within a short time of Nigel leaving, I left as well.'

Bully understands a lot of the difficulties Rod and Nigel had to face whilst running the venue alongside their mother. He observes:

Mrs Blow treated her boys shoddily. I remember Rod coming back on the scene and the two boys were going to do this and that, and the mother played up quite a bit about different things. If them two boys had been left, they could really have done a lot. She ruined it. Looking at it now I'm older, I think they must have got so frustrated with her ways.

There was to be one parting shot, however, as Bully explains:

When one of the boys left, the licence for the bars had been in his name. There'd been a row and he was so frustrated that, to get at the mother, he wouldn't open the bar that Saturday night. As the licensee, he was quite within his rights to do that. I believe the court had to sit on a Saturday afternoon to transfer the licence over to her name so they could sell the drink on the Saturday night. I think, right when it opened at eight o'clock, we could only serve soft drinks because it was still being sorted out until nine or half-past.

David Pegg ('Gaffer') helped out at the Links. He lived in a caravan and walked the dog. He says, 'Mrs Blow was a great old lady – a bit eccentric, but always honest and upfront.'

Ali Farrow remembers one occasion when Mrs Blow thought there were prowlers about so he and another doorman, 'Watty' (David Watts), had to sit in a caravan to see if they could catch them.

Roger Bunting describes Mrs Blow as 'An amazing character: eccentric, you might say. She was bleached, very dramatic-looking. She used to talk about seeing ghosts.' Apparently, when the Blows had lived at East Runton, Mrs Blow said she'd seen the ghost of the miller who used to live there.

The Links itself was said to have been haunted and, before they left, Rod and Nigel had a strange experience, as Rod relates:

We did strongly believe there was a ghost, and we heard it one night. We had Rinty the dog, he used to sleep in the foyer. He always hated being left on his own. On a dance night, he used to be in the back room – a little room adjoining the kitchen. We used to keep him in there. We'd all finished and cleared up and were just about ready to shut up shop, there was only about half-a-dozen of us left there. We went to get Rinty and bring him through and, as we were coming across the dance floor, he dropped his ears, lifted his head, and just howled. It was horrible. You know the story about the hairs on the back of your neck standing on end? Well they did. We thought, what's the matter now? There's something wrong, is he not well? Nothing ever frightened him. Next thing, we heard distinct footsteps going along the balcony, because the balconies were just wooden: wooden floorboards. The footsteps went all the way along the balcony to the end, and that was it. But there was no-one there.

It is said that two American soldiers were killed in the area just after the War when the hotel was still operational. Rumour has it they were drunk and drove a jeep over the big retaining walls. Bully heard the story as well:

There was talk about a ghost there and there were times, you never saw anything but you had a feeling there was something there. Someone said it was something to do with a soldier who was there during the War, when the big hotel was at the top of the hill. Whether it was right or wrong, I don't know. I'm open-minded, I don't know either way, but I've been in there and I've not seen anything, but you could feel something sometimes: cold and eerie. The dog used to howl. Quite often you could see the dog's behaviour was strange, but then it might have been your mind playing tricks.

After Rod and Nigel left, Mrs Arundel-Langley, as Mrs Blow had now become, employed a succession of managers to help run the Links, starting with Paul from Gloucester, who is thought to have been her nephew. Phil Beavis from the agency Norwich Artistes, who had been helping Nigel for some time arranging local bands, was just starting to pick up some of the bigger names as well and he lent Paul a hand with the booking. According to Brian Russell, who now runs the agency, 'In 1972 and 1973 Phil was practically living at the Links.'

One of the stars they secured at this time was Rory Gallagher at a cost, Bully thinks, of £800. Music fan Terry Bunting was there:

I remember when Rory Gallagher came, he was a massive star, and it was a quid to get in, which was double the usual price. We all thought, Christ, that's a lot of money, but it was worth it. His Live in Europe *album had been top three in the summer.*

The advert for the gig confirmed Rory Gallagher's status: 'Proudly presenting the biggest rock event ever to be staged in Norfolk, voted the world's number one guitarist.'

Local band Raw had the unenviable task of supporting Rory Gallagher but they are said to have met the challenge admirably. They had formed in January 1972 with Peter Allen (drums) and John Rosbotham (lead guitar/vocals) – both from Mister Toad – and Pat Wood (bass) from the Continentals. The band's name was made from their surname initials: Rosbotham, Allen and Wood. There was an article in the *Eastern Evening News* of 3 January 1972 announcing their formation and including a photograph.

Raw supported Crow in July when, as a special promotion, the Links was offering a shot of Old Crow Bourbon for 10p. The following year Raw supported Thin Lizzy and Darryl Way's Wolf. Darryl Way was a violinist, who had formed Curved Air in 1970, then left to form Wolf in late 1972. He returned to Curved Air when Wolf finished in September 1974.

John Rosbotham, from Raw, remembers the Links was always hot and sweaty. They also played at the Canary pub in Norwich, at various RAF bases in the area and supported the Crazy World of Arthur Brown at the Gala in Norwich. One summer they did a season at a holiday camp in Yarmouth with jazz saxophonist Derek Cooper. Raw played songs by Led Zeppelin and Status Quo, Rod Stewart's 'Maggie May' and Argent's 'Hold Your Head Up'. Both John and Pat Wood, Raw's bass player, remember supporting Status Quo but Pat said there were no stories he could put in print! Peter Allen, Raw's drummer, remembers going along in the car for the Status Quo gig:

We could hear them rehearsing while we were still a few roads away. It got louder as we got nearer, but when we went in the Links, there was only Rick Parfitt playing. We all used the same dressing room and played their gear. We used their amps etc, because the stage wasn't big enough to get ours on as well.

When he played at the Links, Rory Gallagher's list of requirements did not amount to much more than a crate of Guinness; unlike Gary Glitter who, Bully remembers, had all sorts of requests:

Gary Glitter had a rider about having bouncers all along the front of the stage, his own dressing room, loads of different things. I used to pay a lot of the bands. When I went to pay him his money, he had eye mascara all on his chest hair, to make his hairs look all dark!

Gary Glitter had had a big hit during the summer of 1972 with 'Rock and Roll Part 2' and when he played at the Links in the November his latest single 'I Didn't

Know I Loved You (Till I Saw You Rock 'n' Roll)' had just left the top 20. His booking was, therefore, a bit of a scoop. However, as Terry Bunting relates, he wasn't really suited to the bulk of the Links crowd:

I've never ever been to a gig like it. They were throwing glasses and bottles at him, the stage was awash with things. People there were not interested in Gary Glitter, he was a little girls' band, it was a completely wrong booking, a bit like nowadays putting McFly on at the Download Festival! There were all these young girls at the front shouting, 'We love you, Gary!' The saxophone player had a gold lamé jumpsuit on, and he was letting the girls touch his suit.

Gary Glitter was an old rock and roller with a new image. He did this old croony number called 'Donna'. It went, 'Donna, where can you be?' then it would stop. Every time the song stopped, you ought to have heard the booing. We didn't want that, we wanted Nazareth or Quo or UFO. He used to do this thing where he'd turn his back to the audience, and raise his arms in the air. While he was turned round, a beer glass hit him right between the shoulder blades. He stopped the band at least once and said, 'Some people are just trying to ruin our show, but we're not going to worry.'

I was with some friends of mine up on the balcony and we were buying these packets of peanuts for about 5p, ripping the tops off and lobbing them at the stage like hand grenades.

Barry Pearce, Kevin Dorey and Bob James all remember the infamous night and Joe Barber summed it up very concisely: 'Gary Glitter was bottled off stage. He wasn't playing too well, he huffed and blustered and bottles started to rain down on him. He played a short set that night!'

The balconies, which had been retained during the internal improvements, were a popular feature at the Links, not just for throwing missiles at the stage – although Frank Kinsley also remembers that punters on the balconies would 'drop beer glasses on your skull'. Jan Petty says she liked them because 'you could walk about up there and check out the talent,' and Julie Bunting remembers going 'up the balcony' and having to pick her way 'over the bodies'. She says, 'The boys went to the Links for the music and the beer; the girls went to get the boys – most of them weren't so interested in the music.' It is rumoured that half of Cromer was conceived on the hillside outside the Links – called 'Happy Valley' – although there is, of course, no way of confirming this!

When Screaming Lord Sutch played at the venue, the missiles were coming off the stage, rather than the other way round, as Terry Bunting explains:

Screaming Lord Sutch used to cover the old rock song 'Great Balls of Fire'. He had these cheap plastic footballs and he used to put lighter fluid on them and throw them out into the audience. It wouldn't happen nowadays.

Bully remembers the first time he saw the act:

When the music stopped and the lights went down, there was this big bang, there might even have been a flash of fire, I don't know, I just ran to the office to where the electricity supply was, thinking there was something wrong with the electrics! It really frightened me.

'On one occasion,' recalls Danny Hagen, 'Screaming Lord Sutch set fire to the drapes at the back. I remember someone went up and took them down, bundled them in a ball, and got the fire extinguisher on them. He carried on with the act.'

Inspired by one of his favourite rock and roll acts, Screamin' Jay Hawkins, David Edward Sutch had changed his name to Screaming Lord Sutch in the 1960s. Lord Sutch's stage show had a horror theme. He would usually dress like Jack the Ripper, after the name of one of his singles. He would use knives, daggers and skulls on stage and would often start the act by appearing slowly out of a large black coffin. Brian 'Ringo'Ward remembers his band, Spencer's People, supported Screaming Lord Sutch. They had to carry him in from the hearse in the coffin, and when they laid the coffin on stage, Lord Sutch jumped out with a toilet seat around his neck! David Hines, a glass-collector at the Links, also remembers carrying the famous coffin.

Screaming Lord Sutch became involved with politics and founded the Official Monster Raving Loony Party in 1983. The Party's policies included all day pub opening, which at the time was considered far too ridiculous an idea to be taken seriously! He funded the Party's activities by performing rock concerts, but in 1999, a year after his mother died, Lord Sutch committed suicide.

When Paul left the Links after about eight months as manager, Bully (Steve Bullimore), whose association with the venue had begun as a 10 year old schoolboy collecting glasses and walking the dog, found himself booking the groups. These included Back Door, a three-piece band with legendary bass guitarist Colin Hodgkinson being joined, unusually, by saxophone and drums; Badger featuring Tony Kay from Yes; Stealer's Wheel, with Gerry Rafferty, who had a big hit with 'Stuck in the Middle With You'; and Sassafras, an R & B band who were well-respected in Europe and the United States.

Heavy band the Pink Fairies, comprising Duncan Sanderson (bass/vocals), Russell Hunter (drums) and Larry Wallis (guitar/vocals), came to the Links a couple of times under Bully's tenure. Duncan would appear at West Runton Pavilion in 1978 with his new band Lightning Raiders, supporting Motorhead. Prior to the Pink Fairies, Larry Wallis had been with UFO when they had debuted at the Links in April 1972, described as the 'hottest rock band in London'.

Links regular Terry Bunting remembers that northern band Geordie had a record in the charts entitled 'Can You Do It?', with the B side 'Ain't It Just Like a Woman', when they played the Links in 1973. Geordie were a four-piece band who released a couple of albums and Terry remembers that Vic Malcolm, the lead guitarist, played a white Stratocaster. However, they are probably most famous for having a lead singer called Brian Johnson, who would go on to join AC/DC when their original singer, Bon Scott, died in 1980. Sandra Fishwick (was Bailey) remembers that Brian Johnson appeared in his Malcolm MacDonald number nine football shirt when he came with Geordie to the Links. Geordie were the first band that Rosie Hook saw there. She went with Ronnie Mears, who would later become her husband.

Geordie were supported by local band Hieronymus Bosch, named after a fifteenth century Dutch painter who specialised in depicting religious visions and the torments of hell. The band consisted of Rob Seales (lead guitar), Mick Hudson (vocals), Geoff Hollis (bass) and Ian 'Fritz' Wright (drums). Rob, Mick and Ian would later play in another local band, Spiny Norman; Rob and Geoff would also join the Buster James Band and Ian would crop up again in Zorro.

Brendan Shiels, who had taught Phil Lynott to play bass when Phil had been singer with him in Skid Row, came to the Links with his new band Brush. The band had taken their title from Brendan's nickname, so-called because his beard looked like a brush. Brush were supported on two of their visits by another local band, Scapa Flow, named after the place in Scotland where the Germans scuttled their battleships after the First World War. Scapa Flow also supported Raymond Froggatt, Chicken Shack, Status Quo and Gary Moore. Terry Bunting was a big fan:

Scapa Flow were fantastic musicians, three-piece. They played Jimi Hendrix, Cream covers, stuff by Spirit and other three-piece bands like that. They also did one or two of their own songs. They were a very popular local band, very talented. Ronnie, the guitarist, used to play Hendrix like no other. They were all introverted on stage: they would be very quiet. They were friendly, but there wouldn't be a lot of chat coming off the stage. When you look at some of the bands they were supporting, they were mis-matched, but they were brilliant, my favourite local band.

By 1974 they had changed their name to Cousin David and returned to the Links supporting UFO and Thin Lizzy.

Meanwhile, back in 1973, Phil Lynott was finding success with the original three-piece Thin Lizzy, and returned to the Links in March. Kevin Dorey recalls that Phil Lynott used to stay at the Red Lion in Cromer. Kevin used to see him in there before the gigs, drinking Guinness and champagne. Sandra Fishwick (was Bailey) remembers:

The first band I ever saw at the Links was Thin Lizzy in 1973. 'Whiskey in the Jar' had just been released. What a way to start! I just fell in love with guitarists in tight trousers, there and then.

David Hicks was also there, and although he didn't mention the tight trousers, he did remember them playing 'Whiskey in the Jar' and it being on the top 20 countdown on the radio the following night.

Bully (Steve Bullimore) was walking through Cromer at teatime on the Sunday when he heard a radio being played. 'Whiskey in the Jar' came on and the person in the house shouted, 'We saw these at the Links last night!' Bully says he felt really proud to have been part of it.

Terry Bunting assesses Thin Lizzy:

I saw them as a very young band coming over from Ireland and playing for peanuts. I saw them at the Links two or three times like that, slowly building a following. Then I saw them when they had their hit single 'Whiskey in the Jar'. I remember the guitarist, Eric Bell, wearing this jacket made of silver medallions. He wore it on Top of the Pops and he also wore it for this gig at the Links in March 1973. It was a full house.

Thin Lizzy were supported by local band Shy Fly, named after an old Status Quo song. The band comprised Trevor 'Monty' Baggott (bass), Peter 'Portfleet' Wright (vocals), Alan 'Ginger' Westgate (second guitar), Phil 'Herman' Buck (drums) and Neil 'Arnold' Pitcher (guitar). Jack Howard was lighting engineer and Elton Selfe was sound engineer.

Neil Pitcher recalls jamming with Thin Lizzy bassist Phil Lynott before the gig, 'He played my Deluxe Les Paul Gold Top with mini humbuckers, I played his Dan Armstrong perspex bass.'

Shy Fly were paid £25 for their performance, with 10% given to Phil Beavis as the agent's fee. They paid their roadies £1 each.

Neil's diary entry for the event reads:

We played 'Big Fat Mama' for the first time and it went quite well. When we played 'All Right Now' my top E was way out of tune, it sounded bloody awful. Still, it made them laugh and that, at least, was something.

Local newspaper, the *Eastern Evening News* included a music column every Monday entitled 'Here and Now'. Shy Fly were featured on 26 March 1973:

The band was formed almost a year ago by sound engineer Elton Self and lead guitarist Arnold Pitcher and they play hard rock on the lines of Status Quo with the emphasis on the visual side of their act.

None of the band claim to be great musicians, relying simply and successfully on conveying to an audience their enthusiasm for the group.

Their first really important gig was at Cromer Links and they have always received plenty of encouragement from the audience on their return visits.

When they had played at the venue in January that year, Neil recorded in his diary, 'Used the Links disco columns, 4 x 12 inch Marshalls, which greatly increased the effect of the PA.'

They played the Quo song 'Softer Ride' and during the evening 'Ginge' had used Neil's amp. Neil wrote, 'Every time he gets feedback he grins like a Cheshire cat and says "Listen to that ow' boiy."'

On 7 April they supported Sam Apple Pie at the Links and Neil wrote, 'Phil split a drum skin but it didn't affect the performance at all. We bought a Binson Echorec off Sam Apple Pie's roadies for £60.'

Gary Moore, who would briefly join Thin Lizzy the following year, came to the venue on 12 May with his self-named band. Shy Fly supported and 'played well and received a good crowd,' according to Neil's diary. The following month they had a 'good night all round' and 'really got the crowd going' for Raymond Froggatt; and in August they played 'two very good sets overall' supporting Jack the Lad, an offshoot of Lindisfarne.

Shy Fly were reviewed in *Musicfolk*, a local newsletter of the time, written by someone identified only as 'AB':

All aged between 19 and 23, their music is loud, second generation rock 'n' roll as played by young musicians who were still learning to talk when the first rock records were released, who were too young to be moved by Beatlemania and whose style was ushered in by the re-creators of harsh, thumping blues-based rock such as Led Zeppelin and Ten Years After.

Arnold says, 'If we're working towards anything it's just towards being a respected name in East Anglia. That's all we want to begin with.'

The band is already established as one of the most popular support acts at the Royal Links, Cromer, a 'plum' spot for Norfolk bands. 'Being accepted and liked by the crowd up here did a lot for us,' says Arnold. 'We're very grateful to them.'

Shy Fly don't dream of 'making it'. They just look forward to the next gig and hope it's a good one.

In March 1974 they supported Kilburn and the High Roads, the lead singer of which was one Ian Dury, who would find commercial success in 1977 after recruiting a new band, the Blockheads. Shy Fly received a call from Phil Beavis later in March saying he had heard that Queen would be late and could Shy Fly stand in for them at the Links?

Shy Fly's equipment inventory at the end of 1973 went as follows:

1 x Gibson Les Paul Deluxe gold guitar
1 x Gibson SG Prof cherry red guitar
1 x Fender Jazz bass sunburst maple neck
1 x set Premier 8303 drums
2 x Shure Unidyne III microphones
2 x Shure Unisphere 'B' microphones
1 x Shure Unisphere I microphone
1 x Simms-Watts performer microphone
1 x Hi-Watt 100 watt PA
1 x Impact 100 watt lead guitar amp
1 x Sound City 100 watt Mk 3 lead guitar amp
1 x Sound City 120 watt Mk 4 bass amp
2 x Carlsbro 4 x 12 inch 80 watt columns
2 x Carlsbro 4 x horn 120 watt boxes
1 x Sound City 80 watt 4 x 12 inch lead cabinet
1 x Sound City 120 watt 4 x 12 inch lead cabinet
1 x Sound City 120 watt 4 x 12 inch bass cabinet
1 x Carlsbro 100 watt 4 x 12 inch lead cabinet
2 x Impact 100 watt 4 x 12 inch lead cabinets
2 x Marshall Superfuzz effect boxes
1 x Binson Echorec Echo Chamber

Musician Terry Bunting explains and assesses Shy Fly's gear:

It was pretty state-of-the-art at the time, now light years behind modern stuff in looks, power, size, efficiency and price. Believe it or not, modern stuff is relatively much cheaper.

Les Pauls, SG's and Jazz basses were used a lot in those days. There wasn't such a choice of quality guitars then, although Shy Fly's guitars were Gibson and Fender, the two most famous and respected makes.

The two lead guitar amps would have been 100 per cent all-valve amps and very loud. A lead guitarist would use a Marshall Superfuzz effect box to give him an overdriven sound at relatively low volume. Now most amps have this facility built in.

Judging by the number of microphones, I would suspect that, as well as the vocals, some of the drums would go through the PA. A Hi-Watt 100 watt PA would be seen as very quaint nowadays and most people would be unlikely to even rehearse with one any more.

I would imagine the Binson echo chamber would have been used to give the vocals a bit of reverb, or possibly a guitarist used it for some echo in a solo or two. Modern PA and guitar amps usually have reverb built in, and some guitar amps have echo incorporated too.

This gear set-up would be pretty typical of a working semi-pro band in the early 1970s. The only thing that's a little incongruous is that each instrument had at least 100 watts power (making a backline of 320 watts), and the poor old PA had to try to get over it with its paltry 100 watt output. This wouldn't really happen nowadays. Amplifier and, especially, speaker technology has moved on so much that even local bands have 1,000 watt PA systems for vocals and drums, although guitar amps haven't needed to get any louder. If a band needs loud guitars for a large venue, they will mike them up through the PA.

Shy Fly didn't appear to have a monitor system, which would have enabled them to hear what was coming out of the PA. Pretty much the norm then: nowadays a monitor system is considered a necessity.

Thin Lizzy returned to the venue later in 1973, this time supported by Raw, but Terry Bunting was disappointed:

When they came back, Thin Lizzy were still a three-piece, but they'd gone from being a touring little club band to big stars and I thought they lacked a little bit of fire that they normally had: that little bit of hunger. They eventually got it back, but not after personnel changes. Their star started to fade a little and they started to drop back down, because they never followed 'Whiskey in the Jar' up with another big hit. They had an album Vagabonds of the Western World – released in September 1973 – which sold quite well, but 'Whiskey in the Jar' isn't on there, it was just released as a single.

In July 1973, attendance was down because the admission price had been increased for Lizzy. I remember the only thing that went down well then was Brian Downey's drum solo. The DJ [Bully] stood up and clapped first, then everyone else followed. They had a pretty bad night there. That was probably the worst Lizzy gig I'd seen, because I think what used to happen to people at the Links was, you used to see a band there quite often, every few months, and you used to think they belonged to you. When they became popular and everyone was playing their records and talking about them, you felt a little bit cheated, but sometimes the best kept secrets got out!

Joe Barber used to see Thin Lizzy for the standard admission rate. When they returned to the venue after 'Whiskey in the Jar' had reached the top five, the admission price had gone up, so Joe and his mates went to the pub. He remembers, 'We said we're not paying all that just to see Thin Lizzy!'

A bootleg Trevor Alford has, which was recorded at Birmingham Town Hall during the 1973 tour, has the following set-list:

Gonna Creep up on You
The Nazz are Blue
Suicide
Little Girl in Bloom
Slow Blues
Whiskey in the Jar

The Rocker
One Way Jammer
Things Ain't Working Out Down at the Farm
The Rise and Demise of the Funky Nomadic Tribes

'Suicide' did not appear on an album until *Fighting* in August 1975, but Thin Lizzy guitarist Eric Bell confirms that they used to perform a live version of it in the early seventies involving a lot of slide guitar, although this version was never recorded in the studio. Eric left Thin Lizzy at the end of 1973.

Terry Bunting observes:

The Links would get bands that would play there regularly. Quo were a good case in point: they'd be there every few months and we'd think, Status Quo, that's a good night, we'll go and see them again. As soon as they had a big hit single, they never came back. Nazareth were the same with 'Broken Down Angel'.

Thin Lizzy were pretty much the exception because they had the big hit single but they never followed it up, so they came back again. The bands at the Links were good because they were hungry. If you saw them later, after their hits, often they weren't nearly as good as they had been at the Links. Some bands like Thin Lizzy got even better, but some, after they had had a hit single, tended to lose it a little bit.

Scottish band, Nazareth, appeared at the Links for the third and final time in January 1973, just before they hit the big time with UK top 20 singles 'Broken Down Angel' and 'Bad Bad Boy'. The line-up comprised Manny Charlton (guitar), Pete Agnew (bass), Dan McCafferty (vocals) and Darrell Sweet (drums). Pete North remembers, 'We got invited onto Nazareth's tour bus because my mate, who was Scottish, grew up with Manny Charlton.'

One of Bully's jobs as manager at the Links was to be there on the Saturday afternoons when the bands were setting up. He says:

What I used to love was, when they used to tune up and do a few numbers, sometimes you'd hear them play something – part of a song, it didn't mean anything – then two months later you'd hear it come out as a single.

Dutch band Golden Earring did a memorable sound-check, according to Bully:

I remember a special electric supply had to be put in for them. They had a lot of gear for this quadraphonic sound. When they were setting up on the Saturday afternoon, the drummer was going through all the drums and the chap on the mixing desk was bouncing the sound around the four speakers. I thought, this is going to be incredible. We had a phone call from someone in Cromer who could hear it.

Terry Bunting saw Golden Earring at the Links:

They were the first band I'd seen with quadraphonic sound, two sets of P.A. speakers at the front, two at the back of the hall. They were probably the loudest band I ever saw there. The singer said, after about the first number, 'We're sorry it has to be so loud, go to the toilet and stuff some toilet paper in your ears!' They were really good but they were just unbearably loud, and this is coming from someone who has played loud music for thirty-odd years. Why they had to be that loud I'll never know: it was ridiculous!

Rob James was living in London when Golden Earring came to Norfolk. He went with half-a-dozen friends to see them in Norwich on the Friday, then he saw them at Cromer Links on the Saturday. He spoke to one of the roadies who said the band were travelling down to London for a gig at the Finsbury Park Rainbow on the Monday. Rob was going back too, and the roadie said, 'Come along and ask for John.' So Rob did and he got in free and saw them on the Monday as well.

Golden Earring played at the Links in May and December 1973. Barry Pearce ('Big 'un'), who helped at Links as a bouncer, remembers, 'The second time they were booked, the crowd was queued right back to the golf course.'

Chris Hare says, 'My mate used to stay in one of the caravans near the Links, so we would go over there in the afternoons and help the roadies unload the gear before going to the gig that evening.' Chris saw Golden Earring both times, as did Steve Rowe, who got seven friends to go with him the second time, because the band were so good. Steve remembers that the electric cable, which had been run from the sub-station, had ramps for the cars as it went across the road. With the quadraphonic sound, they used four banks of speakers, rather than two, and rotated the sound around, which he says, 'made some people fall over (although drink probably helped!)'

Golden Earring comprised George Kooymans (lead guitar/lead vocals), Rinus Gerritsen (bass/harmonica/electric piano/organ), Cesar Zuiderwijk (drums) and Barry Hay (lead vocals/flute/guitar).

When they came in December 1973, Golden Earring had just played 'Radar Love' on *Top of the Pops*. As Terry Bunting says, 'They played at the Links at the absolute height of their fame. I remember we were all thinking, is the drummer going to jump over his kit, because he'd done it on *Top of the Pops*.' He didn't disappoint the large crowd and Sandra Fishwick sums it up as her most memorable moment at the Links, 'Who could forget the drummer jumping over his drum kit? Fantastic!'

Steve Rowe's ears were ringing for two days after. He says, 'We drove there in a noisy old banger, but came back in a Rolls Royce, as we couldn't hear the engine!'

Bully was a hard task-master, particularly with family members. He says:

My younger sister used to go in to watch the bands and I said she could go in for free but if I needed a hand, she'd have to work. One Saturday I wanted her to work, she had a date with a boy and wouldn't work, so I told her she had to pay after that. All the staff thought I was rotten. I've found out since they used to let her in for free. In my eyes she should have paid.

Unfortunately, despite his obvious commitment to the Links, it soon all went wrong between Bully and Mrs Arundel-Langley. He recalls:

I reached the top and I had a week's holiday, well, Monday to Friday because I didn't want to miss my Saturday night. When I came back, she'd got someone to work with me or took some of my jobs. When I was younger, I thought she was marvellous, but as I got higher up the ladder, I realised what she was like. I handed my notice in and about 10 days later I got a letter from the solicitors saying I had these keys. I'd handed all the keys into the accountant, because I was honest as the day was long, so she was just being awkward. I was lucky, I only saw it the last bit and I knew the signs and got out of it. I could see what was going to happen. It was a lovely place to work, but after that, I kept out of the way: never went back. I had a big number of albums signed to me, and when I left, I left them there. It's sad really.

It was an amazing place; it made me what I am today. When I started there, as a boy, I used to stutter quite a lot. I wasn't very confident and the only person who really understood what I used to say was my mother. Then I got involved with Rod and Nigel and it just changed my life completely: got me where I am today. It's a shame in lots of ways how it did all end up.

Sam Apple Pie played the night Bully left, in October 1973.

9

Very Hot Chocolate

While he waited for his planning permission to be granted, Frank Boswall continued to host dances at West Runton Pavilion. Old local favourites like Berry and the Tree Tops, Fascinatin' Rhythm and Second Opinion made regular appearances. Second Opinion, featuring Robin Goodyear, came to the venue many times between 1973 and 1978, supporting acts such as the Tremeloes, Freddie 'Fingers' Lee and another local band, Memphis Index.

Memphis Index were a very popular, well-established local rock and roll band formed by lead vocalist and pianist Tony Dee. The earlier line-up had included Francis Wigley (bass) and Grenville Arnold (drums). Bobby Secker, who had been bass player with the Highwaymen, joined Memphis Index in the late sixties and, together with Raver Lee (drums), Louie Paston (guitar) and Mick Robinson (piano), made many appearances at both West Runton Pavilion and Cromer Links. Colin Dodman, one of their fans, remembers Memphis Index playing the Safaris' song 'Wipe Out' which he says had 'a mega drum solo'. They were at their peak in the mid-seventies, as Bob Secker relates: 'We were invited to join forces with some members of another band, which we declined, little knowing we could have become Showaddywaddy!' Memphis Index appeared all over the country, playing 1950s and 1960s rock and roll music and supporting many big names of the day.

Newer bands like First Impression and Sable also started playing at West Runton Pavilion. Richard Hewitt, who had previously drummed in Emblem, was in First Impression with Donny Wright (lead vocals), Sid Fish (lead guitar), Bob Gay (bass) and Tony Powell (rhythm guitar). Tony's previous bands had been the Highwaymen and East Coast Rock. Richard then joined McDivitt playing middle-of-the-road chart and disco music such as Tavares, Four Seasons and Status Quo, with Tom Hill (rhythm guitar/vocals), Will Webster (bass/vocals) and Leon Schindler (lead guitar/vocals).

Andy Gray had been drummer in the band Treble Nine, in which all the other members were policemen and a bit older than him. They had played the local circuit doing Shadows numbers and such like. Andy met Barry Duval in a pub one Friday night and Barry explained that his band, Sable, were looking to replace their current drummer. Their next gig was on the Sunday. Andy loaded his drums and turned up. They had big banks of WEM speakers, plenty of amplifying kit, and looked worriedly at Andy's drum sticks. 'You'll need broom handles here,' he was told, but in the absence of any, turned his drum-sticks round the other way and played like that. Andy remembers the gig was very loud. Together with Colin English (bass), Andy Colk (lead/rhythm guitar) and Barry (lead guitar/vocals) they played several gigs at both West Runton Pavilion and Cromer Links during 1974 and 1975. When Kevin Dando joined as lead singer, they changed their name to Pinto.

Occasionally a famous group would appear at West Runton Pavilion. Back in the early sixties, acts like Chris Farlowe and 'top vocal group' the Emeralds had been booked, and this continued with the odd smattering of famous names amongst the regular local bands. The Tremeloes came in November 1973, Hot Chocolate in February 1974 – a month before their single 'Emma' was released – and the Equals in April 1974.

Meanwhile, over at the Links, Danny Hagen had taken over as manager. He says:

I came out of the Forces in 1973. I went to the Links for a while before I was asked to manage it. I remember the night Elkie Brooks played, with Vinegar Joe, I had to go and man the lifeboat and someone else locked up.

There was another event which stayed in Danny's mind, but for a completely different reason:

While I was manager, I remember one of the staff asked if he could have half an hour off because he had pulled a girl. I agreed. A bit later I was patrolling outside with Rinty the dog. The beam of my torch lit up an old-fashioned wooden wheelbarrow with the tailgate down, and the girl was spread-eagled in the barrow. I will let you guess the rest! I never let him forget that.

The high standard of bands continued at the Links with Edgar Broughton, the Average White Band and Savoy Brown, a blues band featuring keyboard player Paul Raymond who would later join UFO. Savoy Brown were supported by Yarmouth band Ribs, who Links regular Terry Bunting remembers did Black Sabbath and Rory Gallagher numbers as well as general rock covers. On another of Savoy Brown's visits, local band Train provided the support.

Another band Terry particularly enjoyed were the Sensational Alex Harvey Band, who played at the Links in December 1973. Colin Melton remembers the lead guitarist, Art Clemenson, came on stage dressed like a clown, as pictured on their album cover. Terry Bunting says:

Although it was very theatrical, they could really play. Alex Harvey's first album wasn't a massive seller. Then he brought out his second album called Next, *which was probably his most enduring album, with 'Faith Healer' and stuff on it. They were bubbling under. We knew that they were a hot act and popular. Alex Harvey came onto the darkened stage with just a light on him. He was wearing his trademark striped t-shirt. He just said, 'Good evening boys and girls,' in this lovely Scottish accent, 'My name's Alex Harvey and I'd like to introduce you to my band, they're called the Sensational Alex Harvey Band.' Then 'Faith Healer' starts up — they may have used a backing tape, or they could have done it on the keyboard. They were just brilliant. They took my brains out at the beginning and gave them back to me at the end. It was stunning, in my top 10 gigs of all time.*

One band Terry encountered after their Links appearance was Skin Alley:

Skin Alley were quite a big band at the time and they were friends of a girl who lived in my village: her dad kept the shop. I woke up one morning, walked out of my house, looked down the road, and there was Skin Alley's van with all their gear in it, they'd stayed the night in Edgefield!

Chicory Tip had reached number one in the UK singles chart in February 1972 with 'Son of My Father' and were booked to play at the Links at very short notice in January 1974 to replace Budgie, who couldn't come. Bob James remembers it was a 'very good gig'.

Joe Barber thought they had a very weedy keyboard sound which didn't suit the crowd. He recalls they gave up with that, admitted to the crowd, 'We appreciate you don't like us,' and started playing covers of Free, which Joe says saved them from bombardment.

Terry Bunting remembers seeing Chicory Tip on *Top of the Pops* when they wore outlandish stage outfits and rubber masks. When they came to the Links he says they played without make-up. They didn't seem to have enough original material for a whole gig so played songs by other bands. In particular, Terry recalls a cover of 'Blowing Free' by Wishbone Ash. He says:

Chicory Tip did not go down all that well, because audiences at the Links were partisan towards heavy rock, so if it wasn't a heavy or blues band they did not tend to like them.
The support, the Flying Hat Band from Birmingham, blew them off the stage. They could really play. Chicory Tip were pop stars, they could play OK, but the Flying Hat Band were a different class. Their guitarist that night was a guy called Glenn Tipton, who went on to join Judas Priest and became a metal superstar.

Gary Moore had been at the Links with the Gary Moore Band, then he came back there as lead guitarist with Thin Lizzy in March 1974 after Eric Bell had left. Gary Moore left the band shortly afterwards and was replaced by the twin guitars of Brian Robertson and Scott Gorham. Terry Bunting recalls, 'In August 1974 I went to Reading Festival and that was one of the early appearances of the four-piece Thin Lizzy, the one that everyone says is the classic Thin Lizzy line-up.' This new line-up – completed by Phil Lynott (bass/lead vocals) and Brian Downey (drums) – would debut at the Links the following year, although Chris Hare was not impressed:

I'd seen them two or three times and then they came back with two guitarists and I found it a bit loud. We stood near the stage after the gig and I said to my mate that I hadn't liked the band as much with the two guitarists. This voice behind me asked, 'Why, what was wrong with it?' and when I turned round it was Phil Lynott! What he must have thought of this 14 year old – or whatever I was then – who didn't really have a clue, I don't know!

It was usual for the bands to play two sets at the Links, although some of the bigger names would only play one. The support band would normally perform from 8.00pm to 9.00pm and from 10.00pm to 11.00pm, and the main band would be on from 9.00pm to 10.00pm and then from 11.00pm until the venue closed. Joe Barber recalls that Greenslade, in particular, were amazed they had to play twice when they appeared in April 1974, although several members of Greenslade had been to the Links before with other bands so they ought to have remembered the drill. Dave Greenslade (keyboards) had previously played there with Chris Farlowe and his Thunderbirds and Tony Reeves (bass) had been with John Mayall's Bluesbreakers. Andrew McCulloch had probably been the drummer with Manfred Mann when they came to the Links in 1970. Greenslade's line-up was completed by Dave Lawson (vocals/keyboard).

Chris Hare met the band:

I enjoyed Greenslade a lot and met them after the gig to get autographs. The drummer, Andrew McCulloch, could sign his name in mirror writing with either hand, which he did on one of the LP sleeves that were usually pinned up in the front entrance. If only I still had all those autographs!

One very famous gig that Danny Hagen was involved with was the night in March 1974 when Queen played at Cromer Links. He remembers, 'I was manager when Queen were booked. I didn't think they'd turn up because "Seven Seas of Rhye" was just coming into the charts and being played on the radio.'

Pete Mason didn't know much about Queen, but on the Saturday morning of the gig he had heard 'Seven Seas of Rhye' playing in a coffee bar in Holt. One of his mates suggested he should go to see them at the Links, which he did and thought they were incredible.

Queen comprised Freddie Mercury (lead vocals/piano), Brian May (lead guitar), John Deacon (bass) and Roger Taylor (drums).

Sandra Fishwick (was Bailey) names Queen as her 'most memorable gig'. She says:

I vividly recall them playing Ogre Battle. There were two band members in black, two in white – Brian in his famous Zandra Rhodes pleated top – and I remember the sheer brilliance of the music. Freddie passed just a metre in front of me, looking like the rock god he was to become. It was one of the best nights of my life.

Chris Hare remembers:

Freddie came out with this black nail varnish on, Brian May did a big guitar solo, and Roger did a drum solo. There was a big gong behind the drums. I had an idea they were going to be something special.

Terry Bunting recalls:

Freddie Mercury was dressed all in black. Brian May came on stage wearing a white outfit with a small cape on the back. They were absolutely brilliant, blew the place to pieces, they were really polished. They encored with 'Jailhouse Rock' and 'Big Spender' that night. I spoke to the band after the gig. Brian sat on stage and chatted. I asked him if I could have a go on his 'red special' guitar, but he said, 'No, I think the roadies have just packed it away,' which was a real drag.

The band came onto the stage with Freddie walking down the steps to a taped introduction of 'Procession', the first track on their *Queen II* album. They were one of the first bands to use a taped introduction onto the stage. Two other innovations which are now taken for granted at concerts – dry ice and moving lighting rigs – were also pioneered by Queen.

Terry continues:

In those days, if you hung around long enough afterwards, the band would either reappear on stage in their normal clothes or you would catch them outside. Occasionally you could be standing in the toilets next to a rock star! Queen were very nice people. I brought my albums along and they signed them for me, Queen I and Queen II.

Julie Bunting's friend Maggie Key died in 2005. They had been to see Queen at the Links together and, although Julie doesn't recall much about the gig because she wasn't keen on the band, she says Maggie always remembered that Freddie Mercury had bought them a drink at the bar.

Queen were supported by Liverpool band Nutz, who did the British tour with them and appeared at the Reading Festival. They later headlined at the Links. Despite being a heavy band, their vocalist, David Lloyd, famously sang on an advert for a certain chocolate bar. On one occasion, Nutz appeared at the Links with Strife, a heavy three-piece band. Terry Bunting explains, 'You might get two second division bands touring together, and they'd swap headlining duties.'

UFO were frequent visitors to the Links. The band formed in 1969 and early appearances at the venue had featured Phil Mogg (vocals), Pete Way (bass), Andy Parker (drums) and Larry Wallis (guitar), when they were advertised as 'The hottest rock band in London.' Larry had joined Pink Fairies and appeared at the Links with them in 1973. His replacement, Bernie Marsden, appeared there with UFO but left to join Wild Turkey the same year and would later return to the Links with them. Bernie was replaced in UFO by German guitarist Michael Schenker from the Scorpions.

Terry Bunting saw UFO at the Links about half-a-dozen times as a four-piece. He says:

They were awesome, and to think we used to get this sort of thing down the road every week! When I met Phil Mogg at the UEA five or six years ago, I shook his hand and said, 'I used to come and see you twenty five years ago in Cromer,' and he said, 'I'm a Cromer man – I remember it really well!'

The advert for UFO's gig at the Links in January 1974 stated they had had 'five gold albums in Japan'. When they were at the venue in July that year, they were promoting their *Phenomenon* album. Phil Dunning thinks the photos of UFO which appeared on the album had been taken at the Links. Both that album and *Force It*, released the following year, were very successful in the UK.

Bernie Marsden came to the Links again in July 1974, this time with drummer Colin 'Cozy' Powell. Cozy himself was no stranger to the Links. He had appeared with Young Blood in August 1968 with Ken Aston (vocals), Pete Ball (organ), Roy Black (bass) and Chris Moore (guitar). He had left that band shortly afterwards and in November 1973, along with vocalist Frank Aiello and Pete's brothers Dennis Ball (bass) and Dave Ball (guitar), he had come to the venue again under the name Bedlam. The advert read, 'If you think Led Zeppelin's heavy – try these!'

Cozy Powell's single 'Dance With the Devil' had been cut while he was still with Bedlam and had reached the top end of the charts by the time he returned to the Links in July 1974 with Cozy Powell's Hammer. As well as Frank Aiello and Bernie Marsden, this new band also included Clive Chaman (bass) and Don Airey (keyboards). Cozy left for Rainbow in September 1975 and was subsequently joined there by Don Airey in April 1979. Bernie Marsden, clearly liking a change, joined Rainbow's rivals Whitesnake.

Terry Bunting remembers meeting Cozy Powell at the Links:

He had a hit with 'Dance With the Devil', which had the same riff as the Jimi Hendrix song 'Third Stone From the Sun', which had come from the theme tune to Coronation Street. *Right Said Fred also used it for their song 'I'm Too Sexy'. Cozy Powell came to the Links with his band, riding on that hit. I spoke to him afterwards – he was up on the stage, crouching down on his haunches – and he said, 'I love Cromer, I come here for my holidays.' He autographed a drumstick with a black felt pen and gave it to me.*

John Fiddler (guitar/bass/drum) and Peter Hope-Evans (harmonica/Jews' harp) made their second trip to the venue with Medicine Head in April 1974. Their first appearance had been as a duo, but with the addition of Roger Sanders (guitar), Rob Townsend (drums) and George Ford (bass) to the line-up, they had achieved success in the UK singles chart with 'Rising Sun' and 'One and One is One' in 1973. Their latest single, 'Slip and Slide', had just been released. John Fiddler would later join the British Lions and appear with them at West Runton Pavilion. Charlie McCracken replaced George Ford on bass and, together with Roger Sanders and Rob Townsend, would join Duane Eddy on his 1975 UK tour, which would also call at West Runton Pavilion.

Local band Zoe, who had supported Atomic Rooster and Gnidrolog, were back at the Links in June 1974 supporting Blackfoot Sue, who had had a hit single with 'Standing in the Road'. This was the first gig Andrew Turner ever went to, and he was accompanied by his mum! Zoe comprised Terry Cousins (drums) and Alan Fish (bass) – who both went on to play in Poacher – Chai Nanakourn (guitar) and Dave Shirt (vocals). Later, Alan also played in the Groundhogs with Tony McPhee. Music fan, Andrew Pye, remembers seeing the Groundhogs at the Links in July 1974.

Tony McPhee had named his band after an old John Lee Hooker song, and the Groundhogs supported John Lee Hooker on his British tours. In an interview of the time, Hooker called the Groundhogs the 'number one British blues band'. Their fourth album, *Split*, had been the sixth best-selling album of 1971 and contained their only single, 'Cherry Red', which they had played on *Top of the Pops.*

Steve Harley and Cockney Rebel came to the Links in June 1974, having had UK chart success with their singles 'Judy Teen' and 'Mr Soft'. Sandra Fishwick says of Steve Harley, 'He had the best rapport with the crowd of anyone I have ever seen.'

Also in June was an appearance by the Butts Band, formed by John Densmore (drums) and Robbie Krieger (guitar) after Jim Morrison, the lead singer of their previous band the Doors, died in 1971.

In August Bilbo Baggins played at the Links. They were described in the advert as 'Scottish stable-mates of the Bay City Rollers', and had appeared on the children's television programme *Lift Off with Ayshea* hosted by Ayshea Brough.

Despite still attracting the big name bands to the venue, behind the scenes things were not going well at the Links and in August 1974 there was a disagreement over Hot Chocolate's fee. Manager Danny Hagen explains:

They were due to get £350 or 60% of the door, whichever was greatest. You would reckon to get 700 people in and the admission was 95p. At eight-thirty that evening, Mrs Arundel-Langley negotiated a cheaper rate with the band because there weren't many there, so it was agreed to reduce the fee to a flat £250. When they went back out, the place was packed, there were actually 800 or 900 people in that night, but she wouldn't pay them any more.

Rosie Mears (was Hook) went to the gig with her boyfriend Ronnie and their friends Maggie and Nigel. Rosie remembers the place was very crowded but she didn't see Hot Chocolate at all – she just heard them – because her friend had felt unwell and they sat outside on the steps all night. She says, 'It sounded good and Ronnie and Nigel kept coming out to see how we were, then they went back in again!'

Danny Hagen was embarrassed by the whole Hot Chocolate incident and left the Links, but the same month a familiar face returned in the form of caveman guitarist 'FLO', who once again featured in the newspaper advertisements. In February 1973 the psychedelic fish adverts had been replaced by a more subdued arch design, although they had retained their tongue-in-cheek humour with, for example, the one in September 1973 advertising Babe Ruth as 'A fantastic band with gorgeous chick singer!' However, by August 1974 old favourite FLO was back.

Clive and Eddie, from the Norwich nightclub Tudor Hall, were involved with managing the Links at some point, together with Howard Platt, and it is likely they took over when Danny Hagen left since, from July 1974, Howard Platt was billed as the regular DJ. The trio stayed until the end of the year, booking old favourites like Screaming Lord Sutch, UFO and Nutz, as well as promoting local bands Spencer's People, Cousin David and Hoss to the headline spot. The venue was then closed at the beginning of 1975 for more extensive alterations and another complete refit and FLO said, 'I'm hibernating!'

On Friday evenings during 1974-5 various cabaret nights were held at West Runton Pavilion, and ballroom tuition started with instruction by qualified dance teacher Peggy Carr. She had been in the States for 12 years, teaching in Hollywood, and was just starting to build up her business again after returning to England. The Dance Quartet would play and 45 minutes of tuition would be provided in jive, cha cha cha, samba, foxtrot or tango: a different style each week.

Owner Frank Boswall remembers, 'We used to run the ballroom dances on a Friday night. We sometimes had the big names like Victor Sylvester and Ray McVie.' Another big name, in jazz circles, was Chris Stainton, an internationally renowned musician who appeared at Runton with his 'Tundra' band.

Unfortunately, however, these nights were not particularly well attended and the Saturday dances with local bands were also losing their popularity so, in early 1975, Frank began widening his net with nationally recognised names. The Drifters Showband came in January, Peter Oliver from the New Seekers in March, and New Pickettywitch and Marmalade on different nights in April.

Doorman John Mason, who had taken a short break, had returned to West Runton Pavilion when Frank had taken over. John had joined Bob Newlands, the current bouncer, who had done a bit of boxing in his time. Danny Hagen had spent the Autumn of 1974 on the herring fishing boats since leaving the Links, and then joined John and Bob at West Runton. John remembers one of their early nights working together:

One evening Danny and I were talking in the foyer when the hall door burst open and a worried punter shouted, 'Come quickly, Bob's having trouble with a crowd down near the bottom doors.' Danny, having had a lot of experience of this type of job, took a deliberate, leisurely pace through into the hall, followed by me now starting to try to look extra tough. We found Bob standing between the two stages. 'We'll have no more trouble from that lot tonight, they're out and can stay out,' he said. 'We have a problem now,' said Danny, 'You've just thrown out the next band!' Fortunately, the main entrance doors opened almost immediately, and in walked the band, to great cheers from the crowd.

On one occasion, the main act was very late, as John recalls:

One night, in the early seventies, this big coloured bloke in a van turned up to play at about quarter-past 11. I went out to help him with his gear, and he was throwing these huge speakers at me. They were massive and it was all I could do to hold them, and he was throwing them to me! He went on the little shell stage, and started playing really late. It should have stopped at midnight, but he carried on until about one-thirty in the morning, because no-one dared stop him. When he'd finished, I helped him put his gear back into the van again and off he went.

Bob Newlands left a short time after John started working there, and Ronnie Carroll was recruited to the staff. Ronnie says:

I remember how I started at Runton. I went there one night to see a group and Danny was on the door on his own. He had really bad toothache. I drew my fist back, as if to hit his mouth, and said, 'I'll soon sort that out.' Danny was impressed and said I was just the sort of bloke Runton needed. I had an interview with Frank Boswall, and he asked me various questions, what would I do in certain circumstances, and then I was on a month's trial. I stayed there around eight years, finishing up as head bouncer.

Joe Tuck remained as manager and his wife, Nan, worked in the ticket office. Frank Kinsley, another bouncer, remembers that Joe Tuck was always well-dressed with a nice suit. 'Whatever band was on, he always wore a bow tie,' Frank added. Hank Platten, described by Frank as 'a real character', helped out too, although sometimes to the detriment of the other staff, as Danny recalls:

I remember Hank was going mad in the foyer one night. He went to hit Joe Tuck, took a swing but Joe ducked and Hank hit Joe's wife, who was sitting behind at the cash desk. She fell off her stool and Hank didn't know what to do!

Frank Kinsley describes how Norwich nightclub the Samson and Hercules dealt with trouble:

They used to give a voucher for a drink to anyone who was causing a problem. The barman would give them a triple whisky, so they'd get drunk and were easier to put out.

Frank Boswall confided his future plans for West Runton Pavilion to John Mason, who says, 'I remember Frank saying he was planning to build the place up to attract some of the top bands from all over the world, never ever dreamt of in this part of the country.'
   On 9 May 1975, at the height of 'Rollermania', the *North Norfolk News* reported:

More top names have been engaged for West Runton Pavilion but the owner, Frank Boswall, is struggling to bring top performers to North Norfolk. A certain Scottish band asked for £7,000 for a 45 minute appearance.

That band was, of course, the Bay City Rollers.
   Leapy Lee, of 'Little Arrows' fame, came to the venue at the start of May, but the breakthrough was to be on 17 May 1975 when advertisements for West Runton Pavilion announced:

We proudly present our greatest ever attraction. World famous TV, radio and recording stars, the Rubettes. To celebrate this special occasion in a special way, for one night only, the first drink will be on the house.

Frank Boswall confirms:

The first big band we had were the Rubettes. Before that, the bands were booked by Phil Beavis, he used to ring me up and say, 'These will do well.' Most of them came from around here. Then a friend in the music business said he could get me some bigger names and the Rubettes came. We spoke afterwards and he asked how it had gone. I told him they were a horrible bunch. They played me up something rotten and sprinkled Vim all over the dressing room. 'But,' he asked, 'Did you make any money?' I had to say we had, they had packed the place out.

He offered to arrange some other big names and I got a taste for it. I used to really enjoy seeing the youngsters enjoying themselves. It was terrific fun.

The Rubettes had reached number one in the charts the previous year with 'Sugar Baby Love' and had also enjoyed hits with 'Tonight', 'Juke Box Jive' and 'I Can Do It'. Their lead singer, Alan Williams, was apparently worried because he thought the girls at Runton would mob him, so he borrowed a cardigan and woolly hat from Bob James – who had been in the audience – as a disguise to get out of the building.

A month later, the Pavilion was closed for improvements. Graham Curlew, also known as 'Jumbo', who had started out glass-collecting and working behind the bar, helped with the refurbishments. The shell stage in the corner and the little stage in the middle were replaced with one that went from side to side, made of timber and covered with hardboard. Jumbo remembers pinning the hardboard on the stage that evening while the band were setting up. As he finished each bit, the band were putting their gear on top.

The venue re-opened on the 14 June 1975 with glam rockers Kenny. Rick Driscoll (vocals), Andy Walton (drums), Chris Lackison (keyboards), Yan Style (lead guitar) and Chris Redburn (bass) had seen success in the UK singles chart with 'The Bump' and 'Fancy Pants', and their latest 'Baby, I Love You, OK' had just been released.

Frank Boswall was happier with this booking. He says, 'Kenny were all right. The bass player was son of one of my directors!'

John Mason's daughter, Julie, remembers her early visits to Runton:

My dad had started out at West Runton Pavilion as a respectable bingo caller, but as demands changed he became a doorman, complete with velvet bow tie and smart jacket. He would drive off every Saturday evening and return in the early hours of Sunday morning with his clothes smelling strongly of cigarette smoke.

I was only 10 or 11 at the time, and very chart-orientated, so much of what went on at the local music venues had gone over my head. I remember a girl in the chip shop asking her friend if she was going to see Thin Lizzy – prior to their 'Whiskey in the Jar' success – at the Links that evening, and I thought it was a nickname for another of their friends!

However, when Kenny were set to play at Runton in 1975, I knew the time had come at last when I would discover the secrets of Dad's smokey Saturday nights. I was underage, and the owner knew it, so I was taken by Dad, with my best friend, Belinda Mason ('no relation' – as we used to tell everyone), and allowed to watch from the small private balcony upstairs, which was at the back of the hall, facing the stage. Here we met lighting crews, sound engineers and friends, family and hangers-on from the band, and did 'The Bump' to our hearts' content.

After that, we saw all the glam rock bands of the day from our lofty viewpoint, and when they left the stage, if they didn't get straight off back to civilisation, we might be taken into the dressing room to meet them. I remember the Glitter Band, with semi-clad girls all around them, smiling indulgently at these two geeky schoolgirls who came to say 'Hi' but had forgotten their autograph books. Later, after the band had left, we collected the shiny sequins which were strewn all over the dressing room floor.

Kenny had left the building, but had clearly been practising their signatures, and we bagged the signed photos they had left behind. The old autograph book is testament to having met both Hello and the Rubettes, but the actual occasions are lost from memory.

We would walk around the beer-sodden floor amongst the discarded Breaker cans and plastic beakers, looking for money and lost jewellery, while Dad and his co-workers ejected the last of the drunks.

Many a journey home was cheered by following one of said drunks as they negotiated their perilous way in an A40 or a rusty old van and bounced off the verges on either side of the twisty Hunworth hill.

As an illustration of my relative youth, or of my mum's lack of understanding of such things, I remember one occasion when my friend and I were packed off to a gig with a crème egg each. My friend ate hers on the way; I stashed mine carefully in my new burgundy, suede-effect shoulder bag and forgot about it. After an hour or two on the balcony, we decided to go downstairs for a burger. When I put my hand into my bag to get out my purse, I discovered my crème egg had melted into a sticky brown, white and orange mess wrapped inconclusively in ripped silver paper.

The comment could be made that the competition was hotting up, but that would obviously be too corny. Suffice to say, with Frank Boswall's new resolve at West Runton, Cromer Links was now not the only venue to be bringing top bands to North Norfolk and, although it had fought off competition from other venues in the past, the Links was going through a tough time. A succession of managers were finding it difficult to work for Mrs Arundel-Langley and it looked increasingly unlikely that the venue would ever again enjoy the stability which Mrs Arundel-Langley's two sons, Rod and Nigel, had given it.

10

Rivalry And Rumour

When the grand reopening of the Links took place in February 1975, Roger James – from local band Crow – had been recruited to help with the bookings. He says:

I gave the owner of the Links a hand. I can't remember her name, but she reminded me of Barbara Cartland. I helped her book a number of acts to keep the standard of bands up, at what I will always consider to be one of the best venues in Great Britain that I had the pleasure to play at. My main memory is that the Links was the place to play, not just for local bands, but also for bands which went on to be really big.

One of the first bands Roger booked was Mungo Jerry, and he found some familiar faces in the line-up. In November 1973 John Brunning had joined Roger's band, Crow, replacing guitarist Clive 'Buzz' Hunt; and in March 1974 John 'Jimmy' Jewell took over the drum stool from Paul Callaby, joining Chris Warnes on bass and Roger on vocals. Then, as Roger says, 'It seemed like at one point my whole band went to Mungo Jerry!' because when Mungo Jerry appeared at the Links in 1975 they were said to include Jim, Chris and John from Crow.

There were obviously no hard feelings, because Roger booked the band three times. Mungo Jerry were led by singer, guitarist and songwriter Ray Dorset, who had named his band after a character in TS Eliot's *Old Possum's Book of Practical Cats*, which was later adapted and made into the musical *Cats*. Originally a skiffle band featuring an upright bass, washboard and kazoo, there had been several different line-ups and a change to a harder style. 'In the Summertime' had been number one in the UK singles chart for seven weeks in 1970 and 'Baby Jump' for two weeks the following year. In 1972 'Lady Rose' had got to number three as had 'Alright, Alright, Alright' in 1973.

John Brunning and Jimmy Jewell would later leave Mungo Jerry to form local band Boy Bastin with John Tuttle from Kiss.

With the demise of Crow, Roger – also known as 'Buster' – had formed the Buster James Band, recruiting Rob Seales (guitar) and Geoff Hollis (bass), both of whom had appeared at the Links several times with their previous band, Hieronymus Bosch. Tony Smith (drums) and Dick Young (keyboards) completed the new line-up. Roger says, 'We were all set to sign a major contract at one point, but our guitarist dropped out. The next band the company signed were Queen!'

Roger helped out at the Links throughout the summer of 1975 and kept a list of the cost of some of the bands he booked:

Nutz	£110
Kursaal Flyers	£125
Savoy Brown	£150
Judas Priest	£175
Lord Sutch	£250
Heavy Metal Kids	£250
Raymond Froggatt	£250
Budgie	£300
Mungo Jerry	£300
Thin Lizzy	£300
Hot Chocolate	£600

(All plus VAT, which at that time was eight per cent.)

Terry Bunting was a big fan of Budgie. He says:

Budgie were fantastic, they just were great. If you went back to that period and said, 'What are the top heavy bands in the country?' you'd have Led Zeppelin, Deep Purple, Black Sabbath – and Budgie would be in there somewhere. When they were coming to the Links they had had two or three albums which had charted. You would get top 20 album bands coming down in those days because they were going out and touring.

Budgie were what I would call a typical rock band of the time – a bit like Thin Lizzy and Status Quo – in other words, they all piled in the back of a van and just went round and round the country playing gigs. That was great; that was what a proper band was all about – a self-contained unit, writing and playing their own songs themselves. It's not the Spice Girls or Westlife.

I remember going outside after one of their gigs at the Links and Tony Bourge, Budgie's guitarist, was eating a hamburger, so I bought one and wandered over to him. I said, 'I'm really sorry, but I've just got to ask you a question: I really love what you do, but when you play a lead guitar solo, how do you know what notes to play?' And he said, 'You can play any notes you like, as long as you end up on the right one!'

Then my mate and I saw Burke Shelley, the bass player and lead singer, and we went up and said, 'We've just got this band together and we're just starting to do something. Have you got any advice for us?' And he said, 'Yep, get out on the road and do a million gigs, that way you'll get good, you can't fail.' And that's really what they did. I got all my albums signed by them. They had chart albums and I'm out there chatting to the guitarist at the hamburger van – it just doesn't happen nowadays. Budgie were huge at the Links, one of the best-loved bands, always brilliant, always a good night out.

The Heavy Metal Kids were another band who were very popular at the Links. They had formed in 1973 and included front-man Gary Holton with Danny Peyronel, who would later join UFO, on keyboards. Joe Barber remembers seeing the Heavy Metal Kids at the Links:

They were the new wave, first of the heavy metal avant-garde bands. They did spitting long before the punks thought of it. The keyboard man used to hit the singer on his left ear from 25 feet away. Everyone used to get blind drunk and fall over. On their first album they are pictured in a back alley, like the Artful Dodger, dressed in Dickensian outfits with white frilled shirts and black jackets.

This was how the Heavy Metal Kids dressed for their early Links gigs. When they played at the venue in August 1975 they had just appeared at the Reading Festival, and they returned to the Links in October 1975 having supported Alice Cooper on his European Tour. They had released their second album, *Anvil Chorus*, which contained what was to become a favourite live song, both for the Kids themselves, as they were known at that time, and for the many local bands who would cover it. The track was called 'The Cops are Coming' and included the classic line 'his head fell off', which would be repeated over and over by the audience.

Local band Chaser supported both Budgie and the Heavy Metal Kids at the Links. Chaser's drummer, Dave Marshall, remembers:

When we supported the Heavy Metal Kids I sat at the bar drinking with Gary Holton. I was a big fan, they were a cult band, early punk, and I thought they were amazing. They did kicking and fighting on stage well before punk. Gary Holton had a black umbrella, he used it closed as a stage prop – like a cane – then he opened it out, the lights were directed on it and the inside of it was bright pink. It was very effective. I think the roadies nicked my drum stool. I played drums at the time and I'd made the stool at school in metalwork. When we went to unload the van after the gig, the drum stool was missing. That's my claim to fame: the Heavy Metal Kids' roadies nicked my drum stool!

Dave had joined bass player Mike Betts and guitarist Roger Pye in 1972 in an early glam rock band called the Hot. Prior to Dave joining they had supported a couple of bands at the Links with their previous drummer Glen Medler. When the Hot disbanded, Dave and Mike began looking for a guitarist. Meanwhile, John Sparkes had got a summer season at Yarmouth but he was no longer with his group, Silk. He was advertising for a band and the three of them got together as Chaser around 1974 and did the summer season. They supported Showaddywaddy at the Gaumont, Ipswich, in January 1975. Chaser played pop-orientated chart material

WHAT FLO SAID

and a few of their own numbers.

Another band Chaser supported at the Links were SNAFU, who took their name from the American expression used in Vietnam which was an acronym for 'Situation Normal, All F***ed Up.' SNAFU played several times at the Links between 1974 and 1976 and contained members from Procul Harum and Juicy Lucy. Micky Moody, who went on to be in Whitesnake, was the guitarist and Chris Hare remembers him as being 'very impressive'. They released a single called 'Drowning in the Sea of Love'.

On other visits to the Links, the Heavy Metal Kids were supported by Yarmouth band Teezer, who became quite big and had a bit of money behind them. Drummer Ricci Titcombe and guitarist Richard (Ricky) Newson would later join Terry Bunting in Zorro. Teezer also supported Slack Alice, billed as 'The Lady with the Bull Whip.' Chris Hare recalls that 'rather suggestive stickers were available!'

Sailor appeared at the Links and were well-received. Joe Barber remembers they had 'a double sided organ which they played quite nicely.' The following year they would have chart success with the singles 'Glass of Champagne' and 'Girls, Girls, Girls'.

Desmond Dekker was not so popular, and Kevin Dorey says he was 'booed off stage' when he played at the Links in 1975.

Horslips, an Irish band whose music was described as 'folk rock' appeared at the venue in April and October 1975.

The Links introduced a disco as well as two live bands during the summer of 1975, while West Runton Pavilion hosted concerts by Mac and Katie Kissoon – the brother and sister who had had a hit with 'Sugar Candy Kisses' – and 'twangy' guitarist Duane Eddy, who Terry Pardon named, along with the Drifters, as one of the best acts he saw at West Runton.

American guitar virtuoso Duane Eddy had had numerous top 50 hits in the early sixties including 'Peter Gunn Theme' and '(Dance With the) Guitar Man'. In 1975 he had a hit with 'Play Me Like You Play Your Guitar' and put a band together – the Rebelettes – to tour with that hit. The band included Roger Sanders (guitar), Rob Townsend (drums) and Charlie McCracken (bass), who had all previously appeared at the Links with John Fiddler in Medicine Head.

Doorman John Mason met Duane Eddy when he played at West Runton:

I went to his dressing room after the show and he signed a photo for me. I shook his hand and said, 'That was an absolutely fantastic show,' and he knew I meant it. He was a very nice person.

Although Julie Bunting doesn't remember looking at the weekly newspaper adverts

100

and having to make a difficult choice about which venue to go to, West Runton Pavilion and Cromer Links were now in direct competition with each other.

Dawn McMinn (was Lister) says, 'I spent every Saturday night at Cromer and Runton Pavilions. The best nights ever were at Runton and Cromer.'

Jacky Regis (was Griffin) agrees, 'It's great to think of the Links and Runton. I spent many happy times in both.'

Rachel Gray (was Bullimore) used to go with her family – including brother Bully (Steve) – to the Links. She says, 'Later, I used to go to West Runton Pavilion as well. If you'd seen a band at one place, and you liked them, you'd go and see them at the other place if they came there.'

Those who went to both venues tended to prefer the Links, although their methods of getting there were often very different.

Colin Melton comments:

West Runton Pavilion did not have the atmosphere of the Links; the Links was a bit smaller. I used to go in a Bedford van with eight of us in it. My brother was four years younger, 15, and we used to sneak him in.

Colin remembers the plastic glasses at the Links and how they would still taste of pernod if that was what the person before you had been drinking. He remembers seeing the Global Village Trucking Company at the Links in 1974 and describes them as 'hippies with no shoes'.

Jan Petty agrees with Colin about the Links having a better atmosphere. She says, 'People went to the Links, whatever was on. My sister met her husband there, he used to travel from Norwich to Cromer on a scooter.'

Kevin Dorey also preferred the Links. At the age of about 16 he would meet his friend at 5.30pm at the Tyneside Club in Sheringham and have a couple of pints. They would then hitch to Runton, go in the pub there for a game of darts and another pint. Then they would walk to the Links, via Denjo's coffee bar in Cromer.

Joe Barber used to go to the Links in the early days from Fakenham on the free bus and would drink a quarter bottle of whisky on the bus on the way there.

Johnny Wharton went to West Runton on the free bus from Melton. He says:

I was underage at the time and I got a lot of stick from the older ones there. I often used to miss the bus back because I had got so drunk, so I would start walking home. Someone always picked me up and brought me home in their car, I never had to walk all the way. They were great days.

Frank Kinsley alleges it wasn't just the punters that got drunk – he says often the bus drivers would be 'drunk as lords' as well. Runton doorman John Mason remembers the Dereham boys used to come in an old double-decker bus and whoever was least drunk would drive it home. The bus had no back door but a platform and a pole. It was usually packed and people would be hanging off the platform at the back. Frank Kinsley remembers Colin from Black Cat Coaches and Terry Dunthorne from Wells. He says they wouldn't let anyone on their buses during the evening, but Frank had a works minibus and says he used to hire out the back seat for a pint!

Paul Francis started going to the Links when he was 18. When he reached 21 he got a PSV licence and used to drive the bus from Fakenham.

Sandra Fishwick (was Bailey) has fond memories of Cromer Links:

I used to go to the Links and, to a lesser extent (because I was away at college), West Runton Pavilion. I lived in Overstrand in the 1970s so the Links was just down the road and it was a truly great venue.

We girls would go there in our long cheesecloth dresses and drink cider from plastic glasses that always tasted of pernod. There was usually a strong smell of something herbal in the air – I didn't know what it was then but it just seemed to add to the atmosphere! We never felt threatened or worried, it was just a really good night out.

Despite having been born in West Runton, I never really had the same fondness for the Pavilion.

Glynis List (was Taylor) says simply, 'The Links had the better bands.'

Phil Dunning says, 'For me, Cromer Links had the real rock venue feel with an intimate side to it, due to its relatively small size.'

Terry Bunting observes:

Both venues had a knack of getting bands just as they were about to break and make it big. Many people were stars a few months after you'd seen them.

Runton was great because you could go to the bars off at the side and have a drink and still see the band; you could still hear them, but you could talk. The Links was slightly more of a shoe box, but then you had those lovely balconies.

In the struggle for supremacy, however, it seems West Runton Pavilion had an influential ally, according to Frank Boswall:

We were going to have Hot Chocolate one night because her at Cromer had a big band who she'd paid a lot of money for. Hot Chocolate found out and phoned me up and said, 'We want to do the gig on that night if you'll have us,' because they knew they were the bigger pull and they wanted to get their own back. They'd fallen out because she'd stitched them up.

This could well have been the night music fan David Hagen ('Bulla') has called 'Looking back in anger':

It was a warm September evening when Bashy [Philip Basham] said to Bulla, 'Come on, mate, let's go and see Hot Chocolate down at Runton.' So off they went in the trusty Morris 1000 Traveller (0 to 60 in 17½ minutes). They arrived at Runton and the queue was miles long, nearly into Sheringham, so they decided to go to the Links to see Lord Sutch.

When they got there, the place was about three-quarters full, a support band was playing, and the atmosphere was good, as usual, so they made for the bar. Later on, Cookie came to the two boys and said, 'Can you give us a hand to carry Lord Sutch in his coffin onto the stage?' They declined, so off went Cookie to find some other pall-bearers. He eventually found four young lads who were somewhat worse for wear.

The band played the funeral march and in came Lord Sutch in his coffin. How they ever made it to the stage at all was amazing, what with all the staggering going on. Eventually they did and stood the coffin upright on the stage. Lord Sutch's band played louder and louder and he leapt out of his coffin.

Did we all cheer? No, I'm afraid we all burst into fits of laughter. His 'Lordship' was facing the wrong way towards his band, and as we say in Norfolk he was 'suffin' savage'. He soon got his bearings and went on to give a great show. So Lord Sutch was 'looking back in anger' long before Noel and Liam.

Bashy and Bulla had a brilliant night and one they will never forget.

Bashy adds:

I remember that night well. Screaming Lord Sutch used to have a bin with paper in, which he would set on fire while his band played 'Great Balls of Fire'. He would stand on a chair with a watering can putting it out. He would throw some of the paper into the crowd and I remember the boy Kinsley's hair caught fire. We were all slapping him on the head to put it out.

Jumbo (Graham Curlew) remembers that Lord Sutch's dancers wore little more than bikinis. On one occasion Lord Sutch was singing in the coffin when someone grabbed one of the girl's bikini bottoms. Lord Sutch started swearing and said, 'If anyone touches them, I'm off!'

'Cookie', who Bulla explained was struggling to locate sober and willing pall-bearers, was John Cook, who started at the Links as a bouncer and barman. Norman Clowes, who worked with Cookie behind the bar, remembers him as 'a lovely character, larger than life,' and Bully (Steve Bullimore) recalls Cookie using a broom handle as a guitar.

Roger James and Paul Callaby gave Cookie the nick-name 'Spud King'. Roger explains why:

Cookie used to deliver potatoes by lorry and we called him Spud King after the Deep Purple track Speed King! Cookie was such a good friend, I had so much fun with him.

Cookie was another staff member who would end up booking the bands at the Links, probably after Roger James finished there.

One of the last bands Roger booked was Be Bop Deluxe. They had appeared at the venue twice the previous year supporting Merlin and Cockney Rebel, but in November 1975 they were the headline act wearing, as Chris Hare remembers, matching white suits and hats. Terry Bunting has vivid memories of the gig:

When I saw them they were astonishing. They were fantastic at the Links that night and they had a big crowd as well. Bill Nelson, the lead guitarist, was well respected, and is a bit of a legend still. When he held the guitar, it looked like it was part of him. That happens with some of the greatest guitar players, they look like they were born with the guitar in their hands. Bill Nelson was like that, he blew us to pieces. I'd never seen anyone down there play guitar like it.

They were at the Links just before they made it big. In 1976 they became massive – they had a hit single 'Ships in the Night' from their album Sunburst Finish. *I saw them at the UEA, the album was coming out, they had just been on* Top of the Pops, *and they weren't anywhere near as good as they had been at the Links because then they had been hungry.*

The support band at the Links, Bliss, were excellent as well. They played mainly covers. They weren't a local band, came from Birmingham or somewhere, but were very accomplished.

Top of the Pops was a weekly ritual that declined with the advent of the television music channel MTV, and was finally axed in the summer of 2006. During the seventies, everyone who was interested in music would sit in front of what was often the only television in the house and watch the top 20 countdown, which had CCS's version of Led Zeppelin's 'Whole Lotta Love' playing in the background. A select few artists would perform their current hit in the studio or provide a pre-recorded promotional film. A group of five or six – often scantily clad – dancers would come on and perform a dance routine to one of the evening's records, whereupon the whole nation must have echoed to the cry of, 'Dad! They're on!' Pan's People were the most enduring, and probably the most popular, of these dance troupes and debuted on the programme in 1968. In between rehearsing for the following week's dance routine, they would often do cabaret spots in clubs.

They found their way to West Runton Pavilion in October 1975.

Owner Frank Boswall enlisted Jumbo (Graham Curlew) to help with the arrangements, because the girls' contract said they had to be picked up from the nearest mainline railway station, run about wherever they wanted and then taken back to London after the show. Jumbo and Frank picked them up from Norwich Station; Frank was in his Mercedes and Jumbo was in Frank's brand new Ford Escort estate. They took them to Sheringham, where the girls had a meal, then they went back to the Pavilion for a rehearsal. Pan's People did the show then had to be taken back to London.

Jumbo says Frank's wife, Janice, wouldn't let Frank take them back so Peter Burton-Pye did it. He took two of them and their manager, and Jumbo took the other four girls in the Escort. On the way, as they were approaching Red Lodge café, one of the girls asked if Jumbo would like to stop for something to eat. Jumbo hadn't eaten all day because he had been running them about and was starving, but didn't feel he could eat a big, greasy bacon roll in front of the girls. They stopped anyway, and he declined food, just ordering a coffee – which he thought sounded sophisticated – although he actually only used to drink tea. The girls went and ordered the food, and they came back with bacon butties and fried egg rolls for themselves. They all sat there eating them and Jumbo sat there with his coffee, which he didn't like, feeling very hungry.

Glyn Chesney, one of the glass-collectors at West Runton Pavilion, would not have watched the Pan's People act, as John Mason explains:

Glyn was a devout member of the Salvation Army. If ever there were scantily clad women appearing, he would collect the glasses with one hand shielding his eyes from the stage. He would come and find me on the door and say to me, 'I mustn't look at that, must I John?' so, of course, I would have to go and check for him!

John would almost certainly have had to check the nude females who Jumbo recalls danced one night behind a curtain on the balcony, being lit in such a way that they appeared in silhouette.

John's daughter, Julie, remembers watching Glyn at work:

When my friend, Belinda, and I used to watch the bands from the balcony, it was easy to spot Glyn as he made his way among the crowds, collecting the plastic glasses. He wasn't very tall, but as he picked up the glasses from the floor and put them at the bottom of the stack, the stack grew higher and higher. We would watch, fascinated, as it grew larger and bent over with the weight. It would often end up several feet higher than the crowd. Sometimes people would mess about and take a load of glasses off the top and hide them in the crowd, so when Glyn got back the stack was nowhere near as big as he thought it should have been. Sometimes he would go out to my dad at the door and tell him that he was being picked on.

Dad would say, 'Don't worry Glyn, just tell them if they don't stop it, I'll come and sort them out.' And Glyn would go off, happy.

One evening Showaddywaddy were expected but it was getting a bit late and the teddy-boys who had come to see them were getting restless. The DJ put on some rock and roll music and the teddy-boys all got in a line to do their dancing. Suddenly, Belinda and I could see a stack of glasses, at the right-hand end of the line of dancers, attempting to move to the music. Unfortunately, although Glyn was keen to join in, he didn't seem to have much idea what the dancing involved, and as the line of dancers stepped to the right, they kept bumping into Glyn, who was stepping to the left. Eventually, they began to get angry with him, the stack of glasses was getting a bit wobbly, and one of the bouncers had to go in and rescue Glyn before the teddy-boys all set about him!

Showaddywaddy didn't play that night, and it was rumoured they had said the stage was too small for them all to perform, but Frank Boswall has the real story:

Showaddywaddy failed to turn up. That was a real disaster. They were at Leicester watching a football match. They were just awful people. We found out where they were and that made me even more angry.

We were charging £2.75 a ticket for Showaddywaddy, but we had booked them reasonably cheaply at £1,000. You have the advertising costs and so on, so you weren't making a fortune out of it. It would have been £3 on the door, which was very cheap for that kind of band. In the end, the tickets all sold out and you imagine trying to find that odd amount, £2.75, to give to eight hundred or a thousand punters who wanted their money back.

Showaddywaddy did appear at the venue the following year, with what was advertised as, 'A special show for fans, admission £2, free autographed LPs.'

Jumbo recently asked Glyn whether he remembered West Runton Pavilion, and he said he liked 'Showaddywaddywaddy'!

Dick Woodley remembers Glyn's other job:

Glyn was a road-sweeper. He used to wear out no end of brooms. He would push his cart up the middle of Sheringham High Street and stop the cars. In the summer the holiday-makers would have their windows wound down and he would chat away to them. The traffic would be at a standstill but he didn't seem to worry.

The first big band Colin Woodyard saw at West Runton Pavilion were Fox in November 1975. Their single 'Only You Can' had been in the UK charts that March. Colin sent flowers to the lead singer, Noosha Fox, that night and he watched her walk through with the flowers he'd sent. Jumbo remembers the contract had said that no-one was supposed to talk to her unless she approached them first, but says, 'She was lovely, really nice and didn't take any notice of it.'

There were often riders on the bands' contracts, with sometimes bizarre and unreasonable requests. Jumbo remembers that owner Frank Boswall had a rubber stamp made up with the word 'Bollocks' on it. If there was a rider he didn't agree with, he would stamp that on it and send it back. Jumbo says, 'One band wanted the dressing room painted pink, that got the "Bollocks" stamp!'

Chris Farlowe came to Runton with Madelin Bell and Albert Lee. Jumbo remembers that Chris Farlowe was a 'lovely guy'. Jumbo also got on well with Smokie, and Frank Boswall confirms they were 'very nice people'.

Chris Norman (lead vocals/guitar), Pete Spencer (drums), Alan Silson (lead guitar) and Terry Uttley (bass) came from Bradford and were looked after by the Nicky Chinn and Mike Chapman song-writing team. Originally spelling their name 'Smokey', they changed it after alleged confusion with Smokey Robinson.

Frank says, 'They appeared quite often, kept having hits, everyone would ring up asking when they would be on again.' Their early singles included 'Don't Play Your Rock 'n' Roll to Me', 'I'll Meet You at Midnight' and 'If You Think You Know How to Love Me'.

Ann Dennes remembers seeing Smokie at West Runton Pavilion on one occasion. She had just got married and her husband watched a man buy her a drink at the bar. She saw her husband nudging their friends, and she thought it was because she was being chatted up. It wasn't until later, when the band came on stage, that she realised it was because she had been talking to the lead singer of Smokie, Chris Norman, for the last half hour and hadn't known who he was!

Colin Woodyard met Smokie at one of their Runton gigs. Chris Norman had bad toothache and Colin got him an asprin. He says, 'The band were very nice and Terry Uttley showed me how to play the guitar.' Recently, Colin met Terry Uttley again, and asked him if he remembered West Runton Pavilion. Terry said that he did, because one night they had got locked in by mistake and he had to break the toilet window to get out.

Frank Boswall remembers:

I put Smokie on at Yarmouth as well because they wanted to do two dates up here. We used to allow bands to rehearse here. Smokie had about three days here rehearsing, then Friday night they did Tiffany's at Yarmouth and then played Saturday night at Runton, which was handy for them.

They were advertised in the *North Norfolk News* to play at Tiffany's in Great Yarmouth on the Friday 'with local favourites Teezer, £1.30' and on the Saturday they were at Runton 'with zany guests Crackers', for the same price.

Frank had a similar two-night arrangement with the Glitter Band, but their night at Yarmouth wasn't promoted well and they only got about a hundred people in. Runton, the following night, was packed. Their hit singles – without their illustrious leader, Gary Glitter – included 'Angel Face', 'Just For You', 'Let's Get Together Again', 'The Tears I Cried' and 'People Like You and People Like Me'.

Other bands who appeared at Runton in 1975 after success in the UK singles chart included Cuff Links ('When Julie Comes Around') and Wigan's Ovation ('Skiing in the Snow').

David Bowie's band, the Spiders from Mars, put on an informal, free concert one Sunday in December and Jumbo thinks that was probably the latest he ever went home after a concert; it was six o'clock in the morning when they finished packing up.

On Christmas Eve 1975 Terry Bunting's band, the Hunter, supported Sam Apple Pie at the Links. The Hunter had formed in June 1975 and débuted at Melton Constable Country Club in the August. Terry (lead guitar/vocals) was joined by Robert Bishop-Wells (lead vocals/harmonica/guitar), Jamie Durant (bass/vocals) and Jon Kirk (drums). An article in the 'Here and Now' section of the *Eastern Evening News* of 13 October 1975 reported that:

The Hunter call their music a cross between Beethoven and Black Sabbath, which is another way of saying it is different. Terry and lead singer Robert Wells do most of the band's song-writing, although Jamie Durant (bass guitar) contributes ideas and riffs.

Terry explains the importance of the Links to his music career:

When I first started going to the Links I was about 16. For a guy growing up in a village learning to play guitar and dreaming of being a professional guitarist it was amazing.

What used to happen to me was that I would go there and stand as close to the front as I could and I would stare at the guitarist's left hand all night. Nowadays, if kids want to learn to play there are zillions of people like me who teach rock guitar; in my day there were only classical guitar teachers. We can also download guitar tablature off the Internet and you can get tab books, which show you where to put your fingers. If you want to know how to play, say, 'Surfing With the Alien' by Joe Satriani, you can go and buy a DVD now and someone on it will show you in slow motion. In my day: nothing. There weren't really any guitar books unless you wanted to play old folk songs.

So it was a big thing for me and my contemporaries to go to the Links and see what equipment the bands had. I could even tell you what guitars these blokes were using: Chicory Tip's guitarist, if I remember correctly, was using a Stratocaster; Nutz's lead guitarist always used a cherry-red Gibson SG, as did Budgie's Tony Bourge. Manny Charlton, from Nazareth, used a black Gibson Les Paul with three pick-ups. When Hustler played in

December 1975, the guitarist had an Ibanez guitar. It was the first time I had ever seen one.

There were always these bands who were fairly accessible and you could go there nearly every week and watch a class act: a great band, which you don't get nowadays, really. Standards of musicianship were through the roof with a lot of those performers; they would blow the pants off anybody nowadays in equivalent bands touring the clubs. The place was nearly always full, very rare to get it under half-full. I never saw a lot of trouble there, either; it was pretty good.

I think the thing about the Links, with my friends and me, is because we were so young and impressionable things stick in your mind. We were seeing stuff for the first time. When I saw Thin Lizzy down there in 1972 I just stood there and watched them and thought, how could anybody play like that? They were just so tight. Budgie were the same.

Everything is so disposable nowadays. You don't get many bands on the circuit for years making a living like Sam Apple Pie; they never had a massive hit album, but they made a living out of it.

Nowadays I'm very, very fortunate to be able to make my living from playing the guitar, and I'm sure it was those Saturday nights at the Links that made me realise, deep down, that was all I ever wanted to do.

It was a dream come true, then, when the Hunter got to play on the hallowed stage, but Terry tried not to let the occasion overwhelm him:

I remember walking down the steps to the stage and someone in the band said, 'Rory Gallagher and Queen have walked down these steps,' and I replied, 'Yes, and so has Gary Glitter!'

11

Bouncers And Boxer

Thin Lizzy visited North Norfolk early in 1976 as part of their 'Jailbreak' tour, although the exact date of the gig is not known. What is clear is that sources giving the venue as West Runton Pavilion are incorrect. Thin Lizzy fans Terry Bunting and Trevor Alford are both certain that Thin Lizzy never appeared at Runton but they definitely saw them in 1976 at the Links, possibly in February.

Terry remembers the gig:

By 1976 the Links was going through the doldrums a little, but Thin Lizzy came. They played a lot of the songs from the Jailbreak *album, and went down an absolute storm. They had moved up a league by then and it seemed a bit of a surprise to everyone that they were actually coming to play in Cromer.*

Phil Lynott (bass/vocals) and Brian Downey (drums) and been joined by guitarists Scott Gorham and Brian Robertson.

Trevor Alford later bought a bootleg of a gig Thin Lizzy played at Birmingham Town Hall on 15 March. It is likely this is the same set-list as that played at the Links. The recording starts with the sound of jail doors locking, bolts being secured and footsteps walking up stairs and along metal suspended corridors. Then a voice whispers, 'This is it: we're getting out of jail,' before the familiar guitar riff of 'Jailbreak' begins. The other tracks are:

The Boys are Back in Town
For Those Who Love to Live
Wild One
Emerald
It's Only Money
Romeo and the Lonely Girl
Blues Boy
Warrior
Rosalie
Angel From the Coast
Suicide

Sha-La-La (and drum solo)
Baby Drives Me Crazy
The Rocker
Me and the Boys

Another gig at the Links which was much talked about was the night in March
1976 when Boxer played. Terry Bunting did not attend but says:

*I've spoken to people who went there. I know it's not a wind-up because every single person
mentioned the incident. One of the band got really drunk and took his clothes off on stage
and I'd heard he was trying to urinate on the audience.*

Boxer comprised Ollie Halsall (guitar),Tony Newman (drums), Mike Patto (vocals)
and Keith Ellis (bass). Dave Marshall, who had gone to the Links that night with
Pete North, names the culprit as drummer Tony Newman:

*The drummer suddenly came to the front of the stage, turned his back to the audience,
dropped his trousers, bent over and pulled his cheeks apart! The crowd were not impressed.*

Pete North confirms what he calls 'the whole dirty truth: their drummer did do
all those unmentionable things!'

The new year at West Runton Pavilion was no less controversial, with the booking
in January of 'Big Bad Judge Dread'. Kelvin Rumsby remembers the big man
from Kent:

*Judge Dread was a great performer. He did very simple songs, based on nursery rhymes but
full of innuendo: 'Little Bo Beep', 'Mary had a Little Lamb', and he did a version of 'Je
t'Aime'. He said, 'You won't see me on Top of the Pops' – every record was banned. He
came to Runton twice, with a backing band. He was a great showman, a big man with a
balding head. I saw him at Norwich once, in the nightclub near Anglia Square, and asked
him, 'Do you remember Runton?' He replied, 'Cor, f***ing hell!' I'm not sure whether
that was good or bad! They served sandwiches in the nightclub and he turned a paper plate
over and signed it for me.*

Judge Dread holds the record for the most songs banned by the BBC – 11, which
was all his singles. Even when he had recorded under a different name, the BBC
still found out and banned them although not all of them were rude! His real
name was Alex Hughes. He had been a professional wrestler, a bodyguard, and
a bouncer at Brixton's Ram Jam Club, then he had become a DJ and wrote the
rude nursery rhymes with a ska/reggae beat. He was the first white artist to have

112

a reggae hit in Jamaica – they had all thought he was black until he performed there!

As a complete contrast, glam rockers Hello appeared at West Runton Pavilion the following week in their satin trousers and platform boots singing their hits 'Tell Him' and 'New York Groove'.

In February, Eddie and the Hot Rods supported fellow Canvey-Islanders the Kursaal Flyers at Runton. While the gig may have been unremarkable at the time, by the end of the year the Kursaal Flyers would return with their single 'Little Does She Know' and their guitarist, Graham Douglas, would go on to write 'Do Anything You Wanna Do' for the band who had earlier supported them, known in 1977 as simply the Rods.

Terry Bunting saw the Kursaal Flyers on their second visit to the venue. He says, 'They were a quirky rock band and were really happening at the time.' Jumbo (Graham Curlew) remembers that the Kursaal Flyers' singer wore a flying hat and goggles, like Biggles.

One act who were certainly unusual were Shag Connors and the Carrot Crunchers. Similar to the more commercially successful Wurzels, Shag Connors and the Carrot Crunchers were part of the music genre known as 'Scrumpy and Western'. They wore farmers' smocks and straw hats, and the line-up included a white cockerel called 'Stuffin' which wore a red nappy, drank from a pint of beer, strutted about on stage, and 'sang' along with the songs. They released various albums, and in 1976, when they made their two appearances at West Runton Pavilion, the line-up on *Country Capers* was said to include Martin 'Scarecrow' Connor (electric guitar), Barry 'Plonker' Hinchley (organ), Adrian 'Silage' Garland (drums) and Richard 'Cow Cake' Smith (bass). An earlier album, *Furzlin' With Shag Connors and the Carrot Crunchers*, offers an explanation for lead singer and harmonica player Mick Connors' nickname:

[He was] *found drunk with his head resting on a manure heap, which caused a tobacco-like hair to grow on the sides of his face. Shortage of cigarettes on the farm caused him to try some* [of this hair] *in a roll-up, very strong but good. Now everybody smokes it in the village. He says, 'They all know I grow me own tobacco, so they call me Shag.'*

John Mason remembers that the audience was a bit lively:

During one of Shag Connors' shows a large fight broke out in the crowd near the stage. Afterwards, the bouncers apologised to Mr Connors for the disturbance. 'That be all right,' he said, in his thick West Country accent, 'That be the sap rising!'

Jumbo recalls that the band would hand out stickers in the shape of a carrot, about eight inches long. They would be stuck all over cars, telegraph poles and such-like for ages after the concerts.

The bizarre theme continued at West Runton with a Bavarian Oompah Night – which Jumbo remembers, 'was a total flop, but a good laugh. I got very drunk,' – and Mike Batt's Mad Hatters, who were advertised with the warning 'Watch Out, There's a Humphrey about!' This referred to the jingle Mike Batt had written for Unigate Dairies' adverts, which featured a large red and white straw stealing people's milk. Despite being an accomplished composer and performer, Mike Batt is probably best known for writing the theme tune and several hit records for television's furry litter gatherers the Wombles.

Beano, formerly known as the Reason Why, were a bit like the Barron Knights: they mimicked other groups and did other people's songs. Their act included a lot of jokes and they came on stage wearing funny costumes. Colin Woodyard and Sarah Baldwin can remember seeing them several times at Runton.

In April 1976 the Brother Lees appeared, with the advert stating they were currently appearing on television impressionist programme *Who Do You Do?* They had played at the Links in 1965 as Barry Lee and the Planets, but when they started to concentrate on the cabaret side of their act they had become the Barry Lee Show. In 1970 they had changed to the Performin' Lees, and in 1972 Michael Lee had embarked on a solo career. Micky Dyball, Tony Dyball and Roger Reynolds carried on as the Brother Lees, with Angus Jarvis in the background as drummer and musical director. All four of them changed their surname to Lee.

The group did eight series of television show *The Generation Game*, four with Bruce Forsyth and four with Larry Grayson, appearing on the programme 16 times. Impressions they did included Tommy Cooper, Michael Crawford, Blakey from television sit-com *On the Buses*, Max Wall, Rod Stewart, Harold Wilson and Bruce Forsyth.

The Brother Lees were supported at West Runton Pavilion by local band Poacher, who had recently formed with Dave Smith (vocals), David Littlewood (keyboards), Graham Adcock (lead guitar), Alan Fish (bass) and Terry Cousins (drums). Alan and Terry had appeared at the Links with their previous band Zoe. The *Eastern Evening News* carried a review of the band:

With the blond, bubbly-haired Dave Smith fronting them in his various bizarre stage outfits, Poacher could find themselves in the same category as the Heavy Metal Kids, Alex Harvey Band and AC/DC. Indeed, their act features songs recorded by all these groups, with their own numbers such as 'Makes You Blind' and 'Bedtime Stories' in the same vein.

Over at Cromer, things were getting decidedly more serious. There was an announcement in the *North Norfolk News* of 23 April 1976 that the Royal Links Pavilion was being sold to a company in the entertainment and restaurant business, and would be run in future on a much broader basis.

It was said that the venue would be closed for a short time for redecoration, and would then be open every night for dancing, cabaret and food – to provide entertainment particularly aimed at holiday-makers with teenage children.

Owner Mrs Arundel-Langley said she was going to Crete to live and would also be retaining a property in the Isle of Man.

It is thought that the sale did not go ahead. In any case, there were no further public events advertised at the Links during 1976, and in early 1977 the only events mentioned in the *North Norfolk News* were the Henry Lloyd Trio and the Norfolk Nuts in February.

The news came as a mixed blessing to Frank Boswall, owner of West Runton Pavilion. According to Rod Blow, Mrs Arundel-Langley's son:

Frank Boswall had been trying to buy the Links, as a developer. He'd had fairly protracted negotiations with Mother, and she stitched him up. He was involved in a huge amount of expense, putting the package together, and it didn't happen.

However, the announcement that entertainment at the Links would be aimed at holiday-making families would mean less competition with Runton for the local youngsters' custom. In fact, West Runton Pavilion often drew the holiday-makers as well, as doorman John Mason recalls:

Countless holiday-makers stood outside and suggested to me that the top band listed must be a tribute band. When assured that it was not, they would often tell me how they had queued for hours in other parts of the country and still not acquired a ticket to see them elsewhere.

Sweet Sensation, who had a number one hit in 1974 with 'Sad Sweet Dreamer', were one of the top bands who appeared at Runton several times. However, on one occasion they almost didn't make it, as bouncer Danny Hagen relates:

When Sweet Sensation were booked, I didn't think they'd get on the stage. Two of them had gone off with a couple of girls and got their van stuck at Northrepps. We had this call from a phone box and I knew straight away where they were. I went off in my car and pulled their van out of the mud. They eventually went on stage about 10 minutes late.

Jimmy James and the Vagabonds had previously appeared at the Links, but when they made their second appearance at Runton in August 1976 their single 'Now is the Time' was in the charts. Philip Basham can remember supporting them with local band Fandango, named after a ZZ Top album. The band consisted of Philip on vocals, Trevor Hunton (lead guitar), Clive Vardigans (bass) and various drummers, although Philip thinks it was Paul Utting who was with them when they played at Runton. They played a mixture of rock covers and what Philip calls 'good old rock and roll' such as 'Johnny B Goode'.

As with Jimmy James, other bands appeared at Runton following success in the UK singles charts including Jigsaw with their hit 'Sky High'. Both Pauline Willey and Colin Melton remember seeing Hamilton Bohannon, who had a hit in 1975 with 'Disco Stomp', although the exact date of their visit cannot be confirmed.

Another top band who came to West Runton Pavilion were Manfred Mann's Earth Band. They had been going since the 1960s as an R & B band with vocalist Paul Jones. They had played at the Links six years earlier as Manfred Mann Chapter Three, then had faded off the scene a little bit. The band had been re-launched in 1971 as Manfred Mann's Earth Band, to reflect a more sophisticated music style, which was the start of massive success for them.

Terry Bunting remembers seeing the band at West Runton in the hot summer of 1976:

Manfred Mann brought the house down. When they did 'Davy's on the Road Again' the singer held the last note for ages and Manfred Mann came out from behind his keyboards and offered him a glass of water. He drank the water and the voice was still coming out – he was obviously using some sort of trick – and everyone just cracked up. They were brilliant. Within a very short time, a matter of weeks, they were in the top 10 with 'Blinded by the Light'. Runton caught them just before they made it big.

Frank Boswall recalls, 'They had just put the band together and struck a deal so they could use West Runton Pavilion as a practice gig before their tour, not expecting their single to do so well.'

'Davy's on the Road Again' featured in Manfred Mann's live set-list a couple of years before being released as a single, when it too achieved chart success.

Andy Fairweather-Low was another star who used West Runton Pavilion for practice purposes. Formerly from the 1960s band Amen Corner, Andy had appeared at the Links with his band of the time, Fair Weather, and had now embarked on a solo career, achieving a top 10 hit at the end of 1975 with 'Wide Eyed and Legless'.

Frank remembers:

Andy Fairweather-Low spent all week practising at West Runton Pavilion and put on a free gig at the end of it. They all wanted to rehearse there because it was so good acoustically. Word got around in the music business and that's why we used to get phone calls from all kinds of agents.

On another of Andy Fairweather-Low's visits to Runton, Pauline Willey says, 'We only paid 50p because he had a really sore throat.'

Terry Bunting explains why bands liked to practice at the venue:

The thing about Runton was the acoustics were so good. I played there a few times and the sound was spot on. A lot of bands used to go there to try stuff out, because they knew the sound was so good and they could hear it properly. It was a beautifully sized stage but yet there was no echo. The stage was perfect for your average band, too small for Led Zeppelin or Deep Purple, but for someone like AC/DC coming up, it was perfect. It was exactly the right height, depth and width.

A lot of bands used Runton as a warm-up for big tours or festivals. They liked it because the crowd was good, but a lot of bands liked it because of the owner; he was really into the music and that's what really mattered. I used to go as a punter and as a performer and he always had plenty of time for me and my cronies.

Terry Bunting's band, the Hunter, had gone through a few line-up changes since their Christmas Eve support at the Links. Robert Bishop-Wells had left in February 1976 and Jamie Durant followed a month later. Mark Newman took over the vocalist slot and Kevin Longman became bass player, leaving Jon Kirk on drums and Terry on lead guitar. Kevin had come from another local group, the Hat Band, with whom he had been vocalist. The Hat Band had previously appeared at West Runton Pavilion and also supported the Buster James Band at the Links.

Following these changes to the Hunter line-up, the new quartet played their first gig under the name of Zorro at Melton Constable Country Club in May 1976. In July 1976 the *Eastern Evening News* carried a report declaring, 'Exciting, varied music – that's the mark of Zorro.'

Zorro's first ever gig at West Runton Pavilion was on 21 August 1976 supporting Johnny Wakelin of 'In Zaire' fame, who Kevin Longman describes as 'a talent-less prat with roadies to match'. German band Can were meant to headline on 14 October 1976 but cancelled, so Zorro supported their replacement Graham Parker and the Rumour, for which they were paid £35. Terry Bunting says, 'I remember that night really well because our singer, Mark, thumped one of Graham Parker's roadies – flattened him – because we had a bit of an altercation with them.'

In the *Eastern Evening News* of 22 November 1976, Colin Cross described Zorro:

Terry Bunting is a great guitarist who strides the stage and has even been known to lie down flat out, still playing his guitar. Mark Newman, who sometimes appears on stage in a long black cloak and cavorts all over it, urging the group on, possesses an astonishing voice-range, which he puts down to six years opera training. Occasionally he throws in a bit of operatic aria between the songs.

Old flyers from West Runton Pavilion show that Zorro were due to appear with Mott on 7 October, although newspaper advertisements nearer the time listed Lone Star as support. In the event, neither band did it. Although Mott had an album out at the time called *Shouting and Pointing*, from which Zorro used to do the title track, Terry Bunting had gone to the gig mainly to see Lone Star, but he reveals:

Lone Star did not play that night; the stage wasn't big enough for both the bands. Lone Star were a six-piece and they couldn't get their gear on the stage, but they were good enough to sign my album. They had been formed in May '75 by Paul Chapman, ex-guitarist with UFO, and had done the Radio One Saturday afternoon rock show, which had been broadcast during that hot summer of '76. They did a brilliant version of 'She Said, She Said' by the Beatles. They had a couple of albums out, produced by Roy Thomas Baker – who worked with Queen – before disappearing without trace.

Mott, an offshoot of Mott the Hoople, had also formed in May 1975, when Mick Ronson and Ian Hunter left Mott the Hoople to concentrate on solo projects, the latter having a hit that year with 'Once Bitten, Twice Shy'. Remaining members Dale Griffin (drums/vocals), Overend Watts (bass/vocals) and Morgan Fisher (keyboards) recruited Ray Major (guitar) and Nigel Benjamin (lead vocals) and shortened the name to Mott.

Frank Boswall remembers that they, too, came to rehearse at West Runton Pavilion and did a concert there at the end of the week. Mott the Hoople were still big in America and Frank recalls an article by someone he describes as 'a music guru' who claimed there was no street in California at that time which didn't have a Mott the Hoople album in it.

Mott played at Runton twice in 1976 and would return later when John Fiddler of Medicine Head had joined the Mott team in place of Nigel Benjamin. The new band would be named British Lions and would play their 'first ever live gig' at West Runton Pavilion on 11 November 1977, according to local newspaper adverts of the time.

Curved Air were another band who appeared at Runton during the hottest summer for 200 years. Advertised as 'featuring Sonja Kristina', Curved Air were a prog rock band formed in the early 1970s with Sonja and violinist Darryl Way in the original line-up. Darryl had previously appeared at the Links with Wolf. Curved Air released a single, 'Back Street Luv', in 1971. In 1976, when they played at West Runton Pavilion, the line-up included bass player Tony Reeves, who had previously been a founder member of Greenslade. Tony went back to reform Greenslade when Curved Air split, which they had agreed to do at the end of their tour. When the tour reached Newcastle, Curved Air's American drummer, Stewart Copeland, went to see local band Last Exit and was introduced to bass

player and singer Sting, with whom he would form his next band, the Police.
Sixties band the Troggs, probably best known for their single 'Wild Thing', hadn't had a hit in almost 10 years. Terry Bunting saw them at West Runton Pavilion, but preferred their support band, Bethnal, who originated from Bethnal Green. He says, 'Bethnal blew the Troggs off the stage that night. They did a fantastic version of the Who number 'Barbara O'Reily' with all the synthesisers.' Bethnal would be rewarded with a return appearance the following year supporting Hawkwind.

As the bands and the crowds at West Runton Pavilion got bigger, more bouncers were employed over the course of the next few years including Geoff Peck (an ex-policeman), Dave (a wrestler) and Terry Cockrill. Christopher Pegg ('Tiffer'), Patrick Robinson ('Pud') and John Cook ('Cookie') all came over from the Links.
Doorman John Mason remembers how Cookie got the job:

We could never get Cookie out when we wanted to close. I used to laugh that we ought to have a set of wheels fitted to him, so we could wheel him out. In the end, Frank employed him to help get everyone else out, which worked better.

John has many memories of Cookie and of the things that happened when they worked together at West Runton Pavilion:

What a character Cookie was; he deserves a book on his own! In fact, I remember Bryan Daly – who was a local television presenter and guitarist – used to come to Runton quite regularly. One night Bryan was standing near the bar, talking to me and Cookie about this project he had in mind. He wanted to do a series on Norfolk characters and their life stories. He turned to Cookie and said, 'You would make a good subject for one of the programmes.' Cookie looked at him in amazement and replied, 'But I'm only 25!'

I remember once the inner swing doors opening and on the end of Cookie's arm was a little fellow, his feet barely touching the floor. 'Keep him out, John, he's starting to annoy me,' Cookie said. Cookie was not the sort of person you annoyed. I helped the little man out and suggested he came back the next week when he might be allowed in again.

Later that evening, the outside door opened and a large overcoat (like an ex-Second World War army great-coat), buttoned to the top, collar fully up, came walking in. It did not have a head. An arm reached up, no hand, just a pass-out ticket sticking out of the end of the sleeve. I took the ticket but the coat kept going. I grabbed it by the collar and unbuttoned it to find the little fellow who had been ejected earlier, hiding inside the coat. For his cheek, determination and originality, I weakened and allowed him to spend the rest of the evening watching the groups from the small private balcony upstairs, out of harm's way. Some time later, a fairly tall punter appeared at the outside door. 'I have lost my pass-out,' he said, 'and it's f-f-f-f-reezing out here,' or words to that effect!

'I believe you,' I replied, 'the North Norfolk coast is not the place to be when the wind is coming off the sea on a frosty winter's night and you are without a coat. Incidentally,' I told him, 'I apprehended your coat a short while ago trying to get into the dance hall.'

On another occasion, the inner swing doors opened and being carried into the foyer was a punter who had been allowed into the hall having been warned of the dangers of being in there whilst his whole right leg was in a plaster cast. Someone had stood on his bare toes and he looked in agony. We sat him down on a chair and placed his leg up on another chair to help ease the pain – but not for long. His brother came in from the dance hall, pulled the second chair away, and sat down on it. 'Tell me who did it and I'll get them,' he said, as the leg fell to the floor with a crack accompanied by screams of pain from the owner. Even my medically untrained eye knew a knee should not be bent in that direction.

One evening, the police called in and they stood in the foyer talking to me. All of a sudden I heard a police siren and could see blue flashing lights in the car park. 'Is that one of your colleagues?' I asked, as we all looked outside. It wasn't, it was Cookie. They had left their keys in the police car and he was roaring round and round the car park in it, having a great time!

Jumbo (Graham Curlew) laughs, 'The police must have lost count of the number of blue lights which they lost in Runton car park, because in those days, they could be unscrewed!'

Kevin Norton, a good friend of Cookie, remembers an encounter they had with the police one night on their way home from Runton:

We were in Cookie's old Renault 4. He'd often buy old cars for about 30 quid and they weren't much good. Anyway, we'd had a drink with the band at the Golf Club till about 2.00am, as we often did. Cookie was driving through Cromer and went quite quickly round the corner near Denjo's café. Suddenly, his driver's door flew off and landed in the middle of the road. He got out to get it. I looked round and, seeing a policeman approaching, thought, oh no, here we go, because Cookie was very drunk. The policeman recognised him and said, 'Hang on Cookie, I'll give you a lift with it.' He helped Cookie put the door on. Cookie couldn't stand, but he got back in the car and drove off with the policeman waving us off.

Neil Emms, a friend of theirs, used to take Cookie to work at Runton sometimes. He says:

One night we were a bit late. Frank Boswall was working on the door and he told Cookie he would be docked half an hour's wages. Cookie never said anything at the time, but when we came away at 12 o'clock he had all these boxes of frozen scampi, chips and stuff loaded in my car. The chest freezer in the Runton café kitchen must have been empty. Cookie didn't think it was right he'd had his wages docked.

Kevin Norton had gone to Runton that night with Neil and Cookie. He remembers sitting in the back of Neil's Mark I Escort waiting for them at the end of the evening when, all of a sudden, he got smothered in all these packs of frozen chicken bits and scampi. Cookie had raided the freezer and Kevin shivered all the way home.

Head bouncer Ronnie Carroll was there when the empty freezer was discovered by Janice, Frank Boswall's wife, who used to run the burger bar. Ronnie says, 'She knew it was Cookie and said she was going to sack him. I said to her, "Don't sack him, I can't replace him, he's the best man I've got."'

Ronnie was a committed bouncer. Unlike a lot of the bouncers at West Runton who came and went, taking the job as casual employment, Ronnie stayed at Runton around eight years, before moving on to work at the nightclubs in Norwich. He compares the two:

I carted as many women out as I did men at Runton. A lot used to faint with the groups. There wasn't so much trouble with the women when I worked at Norwich, just lesbians fighting.

One night at Runton there were two girls outside having a fight. Ronnie and John Mason decided which girl they were going to apprehend. John grabbed his and held her in front of him with her arms pinned to her sides. Unfortunately, Ronnie did not manage to get such a good hold on his – she got loose and took another swing at the girl John was holding. John's girl ducked and he got hit in the eye. Cookie thought it was very funny and never let him forget it. Years later, Cookie saw John in Greens Restaurant, in Aylsham, and he told everyone at the bar that John had been given a black eye by a woman.

Ronnie remembers Cookie dealing with trouble:

These Asian blokes used to come in. One night there had been some trouble and one of them was getting aggressive, he was doing all the karate moves and everyone stood round watching, wondering what to do. Cookie came along, strode through the middle of everyone, and just hit him – problem solved!

Kelvin Rumsby remembers seeing two men having a fight on the floor. Cookie picked one up in each hand, by their clothing, said to them, 'We don't want any trouble, do we?' and plonked them down on their feet. Kelvin used to stay behind late at West Runton drinking at the bar after the bands had gone and would be waiting just to hear Cookie. He says, 'Cookie would be there, with his braces on, telling joke after joke, one after the other, for hours, like a stand-up comedian.'

Neil Emms says, 'Cookie was the life of the party,' and Geoff Norton recalls another of Cookie's traits:

Every woman he didn't know he would call 'Mavis'. I was out somewhere with my second wife and Cookie came over to us. 'Hello Geoff,' he said to me, and, 'How are you Mavis?' to my wife. He got a very cold stare and I got an ear-bashing, because my first wife's name happened to be Mavis!

Neil Emms comments:

Frank regarded Cookie very highly. He thought that much of him that he let him use his flashy sports Volvo, like The Saint [from the television programme of the same name] had. Cookie had it for weeks, driving it about.

Another of Frank's cars, the Mercedes, which had been used for transporting Pan's People, had been previously owned by Alberto Relva's wife. Alberto, usually known as 'Bertie', ran the Snake Pit bar in West Runton Pavilion. Barman Dick Woodley remembers him:

Bertie had been a steward on a cruise liner around Portugal – his home country – and the Canary Islands. On one of the cruises he had met an American woman who had a lot of money and a house at West Runton, and they had married. During the day Bertie was employed bottling up. His whole job was working there, he hadn't needed another because his wife was rich! Frank bought the big Mercedes from Bertie's wife and used Jumbo as a driver.

John Mason remembers Bertie:

In the early days, every time Joe Tuck's band were playing, Bertie would go and stand near the bandstand and wait for his chance to give a rendition of the song 'Sorrento', which he did very well.

John Lemon, who was a glass-collector, recalls that Bertie ran the Snake Pit on his own, 'Mainly because he was good at it, but also because no-one could work with him.'

Peter List and Glynis Taylor, who later married, remember that people used to try and wind Bertie up. On one occasion, Sam Pointer tricked Bertie by handing him two copied one pound notes in between two real one pound notes, in payment for a round of drinks. The fakes were only printed on one side and were poor copies. Everyone around the bar was laughing because they all knew what was going on. Bertie turned to put the notes in the till and then realised

122

what had happened. Sam went off through the crowd like a whippet and Bertie was so angry that he leapt over the bar after him.

It was sometimes difficult for Frank to keep control of his staff and John Mason recalls what happened one particular night:

On arrival for work one evening, I was told that all the dance hall staff were to report to Frank Boswall in his office, one at a time. Frank was seated behind a large desk. The room had a low ceiling, lattice window and was situated above the Village Inn pub. He told me that, due to drinking and other problems with some of the staff while on duty, he had decided to sack all the bouncers. He apologised and said that it would have to include me. This was something new to me, as I had never been sacked before. He said he was advising everyone that he would be in his office and we would all need to go and see him during the evening to be re-instated on his terms.

I went to work on the door as usual and, having talked with the other staff, I realised it was patently obvious they were not planning to ask for their jobs back, so I went along with them. There were a few big gigs imminent, so they knew they would be needed. I don't think anyone was ever re-instated, they just turned up for work at the next gig and life carried on as normal at West Runton Pavilion.

12

Between Ballroom And Anarchy

The long, hot summer of 1976 continued, provoking complaints from nearby residents that West Runton Pavilion was too noisy. Owner Frank Boswall told reporters he had spent £25,000 on sound-proofing, but doors were being left open because of the heat.

The noise was a long-running problem. Runton helper Jumbo (Graham Curlew) recalls that Frank once had an idea to clean the roof and concrete over it to help contain the sound. Whilst attempting the cleaning, Jumbo tripped over and fell through the roof near the bar. He landed on top of the optics and Frank was not amused. On another occasion, Jumbo says, a whole new ceiling was put in, although he didn't say whether this had been necessitated by further cleaning efforts on his part!

Doorman John Mason remembers that residents from Water Lane, which the Pavilion backed onto, would come and see him on the door to complain that their ornaments kept falling off the mantelpiece.

Not all the acts at Runton were noisy, however, and during the summer a variety show was held for all the family. This featured Johnny Allan from ITV's *Comedians* show, children's magician Malcolm Mallet, and Jon Derek, formerly compère and soloist on Slim Whitman's tour. Unfortunately, the Runton variety show was not a success, as Jumbo relates:

Johnny Allen said to me off stage, 'I'm not going down very well.' He gave me a white coat and said, 'Come and pick me up and carry me off.' So I did!

More successful were the Radio One DJs who often graced the West Runton stage. Local band, Giggles, supported Tony Blackburn and later Peter Powell. Paul Simmons, the band's drummer, takes up their story:

We were the first band to be managed by Tom Watkins, who later managed the Pet Shop Boys, Bros and E17. At the time we first played Runton, we were signed to EMI. We borrowed the original Spiderman outfit from Marvel Comics and one of our roadies, Andy Mason, used to wear it during a number called 'Bazooka'. He would crawl around the stage and throw out 'Bazooka' bubble gum. Tony Blackburn, who we were doing the gig with, freaked when Spiderman walked into the dressing room.

During Tony's slot, he got two guys up on stage who were drunk. He asked if they knew any jokes and one of them said, 'I was on the beach this morning but the tide wouldn't come in.' The other bloke said, 'Why?' The first bloke replied, 'Because Tony's wife was sitting on the sand!'

This was my first time in Norfolk. I remember that the AA were fixing our truck outside during the gig so we could return to London.

We had a six foot stand with press cuttings, photos etc on it. We forgot it that night and I understand it stayed in the entrance for some months afterwards.

The band's publicity blurb went as follows:

The act, like many of their contemporaries, come from Essex. They play a brand of music that carefully avoids any form of musical classification – other than that of '76 and beyond. And – as well as their own excellent material – Giggles are somewhat renowned for their interpretation of standards.

Jeff Carpenter could well become one of Britain's Guitar Greats. An important member of the band, his image as he struts around the stage is one of DISDAIN. Mal Corking, Giggles' vocalist, represents a truly electrifying stage presence which is a forceful front for the band's powerhouse that LOOMS out of the spotlights. Des Brewer on bass and Paul Simmons at 'the kit' – an outrageous rhythm section who, with their stage theatrics, highlight the band's obsession with MARVEL COMIX.

Giggles have already left their mark when they toured Britain with the Sweet, and now they're back to the college and DOWN-TO-EARTH club circuits were they'll turn an evening out (or a quiet drink?) into a truly 'ROCK'-ETING experience.

Funny name, Giggles, rolls off the tongue, and it's easy to remember. A pleasant... nice little word, fun packed with laughs! But a comedy band they're NOT! Giggles spells ACTION!!!

There were attempts to revive the Friday ballroom nights at West Runton Pavilion and Joe Tuck still appeared occasionally with his Al Collins band. However, there was a disastrous night when Syd Lawrence and his band were booked for a ballroom dance from 8.30pm to 1.00am on Monday 27 December. In the words of barman Dick Woodley, 'It didn't work, things had moved on. Only about six people turned up. There were more people in the band than on the dance floor!'

Although the West Runton crowd had clearly left the ballroom days far behind, it seems some of the youngsters were not quite ready for what was just around the corner: punk rock.

On Thursday 19 August 1976 the Sex Pistols appeared at the venue. They had played their first gig earlier in the year at the 100 Club in London. The adverts for the West Runton date declared, 'Front page of *Sounds*, *NME* and *Melody Maker* last week – they must be worth seeing.' However, many people did not know what to make of them. Paul Life recalls the gig where he – as he puts it – 'lost my West Runton cherry!':

The Sex Pistols were my introduction to West Runton Pavilion, during the tinder box summer of 1976. An older school friend, John, suggested a trip to West Runton to see 'a band from London called the Sex Pistols'. As a 15 year old, I was thrilled and a bit anxious. I remember clearly him asking me whether the admission fee of £1.50 was OK, as this was considered at the expensive end for the time.

The tickets had red revolvers on the vertical axis.

I'll never forget the feeling of having 'arrived' on entering 'the Pit' (as we called the Pavilion) and ordering a vodka and lime in a plastic glass. The bar seemed to go on forever. As it was, there was no crush at the bar that particular evening. Who were the Sex Pistols anyway?

The PA was enormous. I'd been playing bass in a band at school for a couple of years, but this was another league. I remember thinking, how loud is this going to be? Subsequently, I saw close on a hundred bands at West Runton Pavilion, but I maintain that the Sex Pistols were among the loudest – if not the loudest – act I experienced there.

The support act was a folk band called Grendel – heavy on the beard side. Grendel were acoustic, save for the vocal and bass, so I was spared the PA for a while. No-one seemed to take any notice of Grendel and I was keen to explore the Pit. It had everything a naïve 15 year old could ever need: two bars, a pinball table and chips/hot dogs. Nirvana. There were girls too – well, a few; it wasn't a Girls' night.

Grendel came and went (never saw or heard of them again). A few more people drifted in. By the time the Pistols came on there were probably a couple of hundred in there, I can't say, but certainly the venue was more empty than full.

Something I'll never, ever forget was when the main PA was switched on there was a 'pop' as thousands of litres of air were momentarily thrust in my direction. This was followed by a loud, menacing, expectant, electric hum. Anxiety confirmed.

And then it began. The Pistols were astonishing – first gig or last gig. Johnny Rotten was wearing bondage gear: his jacket was ripped, it had safety pins on the lapels/shoulders and had 'F*** the Queen' written on the front. Some of the locals weren't impressed – I was too scared not to be! The energy was truly astonishing.

Rotten screamed lyrics and leered at the audience. A few lads at the front (there weren't many) swore at him, which seemed to incite him to antagonise them further. Glen Matlock was a good bass player and he was well in control; somehow different to the other three. Steve Jones, I think, played an ivory Les Paul. Matlock had a Fender Precision Bass. Jones was terrific – arrogant, punchy, great riffs. Matlock was left stage, Jones right. Paul Cook played drums, and that was about it. Again, very tight, plenty of energy.

The set was probably about an hour. Many, if not all, of the songs that ended up on Never Mind the Bollocks *were played that night. No-one really knew what to make of it. The regulars didn't seem to enjoy it at all. I think Rotten referred to them as yokels (or similar) and said that London audiences 'got it'. I don't recall anyone dancing, pogo-ing or engaging with the music at all. They finished, we went home – deafened and confused.*

No-one understood what they'd seen that night and I had nothing to compare it to. When a group of us saw the Pistols (with Vicious) a year later at Cromer Links, everyone understood.

Joe Barber was in the audience at Runton. He confirms:

The place was hardly half-full. On stage they all looked scared. I questioned their ability, it sounded like they had done a 'Play-guitar-with-Bert-Weedon' course for a month. They did a terrible version of 'Substitute' and didn't move about much. I remember Johnny Rotten's glaring eyeballs. My mate got spat on by someone in the crowd. My mate put him against the wall and was told by the lad, 'That's what you do when you're a punk.'

Opinion is divided on the origin of spitting at punk gigs. Some say it started with Johnny Rotten, or John Lydon to give him his proper name, who suffered from bad sinuses and used to spit on stage. Others say it was Rat Scabies of the Damned, who spat in the face of someone who had thrown a can of beer at him. Whatever the reason for the practice, it caught on and punk audiences seemed to think it was a good idea – although many punk bands did not like it and claim to have caught ailments ranging from conjunctivitis to glandular fever from infected spit.

Toyah Willcox, according to Neil Morrell, got extremely cross with the West Runton audience when they started spitting at her a couple of years later, and music fan Martin Chapman was equally perplexed by the behaviour of his punk friend, Guy Wiffen:

I couldn't understand about this spitting. I never went down the front if there was a punk band on, anyone that did would come out covered in drool. I remember at the XTC concert at Runton, Wiffy was hitting himself in the face to make himself bleed, and then spitting it at the band – and he was supposed to like them, they were his favourite band!

John Mason was on the door at the Sex Pistols gig and he remembers people walking out because they were disgusted at the spitting and didn't like being sworn at by the band. Terry Bunting had called in that night to drop some posters off because his band, Zorro, were playing there two days later. He says, 'Frank Boswall told me in the corridor that he would like to employ that lot at 11 o'clock every night to clear the place!'

That night the Sex Pistols stayed at the Red Lion in Cromer. Their van had broken down and Angela Thornton – who helped out at Runton designing, painting and delivering posters – accompanied the band back to Cromer on her own on the last Eastern Counties bus out of the village that night. She remembers, 'They were really quiet. The four of them sat dotted about the bus with one or two members of the public and perhaps a couple of backstage guys.'

A week later, a band appeared at Runton who, according to one music critic, could teach most punk groups a thing or two. Billed as 'The Phil Manzanera Band Featuring Brian Eno', they were otherwise known as 801.

The band consisted of Brian Eno (keyboards/synthesiser/guitar/vocals), Simon Phillips (drums), Bill McCormick (bass/vocals), Francis Monkman (keyboards/electric piano), Lloyd Watson (slide guitar/vocals) and Phil Manzanera (guitar).

The group had got together three weeks before their Runton appearance to rehearse material taken from Phil Manzanera's *Diamond Head* and *Mainstream* albums (the latter recorded with the band Quiet Sun) and from Brian Eno's *Here Come the Warm Jets, Taking Tiger Mountain (By Strategy)* and *Another Green World*. This was not, however, the first time some of them had crossed musical paths. Phil and Brian had Roxy Music in common and Brian had appeared on Phil's *Diamond Head* and *Mainstream* albums. Bill McCormick had collaborated with each of them on their solo albums. Lloyd Watson had toured with Roxy Music in 1973 and appeared on Brian's *Here Come the Warm Jets* album.

The other members were no strangers to the music business either: Francis Monkman had recorded three albums with Curved Air, and Simon Phillips is named by Terry Bunting as 'one of the greatest drummers of all time'.

Their Thursday West Runton appearance was a warm-up for their spot at the Reading Festival on the Saturday. The only other gig 801 ever played was at the Queen Elizabeth Hall, London, the following week. This event was recorded and highlights released in October 1976 by Expression Records entitled *801 Live*. Chris Hare has a copy of the recording and says:

The set-list is a selection of Manzanera's and Eno's work plus stunning versions of 'Tomorrow Never Knows' by Lennon and McCartney and 'You Really Got Me' by the Kinks.

As they only played three dates, it is likely the set-list was similar for each gig:

Lagrima
Tomorrow Never Knows
East of Asteroid
Rongwrong
Sombre Reptiles
Golden Hours
Fat Lady of Limbourg
Baby's on Fire

Diamond Head
Miss Shapiro
You Really Got Me
Third Uncle

Trevor Alford used to attend concerts at West Runton Pavilion and Cromer Links
with his future wife, Rosie Cooper, who often carried a large handbag containing
a tape recorder. The 801 Runton gig was one such occasion and the resulting
cassette recording has captured the band playing their encore 'Third Uncle'.
    Rosie confesses the bag was a bit heavy and she was very worried about
being found out and ejected from the venues, but the handbag and tape recorder
accompanied her to several gigs including both the Heavy Metal Kids and Charlie
at the Links. This was Charlie's only concert there, and one of the last staged by
the venue. The sound is, understandably, a bit muffled, but Charlie can be heard
playing 'I Like to Rock and Roll' which later appeared on their *Lines* LP.
    Charlie were a four-piece band, with two lead guitarists, who never really hit
the big time although they released an impressive array of albums. In addition
to their Links appearance, they played at West Runton Pavilion on five occasions
between 1974 and 1977, three of them during 1976. Their first gig there that year
was advertised as 'a free concert for members' and at that time Charlie were said to
be supporting Bad Company at Olympia.
    The band's line-up on Trevor Alford's first album, the 1976 *Fantasy Girls*,
comprises Steve Gadd (drums/percussion), Martin Smith (guitar/backing vocals),
John Anderson (bass/backing vocals) and Terry Thomas (guitar/lead vocals). Terry
is listed as the main composer. Graeme Quinton-Jones played organ and piano on
a couple of tracks but is not listed as being in the band.
    On their second album of 1976, *No Second Chance*, Martin Smith played on
some tracks but is not included on the sleeve photos and Julian Colbeck has joined
on organ and piano. This album featured the track 'Don't Look Back', which
Terry Bunting says appeared on *Sounds* magazine's compilation album.
    By 1978, when the album *Lines* came out, Eugene Organ had joined the band
on guitar/vocals. According to Trevor Alford's record collection, Charlie were still
releasing albums in 1981, but they had stopped coming to West Runton Pavilion.

Liverpool band Deaf School had won a recording contract in a *Melody Maker*
competition and released their first album *Second Honeymoon* just before their West
Runton appearance in 1976. The band featured 'Cliff Hanger' – otherwise known
as Clive Langer, who is now a successful record producer – and 'Bette Bright'
(Anne Martin) who could now be addressed as 'Mrs Suggs', being married to
Graham McPherson, better known as 'Suggs', from the ska band Madness.
    Bands well-known for success in the singles chart still featured in the Runton

130

line-up. Tavares appeared in October 1976 with their current single 'Don't Take Away The Music' coming hot on the heels of their previous success 'Heaven Must Be Missing an Angel'. The Real Thing were at the venue in September billed as 'Britain's No 1 soul band', again with a current single, 'Can't Get By Without You,' following their June number one 'You to Me are Everything'.

Tina Charles, 'the Country's number one disco lady', who had made the top of the charts in March with 'I Love to Love (But My Baby Just Loves to Dance)', and Australian band Sherbet, following success with their single 'Howzat!', both appeared in the Autumn.

The Strawbs came to West Runton Pavilion in July 1976 advertised as a one-off gig as a warm-up for Cardiff. They had had two hit singles earlier in the decade: 'Lay Down' and 'Part of the Union'. The line-up which played at West Runton Pavilion included guitarist/lead singer/song-writer David Cousins, who was co-founder of the Strawbs with Tony Hooper in the late sixties.

Chart-toppers Slik came to the venue twice. Johnny Wharton says, 'The best band I ever saw at Runton were Slik. They had their single out, "Requiem" and it was great.' Featuring Midge Ure on guitar and vocals, Slik had reached number one in February 1976 with an earlier release, 'Forever and Ever'. Midge would later join the Rich Kids and play at West Runton with them. Slik also included Billy McIsaac (keyboards/vocals), Jim McGinlay (bass/vocals) and Kenny Hyslop (drums/vocals). Kenny would also return to the venue later with another band, Simple Minds.

Not so well-known was blues guitarist Pat Travers, advertised as 'Rock and roll smack between Chuck Berry and Status Quo, credited as the best new act at Reading.' Paul Life witnessed the Canadian's first appearance at West Runton Pavilion in 1976 and became a fan:

Seeing Pat Travers was a big deal – not because of who he was (hadn't heard of him) but because school friends were staying over and I was already a (smug) veteran of two or three trips to the Pit. As it turned out, I still listen to Pat Travers, buy his blues albums when in the US, and marvel at what he can do with a guitar. In my opinion, he still can't sing or write a decent lyric though.

The gig was in early November – already frosty when leaving Sheringham, with coloured rings around the moon.

The support act were Blue Angels – a three-piece band very heavily inspired by Hendrix. The guitarist was black, left-handed and played a right-handed Strat. He had a profusion of effects pedals and used the lot. They were a good band. One of my friends (he knows who he is) was a Hendrix nut and this blew him away. But there was still headroom for him to be impressed that night.

The Pat Travers Band were another three-piece. PT on guitar (his trademark black Telecaster Custom with humbucking pickups) with Mars Cowling on bass (beaten up white Precision). Drummer was Roy Dyke. (Nicko McBrain hadn't joined yet – before subsequently playing with Maiden). I don't remember for sure if it was this gig, but PT threw cardboard cut-outs of his Tele into the audience. I grabbed one and still have half of it (somewhere).

The Pat Travers Band were something else. Very tight, terrific guitar work, and it just kept on coming and coming and coming. In the absence of a rhythm guitarist, PT had to work hard to keep the sound full. He had two weapons: the first was some kind of tape-driven effects loop – similar to a WEM Copycat – which clearly was temperamental (much to PT's annoyance); the second was amazing skill. He was able somehow to play lead and rhythm concurrently. I was just in awe of this guy. Turns out that the tracks with this lead/rhythm trick were 'Makes No Difference' and 'Medley Parts 1 and 2' from his 1976 album Pat Travers. *It may be that some tracks from* Makin' Magic *(1977) also made it into the set. I'm pretty sure he closed with 'Boom Boom (Out Go the Lights)'. We went wild – everyone went wild. This was special.*

Afterwards, we went backstage and met PT. He wore a silver wishbone. I bought one in Norwich soon after and wore it for years. My friend (the Hendrix fan – we will call him 'H') went plain nuts with excitement. I can still hear him drunkenly telling PT, 'Oh Mr Travers – you're better than Jimi Hendrix, Mr Travers!' and PT saying, 'Who the hell is this mad guy?' H begged PT for a souvenir. He eventually gave H his empty Peter Stuyvesant cigarette packet, which did the trick – shutting H up and keeping us in the dressing room for a while longer. H kept that packet for years.

I saw Pat Travers each time he returned to West Runton. He was always a favourite with the Friday night crowd. When I asked Frank Boswall, at the West Runton Pavilion reunion, to name his favourite act over the years, I was delighted that he named PT among the best, not knowing I'd been a fan since that night in 1976. It felt good.

PT still can't sing though.

With a long list of singles stretching back to the 1960s, the Drifters were very popular at West Runton and Frank Boswall booked them several times. He says, 'They were a tremendous draw and I knew their booker pretty well.'

Pauline Warnes was a big fan:

When I left school in 1974 I started working in Fakenham and made friends with Sylvia Coe who lived at Cley. There was a free bus from Fakenham and Sylvia caught her bus at Cley and we met up at the Pavilion and had some of the best times there. We were into the glam rock bands and saw Hot Chocolate, Showaddywaddy, Mud, Mac and Katie Kissoon and, best of all, the Drifters. Needless to say, there wasn't room to dance at the Drifters' show.

In December 1976 the Drifters staged two performances on the same night. The doors opened for the first performance at 6.30pm with the band on stage at

7.30pm. The venue was then cleared and the doors re-opened at 9.30pm with the band on stage at 10.30pm. Admission was £2 for the first show and £2.75 for the second.

When they returned the following spring, the Drifters were supported by local band Ram, who had added one of the Drifters' recent hits to their set-list, as drummer Pete North explains:

When we supported the Drifters we used to play one of their numbers called 'Little Red Book'. We asked if it was OK to play it that evening. They said, 'Yes, as long as you don't do it better than us.'

John Daynes, Ram's lead guitarist, says he has good memories of West Runton Pavilion:

It was a fantastic place to play, brilliant atmosphere, we had a lovely time. It was one of the few places where you'd get your own dressing room. We used to wear silly outfits, we were kind of a show band. Our lead singer, Mick Betts, would wear a dirty cap and mac; I would be Dracula; the other guitarist, Steve Rowe, would have a baseball outfit; and Paul Willis, the bass player, would wear a school-boy uniform. Under the raincoat, Mick would be wearing suspenders and have a camera with the flash on his stomach. He would open the mac and the flash went off. He was the engine of the band and would get into all sorts of situations.

We were a fun band, not technically brilliant but we did silly things. We did Alex Harvey's version of Tom Jones' 'Delilah'. Steve Storey, our tall, lanky roadie, would come on dressed as a woman and would stand beside the vocalist, nudging him. He used to complain about it but really loved doing it; it went down a storm.

We used to do a pee-take of the Drifters' number 'Little Red Book'. The night we supported them Mick went to the microphone in this mac and said in a Norfolk voice, 'The Drifters couldn't come so they sent us instead.' Then we launched into our comedy version of 'Little Red Book'. After the set, we had to walk through the Drifters' dressing room into the support band's little one. We got some very bad looks from them. A lot of blokes had been dragged to see the Drifters by their girlfriends but they enjoyed the show because of Ram – we got better applause.

Another night, when Sam Apple Pie were playing, we walked on stage. This huge roadie said, in a really gruff voice, 'Sam don't like you walking on stage,' so we legged it.

I will never forget playing at West Runton Pavilion. It was a highlight to play there, we used to have such a good time.

Mick Stevens, Ram's lead singer, was no stranger to the West Runton stage, as he had appeared there with Chaser under his other name of Mike Betts.

In September 1977, Colin Cross reported in the *Eastern Evening News* on

Ram's appearance at Norwich nightclub Scamps:

The set by Ram the other week began when vocalist Mick Stevens took the stage clad in dirty raincoat and woollen hat, claimed that he was one of the roadies, and sang a ditty telling us what baked beans do to the digestive system.

The rest of the group then came on stage and went into an exciting version of 'I've Got the Music in Me'. The highlight of the set was the group's tremendous version of the Python Lee Jackson (Rod Stewart) hit 'In a Broken Dream'. Also featured were great versions of songs like 'It's All Over Now', Status Quo's 'Wild Side of Life', a couple of Thin Lizzy numbers 'Don't Believe a Word' and 'Johnny', and Hustler's 'Miranda'.

A touch of light relief came midway through the set when the group broke into a version of 'Sunny Side of the Street' and they also included a couple of Mick Stevens compositions, 'Lay it Down' and 'Keep On'.

Paul Willis later left Ram and was replaced by Rob Smith. The following year Kenny Rivett stepped in on drums.

Guitarist Steve Rowe shares his memories of playing at West Runton Pavilion:

When we played at Runton, we had to set up on stage before the main band and we had to get off as soon as the main band's road crew came on. You could set up after the main band had set up their gear but the trouble with that was they might take a long while then you wouldn't have time. We could use the big PA there but it wasn't so good because of the subtleties of setting it up. It was better if we used our own PA although it wasn't so loud.

We would get there about five-thirty and how much time we had to set up depended on how friendly the main band were. Sam Apple Pie were very helpful. They were a college touring band and gave us more time to set up. One or two others would unplug our equipment at six o'clock and tell us to get off. They were frightened the support band would outshine them but it was rare for this to happen.

We'd usually come off at about six-thirty after setting up and we had a long wait before we could get on and play. There was nothing to do but have a drink, but we had to try to stay sober until we were on stage at about nine-thirty. We often failed miserably. In three hours pacing yourself, you would have three plus pints. People got caught out sometimes by the strength of the beer. Staying sober was a task bigger than most of us. The nerves were containable after two or three years of playing, but we had to find the correct point. The punters would get there about half-eight, nine o'clock, and we'd already been waiting two hours.

Our band had a loyal following – we would play at a pub in Ipswich and people would travel from Norwich and North Norfolk to see us.

Ram appeared at various venues in Norwich including Whites, Toppers, and the

Cat and Fiddle. John Daynes recalls one memorable night when the band played at an American Air Base:

There were Airmen with large rifles at the entrance. When we got inside it was a very posh place, with swivel chairs at the bar and velvet curtains in the loo. One member of the band took a woman into the bushes and she fainted. He came rushing back in saying, 'We've got to go,' and explained what had happened. You have never seen five guys and two roadies load up gear so quickly!

Before he joined Ram, Pete North had played drums in other popular local bands including, in the early days, Berry and the Tree Tops and, more recently, Spiny Norman.

Spiny Norman had been formed in 1975 and Mick Hudson (vocals) and Clive Tully (bass) played in all subsequent incarnations of the band. Pete North was the original drummer, with Pete Sear on guitar. The band were named after the giant imaginary hedgehog who haunted the Piranha brothers, Doug and Dinsdale, in the TV comedy series *Monty Python's Flying Circus*.

Clive handled bookings in the early days and he has letters from Frank Boswall offering a number of support gigs at West Runton Pavilion including the Heavy Metal Kids in January 1976, which did not take place because their lead singer, Gary Holton, was ill. Clive says:

I vaguely remember it took a few false starts before our first appearance at West Runton. I think our very first gig there was either Charlie or Doctors of Madness. We were playing covers of songs, and putting on a rather silly stage act.

This may have been why they were booked to support Alberto y Los Trios Paranoias – who were a kind of comedy band, billed as 'zany' – and the Doctors of Madness who Jumbo (Graham Curlew) remembers had a special effect prepared before the show: 'He used to close his eyes and stick something on the lids. When he shut his eyes on stage, they seemed to go green.'

Not all the accepted bookings took place, as Clive explains:

Spiny Norman were booked to support Status Quo at Runton. It fell through when Quo cancelled. It was in their 'wall of sound' era, and they discovered the stage fell slightly short of the minimum area to fit all their backline equipment.

We were asked to support Can (a fairly last-minute thing), but when we got there, they were taking so long to set up all their techno equipment that we didn't actually go on. I was particularly disappointed, as I'd been to London that day and bought a new amplifier (an Acoustic 370, which I still have) which I was hoping to christen.

At that time, Clive's bass was a red Rickenbacker 4001 stereo, used with each pick-up going through a separate amplifier stack. Later he used a vintage Gibson Thunderbird bass, the growling sound of which has been described as 'awesome'.

Clive arranged a group photo:

The publicity shot was taken at Norwich Airport, borrowing an Air Anglia Fokker Friendship – bet you couldn't do something like that these days! I simply wrote to their PR company in Norwich and that was it. We had a large Spiny Norman sticker which we fixed to the aircraft next to the rear passenger door, although it's partially obscured by Mick and Pete. Not quite the same as the famous Led Zeppelin aeroplane poster, but even in our early days we thought big!

However, the line-up in the photo quickly changed, as Clive relates:

Rob Seales came in for a short stint after Pete Sear left at the end of '76 when we decided to change musical direction. We started getting more 'musical' and writing our own material. In the meantime Brian Wise had joined during '76, which is how we developed our distinctive twin lead guitar sound in the style of Thin Lizzy and Judas Priest.

Towards the end of 1976 Pete North left to join Ram and was replaced by Ian 'Fritz' Wright on drums. Ian, Rob and lead singer Mick had all been in another local band, Hieronymus Bosch, who had appeared several times at Cromer Links. Clive continues:

During 1976 and 1977 we probably played more gigs at West Runton than any other band alive. At that time we kept our equipment in a store room at West Runton Pavilion and we used to rehearse there. We even did an audition there for Arista records on a Sunday morning. The boss arrived with his mate 'Whispering' Bob Harris in tow, who spent his time finishing off the not-quite empties lying around from the night before, while we played.

As Frank Boswall himself says, we were dependable and we had a sizeable following. That was probably what was behind our frequent appearances at West Runton. We were very much Frank Boswall's band. During 1977 we had an agreement that Bryan Daly (local session guitarist who used to do the Tuesday Music Show on BBC East, and who subsequently found fame and fortune as the composer of 'Postman Pat') was going to get us a record deal. Frank Boswall was in the wings ready to be our manager, in conjunction with John Reid (at the time, Queen and Elton John's manager).

Once we'd established our following there, there were many occasions when we were pulled in at the last minute to beef up the bill when Frank had doubts about the pulling power of the main act – and of course gigs like that were rewarded with really amazing supports like Judas Priest, John Miles, Smokie, the Ian Gillan Band and many more.

Smokie appeared on *Top of the Pops* in January 1977 with their song 'Living Next Door to Alice', a number written by the successful song-writing duo of Nicky Chinn and Mike Chapman and originally recorded by New World. With their record riding high in the UK top 20, Smokie appeared at West Runton Pavilion on 4 February 1977 supported by Spiny Norman. The latter also supported Mr Big (not to be confused with the American band of a couple of decades later) when they had their only hit 'Romeo'.

Ian 'Fritz' Wright left Spiny Norman in April 1977 to join Zorro when they went professional, and Pete North returned as stand-in drummer when Spiny Norman supported Judas Priest, which Clive describes as a 'triumphal gig'. Decca's A & R man was there and as a result Spiny Norman did some demo recordings at the record company's main studio in London, which Clive has had cleaned up and placed on CD.

The band then recruited Budgie Burgess as drummer, and Andy Schoenherr came in on guitar after Rob Seales left to join the Buster James Band.

Jenny Haan's Lion came to Runton in June 1977 and Terry Bunting recalls she was 'a really good rock singer'. Clive remembers her for a different reason:

I remember Budgie Burgess, our drummer, coming over all unnecessary when she came off stage after her set, went back into the changing room, and whipped her top off in front of him and some others without batting an eyelid.

Spiny Norman's last gig at West Runton Pavilion was in September 1977 supporting Strife. Clive, Mick and Brian then formed Kamakazee while Budgie joined Rob Seales in the Buster James Band.

Clive concludes:

Spiny's short life was from 1975 to 1977, but we did pack in quite a lot, I guess, including an audition onstage at the London Palladium for New Faces, *a 1970s version of* The X Factor.

13

Damned And Delirious

Apart from an appearance by the Damned in the Autumn, West Runton Pavilion had had little to do with punk since the visit of the Sex Pistols in August 1976. However, the venue began to dabble in the genre a bit more during 1977, the year of the Queen's Silver Jubilee.

'New Rose' by the Damned is widely acknowledged to be the first British punk single and had been released around the time of their first visit to West Runton Pavilion when they had supported the Flaming Groovies, an American rock and roll band. A bizarre billing in February 1977 saw the Damned return as support to glam rocker Marc Bolan during his 'Dandy in the Underworld' tour with his band T Rex. T Rex had topped the UK charts earlier in the decade with 'Hot Love', 'Telegram Sam', 'Get it On' and 'Metal Guru', and had released many other singles including '20ᵗʰ Century Boy', 'Ride a White Swan' and 'Children of the Revolution'. West Runton Pavilion owner Frank Boswall remembers the night they played as 'a busy night'.

Music fan Terry Bunting says, 'The Damned played for about half an hour.' True to their punk ethos they did a song called 'Stretcher Case' and, according to Terry, one of them said, 'We dedicate this to Rod Stewart and hope he dies.'

The Damned's line-up on their first three outings to West Runton was Dave Vanian (lead vocals), Captain Sensible (bass), Brian James (guitar) and drummer Rat Scabies, known only to his mum as Christopher Miller.

Neil Morrell spoke to Captain Sensible at a recent punk festival and says:

The Captain does remember the venue and was telling me how, on one of their early tours, they supported T Rex and they had loads of teenage girls turn up, begging to get in. They thought they were in for a good time, but once the girls got in they all buggered off to find Marc Bolan. He also remembers what he called 'the godawful meal' at the Village Inn.

Rob Aherne comments:

Just as punk was starting to shape most people's opinion on 'pop music' this seemed a very unlikely combination of bands. Lots of people there envisaged T Rex as the dinosaur support to the state-of-the-art punk sound of the Damned: not true.

The pairing had come about because of Marc Bolan's television programme, *Marc*, which showcased a lot of new musical talent. Rob continues:

The Damned started off with a very tight set including 'Neat Neat Neat'. Dave Vanian strutted at the front of the stage looking like an extremely right-wing vampire and Captain Sensible did 'weird' but not quite as obviously as with 'Happy Talk'. In hindsight, the Damned were as much about cabaret as punk – and as such were brilliant – but not as good as the main act.

In my early school days (all of a mammoth two or three years before), you were either a T Rex or a Slade fan; a bit like being either an Ipswich or a Norwich fan. I'd always been a Slade fan but I have to say that T Rex were outstanding. They played all of the latest album – all well and good – but also 'Jeepster', 'Solid Love Easy Action' and much more. I'll always remember Bolan singing 'Dandy in the Underworld' most of all. Great track, great album.

On stage with guitarist/vocalist Marc Bolan was Tony Newman, the notorious drummer who had appeared at the Links with Boxer the previous year and exposed more than his drumming skills. Dino Dines was on keyboards, Miller Anderson on guitar and Herbie Flowers, who would feature elsewhere with John Williams in the band Sky, was on bass.

Colin Woodyard remembers that Marc Bolan said the venue seemed 'like a nightclub' to him. That tour was to be Marc Bolan's last, as he died when his car hit a tree six months after the West Runton appearance, which was one of the last dates on the tour.

Stephen Brady went to see the Damned on their third visit to Runton, in July. This time they were the headline act, supported by the Adverts. He says:

They were the first punks we had seen. We saw lots of London punks wearing badges, and asked one where we could buy them. He said, 'Come and see me after the gig and I'll get you some.' When the Adverts came on singing 'Gary Gilmore's Eyes' we realised that we'd been talking to the lead singer, TV Smith, and we were star-struck! Never did get the badges though!

The single 'Gary Gilmore's Eyes' contained controversial lyrics about the American convict who had recently been executed. In addition to TV (Tim) Smith, the Adverts comprised Laurie Driver (drums), Howard Pickup (guitar) and Gaye Advert (bass), one of the first female punk stars.

In March 1977 a relatively unknown band, the Police, played at Runton as backing group and support to another female punk, Cherry Vanilla, a 34 year old from New York described by the press as a 'brazen punk hussy'. The Police had only recently formed and had played their first ever gig less than three weeks earlier. Bass player and lead singer Graham Sumner – otherwise known as 'Sting' because he once wore a hooped jumper which someone said made him look like a bee – lined-up with ex-Curved Air drummer Stewart Copeland, and guitarist Henri Padovani. Their first single 'Fall Out' was released late in 1977 after which their guitarist was replaced by Andy Summers, an accomplished musician who had played with the likes of Zoot Money. The rest, as they say, would be history.

Punk band the Clash came to West Runton in May as part of their 'White Riot' tour, promoting their self-named album which included the hit single 'White Riot'. The Clash were Joe Strummer (vocals/guitar), Paul Simonon (bass), Mick Jones (guitar/vocals) and Nick 'Topper' Headon (drums). The Jam had appeared on the pre-tour posters but, according to Rob Aherne, they had pulled out prior to this gig. The Slits, the Subway Sect and the Buzzcocks remained on the tour. This is Rob's review:

Thinking back to almost 30 years ago, I'm pretty sure that this was the first real punk event at the Pavilion. Previously there had been the Sex Pistols' initial tour and also a couple of smaller supporting gigs.

The atmosphere was very different from other gigs. For a start the lights were all completely on – a bit like you'd expect at the end of a school disco! There were small groups of people milling round greeting each other, moving on, chilling out in the seats in the tiled area by the side bar. All in all a very cool and laid back manner which was a trend of many punk gigs prior to the band getting on stage.

I was there with an old mate from school, Paul Eaves, and he had arranged to meet another friend – a 'real punk' – there. This friend, who I think was called Trevor, was seriously into the whole scene and had turned up resplendent in a combat suit as worn by Joe and the Clash. He knew everything about The Clash album there was to know.

We had a few beers – Breaker malt liquor was the usual poison – and then the gig started. In hindsight it was an incredible line-up.

On first were the Slits. They lasted approximately 10 minutes before being glassed (plastic) off the stage. Their sound was appalling. It was later blamed on the sound system. I've heard them since and this claim was very justified. However, I can't help thinking that this was the punk public's way of saying, 'Let's get to the meat of the gig.'

Next on were the Subway Sect – fast, great energy – over in 20 minutes to make way for the Buzzcocks – frenetic pre-'Fallen in Love With' angst with real similarities to the Damned.

Then on came the Clash. With one album, The Clash, under their belt they thrashed through it almost song by song, finishing up with 'White Riot' again as an encore. They were very, very raw.

Don't get me wrong – the Clash are probably my favourite genre band, and they always majored on their raw edge, but this was so far from any of the subtleties of any later album that you could feel the hurt. An unforgettable experience.

The Jam came to Runton as the headline act in July. The Boys and the Advertisers were down to support them, but Rob Aherne thinks they were supported by New Hearts, who later became Secret Affair. The doors were advertised to open at 7.45pm and the first 50 tickets were drawn for Jam LPs. Rob missed this, however, because he was in the pub! He explains:

Even though the actual venue was quite small, the whole Pavilion 'experience' – in big inverted commas – seemed bigger than just the gig. Next door to 'the Pit' – as we fondly called the Pavilion – was the Village Inn pub. From the mid-'70s through to the early '80s the 'back bar', a new, slightly less fashionable tile bar with pool table and juke box, was the place that we'd congregate prior to a gig.

This congregation that I'm talking about were the bunch of people – mainly from school – who would pitch up for a beer before the main event. Time to name-check a few of the faithful. Drinking, playing pool or putting 10p into the juke box to play 'Sound and Vision', 'Something Better Change' or 'The Lido Shuffle' there was, from time to time: Jona, Digit, Phil, Juicy, Tulip, Jezz, Bubz, Weedy, Hobbs, Peter, Pete, Dave, Nige, Tim, Stanley, Danny, Andy, Finny, Bridgey, Acko, Jock, Sid, Will, Mike, Ad, Mitzi, Linda, Sue, Dave, Barney, Tim, Timmo, Nick, Nik, Liz, Anneliese, Mandy, Georgie, Cheryl, Jo, Digby, Stables, Paul, Nikki, Shep, Milky, Karen, Diddy, and many, many more. And that was only on the nights that we went to gigs!

Rob was eventually persuaded to leave the pub which enabled him to review the Jam gig in the Pavilion:

I hadn't really heard much by the Jam until a week or so before the gig when I'd taped a late evening Radio One session – possibly John Peel, but I'm not sure – with two bands the Jam and Caravan as featured artists. Almost as bizarre as having the Damned and T Rex on the same bill!

I was possibly a bit overwhelmed by all the other 'new' punk music in the last few months because, whilst they sounded really solid and professional, the Jam did not necessarily stand out – and in fact most of the people that I normally went to West Runton with weren't that interested in the gig. There was possibly something big on that Saturday and people were saving their pennies.

I'd been in the Village Inn for about 30 minutes talking to a group from the year above me at school when I was finally persuaded by a conversation with 'Jona', 'Digit' and 'Tulip' that this was not a gig to miss. I duly filed in past the box office, paid my £1.25, and immediately felt the tension in the air.

This was, with the possible exception of the first Darts gig, the most aggressive atmosphere

I had ever felt in West Runton Pavilion. It was nothing to do with the music, initially, but there were certainly some 'major personality conflicts', as they call it today.

I don't remember much about the first band, as I said I think it was New Hearts who went on to be the leading light in new mod as Secret Affair. The Jam, however, were something else entirely. For once, here was a band that sounded better live than on record.

One thing that I had picked up prior to the event was that the Jam were 'not really punk' and this was carried on for years, certainly with Paul Weller's mod allegiance. Irrespective of where anybody thinks they were — and I'm a long-term fan of mostly everything Paul Weller's done — this was the pure heart of punk.

The shortish set (maybe 15 songs) took in their entire first album with Weller, Foxton and Buckler sparse on chat, heavy on aggression and style. Phenomenal.

Highlights were 'Art School' — played twice I think — 'In the City', and my favourite, 'Away From the Numbers', sounding at the start like 'This is the Modern World'.

I'm told that they also played 'Tube Station', but as this was two albums away and I can't remember it, I doubt it.

The set finished and within 15 minutes everything we'd felt inside the venue boiled over into a big fight outside, probably the nastiest that there had been in the area for a few years. Nothing to do with the bands, but everybody had felt that it was going to happen.

West Runton helper Jumbo (Graham Curlew) recalls what happened at the end of another evening:

One time this bloke came up to Frank and said, 'Is your name Boswall?' Frank, always on guard, says, 'Who wants to know?' The reply was, 'The bloke who wants to shake your hand. Tonight the music was good, the beer wasn't too bad, and we had a f***ing good punch-up at the end!'

Jumbo remembers another time when there was a horrendous fight inside the venue, then it had all gone dark. Manager Joe Tuck had turned the lights out because he thought it would calm the situation down!

A short time later, and for reasons unconnected with this incident, Joe left as manager. Times had moved on since he had played at West Runton Pavilion with his Al Collins dance band and they had stopped the music because someone on the floor had been smoking.

Doorman John Mason was offered the job of dance hall manager but says, 'It would have been impossible to fit in the long hours and commitment required with my full-time job so, reluctantly, I had to turn it down.'

Bouncer Ronnie Carroll often used to stay late to help the bands load up after the gigs. He says, 'Sometimes I was there till three in the morning, helping the groups pack away. I often earnt more loading the gear than I did bouncing.'

Jumbo also helped out when the bands were loading and unloading. He says sometimes he had to get there at nine in the morning. George Hann, manager of the adjoining pub, the Village Inn, would go at lunchtime and Jumbo would sit for hours waiting for the bands to turn up and leave. He says:

One night Frank and me were in the pub afterwards, discussing a Vodka promotion. I said we should have a Russian night, where we all break the glasses. Frank said, 'Let's do it now then,' and threw his glass into the fire at the pub. We did it after each drink. George went ballistic the next morning when he saw all the broken glass.

Jumbo laughs and adds, 'Some people thought I was Frank's rent boy, we spent so much time together!'

Jumbo remembers Frank had a smart set of aluminium steps. One band came along with a wooden set and did their lights. When they left, Frank noticed their wooden steps were still there and his nice aluminium ones were missing. Jumbo jumped in the car and chased the band for miles before he caught up with them to swap steps and get Frank's back.

The bands always left cables, which Jumbo used to collect up. He says he had a bag full of speaker wires. Occasionally he worked the 'follow lights' from the balcony, and sometimes the band's mixing desks would be up there. There was a ledge all round the Pavilion which Jumbo would walk on, putting the cables round.

When the lorry drivers wanted some diesel there was nowhere nearby, so Jumbo would drive their lorries to Bale garage, fill them up and take them back. He didn't have an HGV licence at the time, but no-one seemed to mind!

At the end of the evening, Jumbo would go home to Sheringham and says that the road would be littered with empty Breaker tins. Breaker was launched by Tennent Caledonian Breweries, a subsidiary of Bass Charrington, in 1973. Similar in colour to lager, Breaker was a malt liquor with a longer fermentation which made it stronger than most beers. It was also said to have been smoother and less bitter. Frank Boswall struck a deal with the distributors and got the punters at the Pavilion drinking Breaker. Neil Morrell and Michael Wear remember that 'Runton Ale' was also available, thought to have been brewed by Norwich Brewery, or possibly by Watneys.

Jumbo recalls that one night the distinctive gold Breaker tins weren't all he saw shining on the way home. He was driving his girlfriend, Gail, along Britons Lane in Sheringham, and as they went round the corner his car headlights swept onto the Common, picking up a line of seven or eight people mooning, all the way along the side of the road!

The first time Jumbo had taken Gail to West Runton Pavilion was when John Miles was making his third appearance. On one of his previous visits, someone in the band had had a birthday. Jumbo recalls the birthday arrangements: 'On stage during the act they got him to sit there and tipped a bucket of baked beans over him. He was covered in them.' John Miles' single 'Music' had been in the top 10 when he had first played there in April 1976. On this third occasion, Jumbo and Gail were sitting at the bar when John Miles spotted them and said, 'Hello Graham.' Jumbo replied, 'Hello John, how are you doing?' like old friends. Gail was very impressed that such a famous person knew her boyfriend. She and Jumbo became engaged a few weeks later!

Other artists who had seen success in the singles chart continued to visit the Runton stage including Barry Biggs with his recent single 'Sideshow', the Chilites ('Have You Seen Her?') and David Parton, who had had a number four hit at the beginning of the year with the Stevie Wonder song 'Isn't She Lovely'.

Lionel Richie appeared in March 1977 with the Commodores and Frank Boswall recalls, 'When the Commodores came they rehearsed there for about three days and thought it was marvellous.'

Heatwave came to Runton twice, following UK success with their single 'Boogie Nights' and massive success in America. Their second visit to West Runton was one of only a few selected dates before they returned to the States. Another disco star, Billy Ocean, came to the venue in July, hot on the heels of his chart success with 'Red Light Spells Danger'.

The Sutherland Brothers, who had joined forces with Quiver, appeared a year after their hit 'Arms of Mary' although, as Frank Boswall points out, 'They made most of their money when Rod Stewart recorded "Sailing", it was their song.'

Linda Lewis, who had appeared at the Links with Ferris Wheel, came to West Runton Pavilion in 1977, the year of her success in the UK singles chart with 'It's in His Kiss', as did Jimmy Helms with 'Gonna Make You an Offer You Can't Refuse'.

Frank names the Steve Gibbons Band as 'one of the best bands we ever had', appearing the month 'Tulene' hit the charts.

Another good night was the Doctors of Madness and Pat Travers gig in March. Frank says, 'It was a sell-out. Doctors of Madness had sold the tickets because they had been on *Top of the Pops*, but Pat Travers was a big name.' It was the Canadian's second appearance at the Pavilion and Terry Bunting was there:

Pat Travers was an awesome guitarist in a three-piece rock and blues band. They blew the place apart. He was playing really, really well then he said to the crowd, 'Hey, I'm doing pretty well tonight, I've got a bad throat and I had a penicillin injection up my ass this afternoon.'

He did three encores and they wanted him back again and he said, 'No, I can't do it, the Doctors have got to come on.' The Doctors followed and people were chanting for Pat Travers through their set because the Doctors couldn't play. It was just all hype.

When Pat Travers played on his own in October 1977 he didn't go down nearly as well and I remember him saying to the crowd, 'What's wrong with you f★★★ers?'

Showaddywaddy also made a return appearance in March. They had had several top 20 singles including 'Hey Rock and Roll', 'Three Steps to Heaven', 'Under the Moon of Love' – which had reached number one in December 1976 – and their current single 'When'. They were supported by John Otway and Wild Willy Barrett. John Otway remembers Showaddywaddy's introduction:

They had a big orchestral introduction, which got louder and louder, then this American voice came over the PA and said, 'Ladies and Gentlemen, please welcome the greatest rock and roll band in the world – Show-Waddy-Waddy!' It was the biggest introduction to a band I've ever seen.

Sheila Jones (was Chesney) saw Showaddywaddy and remembers the place was packed:

My friend and I stood on a large crate at the back of the hall to get a better view. We leaned against the wall. The crate had casters on it and it slipped out from under us and we both ended up sitting on the floor!

John Otway had also played in the Village Inn on a few occasions because, as he says, 'We couldn't fill the Pavilion.' Rob Aherne remembers him performing in the pub two or three times, next to the dart board. He says it was sometimes on a Wednesday or Thursday night, and at least once when there was something else happening in the Pavilion as well.

Rob also recalls that around the same time 'exhibition' dart matches were held in the Village Inn against the local 'talent' (although hopefully not when John Otway was standing by the dart board!) Eric Bristow, and possibly John Lowe, pitted their skills against the locals.

Shakin' Stevens and the Sunsets played at the Village Inn in July 1977 before appearing at the Pavilion in the November, although it is rumoured that Shakin' Stevens did not actually appear, but a 'double' stood in for him! The real rock and roller later signed as a solo artist but would not achieve commercial success until 1981 when 'This Ole House' reached number one in the UK charts.

Darts had similarly not achieved chart success on their first visit to West Runton Pavilion, but when they returned in 1978 they were in the charts with 'Come Back My Love', the follow-up to their first hit 'Daddy Cool'. Mike Jervis was a punk fan, but says the only gig he saw at Runton was Darts. He describes the occasion:

West Runton Pavilion – Early Days

Exterior view of West Runton Pavilion approx 1965. Photo supplied by Ray Burton.

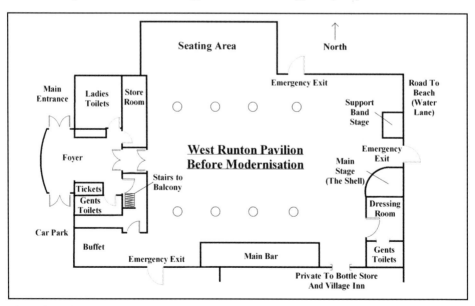

Floor plan of West Runton Pavilion until mid 1970s. Layout by John Mason, graphics by Bruce Fielder.

I

West Runton Pavilion – Early Days

Friends enjoying a night out at West Runton Pavilion approx 1949. Left to right: Maisie, John Cozens, Pam Johnson, Laurie Kendall, Mary Smith, Kenny Bayfield, Anne Dagless, Tony Cox. Photo supplied by Laurie Kendall.

1 September 1954. Bill and Nancy Jervis' wedding reception held in West Runton Pavilion. Photo supplied by Bill Jervis.

DANCING EVERY
SATURDAY

The Pavilion
West Runton

For the month of September

Saturday 4th

Bill McGuffie
Britain's
No. 1 Pianist

Stan Roderick
Trumpet
Star

of Cyril Stapleton's
B.B.C. Show Band

with the PAVILION DANCE ORCHESTRA at 8 p.m.

Your Radio Favourites

8 p.m. to 12.30 a.m

Friday 10th

Norman Burns and his Band

FEATURING

THE "NEARING SHEARING" QUARTET
with DAVID FRANCIS - KERRI SIMMS   Stars of B.B.C. and Esquire Record

Saturday 11th

Al Collins & his Dance Band
with GUEST STAR INSTRUMENTALISTS

Friday 17th **Royal Air Forces Association**

DANCE
8 p.m. to 12.30 a.m

The Pavilon Augmented Dance Orchestra

Saturday 18th # POPULAR DANCE
with GUEST STAR INSTRUMENTALISTS

Saturday 25th # JOHNNY HAWKINS
and his Band
at 8 p.m

SPECIAL FREE BUSES will leave NORTH WALSHAM (Market Place) 7.45; TRUNCH (New Inn) 7.55; MUNDESLEY (Post Office) 8.0; TRIMINGHAM (R.A.F. Station) 8.5; Trimingham Church
OVERSTRAND (Curtis' Garage) 8.15; ADDITIONAL BUS leaves FAKENHAM (Post Office) 7.30; MELTON CONSTABLE (Post Office) 8.0; BRISTON (Post Office) 8.5; HOLT WATER TOWER
WELLS 7.30; (Suttlands Cross Stiffkey) 7.40; BLAKENEY CHURCH 7.30; CLEY (Post Office) 7.55; Arrive The Pavilion, West Runton, 8.30. RETURN BUSES leave after Dances for the above
stops, also to Cromer, Sheringham, Holt and intermediate Stops.

**COMING ATTRACTIONS: Sat., October 2nd, THE ORCHETTE ROYALE (Nottingham); Special London
Attraction—JOHNNIE HOLTON with his Hammond Organ from The Lyceum Theatre, London, W.C.**

Rounce & Wortley, Ltd., Print, Walsham (Road Fitting Works) and Holt.

Poster from September 1954. Supplied by Muriel Ward, singer with the Al Collins Dance Band.

The Al Collins Band – 1950s

Early 1950s. The Al Collins Band, resident at West Runton Pavilion, playing on the 'Shell' stage. Muriel Ward ('Carole') is centre. Photo supplied by Nan Tuck.

1954. Guest musicians Stan Roderick (trumpet), Derek Collins (saxophone) and Bill McGuffie (piano) join the resident band. Photo supplied by Nan Tuck.

Late 1950s. Joe Tuck, leader of the Al Collins Band. Photo supplied by Nan Tuck.

The Al Collins Band – 1950s

1959. Guest singer Mike Redway joins the Al Collins Band. Photo supplied by Nan Tuck.

Pianist Stanley Jennings. Photo supplied by Nan Tuck.

Saxophonists in the Al Collins Band. Note the table lamp top right! Photo supplied by Nan Tuck.

Royal Links Pavilion, Cromer

The Royal Links Pavilion, Cromer. Photo supplied by Rod Blow.

The Links entrance. Photo supplied by Rod Blow.

Royal Links Pavilion, Cromer

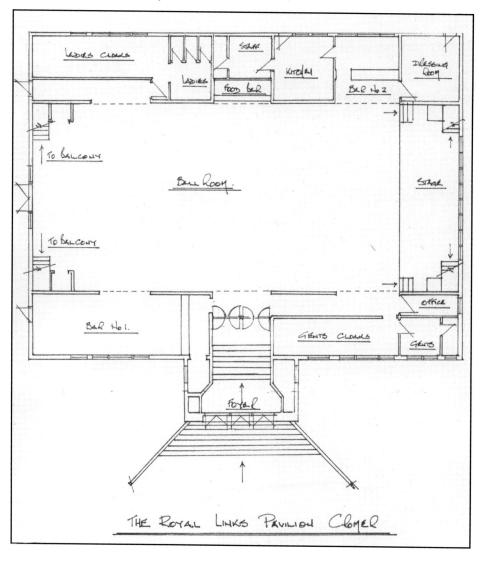

Floor plan of the Links, by Nigel Hindley.

Early Entertainment At The Links

The AJ Band in 1953. L to R: Fred, Ray Gee, Alan French, Derek Page, Arthur Jones, Ollie Scott. Photo supplied by Alan French.

An unknown band on stage at the Links. Part of the wall mural can be seen at the back of the stage. The accordion player is probably left-handed, as he is playing his instrument upside down! Photo supplied by Nigel Hindley.

Entertainment At The Links – 1960s

Beer promotion nights at the Links during the summer of 1965. The balconies and murals can be seen clearly. Photos supplied by Rod Blow.

Links Local Bands – Mid 1960s

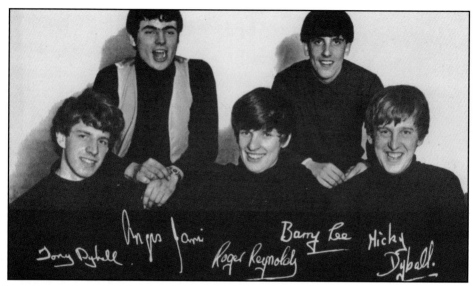

Local band Barry Lee and the Planets appeared at the Links in 1964. L to R: Tony Dyball (lead guitar), Angus Jarvis (drums), Roger Reynolds (bass), Barry Lee (vocals), Micky Dyball (rhythm guitar). Photo supplied by Roger Lee.

Another local band, the Highwaymen, taken in January 1965. L to R: Tony Powell (rhythm guitar), Alan Cannell (lead guitar), Keith Artis (vocals), Hilson Hatley (drums), Bobby Secker (bass). Photo supplied by Alan Cannell.

X

Entertainment At The Links – 1960s

Judging the nobbly knees contest at the Links, summer 1965. Photo supplied by Nigel Hindley and Rod Blow.

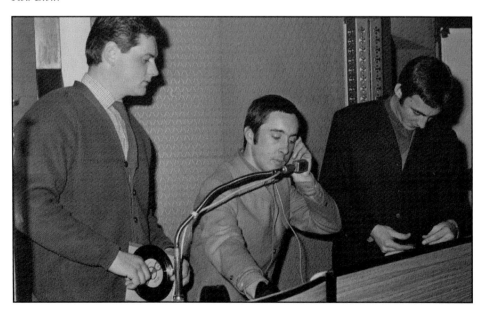

December 1966. The disco phenomenon is born. L to R: Rod Blow (MC), Tim Bartlett (disc jockey), Nick Bartlett (dance instructor). Photo supplied by Nigel Hindley.

Promoting The Links

Rod Blow, Roger Bunting, Nigel Blow and a friend with the Austin A55 pick-up used to promote the Links.

Taking a well-earned rest! Photos supplied by Rod Blow and Nigel Hindley.

West Runton Pavilion Local Bands – 1960s

Berry and the Treetops at Felthorpe Hall, 1969. They appeared frequently at West Runton Pavilion in the late '60s and early '70s, later as The Berries. L to R: Barry Butcher (bass), Ronnie Broughton (rhythm guitar), George Neave (drums), David Waller (vocals), Berry Bambridge (lead guitar). Photo supplied by David Waller.

The Electrons, one of the first 'pop' groups to play at West Runton Pavilion in the early '60s, inspiration for Jimi Hendrix perhaps? L to R Back: Tony Barber (guitar), Jim Baldwin (guitar). Front: Dave Elliot (bass), Terry McDowell (drums). Photo supplied by Jim Baldwin.

Memphis Index in 1969. L to R: Mick Robinson (piano), Tony Dee (lead vocals / piano), Raver Lee (drums), Louie Paston (guitar), Bobby Secker (bass). Photo supplied by Bobby Secker.

Links Poster – 1967

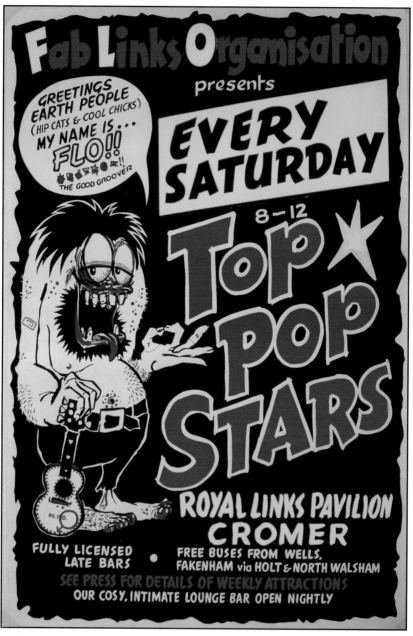

A poster from 1967 designed by Ian Foster, featuring the cave-man character 'FLO'. Poster supplied by Nigel Hindley.

The Who – 1967

The Who on stage at the Links 11 February 1967. Top left: Roger Daltery. Top right: Pete Townshend, with Rod Blow in the background. Bottom left: Keith Moon. Bottom right: Notice how close the audience are to the stars! Photos supplied by Rod Blow.

The Links – Late 1960s

Dancing at the Links in 1969. Photo by John Wells.

Linda Lewis appeared with Ferris Wheel on 10 May 1969. Photo by John Wells.

John Anthony Helliwell and the Alan Bown Set appeared 13 January 1968. Photo by John Wells.

Stars On Stage At The Links

Above:
The Move at Cromer Links, 24 May 1969.
Roy Wood (top left) and Carl Wayne (top right).
Right:
Polly Browne appeared with Pickettywitch on
2 May 1970.
Photos by John Wells.

The Raymond Froggatt Band

Raymond Froggatt (above left) and Hartley Cain (above right) on stage at Cromer Links during 1969. Photos by John Wells.

The Raymond Froggatt Band. L to R: Hartley Cain (guitars), Len Ablethorpe (drums), Raymond Froggatt (vocals and guitar), Louis Clark (bass). Photo supplied by Steve 'Bully' Bullimore.

Links Adverts

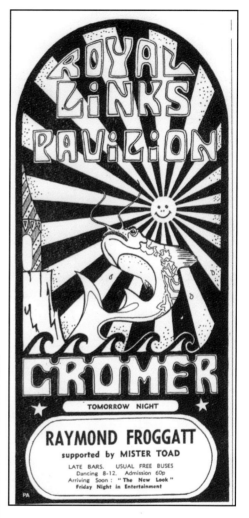

Various advertisements for Cromer Links from the North Norfolk News and Eastern Daily Press.
Above left: 'FLO' from 1969.
Above right: Psychedelic fish from 1972.
Bottom left: A more restrained arch design from 1973.
Reproduced by kind permission of Archant.

Links Local Bands – Late 1960s

Line-up of Eyes of Blond approx 1969-70. L to R: Paul Watts (drums), Phil Wade (rhythm guitar), Phil Dimitri (lead guitar), Neil Applegate (bass). Photo supplied by Steve 'Bully' Bullimore, line-up details from Trevor Jay.

Kiss in 1969. L to R: Dave Howell (lead guitar/vocals), Dave Knowles (bass/vocals), Keith (unknown), Jim Jewell (drums), John Tuttle (saxophone/vocals), Terry Seeley (lead vocals). Photo supplied by Steve 'Bully' Bullimore.

West Runton Local Bands – Early 1970s

East Coast Rock 1971. L to R: Trevor Leeder (bass), John Jarvis (vocals), John Chandler (drums), Tony Powell (rhythm guitar), Mike Green (lead guitar). Photo supplied by John Jarvis.

The band turned professional as a four-piece, under the name of Fascinatin' Rhythm. L to R: John Chandler, Trevor Leeder, John Jarvis, Mike Green. Photo taken in 1973 showing their very loud checked jackets. Photo supplied by John Jarvis.

In 1974, after recruiting a new singer with Alvin Stardust tendencies, they became known as Star. L to R: John Chandler, Peter Collins. Photo supplied by John Chandler.

Links Local Bands – Early 1970s

Mister Toad in 1970. L to R: Steve Kerrison (bass), Roger Mayes (drums), Alex Blythe (vocals), Chris Mortimer (guitar), David Loombe (tenor sax). Photo supplied by Chris Mortimer

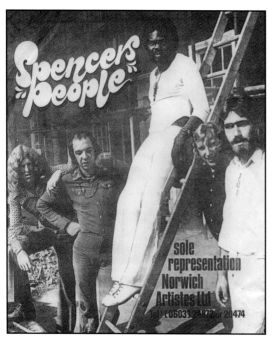

Spencer's People taken at Kings Lynn Docks in 1972. L to R: Brian 'Ringo' Ward (drums), Harry Collins (lead guitar), Tony Spencer (vocals), Alfie Hall (bass) Kenny Philpot (keyboards).
Photo supplied by Alfie Hall, included with permission of Brian Russell at Norwich Artistes.

Local Band Wildfire – 1971

Wildfire supporting Raymond Froggatt at the Links, 8 May 1971.
Top left: Mel Chamberlain.
Top right: Bob Walker.
Middle left: Mervyn 'Coe' Hambling.
Middle right: Brian Kerrison.
Bottom left: The van loaded up and ready.
Photos supplied by Mervyn Hambling, Bob Walker and Brian Kerrison.

Local Band Crow

Paul Callaby (drums).

Roger James (vocals).

Crow appeared at the Links in the early 1970s. L to R: Paul Callaby (drums), Chris Warnes (bass), Clive Hunt (guitar), Roger James (vocals). Photos supplied by Paul Callaby and Roger James.

Local Band Shy Fly And Links Security

Shy Fly appeared at the Links several times in the early 1970s. L to R: Alan Westgate (guitar), Peter Wright (vocals), Neil Pitcher (lead guitar), Phil Buck (drums), Trevor Baggott (bass). Photo taken in 1973, supplied by Steve Andrews and Neil Pitcher.

Rinty the Links security dog being held safely at arms length! Photo supplied by Nigel Hindley.

Links Telegrams – 1972

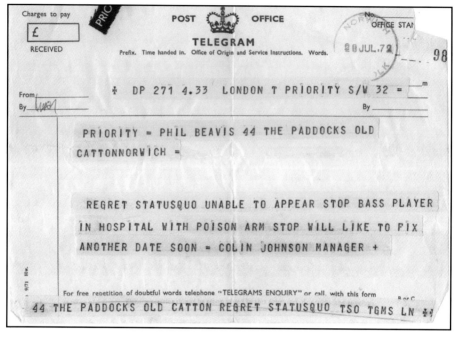

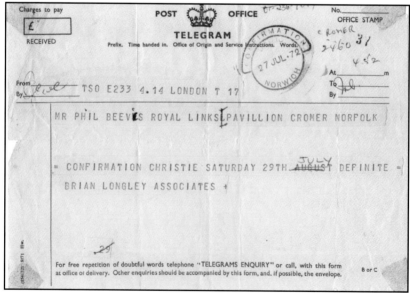

Telegram (top) from 20 July 1972 confirming that Status Quo are unable to play on the 29 July and (bottom) confirmation that Christie will play instead. Supplied by Steve 'Bully' Bullimore.

West Runton Pavilion – 1976 Onwards

West Runton Pavilion showing addition of entrance lobby, accessed from left of building. Photo supplied by Ray Burton.

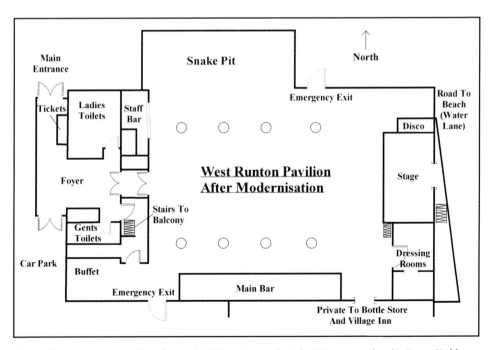

Plan of West Runton Pavilion after mid 1970s. Layout by John Mason, graphics by Bruce Fielder.

Entertainment At West Runton Pavilion – 1970s

The Brother Lees, who appeared at West Runton Pavilion 23 April 1976. L to R: Roger, Michael, Tony. Photo supplied by Roger Lee.

August 1978. Miss Sheringham competition at West Runton Pavilion. Photo supplied by Jane and Tim Joyce.

West Runton Pavilion Bands – 1976

Local band Fandango appeared at West Runton Pavilion in 1976. L to R: Unknown drummer, Trevor Hunton (guitar), Philip Basham (vocals), Clive Vardigans (bass). Photo taken at Thornage Vicarage and supplied by Philip Basham.

Giggles also appeared in 1976. L to R: Paul Simmons (drums), Mal Corking (vocals), Des Brewer (bass), Jeff Carpenter (guitar). Photo supplied by Paul Simmons.

West Runton Pavilion Local Bands – Mid 1970s

Spiny Norman – line-up from 1976, taken at Norwich Airport in front of an Air Anglia Fokker Friendship. L to R: Pete Sear (guitar), Clive Tully (bass), Pete North (drums), Mick Hudson (vocals). Photo supplied by Pete North.

Ram – line-up from 1976-77. L to R: John Daynes (lead guitar), Mick Stevens (vocals), Paul Willis (bass), Pete North (drums), Steve Rowe (guitar). Photo supplied by Pete North.

West Runton Pavilion Local Bands – Mid 1970s

Pinto. L to R: Colin English (bass), Andy Colk (lead/rhythm guitar), Kevin Dando (vocals), Barry Duval (lead guitar), Andy Gray (drums). Photo supplied by Andy Gray.

Kamakazee. Top to bottom: Clive Tully (bass), Dennis Temple (guitar), Pete North (drums), Brian Wise (guitar), Mick Hudson (vocals). Photo supplied by Pete North.

The Sex Pistols

Above left: Money-saving coupon for Sex Pistols gig at West Runton Pavilion on 19 August 1976 (supplied by Terry Bunting).

Above right: Ticket from Sex Pistols gig at the Links, 24 December 1977. This would be the last event at the venue.

Middle left and bottom left: The band on stage at the Links. Line-up: Johnny Rotten (vocals), Sid Vicious (bass), Steve Jones (guitar), Paul Cook (drums). Photos taken by Richard Brooks.

The End Of The Links – 1978

The Royal Links Pavilion on fire, 5 April 1978. Photos supplied by Steve 'Bully' Bullimore.

Zorro – 1978

Local band Zorro.
Above: 29 April 1978, just off stage after supporting Suzi Quatro at West Runton Pavilion (photo taken in dressing room). L to R: Dave Littlewood (keyboards), Terry Bunting (guitar), Ian Wright (drums), Kevin Longman (bass), Dave Smith (vocals).
Right: Terry Bunting.
Photos supplied by Terry Bunting.

Stars On Stage At West Runton Pavilion – Late 1970s

Above and below: The Jam on stage at West Runton Pavilion, 22 July 1977. Line-up: Paul Weller (guitar), Rick Buckler (drums), Bruce Foxton (bass). Photos taken by Richard Brooks. Note the silver foil back-drop which didn't last long!

Gary Holton of the Heavy Metal Kids and Gary Holton's Gems on stage at West Runton in 1979. Photo taken by Pauline Willey.
Autographs signed at West Runton Pavilion – Gary is top of the list. Supplied by Sarah Baldwin.

Stars On Stage At West Runton Pavilion – Late 1970s

Noel Crombie from Split Enz photographed in 1978 by Pauline Willey.

Autographs of the Damned signed at West Runton Pavilion: Rat Scabies (top left), Dave Vanian (top right), Algy Ward (centre) and Captain Sensible (bottom). Supplied by Sarah Baldwin.

Chrissie Hynde of the Pretenders, photographed on stage in 1979 by Chris Hare.

Wilko Johnson photographed by Chris Hare in 1979.

West Runton Pavilion Flyer – 1979

West Runton Pavilion

Friday 30th March	**THE CURE** + BITCH + Ian Mac Disco	Admission £1·20
Saturday 31st March	**BRAM TCHAIKOVSKY** PLUS DISCO	Admission £1·30
Friday April 6th	**PUNISHMENT of LUXURY** + LEARGO + DISCO	Admission £1·30
Saturday April 7th	DON'T MISS **DAVE LEE TRAVIS** ONE OF YOUR FAVOURITE D.J's PLUS MISSING LINK DISCO	Admission £1·75
Saturday April 14th	**SORE THROAT** PLUS DIMITRI + Ian Mac Disco	Admission £1·30
Monday April 16th	**Disco Evening** WITH GUEST D.J. SIMON BATES	Admission £1·00
Friday April 20th	**TOYAH** PLUS DISCO	Admission £1·00
Saturday April 21st	HE'S HERE ONCE AGAIN..... **Raymond Froggatt**	Admission £1·50
Friday April 27th	**IGGY POP**	Tickets in Advance £2·50 at the door £3
Saturday April 28th	**ROKOTTO** PLUS DISCO	Admission £1·30

F.C. BARNWELL - AYLSHAM

Advertising flyer. Supplied by Sarah Baldwin.

West Runton Pavilion – Staff

Graham Curlew ('Jumbo') with Raymond Froggatt in the disco booth, 1978. Photo supplied by Graham Curlew.

Barman Dick Woodley at work, photographed approx 1978 by one of the Woodyard brothers. Photo supplied by Dick Woodley.

Bouncer Philip Basham in 1979. Photo supplied by Philip Basham.

Bouncers Danny Hagen (left) and Geoff Peck in 1980. Photo taken and supplied by Ronnie Carroll.

West Runton Pavilion – Staff

19 December 1980. L to R: John Cook ('Cookie'), 'Harmony', Rodney Whitlam ('Smurf') and Ronnie Carroll, next to the ticket office. Photo supplied by Ronnie Carroll.

West Runton Pavilion bouncers Terry Cockrill (left) and Nigel Slipper ('Whip') in the Snake Pit, 1980.
Photo taken by Ronnie Carroll.

Owner Frank Boswall with his wife Janice, in 1980. Photo taken by Ronnie Carroll.

Stars On Stage At West Runton Pavilion

Steve Hackett, 6 November 1979.   Photo by
Chris Hare.

Toyah Willcox photographed by the Woodyard
brothers, possibly during her 1980 visit to West
Runton Pavilion.

Steve Harley, 19 December 1980.   Photo by
Chris Hare.

Annabella Lwin of Bow Wow Wow, 5 September
1981. Photo by Neil Dyer.

Chuck Berry At West Runton Pavilion – 1980

Chuck Berry on stage 31 May 1980, photographed by Kelvin Rumsby.

Chuck Berry's autograph, signed before he left the venue, supplied by Carol Bishop.

West Runton Pavilion Local Bands – 1980s

Local band Alverna Gunn in 1980. L to R: Steve Gamble (bass), Keith Thacker (vocals/acoustic), Mark Holmes (guitars), Paul Hale (percussion). Photo supplied by Mark Holmes.

A ticket for the gig that never was! The Beat called off and B A Robertson, who replaced them, brought his own support band. Ticket supplied by John Lawson. Winner's support slot was postponed until 23 May 1980, when they supported the Vapors.

Kenny Philpot, keyboard player with Winner.

Winner. L to R: John Lawson (bass), Owen Savory (drums), Harry Collins (guitar). Photos of Winner taken at Runton by William Strong, supplied by John Lawson.

Rock And Roll At West Runton Pavilion – Early 1980s

Top left: Dynamite.
Top right: Crazy Cavan.
Middle Left: Freddie 'Fingers' Lee (note the 'DA' hair-style, bottom right of picture!).
Bottom: Local band White Lightning supported Freddie 'Fingers' Lee on 23 January 1981 (photo taken at another venue). L to R: Steve Popey (double bass/vocals), Andrew Lincoln (drums), Martyn Popey (lead guitar).
Photos supplied by Steve Popey.

Stars On Stage At West Runton Pavilion – 1981

Top left: Lead singer of Matchbox, Graham Fenton, 14 February 1981.
Top right: Gordon Giltrap, 21 February 1981, with fan sporting a Gordon Giltrap t-shirt.
Bottom left: Lesley Woods from the Au Pairs, Feb/March 1981.
Bottom right: Lillian Lopez, singer with Odyssey, 25 March 1981.
All photos taken by John Lemon.

Stars On Stage At West Runton Pavilion – 1981

The Stranglers, 5 March 1981. Above left: L to R: Jet Black (drums), Jean-Jacques Burnel (bass), Hugh Cornwell (guitar), Dave Greenfield (keyboards). Above right: Hugh Cornwell. Photos by John Lemon.

Top Right: 7 March 1981. The UK Subs with lead singer Charlie Harper.
Bottom Right: Bouncer John Cook ('Cookie') on stage second from right, dealing with a crowd invasion at the same gig.
Photos by John Lemon.

West Runton Pavilion – 1980s

Denim were one of the last local bands to play at the venue. This photo was taken in approx 1980. Clockwise from far left: Jimmy Pye (lead guitar), Martin R i c h m o n d (drums), Arthur Watts (bass), Nigel Moy (rhythm guitar), Ady Spinks (vocals). Photo supplied by Ady Spinks.

Motorhead were one of the last bands to appear at the venue. These autographs, supplied by Sarah Baldwin, were signed at one of their earlier visits and feature the line-up of Phil Taylor ('Philthy Animal'), 'Fast' Eddie Clarke, and Lemmy Kilmister. When they played on 1 July 1983, Fast Eddie had been replaced by Brian Robertson.

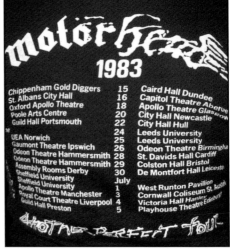

Chippenham Gold Diggers	15	Caird Hall Dundee	
St. Albans City Hall	16	Capitol Theatre Aberdeen	
Oxford Apollo Theatre	18	Apollo Theatre Glasgow	
Poole Arts Centre	20	City Hall Newcastle	
Guild Hall Portsmouth	22	City Hall Hull	
	24	Leeds University	
UEA Norwich	25	Leeds University	
Gaumont Theatre Ipswich	26	Odeon Theatre Birmingham	
Odeon Theatre Hammersmith	28	St. Davids Hall Cardiff	
Odeon Theatre Hammersmith	29	Colston Hall Bristol	
Assembly Rooms Derby	30	De Montfort Hall Leicester	
Sheffield University	July		
Sheffield University	1	West Runton Pavilion	
Apollo Theatre Manchester	3	Cornwall Coliseum St. Austell	
Royal Court Theatre Liverpool	4	Victoria Hall Hanley	
Guild Hall Preston	5	Playhouse Theatre Edinburgh	

Alan Hooker at the Reunion in October 2005, wearing a Motorhead t-shirt from 'Another Perfect Tour' in 1983, showing the West Runton date on the reverse. Photos by Steven Fielder.

West Runton Pavilion Demolition – 1987

Demolition, February 1987.
Top: From the foyer looking into the dance hall.
Centre: Dance hall showing the mural behind the stage.
Bottom: A good indication of how close the Pavilion was to its residential neighbours!
From a cine film taken by Kelvin Rumsby, later transferred to video. Stills extracted by Nat Crosby.

West Runton Pavilion Blue Plaque – 2004

Tony Hall's cartoon featured in the Eastern Daily Press *on 20 July 2004 depicting the unveiling of the blue plaque. Reproduced by kind permission of Tony Hall and Archant.*

John Mason and Julie Fielder at the unveiling of the West Runton Pavilion blue plaque at the Village Inn, Saturday 17 July 2004. The plaque reads: 'West Runton Pavilion hosted concerts by legendary pop, rock and punk artists from Chuck Berry, T-Rex and Black Sabbath to the Sex Pistols and the Clash, before its demolition in 1986.' Photos taken by Steven Fielder.

It was the strangest gig in my entire life. The place was packed. The atmosphere was so hot and steamy their piano gave up and they had to get another one. The band didn't get on till midnight. My mate temporarily lost his eyesight.

Colin Melton went to that gig as well, and remembers that Darts came on stage really late. Andrew Turner observes, 'The venue was so full it's lucky there wasn't a fire.'

Darts were supported by local band Pinto, comprising Colin English (bass), Andy Colk (lead and rhythm guitar), Barry Duval (lead guitar), Andy Gray (drums) and Kevin Dando (vocals). They had previously played without Kevin under the name of Sable.

Andy Gray says:

At the time, Phil Beavis was our agent and got us gigs seven nights a week and Sunday afternoons at Norwich Prison. He pocketed the money from that one as his fee. We played in Manchester and other places. Most of the band turned professional but one carried on working at Cranes for a while, ringing in sick if we had an 'away' gig.

Andy remembers they also supported the Heavy Metal Kids when they came to West Runton Pavilion in December 1977:

We arrived at three o'clock to set up but there was no sign of the main band. We had to wait until they had arrived and set all their stuff up before we could do ours. Eventually, the Heavy Metal Kids' roadie arrived in an old bread van. He unloaded all the gear on his own, then got the 26 inch bass drum and nailed it onto the stage. There was already a hole in it but he put this huge nail through the drum. I nearly cried! The skins on the drum kit were all shagged but they sounded OK. No-one really minded.

There was a round table in the dressing room and the Heavy Metal Kids had cans of lager piled up in a pyramid. When we had finished playing, most of the cans were empty

Earlier in the year, the Heavy Metal Kids had been supported by the Motors. Zorro's lead guitarist, Terry Bunting, recalls:

Zorro were supposed to be doing a European tour supporting the Heavy Metal Kids. The Motors' management came up with more money than our management, and that is how the Motors did that tour.

Roger Peck names the Heavy Metal Kids as one of the best bands he saw at West Runton and recalls that the line-up included Ronnie Thomas (bass), Keith Boyce (drums) and John Sinclair (keyboards). Original guitarist Barry Paul had been replaced by Mickey Waller and then by 'Cosmo', before Barry returned to the band. Their singer, Gary Holton, was quite a character. Terry Bunting says:

I remember Gary Holton was drinking in the Village Inn and had to be picked up and carried out by one of the band so that he could get on the stage for his gig.

They used to do a song called 'Delirious' and Gary Holton came on stage in a strait jacket with his hands tied behind his back. One night at Runton a guy jumped out of the audience and starting singing, and he really could sing it – he was perfectly in tune and he knew all the words – and because Gary Holton was in a strait jacket he couldn't do anything about it.

Barman Dick Woodley remembers, 'Gary Holton leapt about a lot. One night he climbed on the speakers and jumped off. He broke his leg or ankle and was so out of it, he didn't notice and carried on.'

Frank Boswall says:

I remember knocking about £50 off the Heavy Metal Kids' fee one time because Gary Holton pulled all the backdrop down. We had just put up some aluminium foil-type stuff, all across the back, for a bit of a joke. It cost about £200. We only charged him £50, but we couldn't use it again; he wrecked it. I suppose they were meant to behave like that. They were very popular.

Dave Marshall lived at Marsham at the time, the same village as Runton bouncer Cookie (John Cook). The Heavy Metal Kids used to stay with Cookie, and Dave remembers being in the bar at the local pub, the White Hart, and Cookie getting them all drinks.

Kevin Norton says:

The White Hart at Marsham was Cookie's local. I went in there one Sunday morning and there was this bloke with pink and blue multi-coloured hair, like a parrot, ripped t-shirt and jeans, and these massive Airware boots – it was Gary Holton.

Unfortunately, Gary Holton's over-the-top performances led to friction and he left to start his own band, Gary Holton's Gems, who made two appearances at West Runton Pavilion. He then took up acting and played the part of Wayne in the TV series *Auf Wiedersehen, Pet*. He died of drug-related problems in 1985 whilst the second series was being filmed.

Martin Chapman's friend was a big Heavy Metal Kids fan and saw them at West Runton Pavilion every time they were on. Martin recalls:

My mate was wearing an old brown store-man's coat and he had written 'Heavy Metal

Kids' on the back of it. When the band came on he was leaping about, going absolutely nuts, jumping around everywhere and this old coat was flapping about. Next thing, he'd gone. I looked round for him, and there he was, sparked out on the floor; someone had got fed up with him leaping around and had smacked him one!

Another time this same mate turned up at Runton in this tatty old t-shirt, full of holes. I went up to the bar to get some drinks in, and he went off for a pee. When he came back and stood near us, we didn't notice him at first. Then he asked us, 'What do you think of this?' and pointed at this new shirt he was now wearing. We said it looked really nice and asked how he had got it. He said he'd swapped it with someone in the toilet. Apparently, he'd just gone up to this lad and said, 'Give me that shirt, you can have this one!' As he was telling us this, a little lad went past with my mate's old ripped shirt on. He had his bottom lip out, and was looking very pissed off. He had probably been too scared to argue, but I wonder what his mum said when he got home.

One night, we were ready to go home and we couldn't find this mate. We went out to the car and there was this strange noise coming from under it. We looked, and there he was. He had apparently been sitting on the car, slid off it, rolled underneath and fell asleep. It's a good job he moaned otherwise we would have run over him.

Martin had been a big fan of Deep Purple. After they split up, he had followed the career of each of the members with interest. Lead singer Ian Gillan had formed his own eponymous band featuring Colin Towns (keyboards/flutes), Mark Nauseef (drums/percussion), Ray Fenwick (guitars) and John Gustafson (bass). When they came to Runton in May 1977 the advert in the local paper had promised, 'The best in progressive, raunchy basic rock. A bargain at £1.20!' Martin was so delighted that he stole one of the posters out of the foyer! Unfortunately, he wasn't too impressed with the gig:

I wasn't keen on the Clear Air Turbulence *album and most of the stuff he played was from that. He only did about three Deep Purple songs at the end of the gig: 'Black Night', 'Child in Time' and 'Smoke on the Water'.*

Terry Bunting reveals:

I went to that gig and got drunk on Breakers. I went backstage and Frank Boswall introduced me to Ian Gillan. My band, Zorro, had just turned professional and Frank said to Ian, 'These guys are now going out on the road, have you got any advice for them?' Ian replied, 'Be nice to the people on the way up, because you'll meet them again on the way down!' I was so drunk that Ian Gillan, his bass player, and my mate Pivi had to carry me out to the car!

Zorro had added an extra dimension to their sound with the recruitment of keyboard player Dave 'Galen' Littlewood from Poacher in February. Terry explains that Galen was given his nick-name because it was thought he looked like Galen from *Planet of the Apes*! Terry says that at some point during their career Zorro got called a punk rock band and his mum wouldn't speak to him for about a week!

In April Zorro's drummer, Jon Kirk, had left and been replaced by Ian 'Fritz' Wright from Spiny Norman. Zorro were advertised to play with Jack the Lad at West Runton Pavilion in May, but Terry says, 'I don't think we actually played that gig, I don't remember it, anyway.'

In July Zorro supported the Dead End Kids at West Runton. Kevin Longman summaries the band: 'One hit wonders the Dead End Kids were latter-day Bay City Roller wannabies and truly, truly awful!' Their single 'Have I the Right' had been in the charts that April.

The report in the *Eastern Evening News* the following Monday was less harsh:

Some people might shrug off the Dead End Kids as just another group of averagely capable youngsters who have rolled up their trousers and jumped on to the Bay City Roller bandwagon.

True, their audience is mostly made up of young girls in the 14 to 16 age bracket, looking for another BCR or Slik.

But after talking to the five Scots lads who make up the Dead End Kids, I can't help felling that underneath all the teeny-bop pop there is a band of heavies trying to break out.

Appearing at West Runton Pavilion, the other Saturday, the Kids leapt on stage in tatty, frayed denim cut-offs and gave a tight and energetic performance of disco and old rock 'n' roll numbers.

In September, after attempts to start a new band following the loss of Galen, Dave Smith, former lead singer of Poacher, joined him in Zorro.

Local band Fresh continued to make regular appearances at Runton, both supporting and headlining, and frequently played on Bank Holidays and for the Cromer and Sheringham Carnival dances. In February 1977 they appeared on the television talent show *New Faces* and at Easter they were advertised as 'local band made good'.

Another local group, the Buster James Band, had gone through a few line-up changes since their early appearances at the Links. They came to West Runton in December with Roger 'Buster' James (vocals), Rob Seales (guitar/vocals), Geoff Hollis (bass) and Budgie Burgess (drums). A leaflet produced at the time goes as follows:

Since their formation the Buster James Band have devoted much of that time to writing and rehearsing their material. The audiences who have been fortunate enough to catch them 'live' enthusiastically received the band's own brand of high energy boogie-rock written by Seales and James, whose writing talents must give the band the prospect of becoming one of Britain's foremost rock recording bands. Take the opportunity of seeing the band in action and you can be assured they will not disappoint you.

Ian Dury had been advertised to appear at West Runton Pavilion at the beginning of December, then the adverts had changed to Motorhead with two supports, John Otway and the Buster James Band. John Otway says, 'West Runton was a lovely gig,' but on this occasion he didn't appear. As he was quite a folky act, with banjo, fiddle and acoustic – and Motorhead were this heavy rock band – he had suggested it might not be such a great bill, the two acts together, so he didn't do the show. However, someone in the press wrote that he hadn't played the gig because he didn't think Motorhead were good enough. He says Lemmy has never spoken to him since. So Lemmy, if you're reading this, John Otway is sorry for the mix-up!

Ian Kilmister, known to most people as Lemmy – bass player and lead singer with Motorhead – was making his third visit to West Runton with Phil 'Philthy Animal' Taylor on drums and 'Fast' Eddie Clarke on guitar and vocals. Their first appearance had been in August 1977 as part of their 'Beyond the Threshold of Pain' tour and on their return in October 1977 the adverts had read, 'Lemmy's famous Motorhead, come and see what they are all talking about.'

Earlier than this, Lemmy had had connections with the band Hawkwind, founded by Dave Brock in 1969. Lemmy had been with them when they recorded their single 'Silver Machine' but had left them by the time Hawkwind played their first gig at Runton in October 1977. Martin Chapman went along:

Hawkwind are the loudest band I have ever been to. They had these massive speakers. We stood on the chairs at the back of the hall, up against the back wall, and my whole insides were vibrating with the bass. The area in front of the stage was empty, everyone was standing well away from the noise, apart from this one bloke who had his head inside one of the speakers, head-banging. If he wasn't deaf before, he must have been after. My ears were ringing for about two days.

Rob Aherne was also at the gig:

Although it was the just after the 'Summer of Punk' with gigs like the Clash, Sex Pistols and Buzzcocks changing rock music with a passion, the band that I wanted to see more than any was still an early '70's progressive/psychedelic rock band – Hawkwind.

I'd loved the weirdness of their music for about three years straight after hearing 'Silver Machine' for the first time and although I found albums like Space Ritual *(three hours of live space acid rock) pretty hard to get into – certainly without the acid – I loved the great rambling science fantasy themes of their music: a bit like* Star Wars *meets* Lord of the

Rings *on LSD.*

However, with their last album (Astounding Sounds, Amazing Music) *and their latest* (Quark Strangeness and Charm) *the ramble had gone. The music was more focussed and darker with a smaller, tighter five-piece band and cutting-edge light show. This was also probably Hawkwind's most commercial music for quite a while with tracks like 'Quark Strangeness and Charm' even getting into the top 40 and the band playing this on Marc Bolan's pop show* Marc.

West Runton Pavilion felt quite different that evening. I recall parts of the light show being tested as we walked in, framing the venue in purples and whites. The audience was a mix of well-known faces, some hippies and rockers, a few punks, and quite amazingly some 'old people' — well over 30 years old!

We'd queued quite a while to get in and to this day I don't remember the opening band; but I do remember chatting briefly with Brian Tawn — a guy from Lowestoft who edited a Hawkwind fanzine — and then getting as near to the front as I could for the start of Hawkwind's set.

The Hawkwind line-up was Bob Calvert (lead vocals), Dave Brock (lead guitar), Simon House (keyboards), Adrian Shaw (bass) and Simon Powell (drums).

They opened with 'Spirit of the Age' with a manic Bob Calvert wearing a pilot's leather flying cap prancing across the front of the stage like a psychotic pixie against a space backdrop, then bending the mike boom into bike handle-bars to speed along 'Damnation Alley' before brandishing a sabre for 'Hassan I Sabba' — a very dark track about oil, terrorism and the Middle East.

The light show was as amazing as anticipated with one of the highlights being Simon House's haunting violin on 'Wind of Change' set against slides of a tree becoming a forest, being levelled for a building, becoming a city then crumbling to become a tree and forest again. Then Calvert appeared again wielding the Stars and Stripes against a red rocky landscape for the as yet unreleased 'Uncle Sam's on Mars'.

Other highlights that I can remember were Calvert's werewolf impersonation on 'Steppenwolf', and 'Psychedelic Warlords' from Hall of the Mountain Grill.

They didn't play 'Silver Machine', but I did hear it played live when I saw Hawkwind again at West Runton in July 1980. By that time Bob Calvert had left and they had become far more of a 'me too' heavy metal band in the wake of Iron Maiden and Saxon and any old tracks were played that way.

Other artists of note who came to West Runton during 1977 included John Cale — who had formed the Velvet Underground in the late sixties — and the George Hatcher Band, who played rock and blues, although Kevin Plume says they didn't come on stage until about one in the morning.

Colin Woodyard recalls another time a band was expected from London but they didn't turn up and everyone went home. He later heard they had eventually arrived at two in the morning ready to set up and couldn't understand where everyone had gone. They had apparently left London quite late and thought West Runton was a few miles up the road.

Stray were a heavy, three-piece band who played one Friday in October. Frank Boswall says:

On a Friday we would always have more intellectually inclined music. We put Stray on Friday, but because they had had a hit full of bass riffs and people were doing disco dancing to it, they attracted a soul audience. When they came on stage to do their set, soul was the last thing the crowd got!

Another hard-rocking band, Widowmaker, appeared at West Runton Pavilion in April 1977. Guitarist Luther Grosvenor (also known as Ariel Bender), who had been in Mott the Hoople, had formed Widowmaker in 1975. The line-up included Huw Lloyd-Langton on guitar (ex Hawkwind), drummer Paul Nichols (ex Lindisfarne) and bassist Bob Daisley, who had appeared at the Links twice in 1973 with Chicken Shack. Widowmaker's lead singer, Steve Ellis, had played at the Links with his previous bands Love Affair and Ellis.

Camel performed what was advertised as a 'very special concert of material from their new album', *Rain Dance*, at Runton on August Bank Holiday Monday and Renaissance offered a 'preview before they are in concert backed by the London Philharmonic Orchestra', in October. Joe Barber says that, 'Annie Haslam had a nice voice' and Frank Boswall adds, 'Renaissance were nice people, and they could play. They always stayed at the big hotel on the front at Cromer.' Renaissance returned in 1978 after the success of their single 'Northern Lights'.

In the run-up to Christmas, Mud played at Runton and Alan Hooker remembers that they had a Christmas tree near the stage. They played their 1974 number one single, 'Lonely This Christmas', as well as the UK's best-selling single from the same year, 'Tiger Feet', and their other number one hit from 1975, 'Oh Boy'. Frank Boswall says, 'Mud were quite a good draw.' The line-up at the time was Les Gray (vocals), Rob Davis (lead guitar), Dave Mount (drums) and Ray Stiles (bass), although Alan Hooker thinks that when they came to the venue 18 months later, the lead singer was a girl.

Old favourite Screaming Lord Sutch was up to his usual antics. Kelvin Rumbsy remembers his Lordship jumping out of an artificial palm tree onto the stage, dressed up as a vampire.

Chris Spedding, 'Britain's No 1 session musician', who had had a UK top 20 hit in 1975 with 'Motor Biking', came with a new band in September. In October the JALN Band, who changed their name to Souled Out the following year, supported the Four Tops. David Pegg ('Gaffer') says he 'talked to Levi Stubbs and the boys' and got a ticket signed by them. Resident DJ, Gary James, says:

I had to support the Four Tops from the rear balcony alongside the sound engineer as their three articulated lorry-loads of gear took over the stage leaving no room for my tatty gear (which fitted in the back of a transit van).

The Four Tops had had a UK number one 11 years previously with 'Reach Out I'll Be There'.

Frank Boswall had put in an application to build an extension to the Pavilion but the *Eastern Daily Press* reported on 21 October 1977 that North Norfolk District Council's development and leisure services committee had refused to grant permission. The application had proposed alterations to provide added facilities including a coffee lounge on the ground floor, and a first floor extension including lobby, reception, toilets, store and a lounge with bar and viewing gallery.

Frank was reported as saying that he had cancelled punk rock bands which had already been booked – including the Stranglers and the Sex Pistols – because of possible irritation to villagers, but that on the previous Saturday the Four Tops had appeared and parents had gone there with their children. He said he felt that parents would prefer to be upstairs while their children were on the dance floor.

The report revealed that two petitions had been received by the District Council opposing the application, containing a total of 123 signatures – although two letters of support were later printed in the paper, one of which praised the way the entire establishment had been improved over the last three years.

As it turned out, Frank brought the Sex Pistols back to North Norfolk before the end of the year, but it was to Cromer Links, rather than West Runton Pavilion that the punk rebels returned.

14

God Save The Links

Danny Hagen says that West Runton Pavilion bouncer Cookie (John Cook) was instrumental in booking the Sex Pistols at Cromer Links for Frank Boswall. Frank didn't want to put them on at West Runton Pavilion because of their reputation so Cookie approached Mrs Arundel-Langley, who Danny says still owned the Links. 'She never knew Frank was backing it,' Danny says, 'and she would never have let Cookie hire the venue if she had known.'

Simon Dunford reported in the *Eastern Daily Press* in a retrospective feature dated 9 July 2004 that the event almost did not happen. Residents and police were both concerned that there would be 'a riot of profanity at the very least'. Police had told the organisers that 'shouted obscenities' in the group's music were contrary to the music, singing and dancing licence granted to the Links. Local residents were planning to sue on the obscenity clause but had no grounds after the group and its management gave an undertaking not to infringe the Links' licence.

The Sex Pistols appeared at the Links on 24 December 1977 at what was billed as 'a Christmas Eve Party'. Tickets were only available in advance, a maximum of two per person, from the Regal Cinema Box Office in Cromer.

The ticket read:

Randy Enterprises presents The Most Famous Band in the World. Admission by ticket only, £1.75, doors open 6.45pm, performance 8pm. In order that you may witness the above happening and move on to other festivities, the concert will finish at 9pm.

Paul Cook (drums), Steve Jones (guitar) and Johnny Rotten (vocals) had been with the band when they had played at West Runton Pavilion the previous summer but, following Glen Matlock's departure to the Rich Kids in March, John Simon Ritchie had now been drafted in on bass. He was better known as Sid Vicious, the name given to him by Johnny Rotten (John Lydon) after his aggressive hamster, Sid.

Kevin Norton recalls that Cookie would go in the dressing room before the gigs and ask the bands what time they wanted to go on and whether they wanted anything. Kevin would often go in with Cookie and meet the bands. He says that

Johnny Rotten was sitting at the bar with a big box of coloured paper streamers and was throwing them one by one into the crowd. Cookie went up to talk to him and he scowled at Cookie and said, 'Don't bother me while I'm working!' Kevin says, 'They got through three bottles of Jack Daniels on stage that night.'

Steve Baker says:

It had been part of my teenage years to spend Saturday evenings at the Links. It was a fantastic place. We'd been to the more regular groups and it was quite exciting to see the anarchist type of group. I always remember how skinny and insignificant Sid Vicious looked but with this snarl on his face.

Rob Aherne remembers the pre-show music:

It was some very 'thumping' hard-core reggae – I'd never heard anything like it and I do remember what a big impression it made. I went and saw Third World, Osibisa and, I think, Burning Spear as a result – but none were as good live as this was at the gig – it really was the next best thing and very, very new.

Andrew Turner contributed his thoughts to the *Eastern Daily Press* retrospective in July 2004:

We were incredibly lucky young punks in Norfolk. All the top bands of the day played at West Runton Pavilion and of course the band to see were the Pistols. I didn't see them when they played at Runton, it was before they became nationally known, and as they were virtually banned from playing in the UK after the Bill Grundy incident [when the Pistols unleashed a string of televised obscenities] it looked like I never would.

Then in November a 'secret' tour was announced in the music press. The venues weren't listed, but a map of the UK was printed with crosses giving a strong clue as to where they were playing. Imagine our excitement to see a cross right up on the Norfolk coast!

We immediately thought the concert would be at West Runton, but word soon got around that it was at the old Links Pavilion, which I believe had been unused for some time.

Inside the Pavilion it was very shoddy, paint peeling off the walls – and there wasn't a proper bar, just cans of beer being sold over the counter.

The band were encamped on the balcony, Johnny looking especially cool grooving to the dub reggae being pumped out of the PA, wearing an old army pith helmet.

Sid Vicious was wandering around the audience, looking very mean. He spotted a guy wearing a pink tie with a naked lady on it and swapped a t-shirt for it.

The show itself was good, although ultimately it could never quite live up to our expectations. They tore through virtually everything they'd recorded in good style. I can't remember any great witticisms from John, but Steve Jones, the guitarist, passed out half a case of beer to the fans down the front.

Chris Hare has a recording of the gig. At the start Johnny Rotten is complaining that the audience are 'really quiet' – with some reference to it being Christmas Eve – and asking, 'Why can't you be more like us?' presumably because they weren't jumping around much.

Later in the gig, Steve Jones is trying to tune his guitar and makes some comment that although it isn't in tune, the audience 'don't mind'. Someone shouts, 'Play something then,' and he retorts, 'You know where the f***ing exit is,' before launching into the song 'No Feelings'.

The set-list on the recording is:

God Save the Queen
I Wanna Be Me
17
New York
EMI
Bodies
Submission
Belsen was a Gas
Holidays in the Sun
No Feelings
Problems
Pretty Vacant
Anarchy in the UK

Rob Aherne reviews the gig:

I first went to West Runton Pavilion – 'the Pit' as we fondly called it – in November 1976 for the Pat Travers Band, missing the Pistols' gig there by a few months. I did, however, see the Cromer Links Pavilion SPOTS Christmas '77 gig. SPOTS was the acronym for Sex Pistols On Tour Secretly and was supposedly used to stop local councils from banning the band, although in hindsight you wonder how much of this was just 'spin'.

The school bus was buzzing in anticipation of the gig. Rumours were rife that a huge rocker army was on the move to annihilate the local punks and that hundreds of London punks were coming down to support them.

I'll never forget the experience of walking up to the venue from Cromer Bus Station expecting World War Three any second. Our group had all agonised about whether we should be overtly punk – bondage gear etc – but as we didn't own any, most of us just had ripped jeans and old pullovers and t-shirts.

The gig was scheduled to start early and would only last one hour. Most of North Norfolk Constabulary had been mobilised for the occasion – you could see both cars quite clearly!

Once inside the Links you could see why the gig was here rather than West Runton: if the place had been trashed it would have been an improvement. There were warning signs everywhere about not using certain doors and not going on a balcony due to subsidence.

Hundreds of people were milling around, forming an orderly queue for drinks, or just looking worshipfully at Sid and Johnny lolling by the mixing desk. Johnny Rotten seemed to be in his element – by turns sneering and strutting around. In comparison Sid Vicious seemed quite mild – apart from telling one guy to 'f*** off' when faced with the question, 'You're Sid Vicious aren't you?' – quite understandable really!

Then they started playing and it was quite simply one of the best gigs I had ever attended. They were a tight accomplished group, much more than anybody had anticipated.

They played for just over an hour then we all filed out into the early evening. Everybody went home with no trouble, no fighting, and with the feeling that this was something we would all look back upon one day. And then some of us got changed and went and saw Rockotto at West Runton Pavilion.

Mike Jervis came out of the Links that night with a black eye:

The band were throwing cans of beer into the audience. One can still had the plastic ring on, the bloke in front of me grabbed the plastic, the can swung back and hit me in the eye. I had to go home with a black eye and explain to my dad that I hadn't been in a fight! I still have the scar.

Mike would probably agree with Duncan Sutton then, although for a different reason, that the concert was 'an absolute blinder'!

The gig was reviewed in the *North Norfolk News* on 30 December 1977:

The controversial Sex Pistols concert at Cromer, which at one stage looked like being cancelled, took place after all on Christmas Eve.

The group ... played for an hour to an audience of nearly 600 punk rock fans ... and police did not intervene.

Chief Inspector W Aherne said on Tuesday, 'There was no trouble whatsoever. Everyone was well behaved. They went there quietly and they left quietly.'

Mr Robert Lowe, manager of the Links Pavilion said, 'We are very pleased with the way everything went. By about 8.30pm we realised there was going to be no trouble and that everyone was there to enjoy the music.'

He added that the group had played well and among the crowd were a large number of local people.

'Afterwards, everyone went away very peacefully. They were all interested in finding their way home,' he explained.

Some coach parties had come from as far away as London and Sheffield.

Mr Lowe concluded, 'We're hoping that this can be followed with other concerts.'
Mr Trevor Randall, the promoter, pointed out that the Sex Pistols were not the 'naughty
boys' they were made out to be. On Christmas Day they were due to travel to Huddersfield
to attend a handicapped children's party.

The gig at Ivanhoe's in Huddersfield would be the Sex Pistols' last appearance in the UK. They left shortly after for a tour of the States, where the group broke up.

Unfortunately, despite Mr Lowe's hope of staging further concerts, the venue's days were numbered. On the evening of Wednesday 5 April 1978, the Royal Links Pavilion at Cromer burnt down.

As reported in the *Eastern Daily Press* the following day, the fire brigade was called at around 5.30pm and about 30 firemen attended with 4 fire engines. Much of the roof of the building fell in during the fire, which had been put out by 6.32pm. A thick pall of smoke had hung over Cromer, dimming the sun for about an hour.

North Walsham Station Officer S Briggs told the reporter that the flames had completely gutted the timbered roof, but that no-one had been inside the building. Police later ruled out arson and said that the fire was believed to have been caused by an electrical fault.

Mr Geoffrey Coats, who looked after the Links, said he had checked the building on Wednesday lunchtime and found that two bulbs had fused. When he came back he says, 'The whole place was like a furnace.'

Police closed the road to traffic and had to move back a large crowd of sightseers who had gathered as thick smoke and hot ashes poured from the building.

One young girl, who had been one of the first on the scene, described the flames as being 'like a big genie' as they shot through the roof.

The newspaper report said that Mrs A J Arundel-Langley still owned the Links but that it was currently closed, waiting to be sold.

Her son, Rod Blow, was among those watching the fire and he says, 'I stood thinking of all the memories going up in flames.'

Sandra Fishwick (was Bailey) says:

I can say, quite categorically, that the Links changed my life. It was a truly great venue
– small and intimate, with a terrific atmosphere. I feel so privileged to have seen some of the
great bands of the '70s, often before they were famous.

Jacky Regis (was Griffin) agrees, 'I often speak to my friends about all the bands who first started out at the Links.'

Terry Bunting says:

You went out to the Links on a Saturday night and you saw a band that were stunning, that were musically tight, exciting, brilliant and went down a storm. You look at May 1973: UFO, Gary Moore, Chicken Shack and Golden Earring, all in the space of a month – what a line-up, what can you say? March 1974: Budgie, Queen and Thin Lizzy, all in the space of three weeks – crazy!

It seems to have gone on for years and years, but it was only a short time. I think it was because of the amount of bands you had coming in, every week. It was only once a week, which is quite quirky, looking back – they didn't even open on Fridays!

Bully (Steve Bullimore) agrees:

Virtually all the big bands that came to the Links came on a Saturday, except Christmas and New Year's Eve. Saturday night, people went to the Links Pavilion at Cromer, and it didn't matter who was playing, people went. That was the place to go. When Frank got West Runton going, he did it slightly differently; he would get hold of a band, even if it was a Thursday night, or whatever, to get that band there, it wasn't necessarily a Saturday night.

Another quirky thing Terry observes about the Links was that the venue would find a local band as support, not necessarily one that complemented the main attraction. He says:

You would get a heavy rock band supported by a poppy type of band. It didn't matter, because people would go every week, no matter who was on. At Runton some bands were starting to tour with their own support and sometimes, if bands shared a record label, the record company would put the new band out with the established act, to get them exposure.

This meant less opportunity for local bands to perform in front of a big crowd.
Bully continues:

People perhaps don't realise, you have a list of the bands that played at the Links, and a list of the top 20 of the day, how the two would compare. A band would be in the charts and they had just been or were just going to come. It was amazing at the time how that was. Today, you look at the top 20, where could you see those acts?

Some people might wonder why these big groups came to Cromer. Terry Bunting offers an explanation:

When some of these bands first got together they'd come from touring bands like Graham Bond, who'd make their living from gigs, not from record sales – that was for the Beatles, the Rolling Stones and Dave Dee – but from playing up and down the country five nights a week in clubs, making a fairly good living but working hard. They didn't expect to be anything other than a touring band. They didn't expect to become superstars so their managers and agents just took on all the gigs they could. Nowadays, an act will take off and the management or record company will pay off a venue for them not to play. In those days it didn't happen as much, artists tended to honour their contracts.

Roger James originally came from Gloucestershire. At the age of 17 he was playing at the Marquee Club supporting bands like Cream and the Move, before he settled in this area. But he and his band, the Good Goods, were happy to travel from Gloucester, where they lived at the time, to Norfolk to appear at the Links.

He remembers one time they were booked to play at the Orford Cellar in Norwich on the Friday and at the Links on the Saturday. They hadn't made the Norwich gig but came to the Links for the Saturday and when they got there they found they weren't playing. It had been assumed they wouldn't turn up because they'd missed the Friday gig.

Julie Bunting (was Jarvis) says, 'We didn't realise at the time how lucky we were – all the great bands that came there.'

Jacky Smith, who now works in London for the Queen Fan Club, remembers the Links. She says, 'I went to the Cromer Links Pavilion once. Can't remember who I saw, but it was a great venue.'

Ian Foster ('Flo') had so many good times there. 'The likes of Norfolk will never see that again,' he says. 'For a young, single bloke, it was like Christmas every Saturday!'

Ali Farrow agrees, 'From mid-week on you were looking forward and getting excited about Saturday night at the Links and would thoroughly enjoy the night.' He has fond and good memories.

In the 1960s the Links had become one of the country's biggest pop venues outside London and used to be written up regularly by the music press in publications like *New Musical Express*. Nigel Blow (now Hindley), who managed the venue for many years, recalls:

Bands used to say how much they enjoyed playing there, partly because of the atmosphere and partly because of the acoustics. It was like an organised party every Saturday.

Norman Clowes, who had been a barman at the venue, sums up the feelings of many:

I watched the night the Links burnt down and it was like a piece of you dying.

15

We're Here, So Where's The Band?

As if to prove to local music fans that all was not lost, in addition to reporting on the fire at Cromer Links, the *North Norfolk News* of 7 April 1978 included an announcement regarding that evening's entertainment at West Runton:

> *Wilko Johnson, one of England's finest rhythm and blues guitarists, who rose to fame with the Southend band Dr Feelgood, is visiting West Runton Pavilion tonight.*
>
> *This is the first date for Wilko and his new band, consisting of John Potter (keyboards), Stevie Lewins (bass) and Alan Platt (drums) during a nationwide tour of Britain.*

Wilko Johnson returned the following year with the Solid Senders and Chris Hare took slides of the concert. In 1981, John Lemon was there with his camera to record Wilko's third visit. Wilko's former band, Dr Feelgood, played at the venue on two occasions following their 1979 hit 'Milk and Alcohol'.

Rory Gallagher, advertised as, 'Arguably the greatest blues guitarist of all time,' also came to West Runton in April 1978.

Stars from the sixties were in evidence during the year. In March, punters paid £3 for two 45 minute spots by the Supremes, consisting of Mary Wilson, Kaaren Ragland and Karen Jackson; and Billy J Kramer – who had had several hits with his band the Dakotas, including the 1964 number one single 'Little Children' – came to the venue at the end of October.

Shane Fenton and the Fentones had similarly experienced some chart success in the early sixties, but when their lead singer changed his stage name to Alvin Stardust and adopted an image involving black gloves and tight leather cat-suits with flared trousers, a string of hits had followed in the next decade. These included 'My Coo-Ca-Choo' in 1973, and in 1974 'Red Dress', 'You, You, You' and 'Jealous Mind', which had reached number one. He made his second appearance in two years at West Runton Pavilion in 1978 and Eve Mingay, who was a big fan of Alvin's, was pleased when doorman John Mason was able to take her backstage to meet her idol and get his autograph.

1978 also saw Judas Priest's second visit to the venue, following their debut when they had been promoting their third album, *Sin After Sin*, and Joe Barber says, 'They turned their sound down because they had made people's ears bleed at a gig the previous month.' Simon Phillips, who had appeared at Runton with Phil Manzanera and his 801 band, had been session drummer for the *Sin After Sin* album but had declined to join Rob Halford (vocals), Glenn Tipton (lead guitar), KK Downing (lead guitar) and Ian Hill (bass), so Judas Priest had recruited Les Binks as Alan Moore's permanent replacement on drums.

For John Bowen, it was a whole new experience:

I grew up listening to mainly rock music because in those days you were either a rocker or a soul boy/girl and I couldn't stand Motown.

I was either in the fourth or fifth year at school when word got out about a coach leaving Gorleston heading for West Runton to see Priest, and we got our seat booked. A lot of people in our year had heard of the Pavilion but had never been, so this was a chance not to be missed.

After about a two-hour coach ride up the coast we pulled up outside the Pavilion. I thought, what the hell is this place? The only concert venues I had been to before were the ABC in Great Yarmouth (now a pizza place and card shop) and the Ipswich Gaumont, which were proper theatres or cinemas.

I suppose my first impression of West Runton Pavilion was that it was nothing more than an old shack in the middle of nowhere.

In we went and, unlike the two other venues, this place had no seating so most people had pushed in front of the stage awaiting the arrival of the support band, of whom I can't recall their name or anything else about them. Then on came Priest, who were promoting their Stained Class *album. Even though I was only 15 or 16 years old at the time, I was six foot tall which helped me down the front; nowadays it is called the 'mosh pit' but back then it was head-banging and air guitar. You still had to 'look after' yourself considering there were a lot of older guys in there and several massive biker types but, as usual with rock crowds, people didn't go to concerts to fight.*

For the next hour-and-a-half I became a Priest fan, since I hadn't previously heard much of their stuff. Before we knew it, we were heading back home.

Next day at school I was suffering from head-banger's neck — not that I was complaining! All I knew was that I wanted to get the Priest album whenever I could and that I didn't want to do the usual school-boy thing at the time like hanging around down Gorleston sea-front at night; I wanted to go back to West Runton Pavilion more often.

After seeing Judas Priest there I think I became obsessed with the place. One Sunday me and a mate, for some unknown reason, actually push-biked to the Pavilion in some sort of pilgrimage, stopped for about 10 minutes, then cycled all the way back again. To this day I still have no idea why we did this because, after all that cycling, the place was shut!

Malcolm Birtwell's first visit to West Runton Pavilion also took place in 1978 although, unlike John Bowen, Malcolm had some idea of what the place was like as he had lived in the village for three years. He recalls that first gig:

My introduction to West Runton Pavilion was in February 1978, just after my 16th birthday. My parents, somewhat reluctantly, agreed to me going to see XTC only on the grounds that I was 16, and therefore old enough, and because XTC were one of my favourite bands of the time. I'm pretty sure I also tossed 'well it is my birthday' into the mix as well.

Like most of my school contemporaries I used to tune in to John Peel every night between 10.00pm and midnight to catch his show. I used to lie in bed, finger ready on the pause button of my radio cassette player, hoping to catch a recording of one of the new punk/new wave band sessions that the late, great John Peel championed at that time. After hearing XTC on John Peel's show, a friend had bought 3DEP, XTC's first single, which we had all tape-recorded and listened to incessantly until the evening of the gig arrived. Replete in t-shirt, my old school blazer with tastefully positioned safety pins, monkey boots and British Army size one combat trousers, left over from my army cadet days, I headed off to the Pavilion, a five minute walk from my home, and paid around £2.00 to get in. It may even have been less than that.

The atmosphere was exotic and enticing and, although I felt a little self conscious, it was the most exciting moment of my life at that time. There were so many different people with strange spiky coloured hair, dressed in weird and wonderful gear; the great background music was blasting out, lights were flashing and, of course, there were cans of Swan Lager (Breaker if you were feeling flush) to be had at the bar.

The exhilaration reached a crescendo when the lights went down to signal the support band coming on stage and the Secret launched into their first song. My enduring memory of the Secret was a song which seemed to have a lot of f***s in it which, to a fairly innocent middle class youth like me, was pretty shocking.

I could scarcely wait for XTC to come on, but when they did I was not disappointed. I was utterly mesmerised by Andy Partridge. I managed to get right down to the front (a point of honour between me and my friends at subsequent gigs) so I was crushed against the stage with a fantastic, if sweaty and claustrophobic, view. Health and Safety would've had a fit. One thing I also remember: if ever anyone looked like they were being trampled in the fray at the front, there were always disembodied helping hands pulling you up and patting you on the back, and sweat-drenched friendly faces asking you if you were OK.

London band the Secret featured Simon Lester, who went under the stage name of 'Percy Cute'. XTC comprised Andy Partridge (vocals/guitar), Dave Gregory (synthesiser/guitar), Colin Moulding (bass/vocals) and Terry Chambers (drums). XTC returned to the venue in May 1979, just prior to the release of their *Drums and Wires* album containing the hit single 'Making Plans for Nigel', and this time Malcolm met the band:

By this time I was now a seasoned veteran of many gigs, a lot more confident, and after this second XTC gig I managed to get into the poky dressing room at the rear of the stage to meet the band. I had with me a promo poster of their first gig which I had been given by one of the West Runton Village Inn barmen who knew my father. I handed this to my idol, Andy Partridge, and he signed it for me.

John Bowen was keen to get inside the venue again, and was soon making the long journey from Gorleston once more:

How I had waited for this, my second visit to West Runton Pavilion. Mode of transport again was by coach to witness the Heavy Metal Kids featuring Gary Holton who later appeared in Auf Wiedersehen, Pet. As with Priest, I was down the front very close to Gary Holton, who had difficulty keeping all his clothes on. Musically they were OK but nowhere near as good as Judas Priest; but by now Runton was going to be a major part of my life.

After the gig we returned to our coach, which was totally trashed inside by persons unknown. It was littered with Colt 45 cans (very sugary American lager). When the driver went to find out who the culprits were he was told it was the actual band who broke into it. Suddenly, we didn't seem to care. If it was them, then this is to you, the surviving members of the Heavy Metal Kids: you can have that one on us!

Kevin Plume remembers his disappointment, a couple of years earlier, when he had made a long journey to West Runton to see the Heavy Metal Kids but they had not appeared:

I went with a couple of mates on mopeds to see the Heavy Metal Kids. It was raining and it had taken us two hours to get there. When we arrived, we found out Gary Holton had a broken leg and Sam Apple Pie were playing instead. We had seen them at Lynn Tech as third on the bill to Strider and hadn't liked them much. They were prog rock and we had all said, 'This band's crap!' We weren't keen to see them again, but we had struggled through the rain in trench-coats, which were now soaked and hanging down to our knees, and it was still pouring with rain so we decided to stay for the gig. What a change! Sam Apple Pie had turned bluesy and were brilliant. They had transformed into a boogie band playing R & B covers. It took forever to get home but it was a brilliant night. We liked them so much we went and saw them Christmas Eve as well.

Sam Apple Pie had quite a following, although their lead singer did have a tendency, observed by Terry Bunting, to shout out 'boogie woogie' after every song!

New Zealand band, Split Enz, made their second appearance at the Pavilion early in 1978. Pauline Willey remembers, 'They had grey make-up, looked like corpses, and played very unusual music.' She was there with her camera and photographed Noel Crombie who, according to Rob Aherne, 'Did a mean "spoons" solo.' Rob saw him having a beer in the Village Inn and says he was carrying his spoons then! Split Enz were advertised to return in October 1978, but their UK tour was cancelled. Vocalist/guitarist/songwriter Neil Finn formed Crowded House after Split Enz broke up in 1984.

Local band Zorro had continued to have a few line-up changes before they returned to West Runton Pavilion in April 1978. Vocalist Mark Newman had left in September 1977 and been replaced by Dave Smith from Poacher. Dave joined Poacher's former keyboard player Dave 'Galen' Littlewood in Zorro with Terry Bunting (lead guitar), Kevin Longman (bass) and Ian 'Fritz' Wright (drums).

At the beginning of 1978, an article in the *Eastern Evening News* declared that the 'changed Zorro is better still', and went on:

Dave (Smith) has a magnetic stage personality. His natural enthusiasm and bizarre stage outfits are also having a good effect on the rest of the group. Not only do they seem to be playing better together than ever, but they are also becoming more involved in the visual side of things.

Lead guitarist Terry remembers a new stage trick he incorporated which went wrong on a couple of occasions:

We played this place in Norwich called the Kingsway Caves. It doesn't exist now but it used to be on the corner near Carrow Road, backing onto the river. They had fishing nets hanging from the ceiling. I did this trick where I threw the guitar up in the air, and used to catch it and carry on playing. It actually got caught up in the nets and I couldn't reach it, so I had to climb on somebody's shoulders to get up and get my guitar back in the middle of a song.

The other time was at Runton. I took my original cheapo red guitar on stage at Runton for the encore. At the end of the song I threw my guitar up into the air but, because we weren't used to playing in places with so many lights, I lost it in the glare. I couldn't see anything: I was dazzled. It came down, missed me by about two feet, bounced on the floor, came straight back up, and I caught it and carried on playing! As the gig was going well, I smashed the guitar to pieces. Someone picked up all the bits, and at the end of the night they gave them back to me in a cardboard box.

On 29 April 1978 Zorro supported bass player and singer Suzi Quatro on her first visit to West Runton Pavilion where, according to the *Eastern Evening News*, Zorro 'received a very warm reception from a packed audience'.

By this time, the Zorro set included five of their own songs: 'Starfight', 'Rock Fall', 'Rock 'n' Roll on Up', 'Sad Liza, Bad Liza' and 'Back Street Ladies' as well as numbers by the Heavy Metal Kids, Led Zeppelin and Deep Purple.

Of Suzi Quatro, Terry says:

She was really friendly, one of the nicest people I've ever met. There was only time for one band to do a sound-check so she let Zorro do ours, and she didn't do one. That was a top gig, a thousand people in. We were having to hold the dressing room doors shut after the gig because all these kids wanted to come in and get autographs.

Kevin Longman, bass player with Zorro, agrees, 'Suzi Quatro was great fun with no pretensions.'

Suzi, who is Godmother to a young relative of West Runton owner, Frank Boswall, appeared at the venue during each of the following three years. In 1979 the event was advertised as 'a special concert – the only date she is performing before her world tour.' Her hits included 'Devil Gate Drive', '48 Crash', 'The Wild One', 'If You Can't Give Me Love' and 'Can the Can', which reached number one in the UK singles chart in 1973.

Music fan Colin Woodyard used to ring Frank Boswall up once a month to see who was on. Colin recalls:

When he told me that Suzi Quatro was appearing the next Wednesday, I hitched to West Runton the Wednesday afternoon, met all the roadies and helped unload all the gear. I took it in and helped Cookie put the sound stuff up on the balcony. I got paid £10 and got in free. Cookie let me stand on the steps up to the stage to watch them play although Len Tuckey, Suzi Quatro's husband – who was the guitarist in the band – kept trying to turf me off.

On another of Suzi's visits to West Runton, Chris Grief and his friend Cliffie Farrow were invited up on stage and danced either side of Suzi with their arms round her. They were having a great time but Chris says, 'Suzi's husband wasn't at all happy and kept giving us evil glares.'

John Mason worked on the door and remembers volunteering to stand at the side of the stage during one of Suzi's gigs to 'prevent a crowd invasion'. His daughter Julie was sceptical:

Finally, my friend Belinda and I had reached the magic age when we were allowed on the dance floor to join our other friends who had been getting in under-age for years. The view wasn't as good as from the balcony, but the atmosphere was stunning. I remember watching Suzi Quatro and then spotting my dad standing up on the side of the stage, ostensibly to stop a crowd invasion but bopping and grinning admiringly at the short, leather-clad rocker. As I stood in the audience watching the huge grin on his face, I could see how much he was enjoying his job!

Sarah Baldwin remembers, 'Suzi Quatro was so small she had to stand on a beer crate to play the fruit machines, otherwise she couldn't reach the coin slot!'

One night the party didn't end, as Frank Boswall reveals:

I left Runton, I would think about three o'clock in the morning, with Suzi and the band still playing, but to a private audience because they were having a drink in the little 'Hole in the Wall'. I went to Reepham at about half-past seven on the Sunday morning to meet somebody. When I came back to the Pavilion they were all just coming out. They were shielding their eyes from the morning light.

Bouncer Danny Hagen was in the 'Hole in the Wall' at the time:

I remember Suzi Quatro got the piano and was playing and singing rugby songs. Honestly, she knew more rugby songs than I did, and I had been in the Marines!

Ronnie Carroll recalls the occasion as well:

Suzi Quatro's whole group were in the club room – saxophones, the lot. She was playing this white grand piano and dancing on top of it. I think I got home about five in the morning.

The club room was a converted storeroom. Runton helper Jumbo (Graham Curlew) remembers that owner Frank Boswall was trying to sell annual memberships for £10 to local businessmen which would allow them entry to the exclusive 'Private Member's Club'. Jumbo says, 'The décor included a load of Coca Cola lamps!' Unfortunately, the idea did not catch on with local dignitaries and the room ended up as a venue for after-hours' parties. It was commonly referred to as the 'Hole in the Wall' because it was accessed from the dance hall by a sliding door.

Other refurbishments were carried out at the Pavilion. Barman Dick Woodley has a photo of himself taken by one of the Woodyard brothers when the new 'long bar' was opened. Jumbo has a photo of himself and Raymond Froggatt in the newly created DJ booth from which the discos were run. It was to the left of the stage and required a ladder to get up to it. Jumbo says, 'Frank bought a load of lights off Dougie Read, who was in charge of the Number One Club at Coltishall,' so there was a permanent disco set up.

The stage itself continued to be extended until it reached from side to side between the pillars. Dick Woodley says, 'When it was extended, so there was more room for the pop groups, the stage had to withstand an iron ball being dropped on it.' A wall was built outside at the back for sound-proofing, which also meant the bands had access to the stage from the dressing room, without having to walk through the crowd as they had previously.

The area known as the 'Snake Pit' was essentially an old arcon hut, which had

WHAT FLO SAID

been joined to the side of the Pavilion. Jumbo remembers one time the entrance
to the Snake Pit was boarded up for a couple of weeks while the hut was bricked
round on the outside. The old building was then removed through the dance
hall and the new solid walls were plastered. Frank enlisted the help of budding
local artists, twins Mike and Johnny Sanders, to decorate the new area, and they
produced a jungle-themed design. They also painted the mural at the back of the
stage – a space landscape reminiscent of the Roger Dean designs on the covers of
albums by the band Yes.

The Snake Pit discos were held every Wednesday and Gary James played in
the resident DJ line-up – with his Detroit Express Disco – alongside Ian Mac
and Chris Wells. Gary recalls, 'King Cole played there too (what a mover!) as did
David Harris.'

Phil Dunning went to winter discos when Gary James was appearing and
says he remembers, 'Those cold nights with the disco at West Runton when the
heating had packed in.'

Kelvin Rumsby would often go into the Village Inn public house while the
Wednesday discos, or some other events, were on in the adjoining Pavilion. One
night he had gone round to the pub after 11.00pm, sat in one of the alcoves, and
fell asleep. He says it was 12.15am when he woke up. The pub was in darkness,
the staff had gone, and the door onto Water Lane was locked. When Kelvin moved
near to the bar, he set the burglar alarm off. He couldn't stop the alarm and
couldn't turn the lights on, so he waited in the dark while the alarm blared out.
Eventually the manager of the Pavilion came round and let him out.

During the summer holidays in 1978 a family disco was held most nights at
Runton costing 5p, except for the Wednesday Snake Pit discos, which were 50p.
On 16 August 'Rupert' presented 'The All Las Vegas Revue – a tribute to the King,
Elvis Presley, on the first anniversary of his death.'

Barman Dick Woodley recalls:

*In the summer they would have the Cromer and Sheringham Carnival Dances. One night
they would pick the Carnival Queen, then a week or two later would be for the end of the
Carnival.*

1978 was no exception to this tradition and the usual Carnival dances were held.
Jane Starling has a photograph of the Miss Sheringham competition and a cutting
from the *Eastern Daily Press* of Thursday 3 August 1978 announcing that she and
Hilary Smith were attendants to the Carnival Queen, Karin Farncombe. Jane met
her future husband, Tim Joyce, at a disco in the Snake Pit at West Runton Pavilion.
Tim remembers:

It always seemed to be packed, the car park was full, there were occasionally fights, the 'in

170

beer' of the time was Breaker (in cans). The bar was along the right hand side when you went in. The Snake Pit was to the left. There were certainly some terrific bands; I only wish I'd seen more. We made lots of friends there.

Dick Woodley says the venue also hosted regular police dances, when they would have a band. The bar would be really busy on those nights. Jumbo (Graham Curlew) says he remembers the police dances at Runton because there was always a fight!

Marianne Faithfull appeared in the summer although Dick remembers she was slightly worse for wear. He says, 'They carried her on stage, she sang, slowly sinking down, and they carried her off.' Well-known in the 1960s for her relationship with Rolling Stones vocalist Mick Jagger, Marianne had released seven albums during that decade and had chart success with singles including 'As Tears Go By', written by Mick Jagger and Keith Richards. Following a break in the early 1970s, she had moved to Ireland and recorded the album *Dreaming My Dreams* in 1977 which had reached number one in the Irish charts. This was the first of a string of album releases including *Faithless*, which she would have been promoting during her West Runton appearance.

Colin Dodman's brother Peter was there and later told him:

She was very foul-mouthed and her dress kept falling off! She was with an unsuitable support band, and kept singing Jagger/Richards songs. She suddenly stopped singing and asked, 'Has anyone got a fag?' A young boy handed one to her and she retorted, 'Well give me an effing light, then, it's no good without an effing light!'

Osibisa came to the venue several times. Kevin Longman describes them as 'a great afro jazz rock outfit', and Colin Dodman says they were the best band he ever saw. Jumbo remembers, 'There weren't many there when Osibisa played, but Frank liked them.'

DJs from national radio continued to be popular and Gary James supported Paul Burnett when he came and also helped fellow DJ Chris Wells with the Simon Bates gig.

Dave Lee Travis – otherwise known by his initials of DLT or as 'the Hairy Cornflake', in reference to his beard and the fact that for a while he presented Radio One's breakfast show – appeared at the venue twice. Alan Hooker remembers once DLT came on stage dressed as an Egyptian Mummy and had his bandages slowly unwound and once, at the height of the Star Wars craze, he came on as Darth Vader.

Christopher Woodyard got engaged when DLT was on and he had to go up on stage and drink a whole bottle of champagne.

DLT had a Pontiac Trans Am sports car, like the one driven by Burt Reynolds in the 1977 film *Smokey and the Bandit*. DLT took Kevin Norton to Cromer in his Trans Am so that Kevin could show him where the burger bar was. DLT's car is remembered as being black, with an eagle painted on the bonnet.

Julie Mason says:

When DLT came on at the start of one of the Radio One Road Shows as Darth Vader, I was convinced it was the real thing! They had the music, the terrifying asthmatic breathing, the lot.

I also saw DJ Simon Bates at Runton, when our scatty friend Dawn was hauled up from somewhere near the stage to eat rice pudding blindfold, fed by a blindfolded accomplice. Dawn spent the rest of the evening with her top covered in coagulated and sticky rice.

Coincidentally, that was one of the few gigs my future husband Steven went to, although I didn't know him at the time. He says that because he was doing an apprenticeship in Norwich, and some of his friends were younger than him, they couldn't afford to go. An older friend of his claims the real reason Steven didn't go was because he was frightened of getting 'beaten up', although I'm not sure that's entirely true!

Other famous DJs who appeared at West Runton Pavilion over the years included Kid Jensen, Emperor Roscoe, Paul Gambaccini, Mike Read, Noel Edmonds and Andy Peebles. Alan Hooker was at the Andy Peebles gig in September 1979 and remembers that a young band called Def Leppard played while Andy Peebles took a tea break. He introduced them as, 'A band who will go far.' Less than six months later they were headlining the same venue and Frank Boswall remembers, 'Def Leppard were a sell-out, as you would expect.'

Sandra Fishwick's husband saw Def Leppard and bought their self-financed EP, which had cost the band £600 and was released on their own label. John Bowen saw them at West Runton Pavilion when they returned in 1980:

They had released their debut EP and were touring to promote it. I guess they were still teenagers themselves. They were good on stage and we waited around after the gig to see if we could meet them. They emerged later and wandered around the venue. We approached Joe Elliot, lead singer. Big mistake, because he really thought he was a big rock star and acted like one. He was an egotistical twat who thought, I don't have to talk to this rabble. On the other hand, we went up to guitarist Steve Clark who was very friendly, thanked us for coming, and shook hands with us. Unfortunately, he died some years after. I was never a big Leppard fan, but it was good to remember the concert knowing I had seen them in a sweaty, run-down venue before they were doing stadiums.

John Roberts was also there:

This was the first gig I took my wife to see and she hated it. She was into Motown. We stood next to one of the PA stacks and she often asks me, 'What was the name of that band we saw when I couldn't hear for two days afterwards?' It couldn't have done us any harm, though, because we've been married for 22 years!

Hailing from Sheffield, Def Leppard also included Pete Willis (guitar), Rick Savage (bass) and drummer Rick Allen, who was only 16 at the time. He lost his left arm in a car crash in 1984 but continued drumming with the band using a modified drum kit. Guitarist Steve Clark died in January 1991 after a short period battling alcoholism.

Back in 1978, John Roberts had also been to see Trapeze at West Runton Pavilion. They had returned to the venue after a successful tour of America. Bass player Glenn Hughes had, by this time, left the three-piece Trapeze line-up – which had included Mel Galley (vocals/guitar) and Dave Holland (drums) – to join Deep Purple, and Trapeze had become a four-piece with the addition of Pete Wright (bass) and Rob Kendrick (guitar/vocals).

John Roberts went backstage at Runton and met the band:

Typical thing, as a 19-20 year old you think you know what's going on; then you don't know what to say and come out with the same old questions they must have heard 100 times like, 'What's your favourite song?' and they must be thinking, who is this prick?

Dave Holland left to join Judas Priest in 1979 and Mel Galley joined Whitesnake a year later.

Trapeze were supported by local band, Kamakazee – formed after the demise of Spiny Norman – comprising Mick Hudson (vocals), Clive Tully (bass), Brian Wise (guitar), Dennis Temple (guitar) and Pete North (drums).

Clive says:

Trapeze were just back from a tour of the USA, where they'd played their last date in Boston in a football stadium in front of 16,000 people. They came to West Runton and about 200 turned up, at least half of whom had come to see us.

The local advertisements for West Runton continued to be informative, with Brass Construction promoted as having 'sold more imported LPs than any other act in the UK', Rokotto were a 'super funky soul band', Lindisfarne had a 'huge supporting cast' and the Runaways were an 'all-girl American band with their special brand of high-powered music'. Sandra Fishwick says her husband told her, 'The Runaways ran away. They didn't show up to the gig and he ended up getting a very expensive taxi back to Norwich.'

Ex-policeman Geoff Peck, who joined the West Runton staff as a bouncer in 1978, says, 'A lot of the bands were booked and advertised but never actually played.'

The Climax Blues Band were meant to appear with 'special guests Dire Straits' in May 1978, but later newspaper advertisements apologised for the cancellation. Frank Boswall thinks the show must have been rescheduled because he says, 'They were definitely here. I remember I paid Dire Straits 40 quid.' Dire Straits' eponymous first album was released that month. Local band Ram had played the week before the cancelled gig, supporting Memphis Index. Ram's guitarist, Steve Rowe, kept the newspaper cutting advertising the next few weeks' events at West Runton. He says, 'Our claim to fame was our name was written in the advert larger than Dire Straits.' He went on to explain the reason was that his band's name had fewer letters!

The night after the Climax Blues Band cancelled, AC/DC's show was also cancelled.

AC/DC had first left Australia in 1976 and had toured Europe and the States, trying to establish themselves somewhere between the big rock bands who were filling arenas and the punks who were playing in local pubs and clubs. AC/DC headlined many of the clubs and played as support to more established acts at the larger venues. By the time they were lined-up to play in Norfolk, AC/DC had upstaged many of the established acts they had been booked to support and had found some success in the UK charts.

Kevin Plume was at Cambridge Corn Exchange to see AC/DC on the Friday, the night before they were due to play at West Runton. He remembers that Morgan Fisher, from support band British Lions, came on stage and said, 'Sorry, Angus has cut his foot, and they can't play.'

Angus Young, AC/DC's lead guitarist, had an energetic stage routine which meant the tour was curtailed for a while and several dates were postponed. The West Runton gig was rescheduled to Monday 5 June 1978 with a ticket price of £1.50. The *Powerage* album was out and the photo from the cover featured on all the posters. Angus – in his trademark school cap, jacket and tie – looked like a punk which misled several who now know better! He had only been about 14 when the band had formed and used to rush home from school to take part in rehearsals without changing out of his uniform. His older sister had thought it was a good gimmick, so the school uniform – including short trousers – was retained.

If You Want Blood You've Got It, the live album recorded during the tour, was released in November 1978 and gives a good indication of how Angus, his brother Malcolm Young (rhythm guitar), Phil Rudd (drums), Cliff Williams (bass) and Bon Scott (lead singer) rocked North Norfolk that summer.

The set-list from the tour was as follows:

Riff Raff
Problem Child
Hell Ain't a Bad Place to Be
Rock 'n' Roll Damnation
Bad Boy Boogie
The Jack
High Voltage
Whole Lotta Rosie
Let There Be Rock
Rocker

John Roberts was at the rescheduled gig:

I remember going to Runton that night; it was packed out. I didn't know whether to go or not, it turned out to be one of the best nights I had there. It was the original line-up with Angus and Bon, fairly early on in their career. They were doing the rounds although they were obviously well known. It was very hot in there and, of course, Angus starts off all dressed up and ends up taking most of his clothes off. He was very small and they did their party piece, with Bon taking Angus around the audience on his shoulders. It was an impressive evening. We were packed like sardines, drinking Breakers and sweating like pigs. It was an amazing scenario for a little village.

Bon Scott died on 19 February 1980 and was replaced by singer Brian Johnson, who had appeared at Cromer Links with the band Geordie.

The support band at the AC/DC gig, British Lions, had formed in May 1977 when vocalist John Fiddler, from Medicine Head, joined Overend Watts (bass), Dale Griffin (drums), Morgan Fisher (keyboards) and Ray Major (guitar) from Mott.

Morgan Fisher returned to West Runton the following year in John Otway's band with Paul Martinez (bass), Paul Halsey (drums) and Ollie Halsall (guitar). Ollie Halsall had been at the notorious Boxer gig at the Links. John Otway says, 'Ollie was a famous guitarist who had been in *Rolling Stone* magazine's top 10 guitarists for some time.' John enjoyed that tour. He says, 'It was a lovely tour with excellent musicians. It was the one tour when I stayed in nice hotels!'

Lindisfarne stayed at the Weybourne Maltings when they appeared at Runton. Terry Bunting says, 'They were a semi-acoustic folk band. I heard that the morning after the gig they got their instruments out and gave a free performance from the balcony of the hotel!'

John Bowen had made another pilgrimage from Gorleston, this time to see Lindisfarne, and declares:

Not a good night for head-banging, but just a good laugh from one of the best bands for sing-alongs and not having a care in the world. Their brand of folky pop music just made you feel good and made an hour-and-a-half feel like five minutes. I will always have time for Lindisfarne.

They had hits including 'Lady Eleanor', 'Meet Me on the Corner' and 'Run for Home'. In addition to these, the classic sing-along 'Fog on the Tyne' would have had an airing that night.

Wild Horses made their first visit to West Runton in December 1978. The band comprised Neil Carter (guitar), Jimmy Bain (bass/vocals) from Rainbow, Brian Robertson (lead guitar/vocals) from Thin Lizzy, and Kenny Jones (drums). When they returned 18 months later, Clive Edwards had replaced Kenny on drums.

They were supported by local band Boy Bastin. Earlier in the year, the *Eastern Evening News* had given their line-up as John Brunning (lead guitar) from Crow and Mungo Jerry; Peter Phipps (bass); John (Jimmy) Jewel (drums) from Kiss, Crow and Mungo Jerry; and John Tuttle (vocals and saxophone) from Kiss. The newspaper reported that Boy Bastin had just won a three-year recording contract and Terry Bunting recalls that their single 'All the Way Over the Hill' was Dave Lee Travis's single of the week on Radio One.

Bands with current chart singles still featured regularly at West Runton Pavilion during 1978. That summer both Hi Tension and Marshall Hain appeared at the venue whilst their current singles, 'Hi Tension' and 'Dancing in the City' respectively, were in the charts. Colin Woodyard says he kissed Kit Hain, from Marshall Hain, and she signed the album he had taken along.

In October the venue announced: 'We proudly present, to celebrate their chart success, Britain's biggest reggae name and dedicated follower of black soul.' This was Third World and their hit single was 'Now That We've Found Love'. The following week Ma Tumbi were advertised and punters were advised, 'If you thought Third World were good, don't miss these.'

The Motors were together about 18 months and played twice at West Runton Pavilion. They released several singles with their most successful, 'Airport', reaching number four in the charts around the time of their second visit. They were supported on that occasion by the Jolt, a band comprising 'three blokes in suits who were like the Jam', according to Alan Hooker. After the Motors split up, the band's guitarist/vocalist Bram Tchaikovsky returned to the venue under his own name.

Another new wave band, the Rich Kids, played at West Runton twice in 1978. Bassist Glen Matlock had played at the venue in 1976 with the Sex Pistols but had left them in early 1977 to join the Rich Kids with Midge Ure (guitar/vocals), who had also played at Runton before with previous band Slik. The line-up of the Rich Kids was completed by Rusty Egan (drums) and Steve New (guitar/vocals). Local band TNT, featuring Nick Mallet on bass, supported them on their second visit.

As well as an outspoken lead singer, Bob Geldof – who would go on to be a leading light in the Band Aid and Live Aid phenomenon with Midge Ure – the Boomtown Rats had a very distinctive piano player called Johnny Fingers who wore striped pyjamas on stage. Their second album, *A Tonic for the Troops*, had just been released along with their latest single, 'She's So Modern', when they appeared at West Runton Pavilion in April 1978. Their two earlier singles from their first album had been 'Looking After Number One' and 'Mary of the Fourth Form'. Later that year 'Rat Trap', another track from their latest album, would make the Boomtown Rats the first Irish band to have a UK number one single.

The Tom Robinson Band appeared shortly after their success with their single '2-4-6-8 Motorway' and had shocked the establishment with the release of another single 'Glad to be Gay'. They were booked to appear again in May 1980, although the Tom Robinson Band had dissolved in July 1979 and were called Sector 27 by that time, but they didn't turn up anyway. Tom is alleged to have holed up in a hotel in Cromer following a nervous breakdown.

Another non-attendee was ex-ELO member Violinski. David Watts remembers there was a very small crowd and Violinski didn't turn up. Similarly, Frankie Miller, who had recently charted with his single 'Darlin'', failed to appear. The gig was postponed until the end of January 1979 and Frank Boswall was not impressed:

They never realised what damage they were doing to the venue and to themselves when they kept cancelling and postponing. Frankie Miller postponed, well he was always postponing things, didn't do him any good at all. Had he have turned up when he was supposed to, the 16 December, I remember we had quite a decent crowd in. He turns up on the 27 January, weather might not be as good, I don't know, but it puts people off coming, because they remember he didn't turn up the last time.

Motorhead, who were much bigger, would never let you down. We had them probably five times and they would always turn up for the gig. They were always out of their minds most of the time, but they always turned up.

Of course, as with Angus Young and his cut foot, and Gary Holton with his broken leg, sometimes cancellations were unavoidable. Bands often went to great lengths to make sure they attended. Frank says, 'Around this time we had quite a little reggae section going.' It would usually be on a Friday night and included bands such as Tapper Zukie, Reggae Regular and Burning Spear. Geoff Peck remembers an incident concerning one of them:

They had an accident on their way from Norwich to West Runton and when the police arrived they found cannabis in the car and arrested the band. I believe one of the road crew admitted it was his so that the band could go and play. They turned up about 10.30pm and played late.

Someone who never let his audience down was Raymond Froggatt. Froggie appeared at West Runton Pavilion several times each year, as he had done previously at Cromer Links. He and his band were obviously very popular as one Runton advert declared they were returning 'by massive public demand'. Doorman John Mason remembers Froggie being very friendly to the Runton staff. On one occasion, while he and his band were touring America, Froggie wrote a letter to Frank Boswall thanking everyone at West Runton Pavilion for all the help and support they had given him.

At the end of 1978, however, there was a change from the traditional New Year's Eve booking for Froggie and his band, and they played instead on Saturday 30 December with the usual support from local band, Kangaroo Alley, who were an accomplished country rock outfit that included Chris Hawkins on bass.

Radio One DJ 'Diddy' David Hamilton was booked for the following night for a New Year's Eve party costing £2 including basket supper. This, unfortunately, was to join the list of cancellations but 'Diddy' didn't need a note from his mum on this occasion, as there had been a fall of snow and no-one was going anywhere!

16

Plenty For Punks

Inevitably staff changes continued to occur at West Runton Pavilion. Jumbo (Graham Curlew) left at the end of 1978 and doorman John Mason departed soon afterwards. John summarises his time at Runton:

I suffered one or two little knocks and small bruising including a black eye and, on one occasion, I was thrown through a window, tearing my trousers and shirt. After that, I always made sure I had a cricket box and a spare pair of trousers with me! All in all, the comradeship was on a par with that of the armed forces and I never saw any colleague back away from any trouble. After a particularly busy, rough evening, Frank would buy us all a drink and I've heard him say, 'Where else could you have that sort of fun and get paid for it?'

New staff recruits included Kevin Norton, Philip Basham and Louis Leuw.

Kevin Norton's two older brothers had been at school with bouncer Cookie (John Cook) and Kevin started going to West Runton Pavilion with them. One night, when they were a bit short-staffed, he helped out and ended up working there for about two-and-a-half years. Kevin also remembers the camaraderie:

Sometimes we would get called in to help bouncers in Norwich when they had a live group on. When it was a disco, they relied 100 per cent on the DJ to play music to suit the crowd, but it was completely different with a live band.

Head bouncer Ronnie Carroll agrees:

The nightclubs in Norwich used to help each other out if they were short of bouncers on a particular night. They could get 'Charlie's Boys' who were like floating bouncers and would work anywhere. When there was going to be trouble at Runton, sometimes they would ring Norwich and ask if they could send any spare bouncers, but it couldn't be done. They had to be at work in Norwich until two in the morning; in fact some of the Runton bouncers, like 'Smurf' (Rodney Whitlam) and Philip Basham used to finish Runton at 12, then go up to Norwich and help get the people out there when they closed at two.

Philip Basham worked on the door at Runton for about five years and had to stand at the side of the stage when the bands were playing to stop the crowd from invading it. He says he didn't like it when the punk bands were on because he got covered in spit!

The bouncers would often get help from the Runton regulars, as Kevin Norton explains:

There would be 50 or 60 blokes who came there regularly who were 'with you'. The pub would often be heaving as well. I don't think they had any doormen there, but we would get called on if there was any trouble. Usually, by the time we got there, the fishermen had sorted it out.

There was a woman bouncer, called Renie, used to get the girls out of the toilets if they were fighting. Sometimes, she'd be busier than we were!

We would have a can of Breaker when we got there, one in the interval, and afterwards it was a free house. We could have a free burger or some chips whenever we wanted. What more could a 19 year old want? We had the beer, the music, the girls and we were getting paid for it!

Louis Leuw was another of Cookie's friends who worked at Runton in 'security'. He says:

Cookie was a real character, got me the job there. I moved to Hevingham in 1978 and started going to Runton with Cookie. One of the Dereham boys picked on one of my sons, so I went and got into a fight. Frank said to Cookie, 'Go and stop them,' and Cookie said, 'I aren't going to stop them,' so Frank said, 'Well, give him a job here, then.' So that was how it started. It was rough but good. I enjoyed it. There was nowhere like it. There was no trouble with the heavy rock bands: Motorhead, Judas Priest, Iron Maiden. It was when the skinheads and the punks got there we had to try and keep them apart.

Kevin Norton agrees:

The Motorhead and leather jacket lot were fine, no worries, just there to get pissed and listen to the music. Some nights were easy, but the punk nights would need the full team.

On one of the easy nights, Cookie got a hiding. These lads wouldn't go home, and he went up and told them to get out, didn't know this bloke was some army boxing champion. He knocked Cookie down, and some of his mates came over and gave him a kicking. Cookie's head got split open and he had to go to hospital – it left him with a nasty scar.

Ray Spinks had attended the Pavilion during the ballroom days, but he returned to the venue in the mid-seventies, as he explains:

It was in 1975 when I once again started frequently visiting the Pavilion, but this time in a professional capacity as a police officer. By this time the venue was becoming more of a place for bands to play their own type of music to their own fans, sometimes leading to more head-banging than dancing. Some of these gigs did lead to violence, and sometimes several police officers were required to maintain order, with the occasional stabbing and serious injury.

The type of group appearing would dictate the scale of police presence, with the punk and the skinhead era causing the most problems, not least the calls from terrified householders finding weirdly-dressed ravers fast asleep on their front lawns! The bands whose fans caused the least trouble, in spite of their fearsome appearance, were the heavy metal rockers, such as Motorhead, the Tygers of Pan Tang and Iron Maiden.

On one occasion a serious altercation between a group of youths from the north and some local lads led to a coach being stopped at Holt, and some 40 passengers being arrested and brought back to Sheringham police station. As there were only two cells, this did cause a few problems!

Kevin Norton remembers one time Norwich City Football Club were playing at home to Leicester:

There were two coach-loads from Leicester, around 90 supporters, and they had a skirmish with the locals in Cromer. They followed them down into West Runton Pavilion. There were tables and chairs flying, the bouncers formed a human chain up the middle of the dance hall to try and keep them apart. It was horrendous. I came out covered in blood.

Head bouncer, Ronnie Carroll, recalls the Leicester mob:

They used to come down every year in a couple of coaches and cause havoc. Most of the locals were never any bother, they were a nuisance sometimes, but nothing serious because they knew they would be barred and we knew where they lived! But this lot used to come to look for trouble. They went against the Cromer and Sheringham boys and there were about 200 people fighting in the car park. The police were on the road hiding behind the wall, so I pulled them over and told them to help. One of the policemen fell over someone lying on the ground and complained that there was a body there. I said there'd be more if he didn't get on with it. The staff tried to stop the fighting coming into the Pavilion and one bloke's leg got broken in the door – it went off like a 12-bore shotgun.

Another year, Frank Boswall was prepared for trouble and told one of his staff, Dave, who was also a wrestler, to stop the Leicester crowd from coming in. Dave had hit two of them before Frank realised what was happening and had to explain that wasn't quite how he wanted them kept out! John Mason remembers another big fight:

Three or four weeks before, a load of them came in, casing the joint. They had various weapons: piano cord with a handle at each end, knives, the lot. Things were hidden in their shoes and some of them had a kitchen knife down the trouser leg – that was a popular one. We put all the stuff behind the counter in the cloakroom. At the end of the night, as they were coming out, they asked for it back, because they said they were going to Southend and needed to have it.

Then about three weeks later they were back, throwing chairs and tables at the band. They did a runner. I remember the crowd were standing either side, and there was this big rumpus going on in the middle.

John Lemon worked at the Pavilion for four or five years in his late teens as a glass-collector, three nights a week. He lived about 100 yards away and says, despite the occasional fight, the Pavilion 'was a wonderful place to be'. He worked with Martin Lewis, another glass-collector, from Sheringham. John remembers:

When Motorhead or those type of bands were playing, this drone would start in the village at about four in the afternoon. It would get louder, then all these motorbikes would come along, six abreast, and turn into the car park. They would come from miles, because the ride was as much a part of the outing as the music was.

Girlschool had the biggest load of roadies, speakers and lighting. They used so much electricity the power dropped in the village and the lights dimmed. Heavy bands used to have deep speakers, six feet deep; people used to crawl into them, you could just see their feet, and bouncers would be pulling them out.

Tony Lamb was one of the culprits. He says, 'I regularly attended the West Runton Pavilion and once, at a Motorhead gig, I got very drunk, climbed into one of their speakers and fell asleep!'

John Lemon witnessed a strange event while one of the heavy bands were setting up:

They were doing a sound test with these speakers one afternoon when the Pavilion was empty. One chap, who was standing in the middle of the hall, was knocked over with the acoustics. The bass speakers from the heavy rock bands were particularly bad.

Frank Boswall's secretary, Ray Burton, also lived nearby. She had been asked to run the ticket office when Joe Tuck's wife, Nan, had left. Ray helped with the bar and paid the bands. She also remembers the bikers:

One day about 20 bikers came down from Leicester and lined their bikes up outside my house, which also doubled as an office. When Frank came round the next morning, he told me he had just stepped over a biker who was curled up asleep on my doorstop and might like some tea and toast.

When the big house was empty they would stay in there. One morning I woke up and smoke was pouring out of the house. When I went and had a look, I found out the bikers had accidentally set fire to the old wooden staircase.

She remembers Judas Priest and, in particular, Uriah Heep as being very loud.
Barman Dick Woodley comments:

By the time the heavy metal bands started coming, drinks were sold in plastic glasses or in tins. On some nights they would sell the cans by the case and the punters would sit on them on the floor.

Paul Gray was another glass-collector. He says, 'I used to go to Runton on the bus when I was about 15. I used to collect the glasses so it was a way of seeing the bands without it costing much.' He later invested in a moped, but it was not always so easy to get home. He says, 'I remember one night drinking a few cans of Breaker and Swan lager, and then having trouble at Hunworth hill on my moped on the way home.

He laughs about the graffiti in the men's toilets. 'Burst a bag and win a baby,' had been written on the condom machine, and next to a British Standard sign someone had added, '... so was the Titanic.'

Punter John Bowen remembers the sign on the gents' loo:

This I always laugh about, the sign to the gents' WC was not the normal 'boys' or 'gents', but just a piece of card stuck to the door with [a drawing of a penis] *on it. This remained there for quite some time.*

[Author's note – John actually drew the picture but unfortunately it wasn't possible to produce it using the text keys currently available on a computer!]

John continues, 'Inside the WC the hand drier was removed revealing a cable just sticking out of the wall. These days, Health and Safety would have had that place closed straight away.'

Dick Woodley recalls at one time four girls from Runton Hill School used to clear up, wash up, and collect the glasses. He says they were 'very cagey' when they first came, and wouldn't give their names, because they clearly weren't meant to be there. Runton Hill was an independent boarding school and the matron was known to complain about the bad influence the Pavilion had on her girls. Dick says the four escapees gradually became more friendly, but he still has no idea how they used to get out or sneak back. He recalls another helper, a washing-up boy, who went on to join Norwich City youth as a footballer.

Head bouncer Ronnie Carroll remembers other staff:

I think Cookie was the bouncer I worked with the longest. 'Whip' (Nigel Slipper) was there about three years, and 'Harmony' worked in the ticket office. He was called Harmony because we said he used to dye his hair. He wasn't big enough to be a bouncer so, if we suspected trouble, we used to get him to search everyone. The troublemakers would sometimes wear these studs round their wrists. Harmony told one bloke to take it off, he swung it round and knocked poor old Harmony out!

Geoff Peck saved my life. There was a bloke from away, who had been knocked out cold. His mates thought the bouncers had done it. When I went over, people were jumping on this unconscious bloke. His mates came over, thought I was part of it, and pulled a knife on me. Geoff came in the door, walked round the back of this bloke, and took the knife clean off him. It was no problem to Geoff because of his police training.

John Mason still worked there at the time as a doorman, and adds, 'Geoff took this knife out of this bloke's hand so quickly, I didn't see where it went!'

Frank Kinsley remembers that the big pane of glass in the foyer got broken on several occasions.

The *Eastern Daily Press* of 10 November 1979 reported that the venue was issuing patrons with a leaflet regarding searching, spot checks and barring. Frank Boswall stated that they sometimes had 30 bottles of alcohol in the ticket office which had been taken away from people at the door, who were often drunk before they got there. At that time 60 people were barred.

John Mason remembers:

The biggest fear for any of the local punters was being barred, as most of their friends would be inside the hall. This threat proved the best deterrent and was frequently used by all the staff keeping order. I have seen punters who had been banned for several weeks, still arrive on the free buses and stand outside four to five hours in freezing conditions hoping we would relent.

Colin Woodyard, one of four brothers who went regularly to Runton, was leaning on the bar one night with his younger brother, Chris. A drunk came past the bar and knocked Chris over. The brothers were often there, so the bouncers knew them and were concerned about the incident. They searched for the culprit and when they found him he was barred. Chris, Colin, Patrick and Tom were let in free the following week.

John Daynes also had an encounter with a drunk. He recalls:

One night we went to see a band there and I had some chips in a basket. This chap was arguing with some girls – he was a bit loud and a bit drunk. He started chatting up my missus; I carried on eating my chips. He got worse, louder with the missus; I carried on eating my chips. Then he knocked my chips out of my hand and that was it; I knocked him over and jumped on him. This big bouncer came rushing over and lifted me off this bloke. I thought, I'm for it now, but he kicked the bloke out of the door. He'd seen him hit a woman and knew what was going on.

Maureen Chapman (was Wakefield) encountered trouble in the toilets one night:

I'd gone into the toilets and this girl followed me in, called me by the wrong name, and when I turned round, she hit me. I said 'I'm not ...' whoever she'd said, and hit her back. When I came out, my boyfriend, Martin, was shocked to see me. I told him, 'Don't worry, she came off worst!'

While Frank Boswall's wife, Janice, ran the burger bar – helped by Jumbo's sister Gillian Boyce – Frank's brother-in-law Bob Moore worked on the desk. He was known as 'American Bob' or 'Bob the Banker'. John Lemon remembers Bob used to do the book-keeping and wore a printer's green cap. John says, 'He used to take the money and have piles of it on the table, counting it. There was so much he could hardly see over it.'

Barry Woods worked Wednesdays, Fridays and Saturdays for a few years as a barman at Runton. He remembers the famous people he served including the Four Tops, Slade, the Drifters, Bob Geldof, Johnny Rotten, and Darts – who had a top hit at the time.

Deidre Bound first worked behind the bar at the Village Inn, then in the dance hall and the 'Hole in the Wall'. She met many of the stars and collected their autographs. Lynn Bright was another bar-worker.

Sarah Baldwin had started working in the kitchens at Runton when she was 16. She says she had another job which didn't pay much, so she worked at Runton to make up the money. The kitchens closed before the main band came on so she would go up onto the private balcony to watch. 'Pud' (Patrick Robinson), one of the bouncers, used to get autographs for her. Iggy Pop didn't sell many tickets when he came in 1979 – despite being promoted on the tickets as 'world's outstanding cult figure' – so lots of Sarah's later autographs are on the back of those unsold tickets. Iggy Pop signed one of them for her and wrote, 'Stay honest.' Rob Aherne remembers being in the Village Inn and hearing – through the open doors – Iggy playing 'Batman' as a warm-up to his main gig the next night.

Sarah says that Pud would escort the youngsters when they walked home from West Runton to Sheringham, although she remembers one time sampling a different form of transport on one of Slade's visits to Runton. She says, 'Their lead singer, Noddy Holder, took all the girls out for a ride around Sheringham in his pink Cadillac one summer evening, but we didn't see anyone we knew!'

On one occasion, Colin Woodyard took Slade a bottle of Champagne. He remembers:

Dave Hill couldn't get the cork out, so he busted the top off the bottle. I helped him pick the glass up. Dave was worried I would cut myself. Jimmy Lea and Noddy Holder were also there.

Sara Aldis and her friend Joan Lusher saw Slade at Runton and later had a drink in the bar with Noddy Holder and Dave Hill. Rob Aherne remembers one night Noddy Holder served behind the bar in the Village Inn.

Steve Ayers says:

The most memorable night was at a Slade show. I got a bit pissed and was standing right in front of Noddy during their encore and I slowly slid his mike stand away from him as he was singing (with his eyes shut). He must have been puzzled as to why his vocals were getting quieter! We went backstage after the show and shared a curled-up sandwich and a joke with the band. They were really funny guys.

Although Slade still put on a good show and remained very popular when they played live, they were struggling a bit in the charts at this time. Things had moved on and Noddy Holder, with his Dickensian whiskers and top hat with mirrors, and lead guitarist Dave Hill, with his silver jump suits and glittery make-up, had been left behind by punk rock. With the Conservatives coming to power in 1979, led by the first British woman Prime Minister, Margaret Thatcher, the punks felt they had plenty to rebel against.

One of punk's legends, ex-Sex Pistol Sid Vicious, died of a drug overdose on 2 February 1979, at the age of 21. Stephen Brady went to West Runton Pavilion that evening to see Wreckless Eric. Stephen recalls:

As it was the night Sid Vicious died, all the punks were asking for a tribute for him. Wreckless Eric just said, 'He's dead, I'm sorry, but I'm here to play my set.'

Another punk band, the Members, appeared at the venue when their biggest hit single 'Sound of the Suburbs' had just been in the charts, and the Damned returned, this time as the headlining act. The line-up for this gig was Dave Vanian (vocals), Rat Scabies (drums), Captain Sensible (guitar) and Algy (Alasdair) Ward on bass. They appeared at the venue several times and Martin Chapman remembers one occasion when they played a very short set:

The Damned had been on stage about 20 minutes when the drummer, Rat Scabies, put lighter fluid on his drum kit and set light to it. The whole thing went up in flames and he was leaping around the stage on fire. Someone kicked the drum kit over and small fires started. The band went off stage and Cookie, the bouncer, got a fire blanket and sorted it all out. They didn't come back on, but later they were sitting drinking in the bar. The drummer had his hands bandaged up but seemed fine.

Joe Barber says he was also there the night Rat Scabies set fire to himself.

Bouncer Philip Basham remembers being on stage with his colleague Smurf (Rodney Whitlam) when the Damned played:

Their lead singer (or it might have been Captain Sensible) used to get a mouthful of beer and spit it at the crowd, then of course, they'd spit back. It was like a snowstorm in the lights. Then they'd start throwing cans onto stage; it was nasty if one of them hit you in the face. The Captain stripped off, then kicked the drum kit to pieces.

Mike Jervis was away at college but his mates saw the Damned. Mike says, 'It's just hearsay, but I was told that Captain Sensible ended up stark naked as he usually did.'

John Bowen went to one of the Damned gigs but wasn't too impressed:

Punk was the nemesis of all the music I loved, but grudgingly I did like some of the earlier new wave bands, even though I found it hard to admit it. It was a different type of crowd for this one. I got the feeling that the whole place could erupt into violence at any time but I can't recall any trouble or anything musically memorable. Not the best ever gig but a night out anyway, and when you are about 18 years old a night in with Mum and Dad is not what you want!

Martin Bean was there on one occasion as well:

I saw the Damned at West Runton – not sure of the date – probably late '79 or '80. I believe the Damned ran a competition for local bands to support them when they played in their area. When me and my mates arrived, the first act we saw was a Buddy Holly look-alike who played a selection of rock and roll songs. The audience didn't seem to like this, so they started throwing things at him – mainly cans. One projectile knocked his glasses almost off (so that they were hanging on by one ear). He then hid behind the speaker stack, peeping round the corner of the speakers shouting something like, 'I'm f***ing stronger than you lot!'

At this point I thought he was the local support act and thought, poor bugger – he's doing his best and he gets canned off stage. However, later a mate told me his name was 'Auntie Pus' and he was a support act for the Damned (and, I think, other punk bands)

simply to wind the audience up, because most punks hated rock and roll.
The actual Damned gig didn't go well. I think the bass player had stormed off and
refused to play so they had to 'borrow' a bass player. I seem to remember the gig was a
complete shambles and only improved towards the end when they played some Sex Pistols'
stuff. Captain Sensible ended up playing completely naked, after the audience's response
when he shouted, 'Do you want the pants to come off too?'

Captain Sensible was interviewed by 'Bimble' (Dave Parsons) from *Free Radical*
Sounds who asked him to talk about Auntie Pus, 'the lunatic that used to accompany
the Damned on tour'. This is what the Captain told Bimble:

[He was] *Raving mad! We'd park up outside a music shop. I'd go in to get some guitar*
strings and afterwards we'd be sitting there in the van with the engine running saying,
'Where's Pus?' Suddenly you'd turn round and see some worker from Woolworths holding
the shop door open and Pus would come out carrying a whole load of stuff: electric kettles,
toasters, this and that. He'd bung 'em into the van saying, 'Drive off quick I've nicked 'em.'
We'd be saying, 'Well how the hell did you get away with that? They held the door open for
ya.' He'd say, 'Look, if you come out with so much stuff, they don't believe you're nicking it.'
He was actually a brilliant thief. He used to go up and down the queue of people outside
the gigs, selling toasters and stuff. It was absolutely brilliant.

When the Damned appeared at West Runton in June 1979 they were supported
by the Ruts, who headlined at the venue later that year after their single 'Babylon's
Burning' had reached the top 10. The Ruts lined-up with Paul Fox (guitar),
Malcolm Owen (vocals), John Vincent Jennings (bass) and David Ruffy (drums).

John Vincent Jennings is now known as John Segs. He explained that his
nickname 'Segs' originated when he used to be a roadie in the days before he
joined the Ruts. JD Nicholas, who was later with the Commodores, at the time
was in a band called Hit and Run. He used to say John was 'a bit below the segs'
(which is a part of the shoe) and the name stuck.

Segs remembers West Runton Pavilion well:

It was a very strange place. You got there, and you were in the middle of nowhere. You would
go into the pub next door because there was nowhere else to go. Then these coaches would
turn up and everyone would be in the pub with you.

We stayed at the Red Lion in Cromer. I'm not in the habit of taking hotel room keys,
but I must have got pissed at Cromer because I ended up with one of the Red Lion keys.

There was a little boating pond at Cromer. All the Ruts went on it one afternoon before
the gig. One boat went over, and it developed into a full-blown water fight, the boats were
all capsizing, everyone was soaked.

Rob Aherne remembers the boating lake at Cromer: 'One of the guys from school a year young than me – the real punk year – tried to throw himself in there drunkenly after splitting up with a girl. As it was about 30 inches deep, I think he bruised his knees.'

Chris Hare has a book called *Punk Rock: So What?*. The cover photo is said to be the crowd at one of the Runton Ruts gigs. Inside there is a photo from the stage showing the crowd and some of the interior. There are many punkettes (female punks) in the photos with their trademark spiky hair and black eye make-up. Segs says the photos were probably taken at the Damned gig 'because there were loads of punkettes there'. He also remembers photos appearing in the *New Musical Express* of 'stage diving' at West Runton Pavilion. 'Stage diving' (also known as 'crowd-surfing') involves a person being carried aloft by the crowd towards the stage and, nowadays, usually results in them being ejected from the venue once they reach their destination!

When asked about the Ruts' classic hit 'Babylon's Burning', Segs said they just used to get together and jam, so they are all credited with writing it.

Malcolm Owen, their lead singer, died on 14 July 1980 aged 26 from a heroin overdose. The band became Ruts DC, which stood for Da Capo – meaning new beginning – and returned to West Runton in May 1981. Segs says he doesn't remember the Ruts DC gigs much as it was, understandably, a very grief-ridden time.

No date has been found for the appearance of X-Ray Spex at West Runton Pavilion, but Julie Mason distinctly remembers one of her friends, Jo Armes, talking about the concert at school, and Martin Chapman also thinks they played at the venue. Female punk singer Poly Styrene (Marion Elliot) formed her band X-Ray Spex with schoolgirl Lora Logic (Susan Whitby), who played saxophone but then left to continue her studies. Lora was replaced by Rudi (Steve) Thompson. The line-up also included bassist Paul Dean, drummer BP (Paul) Harding and Jak Airport (Jack Stafford) on guitar. X-Ray Spex had several successful chart singles including 'Germ Free Adolescents', 'Identity' and 'Oh Bondage Up Yours'.

Julie remembers:

It was somewhere around this time that another of my friends, Dawn, started spiking her hair and going out wearing a man's shirt and tie – and nothing else! I must admit, the first time she turned up like that I thought she'd forgotten to put her trousers on, but she assured me it was what all the punkettes had been wearing on Top of the Pops *that week. Me, being a bit more square, went for the baggy shirts and ties in a small way, but the trousers stayed firmly on, much to my mother's relief, no doubt!*

The UK Subs had just appeared on *Top of the Pops* with their single 'Tomorrow's

Girls' when they came to West Runton Pavilion in September 1979. 'Stranglehold', which was their biggest hit, had reached number 26 in the UK charts in June 1979. They later recorded their version of the Zombie's song, also a hit for Santana, called 'She's Not There'. Originally known as the Subversives, the band shortened their name to the Subs then found that another band had the same name. They added 'UK' in deference to the Sex Pistols' hit 'Anarchy in the UK', and the UK Subs were born. They made several visits to West Runton Pavilion with lead singer and founder Charlie Harper accompanied by various line-ups.

The Cure, having played at the venue on two previous occasions – being billed on one of those as 'very special guests' supporting Generation X – returned to support Siouxsie and the Banshees in 1979.

Siouxsie and the Banshees had made their first public appearance in September 1976 at a punk festival when they had improvised the Lord's Prayer for 20 minutes. John Simon Ritchie, alias Sid Vicious, who later became bass player with the Sex Pistols, had been on drums.

In August 1978 Siouxsie Sioux, who was born Susan Janet Ballion, had a top 10 hit, 'Hong Kong Garden', with new Banshees Steven Severin (bass), John McKay (guitar) and Kenny Morris (drums). The month before their West Runton date, John and Kenny had left the band. Some tour dates were moved to March before 'Budgie' (Peter Clarke) took over on drums. Guitarist Robert Smith was borrowed from support act the Cure. The Cure were said to have been better than Siouxsie and the Banshees on the night they played at West Runton because she apparently had a sore throat.

After supporting the Clash at Runton during their 'White Riot' tour, the Buzzcocks returned to the venue in November 1979 as the headlining act. Their single 'Ever Fallen in Love With Someone You Shouldn't' had been released the previous year. Steve Garvey had replaced Garth Smith on bass, but Pete Shelley and Steve Diggle remained jointly on guitars and vocals, with John Maher on drums. Howard Devoto, one of the original Buzzcocks, had left them in February 1977 and played at West Runton at the end of 1978 with his new band, Magazine, cryptically advertised as, 'One of the last dates on the tour which has brought critical acclaim for devoto'd fans.'

The Buzzcocks were supported in 1979 by Joy Division, and Rob Aherne says it was a 'great gig'. John Lemon remembers, 'Joy Division were better than the main band.'

Joy Division had formed three years earlier and took their name from the term given by German officers during the War to female prisoners which they kept for their own pleasure. The band's line-up was Barney (Bernard) Sumner (guitar), Peter Hook (bass), Ian Curtis (vocals) and Steve Morris (drums). They used to play their classic track 'Love Will Tear Us Apart' live, but it was not released as a single until April 1980. Ian Curtis, who tried to hide his epilepsy but often found the strobe lights brought on his fits, committed suicide on 18 May 1980 aged 23. The band later changed their name to New Order.

Peter Jay says:

I was a big fan of the Buzzcocks and had only recently heard of Joy Division. Ian Curtis looked very vacant and danced strangely. Their music had an urgency about it but they were only the support act and I was looking forward to the Buzzcocks, who played a cracking set.

Kevin Smith, from Norwich, saw most of the punk bands who came to West Runton Pavilion, including the Clash and the Damned. When punk wasn't on at Runton, he and his mates would venture down to Brixton Academy, in London, on their mopeds, which would take hours. One night a load of them had been to West Runton by car and the driver had had a bit to drink. His car broke down at Ketts Hill in Norwich on the way home and the police turned up. He was frightened he was going to be breathalysed, so he jumped into the nearby river and started swimming across to get away from the police, who thought it was very funny and just stood laughing at him.

There was no advertisement for 6 March 1979 but a live album is available of Robert Rental and the Normal which is said to have been recorded at West Runton Pavilion on that date.

The Normal was Daniel Miller, a DJ who had been working in Germany and was a fan of electronic music by bands such as Kraftwerk. Scottish man Robert Rental (real name William Bennett) teamed up with Daniel Miller during the spring of 1979 to join the independent electronic music scene which was thriving at the time because cheap Japanese synthesisers were becoming available.

The album was released in 1980 on the Rough Trade label as a 'one-side only' album. 'Jim Tones', otherwise known as Tim Jones, a co-runner with Barry Williams on the Fflint Central experimental music label, reviewed the album:

[It] consists of five 'segments', starting with a knocking, ring-modulated rhythm with spits of noise and taped speech fragments. It must have been a bit of a shock for most of the audience present, who were probably expecting some guitar power chords and sing-along action! This opening section suddenly stops to go into a tape of some orchestral swing music, whilst Miller deadpans something about 'dead reptiles'.

The swing fades out to a one-note percussive synth sound – it's like Rolf's 'Sun Arise', but meant for the apocalypse! Rental starts hollering his fears – you can't really understand what he's shouting about, but he sure sounds anguished – while swathes and blasts of white noise slowly lead to a cacophony of taped splinters, before a hovering drone starts to blanket the overall sound. There is a few seconds snapshot of the stuttering 'TVOD', which is then lost into wrestling with the drone. A synth sequence starts to poke out, but once again succumbs to that blanket drone.

The last leg of this 25 minute set has a sharp staccato synth sequence while, once again, Rental bellows with some force into the microphone. At intervals, this electric and puncturing staccato is interrupted by superb, full blocks of shimmering sound and alternately repeats with the juttering sequence to great effect, until the whole thing is wound down like a beast well and truly slain.

I think they won the audience over that night, as a small but healthy enough cheer rouses up with a few shouts of 'more!'

I always got the impression, when listening to this recording, that the performers didn't expect the positive reaction, as you can hear Miller utter a slightly stunned, 'Thank you, goodnight,' with Rental chipping in an even more brief 'G'neet!'

Another lesser known act which appeared at West Runton Pavilion in March was Pierre Moerlen's Gong. The advertisement said, 'Moerlen must be regarded highly favoured indeed as he had the assistance of Mike Oldfield and Steve Winwood on his album'. He appeared with David Sancious who was described as 'Special guest artiste, one of America's top singer/song writers, five top albums in the USA – the most discerning market in the world.'

In April, Toyah Willcox was supported by local band Zorro. Zorro had undergone a few line-up changes since their last appearance at West Runton Pavilion. The previous summer, 'Fritz' (Ian Wright) had left and been replaced by Ricci Titcombe on drums, formerly from Teezer. Guitarist Ronnie (Ricky) Newson joined in January 1979 when Terry Bunting left. Kevin Longman left at the same time as Terry and was replaced by Alan Fish, who had played with local bands Zoe and Poacher. Alan was described by Colin Cross in the *Eastern Evening News* on 12 March 1979 as 'Probably the best and most experienced bass player in the area.' Former Poacher band-members Dave Smith and Dave Littlewood ('Galen') remained on vocals and keyboards respectively.

On leaving Zorro, Kevin Longman says, 'My biggest regret was not playing with Manfred Mann, whose record company decided to supply the support at the last minute.'

Other bands appearing in 1979 at West Runton Pavilion included the Doll, a heavy girl rock band, and the Street Band, who had a hit with their quirky single 'Toast' and were supported by Trimmer and Jenkins, billed as 'ex Burlesque'. The Dickies, who did fast versions of Black Sabbath's 'Paranoid' and the theme to Saturday morning show *The Banana Splits*, and Kandidate, who had a hit with 'I

Don't Wanna Lose You', also graced the Runton stage. Annie Lennox and Dave Stewart came there with their band the Tourists. They later had a hit with 'I Only Want to be With You' and then achieved worldwide success as the Eurythmics.

The Fabulous Poodles were billed as, 'The newest band to have gone and done it big in the States, playing one of few selected dates.' Ian Snell remembers seeing them at West Runton. The same night was the final of the Miss Disco '79 competition. It was stated that, 'Judging will be based on appearance and dancing ability. Personality and conduct at interviews will also be taken into consideration.'

Disco diva Chaka Khan started out as a singer with 1970s funk band Rufus, who released the single 'Ain't Nobody Does it Better'. Her first solo hit single, the classic disco anthem 'I'm Every Woman', was released at the end of 1978. Maureen Chapman (was Wakefield) is sure she saw Chaka Khan at West Runton Pavilion because she remembers hearing the song, although no date has been confirmed for the appearance. Maureen's husband, Martin, is equally sure he saw Chaka at the venue, although he did not mention the music but referred to a couple of her large physical attributes which had stuck in his mind, so to speak!

From his vantage point in the back bar of the Village Inn, Rob Aherne saw the Merton Parkas before they appeared on stage in August 1979. He says, 'They seemed younger than us and we were only 20!' Rob thinks this was probably the first time the mods took over.

Local band Running Dogs supported the Only Ones in March. A report in the *Eastern Evening News* at the time declared:

Running Dogs ... have to be the best local band around at the moment. The memorable songs of singer Julian Wilde are played fast and sharp with the rhythm guitarist, the oh-so-cool Tim Greenhalgh, holding everything nicely on the edge.

As the year moved on, some established artists took to the West Runton stage. Terry Bunting saw Judie Tzuke and says, 'She was massive at the time, had a hit album and single out. I remember that gig well. It was a really hot night, even though it was in October.'

David Ward was a big Judie Tzuke fan and a member of her fan club. He comments, 'She had lovely, long hair and a beautiful voice. What more can I say?' He kept a press cutting reviewing her concert, which was written by Chris Wise, who began by describing Judie's 'spellbinding performance' as 'magic'. The review continued:

Her beautiful voice ... was perfectly complemented by a thoughtful and highly proficient backing band, to provide Runton's musical night of the year so far.
Her crystal-clear voice seems just as much at home with raunchy numbers like 'Making

New Friends' as it does with slow, heart-rending ballads like the tender 'For You'.

The crowd loved her, and Judie and the band seemed genuinely moved by the reception they received. They had run out of numbers by the time the audience called them back for the third time, and – to a deafening cheer – they chose to do the exquisite single 'Stay With Me Till Dawn' again.

Moving moments at rock gigs are rare these days, but as the diminutive Judie – who has been described, with great poetic accuracy, as an English rose – stepped forward and led the band into that most beautiful of songs it must have left a lump in many throats.

All in all it was a refreshing evening of high-class musical entertainment.

West Runton regular David Wright – who bears the unfortunate nick-name 'Shite' – describes the atmosphere at the Judie Tzuke gig as 'electric' and says it was one of the best nights he had there.

Ian Gillan returned to Runton in 1979, after a change of line-up and two-and-a-half intervening years. The band name had been shortened to just Gillan and the line-up included Colin Towns (keyboards), Bernie Torme (guitar), John McCoy (bass) and Mick Underwood (drums).

John Bowen had now passed his driving test, so he did not have to rely on the coach to get him to West Runton, just an old Ford Cortina. His journey from Gorleston, a distance of some 45 miles, could take anything up to an hour-and-a-half, because of the roads. He says there were often three car-loads and, once, he remembers one of his mates hitting a bend and nearly putting his Hillman Avenger on its roof.

The Gillan gig was certainly worth the journey, as John reports:

This is more like it: we were going to see a major rock star, and they don't come much bigger than the ex-singer of the classic Mark 2 version of Deep Purple.

Somehow, while jostling for the best position down the front, before they came on stage, I noticed a large box or container like a flight case for a speaker or some band equipment. This would give me a great vantage point to see the band, so I climbed up on it unchallenged and knelt on it with no-one asking me to get down. I was set for the concert.

When the band came out on stage, Ian Gillan came up to me and shook my hand. Jesus Christ, I thought, Mr Ian Gillan, singer of 'Highway Star' etc, shaking my hand before even saying anything else to the crowd. It couldn't get any better than this.

This was the Mr Universe LP tour and in the band was this scary looking bloke on bass, no hair, just a massive beard. I think his name was John McCoy.

After the gig my mates were saying did I know Ian Gillan before this gig as he came to me like an old mate when he came on. I just think I had the best spot on the night, but this memory of Gillan I won't forget.

Neville Beck remembers Ian Gillan for a totally different reason:

Ian Gillan fell on top of me! Someone was pulling his trouser leg and he fell off the stage into the crowd. I pushed him back on and this bald bloke from the band came after me because he thought I was the one who'd pulled Gillan off the stage.

Julie Mason remembers her first glimpse of John McCoy:

We were standing towards the back of the hall, near the entrance doors. The stage was in darkness, then a single spotlight picked out something round and shiny about six feet above the stage. We craned our necks trying to work out what it was. When the rest of the stage lights came on the object was identified as the bald bass player's head! That was one of the most memorable starts to a concert I've ever seen.

Gillan was supported by Randy California and Friends, and by the Speedometers, who Alan Hooker remembers were 'really loud, possibly out of tune!'
Frank Boswall explains:

Quite often you would have to book the support band with the main band, because the record company wanted to promote the small band. When Gillan came, we were sold a package: Randy California and Speedometers.

Terry Bunting recalls:

Randy California was the guy in Spirit. He was a legendary guitarist who played in Hendrix's band Jimmy James and the Blue Flames. Actually, it was Hendrix who gave the young Randy Wolfe the name of 'Randy California'. Randy is dead now – drowned while trying to save his son's life in the sea.

Steve Hackett, another ex-member of a popular band, appeared at West Runton Pavilion in November 1978. Chris Hare was a Genesis fan and had Steve Hackett's albums from when he left them and went solo around 1975. Chris says:

I lived in Cromer then. I went up to the venue in the afternoon when they arrived and got him to sign a whole pile of albums. I told him it was a big surprise, him playing here and he said, 'Yeah, we're surprised as well.' Apparently, he'd heard the venue had a reputation for trouble, which I told him was a bit unfair.

With guitarist Steve Hackett were Pete Hicks (vocals), John Shearer (drums), Dick Cadbury (bass) and Steve's brother, John (flute/guitar/bass pedals).
Their album *Spectral Mornings* had been recorded at the beginning of 1979 and

was a big success in the UK and Europe, where the band toured extensively during the year, including a headline spot at the Reading Festival that summer.

In the queue to get into the concert, Richard Fryer met someone who was to become a life-long friend. He told Richard he had just moved to Norwich, got his first car, and had wanted to see Steve Hackett but hadn't known where West Runton was. He had set off in the car that evening in the general direction of the coast but became unsure of where to go so he had pulled over. A car had gone past playing Steve Hackett music so he had followed it and it had led him to Runton. It turned out Richard had been driving the car!

Caravan had been to the venue the two previous years and John Bowen caught up with them on their third appearance:

While this band were never likely to ever be my favourite, I did like them quite a bit as I had their Canterbury Tales *'best of …' double LP, so I knew a few of their songs and we had to go and check them out.*

This was the strangest atmosphere I have seen at West Runton Pavilion as everyone sat down on the floor for this gig. Every now and then a few people would get up, dance around a bit and then sit down, as if there was a time limit on them being on their feet.

Sometimes, when the music is this good, it is nice to sit and not have to crane your neck just to see. From what I remember, they went down very well. All in all a very enjoyable night.

Caravan had been formed in the late 1960s, as had Fairport Convention, one of the founders of which, Richard Thompson, appeared at the venue the following week with his wife Linda. Frank Boswall says, 'They didn't draw a big crowd and yet they were pretty good.' The advert for the gig said that Fairport Convention's music was currently the theme to *Kiss the Girls and Make Them Cry*, which was a television programme.

The year was rounded off in the usual way by Raymond Froggatt, but this was to be his last appearance there. In 10 years he had appeared at West Runton Pavilion and Cromer Links a total of 40 times, more than any other touring band. From the early days when, as Terry Pardon remembers, 'Raymond Froggatt used to have an army tent and stayed the night on the cliffs, before he had any money,' he had gone on to have a successful career on the country and western scene.

Terry Bunting comments:

His appeal crossed musical boundaries. Friends of mine who weren't that keen on the 'heavies' – like Quo and Nazareth – preferred Froggie, although many hard rock fans liked him too.

Froggie's song 'Roly's Going to Get Married' typified the feel-good atmosphere of a Raymond Froggatt concert, but as he ushered in the new decade, few could have foreseen the changes the next few years would bring to West Runton and its Pavilion.

17

Heavy Metal Heaven

Often now, on Saturday nights, there would be a disco rather than a band at West Runton Pavilion. The Ian Mac Disco in January 1980 offered 'Good prizes, including the final of the disco dancing competition.' The mid-week Snake Pit discos were still popular and in April there was a special Tramps Ball with 'Free supper and prizes for the best dressed Tramp.' Usual admission to the Wednesday discos was 50p, with all girls admitted free until 10.30pm.

However, as owner Frank Boswall later told the *Eastern Daily Press,* the music was fragmenting. No longer did people go to the Pavilion every Saturday night no matter who was on – now there were punk bands, new wave bands, heavy metal bands, new wave of British heavy metal bands. Amongst it all, however, fans of rock and roll music were still showing amazing tenacity.

Richard Howard used to cycle from Norwich to West Runton in his full teddy-boy outfit to see the rock and roll bands who still frequently appeared. He wore drainpipe trousers, a long teddy-boy 'drape' (jacket) and brothel creeper shoes. One night he was asked by one of the established teddy-boys where he had bought his new creepers from. The chap asked if he could fit one of them on and he disappeared with it. Richard spent the entire evening wearing one shoe and at the end of the night Cookie the bouncer retrieved his other shoe for him.

Another night, the pin went on one of the pedals of Richard's bike which meant the pedal slipped on each revolution. He had to go all the way back to Norwich using one pedal. He says it took hours and he was shattered when he got home. One time, when it was snowing, he stopped in the bus shelter at Aylsham and fell asleep before venturing home at daybreak. He must have been freezing!

Richard says he enjoyed the atmosphere at Runton and met a lot of friends there, both rock and roll fans and also bikers. He saw a variety of bands including the Clash, John Miles and Motorhead, but on that occasion he took his 'drape' off and left it round the back of the pub with his bike!

Kevin Roye ('Big K') was a rock and roll fan who organised buses from his home village of Foulsham when his favourite bands were playing at the Pavilion. These included Johnny Storm and Memphis in February 1980, and the Flying Saucers the following year. He also arranged charity events. On Saturday 7 July 1979, with Graham Alford from Booton, he had organised a festival in aid of Action for the Crippled Child which raised almost £500. A special licence had been granted by Cromer Magistrates in order that the event could run from 3.30pm until midnight. It had included the Oregon Rock Disco and six top groups: Crazy Cavan and the Rhythm Rockers, Wild Angels, the Riot Rockers, the Jets, and Memphis Index. Rock and roll star Freddie 'Fingers' Lee topped the bill.

Freddie was a piano player along the lines of Jerry Lee Lewis and he appeared at West Runton several times with his band. He wrote his own songs including 'I'm a Nut' and 'Boogie Woogie Fred', and was known as 'The One Eyed Boogie Boy' because he had a glass eye over which he wore a patch. Born Fred Cheeseman, he had played piano for Screaming Lord Sutch in the 1960s. Freddie's eccentric act included setting fire to the cowboy hat he habitually wore, and dropping his glass eye into his beer or a glass of water and 'drinking' it. Kelvin Rumsby went to one of Freddie 'Fingers' Lee's concerts and remembers what a great showman he was.

Steve Popey formed local band White Lightning in 1976 with three friends and supported Freddie 'Fingers' Lee at one of his West Runton performances. Steve says:

We supported Freddie 'Fingers' Lee on 23 January 1981 at West Runton Pavilion, the one and only time we ever played there. I remember the gig well. Freddie had a very crazy stage act at that time. I remember him setting fire to his hat and then running on stage, only to be extinguished by the Runton staff (must have broken a few fire regulations with that one.) At the end of his set he would come onto the stage and try to chop up his piano with an axe. When this failed he would then bring on a petrol-driven chainsaw and would succeed in dismembering his instrument while throwing the pieces into the crowd as his band played on (he must have broken every Health and Safety rule in the book), with bits of splintering wood and wire flying into the crowd.

Freddie was the only man I have ever seen who could play the piano while standing on his head; the man could also play with his feet!

Also, in his act that night, he took out his glass eye, dropped it in his pint glass, drank his beer, spat out his eye and replaced it in his eye socket.

The White Lightning band comprised Steve (vocals/double bass/bass guitar), Martyn Popey (lead guitar/backing vocals), Andrew Lincoln (drums) and Dave Lincoln (rhythm guitar). Steve recalls:

We were four friends with the liking of rock and roll music. None of us could play an instrument but with lessons, and a lot of hard work and practice, the band came together. We played rock and roll and rockabilly music, playing cover versions and our own original material as well.

In the summer of 1980, another charity rock and roll festival was held, from 2.30pm, which included Crazy Cavan and the Rhythm Rockers, the Jets, Dynamite, and the Blue Cat Trio. Dynamite were a London band with Clive Osbourne on saxophone. He guested from time to time with White Lightning, eventually forming a swing band with them, playing Bill Haley, Tommy Steele and similar songs.

Bill Haley himself was booked to appear at West Runton with the Comets. The tickets had been printed, but Kevin Roye remembers being on a bus coming back from London in February 1981 and hearing that Bill Haley had died. North Walsham band Beaky and the Bobcats had been due to support Bill Haley, having appeared at the venue in January 1980. The band comprised Graham Blyth ('Beaky') (vocals/washboard), Tony Blyth (bass), Ronnie Pratt (drums) and Simon Goodyear (guitar).

One of the rock and roll greats who did make it to West Runton Pavilion was Chuck Berry. Kevin Roye was allowed on the balcony to tape the concert and remembers Chuck Berry's daughter singing with Chuck on stage.

Policeman Ray Spinks was often called on to sort out trouble, but he says, 'Attending these events did have its compensations, however, as if things were reasonably quiet, I was able to climb into the balcony and watch some of the acts. One I remember was a hero of mine, Chuck Berry.'

Chuck Berry had had chart success in the UK with 'No Particular Place to Go' and 'Memphis Tennessee' in the 1960s, and had reached number one in 1972 with 'My Ding-A-Ling'. Other tracks, like 'Johnny B Goode', 'Sweet Little 16' and 'Rock and Roll Music', had been released for the American market.

Frank Boswall remembers the night Chuck Berry played at West Runton Pavilion:

We paid £6,500 for 40 minutes. We were told if we wanted him to play longer we'd have to give him more money. In the end, he didn't want to come off stage. Ticket sales were a bit low because the ticket price had to be high. We got about 450 people in, we needed over 1,000. I spent a lot of money on television advertising the week before he came. He only played there once; I couldn't afford him again!

The *Eastern Daily Press* of 2 June 1980 carried a review of the concert:

Rock superstar Chuck Berry, on stage at West Runton Pavilion Saturday evening, told the audience he liked it in Norfolk so he performed for almost an hour longer than arranged. Members of the band appearing with him – the Red Lightning Boogie Band – were all from either Norwich or Ipswich. John Green from North Walsham is their manager.

Carol Bishop got in free because her boyfriend, Jamie, knew John Green. Carol says after the concert she saw Chuck Berry sitting in his Cadillac outside and she was able to get his autograph just before he left. It was on a scrap of paper that she or Jamie had in their pocket. She kept it safely in her old autograph book. The Red Lightning Boogie Band, which had originally been called Zorro, supported Chuck Berry on his tour.

Former Zorro guitarist Terry Bunting explains:

When Chuck Berry came over to England to tour he often didn't bring a band with him, he used to pick up a band to play. Basically, I don't know how this came about – it must have been through management – my old band, Zorro, became Chuck Berry's backing band and were picked up to play on the tour. I didn't really know the rest of the band, except Galen (David Littlewood) and Alan Fish, because it had changed so much.

As well as Alan on bass and Galen on keyboards, the Red Lightning Boogie Band included Paul Stevens (guitar) and an Australian on drums who Alan simply remembers as being called 'Hoppy'.

Brenda Walker and David Howell both remember that Chuck Berry fired the keyboard player on stage. David says it was because he was playing too loudly.

Kevin Norton remembers that bouncer Cookie (John Cook) hit it off with Chuck Berry:

He actually introduced Chuck Berry on stage. Cookie went on wearing a beret to one side and said he was going to do an impression. Everyone was expecting Frank Spencer, then he took the beret off and threw it into the crowd as he announced, 'Ladies and gentlemen, Chuck Berry…!'

Cookie also got on well with Suzi Quatro's husband and guitarist Len Tuckey. Julie Bunting (was Jarvis) remembers that Suzi Quatro and Cookie once went round Julie's future husband's house for coffee. Julie is quite short and says that Cookie would often put her on his shoulders during the concerts so she could see the bands.

He was good friends with Raymond Froggatt and with Lemmy Kilmister from Motorhead. When Motorhead came to Runton, Cookie used to spend a lot of time with Lemmy, drinking and playing on the fruit machines. Chris Taylor says she once saw Cookie in the pub in Marsham having a drink with Lemmy. Cookie died of a heart attack on Good Friday 1991 aged 41. It is rumoured that both Raymond Froggatt and Lemmy attended his funeral.

Ray Burton, Frank Boswall's secretary, says the back room of the Village Inn was known as the 'beach bar', where children could go when it was raining. It was connected by a door to the Pavilion. She and Frank played pool in the beach bar

against Lemmy and his drummer, Phil Taylor, after one of Motorhead's gigs.
Rob Aherne was another of Lemmy's opponents on the pool table. Rob says,
'I spent five minutes asking Lemmy about which numbers he would be playing,
before finding that he was deaf in that ear and hadn't heard a word!'

Lemmy's deafness isn't surprising if one takes into account Chris Wise's review,
in the *Eastern Evening News*, of Motorhead when they played at West Runton in
March 1981. In addition to Lemmy and Phil Taylor, Motorhead's line-up at the
time also included guitarist Eddie Clarke, nick-named 'Fast Eddie'. Drummer
Phil was fondly known as 'Philthy Animal'!

*The noise is deafening, the heat is suffocating but still the band ask if the music is loud
enough. The packed audience at West Runton Pavilion say 'no' and after a few adjustments
the next number is even more ear piercing. Despite the humidity, leather jackets are kept on
as heads shake, hair flows and fists are clenched. Yes, those maestros of heavy metal mayhem
Motorhead were back in town with a vengeance last Friday.*

*Lemmy, Fast Eddie and Phil make up for what they lack in finesse with sheer
unadulterated noise – and the head-bangers love them for it. The first number 'Ace of
Spades' sets a fast and furious pace which is to last for the next one-and-a-half hours. To
my untrained heavy metal ear every number sounds the same but the audience – some of
whom had been queuing most of the afternoon to get in – aren't complaining as hits such
as 'Bomber', 'Leaving Here' and the aptly-entitled 'Overkill' are peeled off. Lemmy sounds
like he's singing through gravel half the time but his voice fits in well with Fast Eddie's manic
guitar work and Phil's thudding drum beat – Motorhead hit you hard, there's no doubt about
that. They're good at what they do and lack the ridiculous posturing that so many heavy
groups seem to adopt these days. And although you have to go through a physical pain
barrier to get through their set – I'm sure the band must be half deaf by now – Motorhead
offer good, honest entertainment, and that's that. Ask the packed audience who paid £5 a
head to go and see them.*

Kevin White saw Motorhead at West Runton. He says:

*Three of us hitch-hiked from Fakenham on the Friday afternoon (and I guess one of our
parents came and picked us up). We got to the pub outside the venue and who was there but
Lemmy – just hanging out normally (although he was too much of an icon for us to approach
him). The concert was awesome and deafening.*

Julie Mason was persuaded by her friend, Dawn Taylor, to go to one of the
Motorhead gigs at Runton. Julie says, 'This glam rock fan was in for a shock when
she arrived to see girls severely outnumbered by long-haired male rockers wearing
leather jackets with sleeveless denim jackets over them.'

Jackie Punchard was in a similar situation when her boyfriend, Mick Cross-

Gower, took her out on a date. She laughs:

I only went to West Runton Pavilion once. Mick took me to see Motorhead. I thought I was the bee's knees in my leather jacket and jeans, a real rocker, and we stood right up at the front. But I was worried about drugs, and all these blokes with long hair. When the band came on, everyone started to sway and I got really frightened. We had to move to the back and Mick was so annoyed he never took me there again.

He did marry her, though!

Motorhead had embarked on their 'Bomber' tour in late 1979 supported by Saxon. Then, in March 1980, they came to West Runton Pavilion for what was advertised as, 'The only gig in the country. A one-off by our old friends, for a very special reason – come and find out why.' Alan Hooker says the band recorded a four-track live 12 inch EP there that night, and both he and Duncan Sutton have copies, although it does not say on it where it was recorded. The tracks are 'Leaving Here', 'Stone Dead Forever', 'Dead Men Tell No Tales', and 'Too Late Too Late.'

Owner Frank Boswall has an explanation for why the EP might have been recorded at West Runton Pavilion:

I remember when Lemmy was being interviewed by David Hamilton once on the wireless and he asked him, of all the venues, which was his favourite. Lemmy said, 'Absolutely no argument, West Runton Pavilion, it's got to be tops.' He was a very nice man.

The night Motorhead recorded the EP, local band Subway supported them. Subway comprised Ricky Masters (lead guitar), Kevin Rudrum (keyboards), Peter Smith (bass/vocals/12 string) and Andy Mickleborough (drums).

Martin Bean saw Motorhead at West Runton in 1980. He says:

It was a cold day and we queued up for two hours or so. Two or three of our crowd would run back to the cars every now and then to warm up. I remember I lit a cigarette and my mates all put their hands around the lighter as if to warm their hands on the flame. I was sitting in one of the cars when a Mark 4 Ford Cortina (green, I think) drove into the car park and Lemmy, Eddie and Phil casually got out and went into the Pavilion. I remember thinking how there was no fuss, no big entrance – it was like they were 'the Peoples' Band'.

When we got in, we bought programmes and while wandering about we bumped into 'Fast Eddie' and he autographed our programmes. We asked Eddie if, when Motorhead got on stage, he could say 'NOR' for us ('NOR' was our catch-phrase/buzzword at the time). He said he'd try, but he didn't get to use the mic much and he could ask Lemmy but he'd probably be too stoned to remember. We saw 'Philthy Animal' Taylor and he autographed our programmes. Then my mate (Llama) and I went looking for Lemmy. We found him in

204

a little back room playing on the pinball machine. My mate Llama was a friendly, quiet, polite lad, and I remember him approaching Lemmy and saying something along the lines of, 'Hello Lemmy, mate. When you go on stage could you do us a favour, please?' Lemmy answered, 'Yeah – what's that mate?' Llama then replied, in his polite voice, 'Could you say "NOR" for us please?'

Lemmy's response was something like, 'OK mate – NOAH.' So Llama replied, 'No, no not Noah, that's NOR, N-O-R.'

Lemmy said he'd see what he could do, and we left him to his pinball.

When Motorhead came on stage, Eddie was right, Lemmy must have been too stoned to remember, so Fast Eddie went straight up to Lemmy's mic and said, 'This is NOR' (or maybe, 'This is the NOR') and we all cheered accordingly. The funny thing was that I didn't actually hear what he said, but cheered anyway as all my mates did, and then said, 'What did he just say?'

Another Motorhead fan, nick-named 'Age', stayed behind after one of their Runton gigs and was talking at the bar with Lemmy. He got Lemmy's autograph and told him he would like to get 'Fast Eddie' and 'Philthy's' as well, but Lemmy didn't know where they were. Suddenly, there was an altercation near the stage. Apparently, the venue had meant to be providing a number of staff to supplement Motorhead's road crew, but only one chap had turned up. 'Philthy Animal' was annoyed that the roadies had insufficient help and, venting his anger on the one helper they did have, 'Philthy' had punched him and knocked him out cold. Lemmy turned to 'Age' and said something like, 'Oh look, he's over there, you can get his autograph now.' 'Age' was, understandably, a bit dubious about approaching 'Philthy', having just watched him flatten one of the staff!

Girlschool had supported Motorhead on their 'Overkill' tour, with West Runton the first date on the tour in March 1979. The *Eastern Evening News* in January 1979 had stated that Girlschool were 'Rated by music critics as the top all girl band in the UK.' Later that year, Girlschool headlined at the venue and returned in 1980 and 1981.

John Bowen went to one of their later concerts:

Got to be honest about this one, we only went because they were a heavy metal band and I think Tygers of Pan Tang were supporting. This was right in the middle of the New Wave of British Heavy Metal era. It was good to see two UK bands starting out. Tygers were good but Girlschool, I'm afraid, were very average at best, and I am being generous about my verdict because they were only young themselves.

The Tygers of Pan Tang appeared at West Runton Pavilion several times, both supporting and headlining, with various line-ups. Terry Bunting remembers,

'Once the Tygers played without a bass player.' On one occasion they were supported by local band Shock Treatment and they appeared at the venue twice with Magnum.

Shock Treatment comprised Mike Carr (vocals), Lloyd Evans (lead guitar), Nick Ward (rhythm guitar), Doug Raymond (bass) and Dave Alden (drums). In an *Eastern Evening News* review of one of Shock Treatment's gigs at Cromwells nightclub in Norwich, Colin Cross wrote, 'A gutsy sound was predominant throughout the set.' They played rock and blues covers as well as the original numbers 'Fire' and 'Flaming Hell'. Terry Bunting describes Shock Treatment as, 'A good local heavy rock band in the AC/DC mould.'

Magnum were frequent visitors to Runton. John Bowen wasn't a fan but went along to see Magnum anyway:

They had been around for some time. I was not that keen on them but my mate, Martin, was. He had decided that before we went he wanted 'MAGNUM' stitched on the back of his denim jacket, but his mum only had time to do the first two letters. Off we went, Martin in his 'MA' jacket, and I thought it was an OK gig. Martin loved it. Magnum were one of those bands you had a feeling would never really make it big. There were other bands who did the same thing, but much better.

Magnum supported Def Leppard at the venue in February 1980 then, following the release of their third album, Marauder, returned to West Runton the following month with the Tygers of Pan Tang supporting them. In a reversal of fortunes, the Tygers were supported by Magnum at the venue in 1981.

Other members of the 'New Wave of British Heavy Metal' genre who played at Runton included Witchfynde, Gaskin, Bastille and Trespass, the latter of whom came from Suffolk. Terry Bunting says that Trespass used to get on the *Friday Rock Show* quite a bit but never really hit the big time. The *Friday Rock Show* was a late-night radio programme hosted by Tommy Vance. Several compilation albums were released show-casing the bands who had featured on the programme.

Another series of albums was released under the *Metal for Muthas* title, with bands touring under the same heading. Saxon, who had just completed the UK tour with Motorhead, came to West Runton in February 1980 as part of one of the 'Metal for Muthas' tours. Saxon had formed in 1979 with Peter 'Biff' Byford (vocals), Paul Quinn (guitar), Steve Dawson (bass), Graham Oliver (guitar), and Pete Gill (drums). After their self-titled first album and their second, now-classic, *Wheels of Steel*, Saxon were starting to get noticed. Their support band, too, were gaining recognition, although they were not even advertised when they came to West Runton with Saxon on the 'Metal for Muthas' tour. Despite this, they were soon headlining their own tour – with two further visits to Runton in 1980 – and playing at the Reading Festival that summer as special guests of UFO. The band were Iron Maiden and John Bowen was there to see them at one of their headline gigs:

This was perhaps the biggest night out at West Runton Pavilion. At the time Maiden had come out of the New Wave of British Heavy Metal and left all the others behind in terms of record sales etc.

I have never seen the Pavilion so packed as it was this night; it seemed like the whole of Norfolk was in there. Once you found your spot near the front you would not dare leave it to go to the bar or the gents because you would lose it instantly and never get back in.

The following might be an unpleasant account of what happened but just goes to show what sort of place it was and also what the crowd were like. Since it was so tight in there that night, before Maiden came on some guys were so scared of losing their spot on the floor if they went to the gents they just urinated where they stood, in fact aiming for their own trainers so as not to splash the person in front of them.

As for the band, this was a classic night of heavy metal, total head-banging, not just the first few front rows but the whole place was jumping.

Afterwards, you had to spare a thought for the venue's cleaners (if they had any!). The floor was awash with spilt beer and urine. What a night! You didn't have to be a massive Maiden fan to really enjoy this night, but they would have won over many people on this showing.

Iron Maiden were a four-piece at this time with Dave Murray (guitar), Paul Di'Anno (vocals), Steve Harris (bass) and Dougie Samson (drums). They released their self-titled debut album in February 1980 with their first single 'Running Free'. They appeared on *Top of the Pops* which they insisted on doing live, contrary to most bands who mimed to a recording of their latest song.

Their album got to number four in April and they released their second single, 'Sanctuary', in May. The picture sleeve was designed by Derek Riggs, as was all their subsequent artwork, and controversially featured the character 'Eddie' – the band's terrifying humanoid mascot – with the British Prime Minister of the time, Margaret Thatcher, lying dead at his feet clutching an Iron Maiden poster she had just ripped off the wall.

Martin Bean saw the band in action:

My favourite gig at West Runton (and possibly my best gig ever) was Iron Maiden in June 1980. They just had their first album out and me and a mate from Norwich College (Rat) and John Bowen got right down the front and had a brilliant night. There's not much more to say about that night; nothing special happened, apart from Iron Maiden playing a brilliant set.

Local band the Angels supported Iron Maiden when they returned to West Runton in August and Chris Taylor recalls a story about them:

The bass guitarist in the Angels, Jamie, became friendly with the bass player in Maiden and he used to send Jamie his old bass strings even when they were playing abroad. Iron Maiden only used their strings once, but they would be OK for other bands who were glad of the help.

The association between the two bands lasted some time and, in a turn of fortune, Iron Maiden, having built on their success, were able to secure the Angels a slot at the Reading Festival two years after they themselves had been helped to get on the bill by a more established act.

Jamie Durant, the Angels' bass player, had played at the Links in the mid-seventies with local band the Hunter. The Angels also included Paul Rhodes (lead guitar), Ozzie Coulson (rhythm guitar), Neil Westgate (drums) and Richard Hill (vocals). Ozzie used a rhythm guitar shaped like an axe.

Jamie spoke to the *Eastern Evening News* in August 1982, just before the Angels' appearance at the three-day Reading festival in front of thousands of rock fans, and explained how the Iron Maiden connection had begun. He said, 'We first got to meet them when we supported them at West Runton. We went back to the hotel and had a few drinks, and really hit it off well.'

The article reported that the Angels thought they were the first Norfolk band to ever appear at the Reading Festival.

London DJ Neal Kay appeared at West Runton Pavilion with Iron Maiden and Praying Mantis in June 1980 and Tony Walsh observes, 'DJ Neal Kay was a big fan and promoter of the New Wave of British Heavy Metal. I even got a pound note autographed by him, long since spent!'

Neal Kay was involved in the *Metal for Muthas* releases, which included other bands who frequented the Runton stage such as Sledgehammer, Chevy, Trespass and Samson.

Alan Hooker remembers that controversial Samson drummer 'Thunderstick' (Barry Graham) used to play his drums on stage in a cage, whilst wearing a rapist mask. The band also included Paul Samson (guitar), Chris Aylmer (bass) and vocalist Bruce Dickinson, who later joined Iron Maiden. Samson supported Uriah Heep at West Runton in November 1980 and the *Eastern Evening News* carried a review of the concert:

Uriah Heep, perhaps one of the top five rock bands of the late sixties and now enjoying a revival through the current heavy metal craze, kicked off a nationwide tour with a Guy Fawkes' night concert at the Pavilion.

They brought along two of the up-and-coming rock bands of the moment, Spider and Samson, to make it a three-and-a-half hour, head-banging extravaganza.

Spider were the first on stage and the four Liverpudlians made up for a slick lack of ability and inventiveness with a show of great energy and determination.

Samson produced a much more original set and tracks such as the mean-beated 'Vice Versa', fronted by their forceful vocalist, should make them one of the big rock bands of the future.

But it was Uriah Heep the leather-clad audience had come to see and from the moment they burst on stage, with a firework display of their own, they produced a brand of music above the 90 mph stuff that had gone before.

Uriah Heep were said to have been very loud, and another loud band had returned to the venue that summer. They were Hawkwind, although they had undergone several line-up changes since their last visit in 1977. Nik Turner, saxophonist and vocalist with the original Hawkwind, came to West Runton Pavilion in October 1980 with his new band Inner City Limit.

Hawkwind had just recorded their new album *Levitation* which was one of the first albums to be recorded using digital instead of analogue equipment, and featured the legendary Ginger Baker on drums. Mark Holmes, who was guitarist with the support band, Alverna Gunn, recalls the difficulties Hawkwind had getting their sound right at Runton for the 1980 gig:

We all stood around watching the band set up, each member in turn sound-checking his equipment. When it got to the keyboard player, he decided he would sound-check for the next hour, giving us no time whatsoever to get our gear on stage. At this point our gear was still in the van because we weren't allowed to bring it in until they finished setting up.

By this time the venue doors had opened and the very large crowd outside had started to filter in. We thought we weren't playing, then eventually the stage manager said for us to get our gear in. I will always remember every single piece of our gear being transported by the crowd overhead onto the stage. What a reception we got! It was awesome, and we went down a storm. It was a great moment.

Alverna Gunn came from Lowestoft and, along with Mark Holmes, lined-up with Keith Thacker (vocals/acoustic guitar), Paul Hale (percussion) and Steve Gamble (bass).

Mark says:

We played mainly our own material with a smattering of Budgie covers thrown in. We were big Budgie fans at the time and managed to get support gigs with them which was a dream. Being a local band on the up, we used to telephone West Runton Pavilion every week for a support slot and fortunately we managed to get a few. I wish I could remember every single gig, as they were all great moments for us.

In December there was a concert at Runton to showcase local bands and four were advertised: Wildlife, Alverna Gunn, Angels and Winner. Unfortunately, Winner did not play, as John Lawson, their bass player, explains:

As we were fourth on the bill, we had to set our gear up last, and with three drum kits and all the other bands' equipment already on stage, we didn't have room for our Hammond organ. We were told we could play on the dance floor at the front of the stage, but we felt we would look like an after-thought, so we decided not to do it. We did stay for the gig though.

John had answered an advert in the *Eastern Daily Press* for a bass player for a band. After an audition with Harry Collins (guitar), Kenny Philpot (keyboards) and Nigel Widdowson (drums), he was offered the job. Harry and Kenny had played together in the early seventies with local band Spencer's People and performed many times with them at Cromer Links. Their new group needed to invest considerably in PA equipment etc, with each member making a financial contribution. John had just finished University and had no money, so he answered another advert and took a bass job which required no financial commitment. About a year later he was contacted by the first band again, and asked to join on a different (non-financial) basis, which he accepted. Owen Savory ('Sos') was recruited to play drums and the line-up for Winner was complete. Nigel Widdowson went on to play drums for Toyah.

Winner's first gig had been in 1979 at the Ark Royal pub in Wells. They regularly played at Fakenham Community Centre and other venues throughout Norfolk and Suffolk. They won a 'Battle of the Bands' competition which was held at the Vauxhall Caravan Park; the prize was two days at Family Tree Recording Studios in Caister. After the first day, doing rough demos of two original songs, they had to wait a couple of months before their second day was booked, at which they planned to produce final recordings. Unfortunately, the recording studio went bankrupt and they were unable to have their second day.

Winner were due to support the Beat with Sam Apple Pie on 5 April 1980 at West Runton Pavilion but, because the Beat were heavily involved in promotional work for their new single, B A Robertson was booked instead. Unfortunately, he brought his own support band, the Film Stars, so Winner's support slot was postponed to the following month when the Vapors headlined. Their single 'Turning Japanese' had just been in the charts.

Winner's set was extremely well received and an added bonus was the support they had from the Vapors' road crew. During a number early in the set, Winner's guitarist, Harry, broke a guitar string. The Vapors' roadie rushed on stage and handed him a Gibson SG, one of his band's spare guitars. Harry played with the loaned guitar and, when the song had finished, the roadie came on and handed him back his Telecaster, which he had restrung for him.

210

Alan Hooker remembers that when B A Robertson came, on the date of Winner's original booking, he sang an old number which the crowd enjoyed. Alan says that B A commented afterwards, 'It's good to know that the music hall is alive and well in a shed in West Runton!' B A Robertson's hits included 'She Knocked It Off' and 'Bang Bang'.

The date B A Robertson appeared, 5 April 1980, was the first night of West Runton Music Club. Tickets stated: 'Please note that admission to this concert is only open to members of the West Runton Music Club. Please fill in your application form which can be obtained from the usual ticket outlets.' These outlets were Topdeck, Norwich; Robins Records, Norwich; Treble Clef, Fakenham; Holt Record Shop; Bayes Recordium, Kings Lynn; and Downham Market Record Shop.

The reason for the membership requirement was that owner Frank Boswall had been having trouble renewing his licence. The *Eastern Daily Press* of 22 February 1980 reported that Cromer licensing justices had refused to renew the music, singing and dancing licence for the Pavilion 'due to complaints from village people over vandalism in the Churchyard and in the grounds of Runton Hill School.' Frank appealed against the decision and on 18 April it was reported a fresh licence had been granted for six months. The music had to stop at 11.30pm, there were to be no paying customers admitted after 10.00pm, and the capacity was reduced from 1,040 to 800.

Frank was in a difficult position. At the same time he was trying to obtain planning permission to demolish the Pavilion and replace it with flats. A public meeting held in February 1980 had, according to the *Eastern Daily Press*, 'agreed overwhelmingly the Pavilion should go,' but the public and the Parish Council were unhappy with the proposal for the design and number of flats.

However, a more positive article in the newspaper the previous week had reported on two successful concerts at the Pavilion:

Hundreds of rock fans swarmed to West Runton this weekend. On Friday the Pretenders were on stage – they have recently topped the singles chart – and on Saturday it was Rockpile. The crowds were well-behaved, car parking in the village was the only problem.

The Pretenders had been to Runton a couple of times before, but when they appeared in February 1980 their single 'Brass in Pocket' had just been number one in the UK singles chart and they were also number one in the album chart. Frank Boswall says:

They had been booked before they were famous but they honoured their contract and appeared. They came with UB40 supporting them. It was for a record company promotion

211

because they wanted to get UB40 on the map. It was a tremendous sell-out that night.

Chris Wise, reporting later in the *Eastern Daily Press*, recalled that he 'had seen an unknown reggae band support the Pretenders and get called back for two encores. They were UB40 but at the time, no-one had heard of them.'

The association between the two bands lasted because, years later, American Chrissie Hynde, lead singer with the Pretenders, recorded two singles with UB40: 'I Got You Babe' in 1985 and 'Breakfast in Bed' in 1988.

The other members of the Pretenders were Martin Chambers (drums), Jim Honeyman-Scott (guitar) and Pete Farndon (bass). Pete and Jim both died of drug-related causes in 1982.

Colin Woodyard remembers, 'When the Pretenders and UB40 played the crowd were queued past the Church.'

Bouncer Kevin Norton laughs, 'When the Pretenders played, about 80 people got in through the fire doors. There must have been a good thousand people in there that night.'

UB40 returned later that year as the headlining act, having had two UK top 20 singles during the summer: 'King'/'Food for Thought' and 'My Way of Thinking'/ 'I Think It's Going to Rain'. Both were double A-sided releases, which meant either side would be played on the radio or would feature on *Top of the Pops*.

Colin Woodyard was at West Runton Pavilion to see guitarist Dave Edmunds and bassist Nick Lowe in Rockpile, the night after the Pretenders gig. Nick Lowe was outside the venue and Colin remembers, 'My brother said "Look, there's old Nick," and Nick replied, "Less of the old!" We got his autograph and Dave Edmunds' as well.'

Dave Edmunds had reached number one as a solo artist in 1970 with 'I Hear You Knockin" and had a more recent hit in 1979 with 'Queen of Hearts'. Nick Lowe had recently released two singles, 'Cruel to be Kind' in 1979 and 'I Love the Sound of Breaking Glass' in 1978. The band also included Terry Williams on drums and Billy Bremner on guitar. Kevin Norton enjoyed the evening and says, 'We had a big piss-up in Dave Edmunds' massive coach!'

Guitarist and vocalist Elvis Costello had had hits with 'I Can't Stand Up For Falling Down', 'Oliver's Army' and 'Watchin' the Detectives'. He came to West Runton Pavilion in March 1980 with his backing band the Attractions, comprising Steve Nieve (keyboards), Bruce Thomas (bass) and Pete Thomas (drums). Pete had played drums with a popular 'pub rock' band, Chilli Willi and the Red Hot Peppers, who had played at the Links a couple of times in 1973. The Elvis Costello concert at Runton was a sell-out, as was Adam and the Ants in November. Neil Morrell says, 'Adam and the Ants was absolutely rammed, with even more people outside.'

John Lemon remembers:

212

The queue for Adam and the Ants was over the railway bridge, towards Beeston Regis, three to four hundred yards. People had come from all over the country, and it seemed like all of East Anglia had made a bee-line for the place. They were crammed in and there were still lots outside.

The concert was a memorable event for Kevin White:

In 1980 (aged 16) I attended my first ever concert – Adam and the Ants at West Runton Pavilion. This was just before they hit the big time. They had just released 'Dog Eat Dog' as a single and the Kings of the Wild Frontier LP. My biggest shock was when I was queuing to get in and finding myself totally surrounded by punks in all their Mohawk glory and with the strong smell of hair gel/soap in the air. I have never felt so square (normal) before with my seventies fringe, jumper and anorak. This feeling of being straight was not good and it had a lasting effect on my later image (which was to be pierced ear, spiky hair and ripped jeans.)

Anyway, the concert was incredibly exciting and the fans worshipped Adam Ant. It was standing only with loads of pogo-ing and jostling. However, what I found here – and in subsequent rock and punk concerts – was the (generally) good nature of the crowds; if someone fell down during the dancing, the crowd parted and they were helped up. I never saw any trouble amongst the leather jacket brigade, unlike the atmosphere in some (disco) nightclubs with all the posers.

Vocalist/guitarist Adam Ant, whose real name was Stuart Goddard, was an early exponent of what was to become the new romantic movement. He wore flamboyant, frilled shirts and various costumes including a Red Indian outfit, and later appearing as the 'Dandy Highwayman'. He was at Runton with a new line-up of Terry Lee Miall (drums), Marco Pirroni (guitar/vocals), Merrick (drums) and Kevin Mooney (bass/vocals), after three of his original band had left him to join Bow Wow Wow, who played at West Runton the following month.

Steve Harley and Cockney Rebel came to the venue twice in 1980, and Frank Boswall remembers he was popular as one of the concerts was on a Thursday and the tickets sold out. The band had reached number one in 1975 with 'Make Me Smile (Come Up and See Me)' and, prior to that, had appeared at Cromer Links.

Chris Hare took his camera, as he often did, and photographed Steve Harley's December concert at West Runton Pavilion. Bouncer Ronnie Carroll had his camera there that night as well, and took several photos of the West Runton staff.

One reason Frank gives for the good attendance was the fact that the free buses were still being provided, which would bring in around 200 people. Elaine Morrell (was Frior) used to go to West Runton Pavilion from Briston on the bus. She remembers on one occasion her sister Sharon's boyfriend 'got thumped on the bus for some reason or other on the way back.'

Unfortunately, not every concert was well attended. In May, Gary Glitter and the Glitter Band reunited for a come-back and Colin Woodyard reckons there were only about 200 people there. Since his poor reception at the Links, Gary Glitter had released several successful singles including 'I Love You Love Me Love' and 'I'm the Leader of the Gang (I Am)', which had both reached number one in 1973. Despite the low attendance at West Runton Pavilion, Kelvin Rumsby enjoyed the show and remembers Gary Glitter telling the audience, 'It's good to be back' and asking them, 'Did you miss me?' – which were lines from his songs.

Generation X appeared at the venue twice with lead singer William Broad, alias Billy Idol. The band also included Tony James (bass), Mark Laff (drums) and Bob Andrews (guitar). Their first appearance in 1978 had included 'goth' band the Cure as 'very special guests supporting'. Generation X returned in December 1980 having achieved success in the singles chart with 'King Rocker'. This second gig was poorly attended, but for good reason, as Steve Curtis explains:

I remember travelling up by car, just before Christmas 1980, in a snow blizzard. We arrived quite late due to the weather and I cannot remember seeing any support bands. There must have only been about 50 to 100 people at the gig but Billy Idol gave a tremendous performance that I will never forget.

Steve also saw Adam and the Ants at West Runton, and the Damned. He particularly remembers, 'In July 1980 my friends and I travelled up from Lowestoft to see Stiff Little Fingers.'

Stiff Little Fingers originated from Northern Ireland, taking their name from a track by another punk band, the Vibrators, who had played at West Runton in 1977. Stiff Little Fingers comprised Jake Burns (vocals/guitar), Henry Cluney (guitar), Ali McMordie (bass) and Jim Reilly (drums). Neil Morrell remembers their gig at West Runton and says, 'I had an asthma attack and ended up sitting outside near the t-shirt stall!'

Peter Jay's Stiff Little Fingers story is also connected to clothing:

I travelled to West Runton during the day with some friends and hung around for hours – don't know why, we just did. I was wearing a biker's leather jacket – the sort the Clash or Sid Vicious wore. It had cost a week's wages, £35, and it was top; I thought I looked so cool! We got talking to some girls in the queue and continued to stand with them inside; one in particular was very pretty, I seem to recall. The gig was extremely hot and after a couple of ventures 'up the front' – as the mosh pit used to be called – in extreme heat, I decided to take my jacket off and leave it, very trustingly, with our new-found friends (you can see where this is going!). The gig finished and I returned to our spot feeling elated, only to find the girls gone, along with my bloody jacket. I was devastated, and learnt a harsh lesson.

Another punk band, the Dead Kennedys, came to Runton in October 1980. Neil Morrell has a bootleg recording of the gig which gives the set-list as follows:

The Man With the Dogs
When Ya Get Drafted
Stealing Peoples Mail
Kill the Poor
Funland at the Beach
California Uber Alles
Halloween
Police Truck
Bleed for Me
Too Drunk to F***
Holiday in Cambodia

Formed in California, the Dead Kennedys maintained that their name was not meant to insult President John F Kennedy and his brother Robert, who had both been assassinated in the 1960s, but as a reminder of how the American dream had been destroyed. That autumn at Runton they were promoting their first album *Fresh Fruit for Rotting Vegetables* which reached number 33 in the UK album charts.

There was a low attendance the following week when Simple Minds appeared. Louis Leuw comments:

Simple Minds came, we counted 30 people there, look how big they became. Frank got the bands just before they made the big time, he had the contacts.

The commercial break-through for Scottish band Simple Minds was to come with the release of their fifth studio album, in September 1982, entitled *New Gold Dream (81-82-83-84)*. In addition to singer Jim Kerr, the band included drummer Kenny Hyslop, who had played at West Runon Pavilion twice before with Slik.

The Q-Tips, who came to West Runton Pavilion in August 1980, featured Paul Young, who had been there the previous year with the Street Band. He went on to have solo success later in the decade.

The venue was still attracting chart acts. Odyssey appeared straight after 'Use It Up and Wear It Out' had been number one, and mod band the Lambrettas had had a hit with 'Poison Ivy'. Splodgenessabounds had recently achieved chart success with their comedy double A-sided single 'Simon Templar'/'Two Pints of Lager and a Packet of Crisps Please'.

Colin Woodyard recalls that, when Dennis Waterman released 'I Could be so Good for You', Frank Boswall was going to book him but as the record did so well in the charts, the fee went up and Frank couldn't afford him.

Another big star, Denny Laine, appeared at West Runton Pavilion in August 1980. He had formed the Moody Blues in the 1960s and had played at the Links in 1967 with the Denny Laine String Band. More recently, he had been co-founder of Wings with Paul McCartney and also co-writer for many of their songs. The advert explained that Wings had not broken up:

Denny Laine and Paul McCartney are doing their own ventures for a couple of months. Denny Laine is teaming up with the drummer of Wings, Steve Holly, together with Jojo (Mrs Laine), Andy Richards (Strawbs), Gorden Sellar (Alex Harvey) and Mike Pittot.

Atomic Rooster had an unexpected star with them when they played at West Runton Pavilion in September 1980. Originally formed in 1969, they had played at Cromer Links in 1972. In late 1979, John DuCann (guitar/vocals) reunited with Vincent Crane (organ) to reform Atomic Rooster. They recorded a self-titled album with session drummer Preston Heyman, who couldn't make the subsequent tour so Ginger Baker, the former Cream legend, stepped in.

One gig in September 1980 was cryptically advertised as 'Law'. The advert read:

We are privileged to have a new band called Law. Those of you in the know will know who this is – those of you that don't and want to know phone West Runton 203.

A fantastic night for Metal fans. They couldn't do Reading because Ozz thought they weren't ready. They embark on a massive UK concert hall tour the week after this gig. Be the first in the queue to see in public – Law. Please ring for their real name.

The band was called Blizzard of Ozz, they had a single out called 'Crazy Train' and the lead singer was Ozzy Osbourne, formerly from Black Sabbath.

Terry Bunting says:

Sabbath had fallen away quite a bit and that was the first gig Ozzy had played as a solo artist. He stayed in a hotel in Cromer and a drummer friend of mine ended up playing pool with him at the end of the gig that night.

This was another concert that John Bowen attended:

I was a massive Sabbath fan at the time and had seen them before elsewhere, complete with Ozzy. So, from Great Yarmouth we went off to West Runton Pavilion in a convoy of Cortinas, Vivas and Hillman Avengers to see what promised to be a mighty gig.

I must admit to having mixed feelings about the actual concert. While I was watching a hero of mine, I was not keen on any of Ozzy's recorded music after Sabbath so I suppose I enjoyed the event rather than the music.

The place was rammed to the rafters. Despite the coded advert for the gig, people were not fooled by a slightly misleading band name and had turned up in their hundreds. After encores we waited at the stage door in slight hope Ozzy could be enticed out to meet his adoring fans. Then, the big shock of the night, he came out and chatted happily to those who kept behind. Top man. Here was a guy who has legendary status, who you would have thought would have left town as soon as he stepped off stage, mixing with us like we were all equal.

Martin Bean was there as well:

We got down the front. At one point I touched Randy Rhoads' spotted Flying V guitar. We went backstage to meet the band afterwards. I thought the band were so loud that I couldn't hear the songs properly but, even so, I shook Ozzy's hand and said, 'F★★★ing good gig mate.' He said, 'Thanks,' and gave me his autograph. I remember getting the whole of the band's autographs on the back of my West Runton Music Club membership card.

In October, Frank Boswall was granted a new licence, again to run for six months. However, renewal looked extremely unlikely after the events of 13 December 1980 when Bad Manners, led by the skinhead with the big tongue – Buster Bloodvessel – were set to play, following recent chart success with their singles 'Lip Up Fatty' and 'Special Brew'.

Many observers have named this as the worst night at Runton for trouble. Chris Grief was there and says, 'Bad Manners never got a chance to play. A riot broke out from different groups of people. Tables, chairs etc were thrown and the gig was cancelled.'

Stephen Wakefield remembers a coach-load of National Front supporters were there. He says:

The crowd didn't like the support band [called Shock] and started smashing their gear. Cookie went on stage wielding a baseball bat and there was a lot of blood. I looked in the stream under the nearby bridge and saw a policeman's helmet floating by!

John Lemon also mentioned coach-loads of National Front supporters, who he believes came from London. He says every coach window in the car park was smashed. Inside the venue things were no better:

The bouncers were knocking people out. Cookie was at the top of the stage steps, hitting rioters one at a time as they came up, and two bouncers were picking them up by their belts and collars and throwing them past the glass-washing machine near the bar where I worked. The police were on the balcony, on their walkie-talkies, watching and letting the bouncers sort it out.

Pud (Patrick Robinson), one of the bouncers, remembers, 'They put poor old Cookie's head down the toilet and pulled the chain that night.'

Barman Dick Woodley worked at the Pavilion for around 10 years and left just before the last gig. He says, 'The only time I put the shutters down was when there was the massive fight at the Bad Manners gig. I wasn't being paid danger money!'

Steve Little, who lived nearby, had gone to the gig, and can remember 'hiding up', wondering when it would be safe to 'leg it home'.

Another resident, Wendy Lemon, lived nearby but says she didn't know anything about it all until the next morning, despite the police presence and the attendance by several ambulances.

The *Eastern Daily Press* of 15 December 1980 carried a report on the incident headlined, 'Fans rampage, four arrested.' The piece stated that police had attended from all over North Norfolk and that Bad Manners had barricaded themselves into the dressing room as a precaution. The report continued:

The management turned 500-600 people out of the Pavilion just before 9.00pm, some threw stones and bricks, a coach was stoned and fans were injured. However, by 10.00pm the trouble was over and people were just standing around waiting for lifts home.

Mike Jervis, who used to live in the village, expresses the view held by many residents, 'It seemed to them like Frank Boswall wanted to get the flats built and he was putting on every reprobate band he could!'

18

Mayhem And Madness

The first band to appear at West Runton Pavilion in 1981 were the Look on 17 January. They had just appeared on *Top of the Pops* with their single 'I Am the Beat'. At the end of the month Toyah made her third visit to the venue. The concert was reviewed by Colin Wilson in the *Eastern Evening News* on 2 February 1981:

The diminutive Toyah Willcox took the stage at West Runton on Saturday night with her newly formed band. The only original member is guitarist Joel Bogen, now joined by Phil Spalding (bass), Adrian Lee (keyboards) and Nick Glotker (drums).

As for all the publicity about Toyah's 'new' band – well I couldn't see much of a difference in sound.

The group, backed by a very colourful lightshow, opened with some of their earlier material, outstanding songs being 'Indecision' and 'Our Movie'.

The physical energy you come to associate with Toyah Willcox was there coming to a forefront with the single 'Danced', which, combined with the lightshow, resulted in a very visual performance.

The older numbers were executed with efficiency and these still remain the most powerful songs. They moved on to play tracks from the album The Blue Meaning *before ending with the singles 'Tribal Look' and 'Victims of the Riddle'.*

A mention of support band Huang Chung, who, for no apparent reason, played only three songs.

Huang Chung (Chinese for 'perfect pitch') later changed the spelling of their name to Wang Chung and had a massive hit with 'Dance Hall Days', perhaps inspired by West Runton Pavilion!

On 14 February 1981 Motorhead and Girlschool released the *St Valentine's Day Massacre EP* as a joint venture, containing the tracks 'Please Don't Touch', 'Emergency' and 'Bomber'. They appeared on *Top of the Pops* as 'Headgirl' with Denise Dufort from Girlschool playing drums because Motorhead's 'Philthy Animal' Taylor had broken his neck. As he recovered, Motorhead appeared at West Runton the following month during the aptly named 'Short Sharp Pain in the Neck' tour.

Motorhead were recording material for their live album *No Sleep 'Til Hammersmith*, although none of the gigs were in London. They played at West Runton on 27 March, Leeds on the 28th, and on the 29th and 30th they were in Newcastle. In his autobiography *White Line Fever*, Lemmy writes that they chose songs from the last three shows because they were the best, so presumably the West Runton recordings did not make it to the finished album.

Motorhead were supported on this short tour by Tank, who had been formed in 1980 by Algy Ward, former bass player with the Damned. Tank had also supported Girlschool and Angel Witch in November 1980 at West Runton Pavilion, and would headline at the venue in 1982. Algy was joined by Mark Brabbs (drums) and Pete Brabbs (guitar/vocals). Meanwhile, his former band, the Damned, acquired bassist/vocalist Paul Gray from the band Eddie and the Hot Rods. Together with Dave Vanian (vocals), Rat Scabies (drums) and Captain Sensible (guitar) they played two further gigs at West Runton Pavilion in 1980 and 1981. In 1980 they had been supported by Straps and East Anglian band the Adicts, who returned to the venue twice in 1981. Terry Bunting remembers:

The Adicts dressed as 'droogs' from A Clockwork Orange [a book by Anthony Burgess, subsequently made into a film by Stanley Kubrick]. The Adicts were bubbling under, had a bit of money behind them. 'Geordie' was the father of one of the band and was their manager. He ran this youth club in Ipswich. My band did a gig there one night as part of a British tour. They let us sleep in the bar, which was a stupid thing to do. Geordie came running in about 8 o'clock the next morning in a track suit and said, 'Who wants to go for a jog?' and he slid on a trail of sick. We got banned from every youth club in the country for that.

Glass-collector John Lemon had saved enough money to buy himself a camera, and took it along to several of the Runton gigs in February and March 1981. He photographed Matchbox in action on their latest visit, following an appearance in December 1979 when they had just had chart success with their single 'Rockabilly Rebel'. 'Midnight Dynamos' and 'When You Ask About Love' had been hits in 1980.

John also photographed the UK Subs, the Stranglers, Odyssey and Gordon Giltrap, who was making his second visit to the venue. John Bowen went to see him:

All I knew about the guy was that he was an accomplished guitarist who did 'Heartsong' which at that time was the theme music to the BBC holiday programme. I was at a stage in my life that I would go to nearly any rock gig I could, so off we went again to West Runton Pavilion. Once there it became clear that this gig was not going to be a classic night out, as the music was technically fine but dull and our little crowd from Yarmouth were about the only people there.

Martin Bean was there with John and remembers:

There weren't many people there and Gordon Giltrap commented on what a 'romantic' lot the audience looked in our leather jackets and heavy metal t-shirts.

'Heartsong' had been released in 1978 but had just failed to make the top 20 in the UK singles charts.
Richard Fryer reviewed the gig for the *Eastern Evening News* on 21 February 1981:

Many talented progressive and classical rock musicians tend to receive little or no attention from the media. One such act, the Gordon Giltrap Band, played at West Runton Pavilion on Saturday.

With a line-up of Giltrap (acoustic and electric guitars), Bimbo Ackock (flute / sax / keyboards), Rod Edwards (keyboards) and ex-Jethro Tull drummer Clive Bunker, they began the set with a lively, beautiful instrumental entitled 'Roots / Magpie Rag'.

'Black Rose' followed, a sentimental, melodic piece of music that featured some excellent guitar work from Mr Giltrap.

Melody seems to be the keyword in his musical dictionary. This was certainly the case on 'For the Four Winds', a haunting melody played on 12 string guitar.

A stage and recorded favourite soon followed in the form of the enchanting 'Heartsong'. The crowd loved it. 'Night Rider' completed the set, a raunchier composition that came over exceptionally well, but would have sounded fuller if they had a bass player.

Richard used to write music reviews for the *Eastern Evening News* and the *Eastern Daily Press*. He lived in Norwich and mainly reviewed gigs there but occasionally he visited West Runton as well. He says, 'I mostly went to punk/new wave/jazz gigs in Norwich but prog rock gigs in West Runton, as my friends who were into that style of music had cars, but the ones who were into punk did not.'
Another gig at Runton which Richard reviewed for the *Eastern Evening News* was Renaissance in October 1981:

After a long break Renaissance returned to play West Runton on Saturday. They have retained their distinctive melodic sound yet they seem to be much more powerful nowadays Annie Haslam's voice is still one of the most enthralling in rock music, and the musicians are all very talented.

The new compositions sounded promising, so the new LP should be enjoyable. An excellent set – welcome back Renaissance.

The Stranglers played at the venue in March and lined up with Dave Greenfield (keyboards/vocals), Jet Black (drums/percussion), Hugh Cornwell (guitar/vocals) and Jean-Jacques Burnel (bass/vocals). They had achieved success in the singles charts at the height of the punk rock boom of the late seventies, with numbers such as 'No More Heroes' and the double A-side 'Peaches'/'Go Buddy Go'. They still attracted punk rock fans who carried on the tradition of spitting at the band. Unfortunately, the Stranglers were not keen on this particular display of affection. Matt Howchin remembers people were jumping and spitting and the band asked everybody to stop.

Bouncer Geoff Peck recalls:

When the Stranglers played, JJ Burnel got fed up with a bloke who kept spitting at him so he jumped off the stage, nearly knocking someone out with his guitar. There was a scuffle and the band carried on playing while JJ set about this guy in the crowd.

Stranglers fan John Lawson kept a press cutting from the *Eastern Daily Press* the day after the gig, headlined 'Rock star in Norfolk gig row':

Notorious rock group the Stranglers walked into more controversy at West Runton Pavilion last night.

According to eye-witnesses, Jean-Jacques Burnel, the group's bass guitarist, leapt from the stage and chased a member of the audience from the Pavilion during the concert.

Mr Kevin Piper said: 'The group were annoyed at people spitting at them. Half-way through a number, Burnel suddenly stopped playing and gestured to a youth to go on stage for a fight. Then he just put his bass down, jumped into the crowd and ran after this youth. The lead guitarist, Hugh Cornwell, cooled the situation by cracking jokes with the audience.'

Mr Frank Boswall, owner of West Runton Pavilion, said yesterday's incident was 'nothing at all'. He said he did not see Burnel leave the stage, although a youth did run to the back of the Pavilion when the bass player gestured at him.

The police said they knew nothing about the incident. Although police were out in force at the concert they were not needed, said a spokesman.

The culprit, Nigel Greenstreet, gives his version of events:

He spat at me, I spat back. He chased me out. He didn't hit me and I came back. This is my one claim to fame and people keep telling me about it!

Nigel played the whole incident down and says he didn't even know it had been in the newspaper.

Chris Hare met JJ Burnel years later and asked if he remembered playing in

North Norfolk. Chris reveals, 'JJ said he remembered the Runton gig well, he had chased someone out who kept persistently spitting on him!'

Nigel says he was about 15 when he went and saw his first band, the Members, and it carried on from there. His mate, Matt Howchin, who was with him at the notorious Stranglers gig, used to go and see all the punk bands at Runton and described it as a 'fantastic place'.

There was trouble, according to bouncer Louis Leuw, at one of the Theatre of Hate appearances as well. He says, 'There were lots of police about for that one.' In October 1981 they were supported by King Pleasure, advertised as 'ex Shock'. It may be a coincidence, but Shock had been supporting Bad Manners the previous year when rioting had occurred. Theatre of Hate were a gothic post-punk band formed by singer Kirk Brandon.

John Lemon has several photographs of the Au Pairs playing at West Runton Pavilion at the end of February 1981, although the gig was not advertised. The band consisted of Lesley Woods (vocals/guitar) Jane Munro (bass), Pete Hammond (drums) and Paul Foad (guitar/vocals).

The Undertones, with lead singer Feargal Sharkey, appeared in May, having had a hit the previous year with the single 'My Perfect Cousin'. They had released several other singles which had hovered outside the top 20 including 'Jimmy, Jimmy', 'Teenage Kicks' and 'Here Comes the Summer'.

The New Wave of British Heavy Metal continued to be represented with Diamond Head and Silverwing appearing in June. Alan Hooker says that 'Silverwing wore crazy outfits, like American rock band Kiss, but came from Macclesfield!'

In July, heavy rock band More appeared as the live attraction on the Sounds Atomic Road Show, organised by *Sounds* music magazine. The show included films of AC/DC, Foreigner and Blackfoot, with competitions and free t-shirts.

Later in the year 'Heavy Metal DJ Demons' the Bailey Brothers came to the venue with their twin turntables in a coffin.

Most nights during the summer featured a disco, including Saturdays, but on 18 August 1981 'Soft White Underbelly' were advertised to appear. This was another cryptic clue, since Soft White Underbelly was the original name under which American band Blue Oyster Cult had first performed.

There were obviously plenty of people who were in on the secret because West Runton Pavilion was packed.

Frank Boswall says:

Blue Oyster Cult came over for a record promotion and to appear at a festival. They told a friend of mine, from Cowbell promotions, that they wanted to play one gig before that. Everybody that knew turned up, and it was a sell-out.

Alan Hooker recalls that the band were very big in the States at the time. He says:

They had just done the 'Day on the Green' gig at San Francisco, supporting Heart, when a lot of the audience had left before the main act came on. They played Runton as a warm-up for the Monsters of Rock Festival at Donington. Fans were climbing in the windows at Runton trying to see the band and the place was packed. People were jammed in right up against the back walls.

Joe Barber remembers:

There were three bands on that night including Quartz. When I saw and listened to Blue Oyster Cult it was like standing in a hurricane – they had a harmonic sound but they were trying it out for a big festival and it blew straight through you. It sounded better when you went to the toilet with a wall in between.

Terry Bunting says that Golden Earring were the first band he had seen with quadraphonic sound, when they had appeared at Cromer Links, and the only other one he'd seen round here were Blue Oyster Cult at Runton. He describes the Blue Oyster Cult gig:

They did a song called 'Godzilla', about a giant lizard, obviously. The singer goes into this big spiel about how the dinosaur lizard was awoken from its slumber in the ice after the Americans did an atom bomb test. He goes, 'I can hear something, it sounds pretty big, it's coming this way,' and because it was quadraphonic, behind you were these giant footsteps. They had all the stroboscopes on the band with all the coloured lights, then it all went dark on stage and this drum solo was going on. When the lights came up again the stroboscopes were on and the drummer was wearing a lizard's head. It was very well done.

They were absolutely brilliant. There were massive cheers and applause after every song; everybody was really into it. It was a fabulous night.

It was not without its problems, however, as Terry explains:

The band came over to England for this very short tour where they were going to play Runton and Donington. The drummer had allegedly fallen in love with a girl and instead of travelling with the rest of the band, he had hired a car and was driving around with her. He didn't turn up for this gig, so the lighting engineer played drums.

The manager came on and explained. He said, 'The drummer hasn't turned up but we're going to go ahead with the lighting guy.' So this little man got up on the drums and we all thought, oh God, here we go; but he was brilliant. He knew all the songs because he'd been their lighting man for so long. Half-way through, the drummer turned up and played the second half of the set, and he was even better! There was a lot about it in the music press at the time. Some time after this they threw the drummer out of the band and the lighting engineer became their new drummer.

The line-up was Eric Bloom (vocals/guitar), Buck Dharma (guitar/vocals), Allen Lanier (keyboards/guitar), Rick Downey (drums for the first five songs), Albert Bouchard (drums for the remainder of the set) and Joe Bouchard (bass). Buck Dharma was the stage name chosen by Donald Roeser.

The set-list was as follows:

Dr Music
ETI
Heavy Metal
Joan Crawford
Burnin' For You
7 Screaming Diz-Busters
Last Days of May
Me 262
Hot Rails to Hell
Godzilla
Born to be Wild
Cities on Flame
(Don't Fear) The Reaper
Roadhouse Blues

Steve Green says, 'I attended many excellent gigs at the Pavilion in the late seventies and early eighties – most memorable being Ozzy's Blizzard of Ozz and Blue Oyster Cult.'
Steve Andrews was impressed with Blue Oyster Cult. He says:

I was there and what a gig. I had only got into Blue Oyster Cult about a year before with a copy of Tyranny I swapped with a mate and nearly wore up.

We couldn't believe it when we were eagerly scanning Runton's gig list and there was Soft White Underbelly. The year before we had seen Ozzy with what I believe was his first Blizzard of Ozz date, and now a chance to see Blue Oyster Cult; well, I still get a buzz from it today.

I was 15 and mad about bands and gigs. I went to school at Wroxham, just a short

225

train journey away from the Pavilion. School-day gigs were great; we all used to tell our parents that our mate's dad was taking us to the gig, and arrange for one of them to pick us up. Then we would bunk off for the day, get the train from Wroxham station, and head to the Village Inn at West Runton to get into the spirit of things. This usually was followed by a good pratting about on the beach, then making sure of staking a claim to the position at the head of the queue, and digging in for the door opening.

Sometimes we even helped out with humping some gear for the bands. I regret never taking a camera, but I think the combination of everything being drunk and smoked – leading to many dubious situations – I doubt any camera would have survived.

Saying all that, I can't remember how I got to the Blue Oyster Cult gig, but we were at the head of the queue with all senses intact – I wasn't going miss out on this one.

From what I can remember, the songs were all full or extended versions and I wasn't disappointed with the selection that they played.

I remember getting a couple of Buck's personalised plectrums – very impressive – which I very much regret I have lost and, if my memory serves me well, a can of Breaker lager that Eric had drunk from. This last item is also not in my possession – I'm not that sad yet – but I do still have one of the drumsticks Albert launched into the crowd, I think during 'Godzilla'. I always remember the story about it being one of his last gigs.

I have a memory, rightly or wrongly, of Buck playing a solo and finishing with breaking, one by one, the strings on his guitar as he finished, or did I imagine it?

We were at the front all the way through the gig and to say it was awesome is an understatement.

The *Eastern Evening News* of 24 August 1981 carried a review:

… American giants Blue Oyster Cult played a two-hour gig. This concert, from one of the States' biggest bands of the moment, must rate as a major coup for organisers at West Runton, especially as the 700-strong audience loved every minute and decibel of the concert.

Simon Goodyear says, 'I helped load two artics for Blue Oyster Cult with my mates, we got £10-£15 each. It was a horrendous gig because it was so loud.'

The following week's newspapers carried another cryptic advert for a concert featuring 'Loch Ness Monster' ('Loch' was deliberately underlined in the advert) and punters were again invited to telephone the venue for clues. However, the gig was cancelled before the mysterious band could make their appearance.

As well as regularly advertising in the local newspapers, Frank Boswall would often place adverts for West Runton Pavilion in the national music press, in publications such as *Sounds* and *New Musical Express*.

After the summer, bands were again regularly booked for Saturday nights and occasionally on Fridays. The first of these, Bow Wow Wow, were advertised as, 'Heading up the charts again.' In January 1980 Dave Barbe (drums), Leigh Gorman (bass) and Matthew Ashman (guitar/vocals) had left Adam and the Ants after seeking advice from former Sex Pistols' manager, Malcolm McLaren. A friend of McLaren's overheard Myant Myant Aye, a 14 year old immigrant from Burma, singing to the radio in a London dry-cleaners where she worked. He told her about the new band which was being formed and she joined, changing her name to Annabella Lwin.

The band called themselves Bow Wow Wow and produced songs full of tribal rhythms. Their first single 'C30, C60, C90, Go' was only released on cassette at first but public pressure meant a more usual vinyl format was issued a short time later. They had appeared at Runton at the end of 1980 and on their return in 1981 were supported by the Higsons.

Neil Dyer was a member of Norwich band Screen Three who had supported Bow Wow Wow elsewhere in the country. He travelled to the gig with the Higsons and sat in the pub with both bands before watching the concert, when he took photographs of the bands on stage.

The Higsons had formed in Norwich the previous year with Charlie Higson ('Switch') (lead vocals/harmonica/piano), Terry Edwards (guitar/trumpet/saxophone/piano/vocals), Simon Charterton (drums/vocals), Stuart McGeachin (guitar/vocals) and Colin Williams (bass/vocals). They did several Radio One sessions for John Peel and released a single called 'I Don't Want to Live With Monkeys'. The group disbanded in 1986 and Charlie Higson later found fame as a comedy writer and actor in TV's *The Fast Show*.

Echo and the Bunnymen came to West Runton at the end of September 1981 and Chris Wise was at the gig, reporting for the *Eastern Evening News*:

Technically brilliant their music may be but their moody sound is by no means immediately accessible – definitely a band to listen to on vinyl before seeing live, I feel.

Highlight of their hour-plus set was 'Rescue', for me one of the best singles never to have made the charts. Even a complete stranger to the Bunnymen sound would have appreciated Friday's superb rendition, with vocalist Ian McCulloch and guitarist Will Sergeant in fine form.

Not surprisingly their new album was given a good airing with 'A Promise' and 'All I Want' the pick of the seven selections.

Ian McCulloch and Will Sergeant had made demo records using a drum machine which they are said to have named 'Echo'. They recruited bass player Les Pattinson for their debut single and, having replaced the machine for a human drummer – Peter de Freitas – they recorded their first album, *Crocodiles*, in 1980. *Heaven Up Here,* their second album, had been released in May 1981.

Nazareth came to West Runton Pavilion at the end of October and, according to Terry Bunting, it was a disappointing night. He says, 'That gig was a bit sad; they seemed a bit old. Well, not old compared to me now, they were probably about 38!'

Scottish band Nazareth had played at the Links in February 1972, and their success in the UK singles chart – including top 10 hits 'Bad Bad Boy' and 'Broken Down Angel' – had been the following year. Although they continued to release singles and albums – their twelfth album was out at the beginning of 1981 – their success in the UK was limited by the fixation with punk rock. However, the band were still popular in Europe, America and Canada. The original four-piece line-up of Manny Charlton (guitar), Pete Agnew (bass), Dan McCafferty (vocals) and Darrell Sweet (drums) was augmented during the tour when they came to Runton by Billy Rankin (guitar) and John Locke (keyboards).

In April quirky band the Spizzles had appeared, following success with their single 'Where's Captain Kirk?' in 1979 under their name that year of Spizzenergi. In 1980 they had been known as Athletico Spizz 80. As the Spizzles, they were supported at West Runton Pavilion in 1981 by Department S, whose single 'Is Vic There?' had just been released.

Ten Pole Tudor appeared later in the year, having had a hit in May with 'Swords of a Thousand Men'.

'Lay Your Love on Me' and 'Some Girls' were recent hits for pop band Racey, who also played at the venue in 1981.

Throughout the summer, ska band Madness were advertised to appear but this initially failed to materialise, with several cancelled dates. They were originally booked for Monday 29 and Tuesday 30 June, with tickets selling at a special price of £3.50 in advance, by arrangement with the band. This was postponed to Wednesday 15 and Thursday 16 July, but this was once again cancelled. After that it was announced the band intended to make it good to all fans with tickets by issuing refunds and 'a parcel of goodies'. Fans were urged in an advert in the *Eastern Daily Press* to 'return your ticket from whence it came'.

On 4 September it was announced, 'People still holding Madness tickets need not necessarily return them as they will be valid on the night of their new date, Thursday 29 October 1981.' Thankfully this time the concert went ahead.

Bob James drove a piano tuner who used to tune pianos for the bands. His nine year old son had a game of football inside West Runton Pavilion with Suggs from Madness while their piano was being tuned.

The actual concert was memorable for Colin Woodyard who says:

When Madness played, all of them except the drummer got off stage and danced round the hall, still playing all their instruments, saxophones etc, and singing. I was really shocked, because I was sitting at the bar. I looked up at the stage and there was no-one there. The music was still going on but the band were walking past me!

Madness had had success in the singles charts with a string of hits including 'Baggy Trousers', 'One Step Beyond', 'Embarrassment', and their current release 'Shut Up'. They lined up with Suggs McPherson (vocals), Mark Bedford (bass), Mike Barson (keyboards), Chris Foreman (guitar), Lee Thompson (saxophone), Dan Woodgate (drums) and Chas Smash (vocals/trumpet).

Not surprisingly, after the Madness debacle with advance tickets, from 25 September 1981 it was announced that all concerts would be pay on the door because, as Frank Boswall says, 'There was a feeling that if you bought tickets in advance, you ran the chance of the band not turning up.'

Despite this, however, fans were still disappointed by the cancellation of concerts and the non-appearance of some bands. Nine Below Zero, Rose Tattoo, and the Lightning Raiders all cancelled their advertised shows and Stray failed to turn up in October 1981. Fortunately, John Bowen did not waste too much petrol that night. He says, 'Stray were a very influential band to many but never got much recognition. My car broke down on the way so I got no further than Stalham.'

One band who were always reliable were Slade. They had appeared at both Cromer Links and West Runton Pavilion several times. They had released 'Merry Xmas Everybody' back in 1973 when it had reached number one. It is one of the great festive rock songs which is played every Christmas and has often been re-released. There is a popular and often-quoted belief that Slade played at West Runton Pavilion on Christmas Eve. There is no record of this, however, and the nearest they got to it was in 1981 when they played on 3 December. They were supported by Spider, who Alan Hooker describes as 'like Status Quo'. His friend Alvin Flowerday has kept his ticket from that night, on the back of which is written 'burgers 55p' and 'hot dogs 35p'. The ticket cost £3.50.

Music fan Terry Bunting explains that Slade were undergoing a revival because of their appearance at the Reading Festival in 1980. They had got on the bill at the last minute when Ozzy Osborne had pulled out. Terry says, 'Slade turned up at Reading in an old Ford car and no-one would believe who they were.' However, when they hit the Reading stage there was no doubt, as Terry continues:

They blew the place to pieces because they always were a great rock band. They cut their teeth playing the clubs, that's why they were so good. Bands like that won't go away. Nowadays a band will get together, do two or three gigs, submit a CD and become big stars, then they fall to pieces and you never hear of them again. But bands like Slade actually made their name by constant touring, like Thin Lizzy and Status Quo did. That's why they still stick at it, because that's all they know.

Slade had followed their Reading appearance in 1980 with a visit to West Runton in the Autumn. The *Eastern Evening News* carried a review of the concert:

Things seemed strangely unchanged when Slade took the stage at West Runton Pavilion on Friday. All right, their music and their fans have matured somewhat since the early days and their lighting certainly seems more impressive. But the music is still loud, the rhythm is still strong and the atmosphere is just as electric.

The new set contains a lot of well-executed new material, but the fans who go to watch are much happier when their heroes are playing old stuff – and I think the group is happier then as well.

After a lean period in the singles chart, Slade had returned to the top 10 early in 1981 with 'We'll Bring the House Down', and their festive appearance at West Runton Pavilion at the end of the year was extremely well received.

Terry Bunting says:

Slade were absolutely fantastic – what a gig! Full house, I'll never forget it. They did about four encores. At the end of the gig they went off stage and it was all in darkness. You could hear Noddy's voice going, 'What do you want to hear? What do you want?' Because it was December, everyone's shouting, 'Merry Christmas Everybody!' The lights come on, Noddy's dressed up as Santa Claus. He says, 'Thank f*** for that, it's just taken me 10 minutes to get all this lot on.' They were brilliant. Jimmy Lea, the bass player, could play the fiddle and he did two fiddle tunes. He was dancing, running along the top of the amps with this fiddle, playing these jigs. They were absolutely stunning. When they finished, the noise from the crowd was incredible. That one's in my top 10 gigs of all time.

Martin Bean says:

Slade came on and did a brilliant set. At the end they did 'Merry Christmas Everybody' and we were all at the back so we got on to chairs to see the band. My mate Yog's chair collapsed – maybe he was on it with someone else – so he jumped onto my chair and that collapsed, so we got on other people's chairs and they collapsed because they were unable to take the weight of more than one person. We must have (unintentionally) broken eight or so chairs.

At one of Slade's earlier appearances, bouncer Danny Hagen remembers:

I played pool with Noddy Holder in the pub after one of their gigs, playing for £20 or £30. We were both pissed. Noddy played with the wrong end of the cue, and he still beat me! When I left Runton I spent two or three months driving a truck for Slade around France, Holland and Germany.

Danny had left in the Pavilion 1979 after an altercation with the manager. John Mason remembers:

A new manager was soon to learn, the hard way, that he did not possess the necessary skills for motivating a very volatile staff. He was knocked to the floor by Danny, who found it hard to take orders when they were shouted at him. I feel, had I taken the management job when it had been offered to me earlier, I might have used a more subtle approach. I remember the manager sliding along the floor. He got up and went and found Frank Boswall. Danny was sacked on the spot.

Danny was later asked to return. He says:

I knew all the police in the area and when Frank was having trouble renewing his licence, because there had been a lot of trouble and complaints, the chief officer came and saw me and said Frank would only get his licence if I went back to work there. So Frank let me back, but I didn't stay very long that time.

When the licence had been up for renewal at the beginning of 1981, the policy and resources committee of North Norfolk District Council had recommended opposing it, in support of the Parish Council, but a large majority of District Councillors voted not to oppose. The Parish Council had said the internal running was quite good but they objected to what took place afterwards outside.

Music fan John Bowen has some sympathy with the villagers:

I remember coming out of the car park and onto the main road. This road went right through West Runton which, from what I can gather, was a nice tranquil coastal village. Then, at various nights at about eleven o'clock, several hundred long-haired yobs spilled out onto the street, with many urinating up these lovely garden walls. The residents must have loved it when it closed down.

Unfortunately, Cromer residents were not spared either, and John was one of the culprits:

We were young and a bit stupid at the time, and we used to love driving around shouting out of the car window at pedestrians — nothing too abusive. Reactions ranged from them taking it all in good spirit and laughing, to giving us various hand signals and threatening to kill us if we stopped at red traffic lights. Since we had to drive through Cromer to get to West Runton Pavilion we always found a few 'victims' there.

West Runton resident Wendy Lemon remembers on one occasion she was walking her dog when the train came in from Norwich full of people bound for West Runton Pavilion. It was obviously a punk night, because the music fans had Mohican style hair dyed in various bright colours, but as they walked over the bridge towards her, she says they all smiled politely and walked quietly past.

John Lemon says:

Lots of the villagers coped well although a few complained a lot. The elderly residents, who had been through the War, got used to tending the Pavilion casualties who were lying around in the mornings on the pavements and in gardens. They would ring the ambulance if they were concerned about someone who was in the hedge. Miss Bridgewater had been a Queen Alexander's nurse during the war. She would walk up to the bodies and prod them with her walking stick. If they showed signs of life, she would move onto the next one.

On 24 December 1981, the *North Norfolk News* reported that North Norfolk District Council's planning committee had approved plans to develop the 'controversial' West Runton Pavilion site. The article continued:

The committee gave the go-ahead to plans to demolish the Pavilion – one of Norfolk's leading pop music centres – and build 34 flats. However, the owner, Frank Boswall, who has been trying to develop the site for eight years, is not sure now if he wants to go ahead because he says that the scheme is only just viable.

Although many of the residents didn't want the Pavilion, they didn't want a large number of flats either. While Frank debated whether it would be worth developing the site with a fewer number of flats, he would continue to try and make the best use of the building by offering a new type of entertainment.

19

The Other One Bites The Dust

1982 got off to a quiet start at West Runton Pavilion and the first act of the year, Freddie 'Fingers' Lee, did not appear until 9 January. Sad Café were on stage later that month, playing their 1979 hit 'Every Day Hurts'. There were no advertised concerts for a further month until the Tygers of Pan Tang returned at the end of February, with rock and roll favourites Crazy Cavan the following week.

Theatre of Hate came in early March. Their single 'Do You Believe in the West World' had topped the alternative chart. Magnum returned to West Runton Pavilion the following night and Alan Hooker laughs:

Each time they played there they kept talking about their Chase the Dragon *LP. They had been talking about it for two years and much of the material from it formed part of their live set-list.*

Chase the Dragon, Magnum's fourth album, was finally released around the time of their 1982 visit to Norfolk, and peaked at number 17 in the album charts. The band formed in Birmingham in 1976 and released their first album *Kingdom of Madness* in 1978. They toured regularly with big names such as Blue Oyster Cult and Whitesnake, and had made previous appearances at West Runton with Def Leppard and the Tygers of Pan Tang. The line-up of Bob Catley (vocals), Tony Clarkin (guitar), Colin 'Wally' Lowe (bass) and Kex Gorin (drums) had been supplemented by the addition of Mark Stanway on keyboards.

The *Eastern Evening News* looked forward to Magnum's concert:

Magnum, who spice their heavy metal with a more subtle 'pomp rock' sound, are on stage at West Runton Pavilion on Saturday.

In adopting a less rigid approach to heavy metal than many of their less subtle contemporaries, Magnum have emerged as a band with both wit and sophistication – as well as maintaining the more basic elements of hard, driving rock.

John Bowen paid another visit to the venue mid-March when King Crimson appeared:

I was the owner of every King Crimson LP. The music was incredible. I was heavily into prog rock. When they played songs like 'Red', 'Larks Tongue in Aspic' and the magnificent 'Court of the Crimson King', few bands could come anywhere close to equalling them. On the other hand, some of their songs leant a little bit too near to jazz for me but, all the same, I loved this band and still do today.

I came home from work one Friday and picked up the Yarmouth Mercury *to see if any good bands were on that weekend at West Runton Pavilion, and there it was, playing that night, King Crimson. Nothing else mattered then; I was straight in my car and bombing up to North Norfolk as quick as I could. This was going to be one of the greatest concerts of my life.*

This was a different King Crimson to their earlier LPs; gone were the half-hour mellotron solos and nonsensical lyrics which I loved, replaced by a stripped down band featuring Bill Bruford on drums, a bald guy who played a bass guitar which looked like a floorboard with strings on it [Tony Levin], an ex-member of Talking Heads on guitar and vocals [Adrian Belew], and the legendary Robert Fripp on lead guitar. I always thought Mr Fripp was a God and here he was in front of me, sitting on a stool playing. I was mesmerised from start to finish. I thought that if I were never to see another band, then at least I have seen King Crimson.

The New Romantic band Classix Nouveaux appeared at West Runton Pavilion in April, just as their single 'Is it a Dream' was entering the UK top 20. The band had been formed by Sal Solo and Mike Sweeny, with ex-members of punk band X-Ray Spex: BP Hurding and Jak Airport.

The New Wave of British Heavy Metal was well represented with return visits for Tank, Angel Witch and Vardis, featuring lead singer/guitarist Steve Zodiac.

Bryan Durham was pleased to see his favourites Wishbone Ash play at the venue in May, lining up with Andy Powell (lead guitar/vocals), Steve Upton (drums), Laurie Wisefield (guitar/vocals) and Trevor Bolder (bass/vocals). Formed in 1969, they were pioneers of the 'twin-guitar' sound. Trevor Bolder had just joined the band from Uriah Heep, following the departure from Wishbone Ash of founder member, bassist and lead singer Martin Turner.

Unfortunately, however, things were not looking good for West Runton Pavilion. The week before the appearance of Wishbone Ash, veteran band Camel had received a low attendance which meant that owner, Frank Boswall, had lost £1,000 that night. It was not the first time this had happened. Doorman John Mason remembers that the takings would sometimes not be enough to cover the cost of the band, and Frank would dip into his own pocket to pay them. Bouncer Ronnie Carroll remembers, 'One night Frank told me he'd lost enough money that one night to buy a bungalow! I can't remember who the band were, but it was a lot of money.'

There was competition from elsewhere, too. In April 1982 the University of East Anglia (UEA) had advertised gigs featuring Blackfoot, the Boomtown Rats, Altered Images, and Kid Creole and the Coconuts. Music fans who had previously travelled from Norwich to West Runton were now able to see bands closer to home.

Following a month's break, it was announced that reggae band Talisman would play at the last ever concert at West Runton Pavilion on 19 June 1982. Chris Wise reported on the situation in the *Eastern Daily Press*:

Frank Boswall has said enough is enough after four-and-a-half years of losing money. At the beginning it was a successful money-making venture, but as the years went by it began to change. Frank Boswall explained: 'In the old days people used to just come and see a pop band, but nowadays the music business has become too fragmented. People want to see a heavy band, or a futurist band, or a reggae band, so you're only ever appealing to say 12 per cent of the music listening public.'

Situated 20 miles from Norwich, the cost of petrol and public transport have added to the difficulties, especially with the recent success story at the UEA.

After the weekend the venue will be turned over to roller-skating. Frank Boswall said it is 'more in line with what the community wants'.

Terry Bunting says:

I remember Frank Boswall being interviewed about what happened, about the bands, and he said the reason why he stopped wasn't really a business decision as such but was because people weren't supporting it. He said, 'People aren't supporting it any more, I guess the kids would rather have a roller disco,' and that's why he did it.

Bouncer Kevin Norton volunteered to work Wednesday nights and Sunday dinner times when the roller-skating was on to earn a bit of extra money.

Julie Mason says:

When Sunday roller discos became the only entertainment on offer at Runton, we went a couple of times, but it seemed the atmosphere was different and many people regretted that the thrill of popular live bands in our little corner of North Norfolk had been lost forever.

For Elaine Morrell (was Frior), the pain was very real:

I used to go to the roller discos with my friend Gina Eke. Afterwards, we would go for a drink at the Village Inn. Unfortunately, one day I broke my kneecap on one of the concrete pillars when skating as part of a chain. I still managed to drive home, then spent several weeks in plaster!

The Pavilion opened its doors again in July 1982 for the mid-week Sheringham Carnival Dance with local band Denim. They had formed around 1979 and first used to play at the Marsham Plough on Sundays nights. The original band comprised Ady Spinks (lead vocals), Arthur Watts (bass), Nigel Moy (rhythm guitar), Jimmy Pye (lead guitar) and Trevor Hewitt (drums). Trevor was later replaced by Martin Richmond, who was subsequently replaced by Paul Dack. They played a variety of seventies music from Supertramp to heavy rock, including Smokie and the Eagles.

Arthur Watts thinks they supported the Four Tops when the Motown favourites returned to West Runton Pavilion in March 1982. Tickets were advertised as 'only £4 advance for UB40 holders' [unemployed]. 'Reach Out I'll Be There' had been a UK number one hit for the Four Tops in October 1966.

Ady Spinks and Jimmy Pye both used to go to West Runton Pavilion to watch the bands. Denim was Jimmy's first band and they progressed to be semi-professional. He remembers sitting in the dressing room, waiting to go on stage:

I looked at all the graffiti on the walls – the Cure, Siouxsie and the Banshees etc – all the famous people had scribbled on the walls. It was an eerie feeling to walk out onto the stage; I couldn't help feeling what a shame it was all going to be knocked down.

You can understand, though, how difficult it must have been to get bands to come to Norfolk when they were on tour. Norfolk was a difficult place to get into, with its single lane roads.

Stewart Meakin, of Sheringham and Cromer Round Table, organised a fund-raising concert in aid of the charity Spinal Research. It was part of an appeal by Round Table UK, which overall raised £60,000 to help the recently-formed charity. The West Runton event was held on Saturday 28 August 1982 and featured Marty Wilde and the Wild Cats, with support provided by Fourmost.

The new venture of roller-skating combined with a disco continued with moderate support. Then, in March 1983, it was announced that heavy metal band Magnum had been booked to play on 20 May, supported by Stanters; and Motorhead would appear on 1 July, supported by Anvil. It was stated that a proper stage would have to be built, presumably because the old one had been dismantled to provide more room for the skating.

For both concerts the doors opened at 7.00pm, the support band was on stage at 8.00pm and the main band played from 9.15pm.

Earlier in the year, guitarist 'Fast Eddie' Clarke had left Motorhead and been replaced by Brian Robertson from Thin Lizzy. Motorhead released their new album, *Another Perfect Day* and embarked on what they named 'Another Perfect Tour', appearing at the UEA the month before they came to West Runton.

Martin Bean says:

The 1983 Motorhead gig at Runton was more low-key than the 1980 one. I seem to remember that there was no beer on tap, just cans, so we were drinking Swan lager all night. Six of us went and decided to camp at the camp-site about quarter-of-a-mile from the Pavilion so we could all drink as no-one had to go home that night. One of our crowd, a girl called Janice, had taken some antihistamines that night for hay fever and, after a few beers, was crawling along on the floor, in a drunken state, collecting ring pulls from beer cans to make me a necklace.

We didn't really see much of the band, but I remember Lemmy had a bottle thrown at him and he said something like, 'You think you're clever throwing stuff at me when I can't see you, but if anyone saw who it was, give him a smack in the face from me.'

Magnum were booked to return later in the year, but the concert was cancelled. The following week, on Saturday 17 December 1983, Hanoi Rocks played at what was to be the last ever live music gig at West Runton Pavilion. They were supported by local band Saigon. Hanoi Rocks originated from Finland, but had recently relocated to London. They achieved great overseas success, particularly in Japan.

Saigon lined up with vocalist Mark Newman (who had previously been with Zorro), Gerald Brown (bass), Ian Gosling (guitar), Ricky Masters (guitar) and Paul Youngs (drums).

Christmas Eve and New Year's Eve discos were being advertised initially, but nearer the time they seemed to have been cancelled.

Ray Spinks, who had attended ballroom dances there in the early years, summarises the changes which had taken place:

The big-name groups were used to playing to huge audiences in much larger venues and obviously became out of the range of a small Norfolk hall. By this time the wheel had turned full circle and my teenage son had spent many a happy Saturday night watching his favourite heavy metal group at West Runton Pavilion. Then the fateful announcement came: the venue would be playing its last gigs, much to the consternation of my daughter, who had been told she could go to the Pavilion when she was 16. This day was rapidly approaching, but the final concert was held before her birthday. However, my wife and I relented and allowed her to go. She need not have bothered as there were a number of 'final' concerts before the curtain at last came down.

On 4 January 1984 the *Eastern Daily Press* carried a report on the forthcoming closure of the venue:

West Runton Pavilion, which has been a popular nightspot for young people for nearly 40 years, closes its doors for good next week. Over the years many people visited the Pavilion for concerts, discos and more recently roller-skating. Planning permission was given three years ago and it will be demolished at the end of the month and 44 flats will be built.

The last roller-skating evening was on Saturday 7 January and the last disco was held on Wednesday 11 January 1984.

Demolition did not happen quite as soon as expected, however, and the building stood empty for the next three years, suffering some vandalism and the inevitable graffiti.

Then, one day in February 1987, Kelvin Rumsby was driving through West Runton on his way home from work and saw smoke rising from the site of the Pavilion. He pulled over to take a look and saw that the building was being dismantled. Fortunately, he had his cine camera in the car and, together with John Lemon, who lived nearby, they recorded a nostalgic trip around the derelict building.

John recalls that the stage door had hundreds of signatures on it.

The *North Norfolk News* of Friday 27 February 1987 included an article confirming that the Pavilion had finally gone. It was headlined, 'Glory days come and go at West Runton Pavilion.' The report continued:

West Runton Pavilion's era as one of Norfolk's top music venues is now just a memory. The building has been demolished and there are plans to build flats with car parking spaces on the site.

Ray Spinks comments on its demise:

It was the end of an institution which had enabled thousands of young and not-so-young people to enjoy fabulous nights out in what otherwise would have been an area devoid of the music which contributed so much to their growing up, and which is still enjoyed avidly by so many of them.

20

Long Live The Memories

The flats were eventually built on the site of West Runton Pavilion and Ray Spinks comments:

It is very appropriate that the name of a group which, like the Pavilion, lasted for many years, is remembered in the name of Slade Court – a block of flats built on the very ground where the illustrious building once stood.

Steve Ayers, who says he spent many a night in the back of a mini-van sleeping off the effects of Breakers and Colt 45s, suggests, 'Maybe we could get a big PA together and get Slade back to the old Runton site (Slade Court, as it's called now) and wake up the neighbours!'

It is thought that a piece of the building lives on, as Bernie Galasky says that part of the West Runton dance floor was removed and placed in a barn conversion in Thornage, and Simon Goodyear thinks another part is in a barn conversion at Felmingham.

Mark Holmes, who was guitarist with Suffolk band Alverna Gunn, says, 'I'll never know why they shut down such a great venue, the likes of which we'll probably never see again.'

Carol Bishop remarks, 'It was a shame when Runton went.'

John Bowen says, 'I will always think that West Runton Pavilion was part of my growing up, as it spanned the years from school to my early twenties.'

Colin Woodyard has fond memories of Runton. He says, 'The place was usually packed and there was a very friendly atmosphere.' He met a lot of the bands and they would often recognise him on later visits and come and his shake hand.

Martin Bean agrees that the venue had, 'A really good atmosphere.'

As well as meeting his idol Andy Partridge from XTC at West Runton, Malcolm Birtwell says:

I met quite a few famous people there: Chrissie Hynde, Toyah, Dave Stewart and Annie Lennox, Siouxsie, but I guess I am most proud of my John Peel autograph as he brought me so much musical pleasure when I was tucked up in bed on school nights, listening to the punk/new wave band sessions on his late night show. I met him at the Pavilion when he came to see Stiff Little Fingers. He and West Runton Pavilion gave me many happy times and made an indelible mark on my life. I loved the Pavilion and was very sad to see it go.

Like many couples, Andrew Turner and his future wife, Charlotte, met at West Runton Pavilion. She says, 'We used to have such great times there.'

In the *Eastern Daily Press,* Chris Wise described West Runton Pavilion as, 'One of the country's most unlikely venues,' and his colleague, Simon Dunford, wrote that it was, 'the unlikeliest rock venue in the world, perched between the boozer and the sea.'

In July 2004, Simon Dunford interviewed Frank Boswall for the *Eastern Daily Press* and explained why bands used to come to Runton:

The venue was unusually large, yet far from the London limelight. This meant successful bands could perform, try out new ideas, and have a lot of fun, safe in the knowledge that the music press reviewers and record company bosses would not be watching. West Runton Pavilion became a notorious warm-up gig at the start of a tour or prior to a big London date.

First night shows at the venue fitted in with bands going north to play in Leicester, Sheffield or Newcastle.

Michael Wear believes it was, 'The greatest venue ever – a small village attracting ground-breaking bands.'

John Mason, bingo caller and doorman at West Runton Pavilion during the seventies, says:

It was a great experience and I met lots of people, including many stars of the day. Little did I know when I started that the next decade was to stay in my memory for the rest of my life, and over 25 years later I meet colleagues and punters and we immediately find common ground talking about the Pavilion.

As with the West Runton Pavilion site, the area in Cromer where the Royal Links Pavilion once stood now contains housing. The development was not without controversy, however, and the *North Norfolk News* of 4 August 1979 reported on a meeting of Cromer Town Council which had described the chalet development as a 'tragedy'. They felt the buildings had broken the skyline and spoiled a beauty spot but, as the newspaper pointed out, back in July 1978 the Town Council had supported the plan believing it would be an improvement on the existing caravan site. At the time the Council were reported as being 'pleased that Cromer was not getting another Links Pavilion'.

Unfortunately, this now means, as David Pegg ('Gaffer') points out, 'There is

nothing for kids now in Cromer.'
Sandra Fishwick (was Bailey) says:

We still go to gigs but East Anglia no longer has a decent rock venue. We find we have to go to London or Birmingham, unless the UEA gets someone of note we want to see, which isn't often. We listen to Planet Rock and occasionally a forgotten band comes on, like Atomic Rooster, and I'll say, 'I saw them at the Links.'

Phil Dunning agrees, 'I have seen some good acts at the UEA, but it ain't Cromer Links.'

Musician Terry Bunting says of the two venues, 'It's a shame they don't have anything like them now. The amount of talent that was on those stages is ridiculous.'

Despite the absence of the buildings, there are often references to the venues in the local newspapers, and the *Eastern Daily Press* and the *North Norfolk News* have both carried articles about them in recent years.

The interest is not confined to the local press. Kevin Plume recalls seeing in *Sounds* magazine an ariel photo of the huge crowd watching the Who on stage at Wembley. The caption read, 'Just another night at West Runton Pavilion.'

Q Magazine, in September 1996, carried a nostalgic feature on legendary music venues entitled 'West Runton, you were great' – over 12 years after it had closed.

There are often phone-ins on local radio stations including Radio Norfolk and North Norfolk Radio when the venues and the many stars that played there are discussed.

In the summer of 2004 the *Eastern Daily Press*, in conjunction with Norwich School of Art and Design, awarded blue plaques in memory of the bands who had played at the two venues. The West Runton plaque was placed on the wall of the Village Inn pub, which is still a thriving part of the community. It was unveiled by Steve Baker, head of leisure and community services at North Norfolk District Council, who revealed he had spent many happy nights in both places. The Links plaque was accepted by Denise Bussey and Lyn Mayes, employees of Cromer Country Club, where the plaque is displayed. The Country Club stands on part of the site of the old Royal Links Hotel, the reception area being formed from a small fragment of the ruins of the old hotel.

The Links plaque reads:

The Sex Pistols played their penultimate British gig to a capacity crowd of fans and police at the Links Pavilion that stood near this site, Christmas Eve 1977.

On Saturday 15 October 2005, a Reunion was held at the Lighthouse Inn, Walcott, which is run by former Links glass-collector and later manager, Bully (Steve Bullimore). Music was provided by another Links regular, Dave McNeir, with his Moods Disco, featuring records by bands who had played at the venues. Over 200 people attended the event and many brought along photographs, old tickets, flyers and records. The wall displayed a list containing the names of over 1,200 bands who had appeared at Cromer Links Pavilion between 1964 and 1977 and at West Runton Pavilion between 1973 and 1983.

The main former owners of the two venues attended the Reunion. Frank Boswall says he is 'still a budding entrepreneur!' Nigel Blow, who is now known as Nigel Hindley, practices as a chartered structural engineer and his brother, Rod Blow, is involved with a motor racing team touring the Continent.

Many of the local musicians who played at Cromer Links and West Runton Pavilion continue to play in bands appearing in pubs, at summer festivals and occasionally supporting bigger names at venues like the Waterfront in Norwich. Some work as music teachers or can be found in local shops, selling a range of goods from musical instruments to pipe-fittings.

The ex-staff are often still involved with the entertainment industry in some way, running pubs, social clubs and discos, although a number have branched out as driving instructors, timber merchants and plasterers. Unfortunately, there are some who are no longer with us, including Joe Tuck and Cookie (John Cook).

There is no doubt that wherever you go in North Norfolk, there will always be someone there who went to Cromer Links or West Runton Pavilion. From the days of the strict tempo dances, the ballroom and the 'steam bands', through the various music crazes of the sixties, seventies and early eighties, the venues brought a wide variety of people together with a common interest in music. The fondness felt by the youth of the time towards the venues that were providing them with top entertainment, week after week, is palpable.

The final words go to John Mason, without whom this book would not have been written. Although he is speaking about West Runton Pavilion in the 1970s, his words could apply equally well to either venue at any time, and express the feelings of many as they look back nostalgically to when the people of North Norfolk had two music venues of which, justifiably, they could be very proud:

It was a time never to be forgotten: sadly gone forever.

Sources and Bibliography

I would like to acknowledge the following sources which proved invaluable in cross-checking my research and which I would recommend to readers:
Pete Frame, *Rock Family Trees*, Omnibus Press, ISBN 07119.0465.0 OP42811
Dave McAleer, *Hit Singles Top 20 Charts From 1954 to the Present Day*, Carlton Books, ISBN 1-84442-824-9, 2003 edition
Wikipedia, the on-line encyclopaedia, at www.wikipedia.org

Much of the information in Chapter One was taken from an article which appeared in the *North Norfolk News* dated 31.1.1969

Thanks to Pamela Sutton, Personal Manager to Mr Acker Bilk MBE, at Acker's International Jazz Agency for permission to use extracts from their website. E-mail: pamela@ackersmusicagency.co.uk
Robert Rental and the Normal review included by kind permission of Tim Jones, a co-runner with Barry Williams of the Fflint Central experimental music label (www.fflintcentral.co.uk).
Captain Sensible interview reproduced by kind permission of Dave Parsons – bimble@freeradicalsounds.com

Articles from local newspapers the *Eastern Daily Press, Eastern Evening News, North Norfolk News, Journal* and *Chronicle* reproduced by kind permission of Archant Regional Limited.
Gig dates were largely taken from advertisements placed in the *Eastern Daily Press* (viewed on microfilm at the Norfolk and Norwich Millennium Library) and in the *North Norfolk News* (viewed as original editions at their offices in Cromer).

Other books mentioned in the text:
White Line Fever, Ian 'Lemmy' Kilmister, Pocket Books, ISBN 0-671-03331-X
XS All Areas, Rick Parfitt and Francis Rossi, Pan, ISBN 0330 4196 25
Punk Rock : So What? Edited by Roger Sabin, published by Taylor and Francis Group, ISBN 0415 1703 03

Appendix A

Bands Advertised to appear at
The Royal Links Pavilion, Cromer 1964–1977

Headline band shown first, support band indicated by '+'.
All dates are Saturdays unless otherwise stated.

1964

27 Jun	The Outcasts
4 Jul	The Challengers + The Ronnie Mack Quartet
11 Jul	Mervyn & the Falcons + The Bernard Quartet
18 Jul	The Outcasts + The Ronnie Mack Quartet
1 Aug	The Highwaymen + The Ronnie Mack Quartet
8 Aug	The Mi££ionaires + The Ronnie Mack Quartet
15 Aug	The Korvairs + The Ronnie Mack Quartet
22 Aug	The Planets + The Ronnie Mack Quartet
29 Aug	The Planets + The Ronnie Mack Quartet
14 Nov	Sonny Childe with The Elders Consolidated
21 Nov	No-Names + Beats Ltd
28 Nov	Original Redcaps + Etc Incorporated
5 Dec	Paul Raven & the Pack + Lee Bryan & the Boscats
19 Dec	The Loose Ends + Maniax
26 Dec	Danny Storm & the Strollers + The Challengers
31 Dec (Thurs)	The Star-men Dance Band

1965

2 Jan	Yarramen + The Ivy League
9 Jan	The String Beats + The Blackjacks
16 Jan	The Mistral-tuacs + The Brokers
23 Jan	The Symbols + The Rocking Roosters
30 Jan	The Combo D'Ecosse + Larry Bond & the Trojans
6 Feb	The Dyaks *(Gene Vincent's backing group)* + Mervyn & the Falcons
13 Feb	The Loose Ends + Trends

20 Feb	The Herd + Dave Quinton & the Cheaters *(The Herd were ill and did not play)*
27 Feb	Mystine & the Coleradoes + The Challengers
6 Mar	The Home Grown + The Devil's Coachmen
13 Mar	The Herd + Mervyn & the Falcons
20 Mar	The Subjects + Larry Bond & the Trojans
27 Mar	Sonny Childe with the Elders Consolidated + Dave Quinton & the Cheaters
3 Apr	The Epics + Jane Seymour & the Boys
10 Apr	The Impacts + The Challengers
17 Apr	The Prophets + The Mi££ionaires
24 Apr	The Knives and Forks + Dave Quinton & the Cheaters
1 May	Malcolm James & the Callers + Larry Bond & the Trojans
8 May	The Preachers + Mervyn & the Falcons
15 May	The Dyaks + The Challengers
22 May	Sound Trekkers + The Blackjacks
29 May	Brian & the Brunelles + The Devil's Coachmen
5 Jun	The Symbols + Dave Quinton & the Cheaters
12 Jun	Bobby Jean & the Combo D'Ecosse + The Mi££ionaires
19 Jun	The Quick and the Dead + Larry Bond & the Trojans
26 Jun	The Tramps + Mervyn & the Falcons
3 Jul	Ray Ford & the Statesmen + The Devil's Coachmen
10 Jul	Alan Wade & the Hawkers + The Blackjacks
14 Jul (Wed)	Carnival Dance with Chic Applin Trio *(Babycham promotion)*
17 Jul	The Invaders + The Trojans
21 Jul (Wed)	Chic Applin Trio *(Harp Lager promotion)*
24 Jul	Doug Gibbons & the Outsiders + The Cheaters
28 Jul (Wed)	The Colin Copeman Combo
31 Jul	The Herd + Mervyn & the Falcons
4 Aug (Wed)	The Colin Copeman Combo *(Worthington E promotion)*
7 Aug	Plus Four *(personal backing band of John Leyton)* + The Mi££ionaires
11 Aug (Wed)	The Colin Copeman Combo *(Bulmers' Cider promotion)*
14 Aug	Cherokees + The Challengers
18 Aug (Wed)	The Colin Copeman Combo *(Harvey's of Bristol promotion)*
21 Aug	The Symbols + The Moggs
25 Aug (Wed)	The Colin Copeman Combo *(Guinness promotion)*
28 Aug	Brent Peters & the Chessmen + Dave Quinton & the Cheaters
4 Sep	The Cool School with Sonny Childe + Mervyn & the Falcons
11 Sep	The Various Others + The Style
18 Sep	Billy Storm & the Falcons + The Mi££ionaires

25 Sep	The Trend Setters + The Charades
2 Oct	Bryan & the Brunelles + The Devil's Coachmen
9 Oct	Peter Jay & the Jaywalkers
16 Oct	Grant Tracy & the Sun Sets + The Moggs
23 Oct	The Action + The Cheaters
30 Oct	The Cheaters + The Mi££ionaires
6 Nov	Paul Dean & the Soul Savages + The Devil's Coachmen
13 Nov	Riot Squad + The Style
20 Nov	Abject Blues + Ultimate
27 Nov	The Roulettes *(Adam Faith's group)*
4 Dec	The Rockin' Berries + The Charades
11 Dec	The Sons of Fred + Ultimate
18 Dec	The Tribe + The Devil's Coachmen
24 Dec (Fri)	Johnny Kidd & the Pirates + The Charades

1966

1 Jan	Group Survival + The Style
8 Jan	Bo Street Runners + The Mi££ionaires
15 Jan	Peter Jay & the Jaywalkers + The Cheaters
22 Jan	Phase 5 + The Moggs
29 Jan	Lynton Grae Sound + Roosters
5 Feb	James Royal & the Royal Set + The Devil's Coachmen
12 Feb	Paul Dean & the Soul Savages + The Mi££ionaires
19 Feb	Hamilton Movement + Ultimate
26 Feb	Prophets + The Cheaters
5 Mar	Majority + The Moggs
12 Mar	Swinging Blue Jeans + Ultimate
19 Mar	Fairies + The Cheaters
26 Mar	Riot Squad + The Style
2 Apr	Sapphires + Trends
9 Apr	Plus Four + Roosters
16 Apr	Profile + The Style
23 Apr	The Felders Oriels + Ultimate *(Cromer Football Club Queen Competition)*
30 Apr	Beat Men + Challengers
7 May	Billy Fury & the Gamblers + Ultimate
14 May	Gaylords + The Style
21 May	Tornados + Roosters
28 May	Quiet Five + The Devil's Coachmen
4 Jun	Mike Berry & the Innocents + The Style

11 Jun	George Bean & the Runners + Ultimate
18 Jun	The Gamblers + Roosters
25 Jun	Time Box + The Devil's Coachmen
2 Jul	Soul of Lynton Grae + Ricky Lee & the Hucklebucks
9 Jul	Alan Price Set + The Style
16 Jul	Creation + Roosters
23 Jul	Geneveve & the Pirates + The Devil's Coachmen
30 Jul	MI5 + Ultimate
6 Aug	Eyes + Challengers
13 Aug	Heinz & the Wildboys + The Style
20 Aug	Merseys + Fruit Eating Bears + Roosters
27 Aug	Stormsville Shakers + Ultimate
3 Sep	Fenmen + Challengers
10 Sep	Some Other Guys + The Style
17 Sep	Fleur de Lys + Roosters
24 Sep	Tiffany & the Thoughts + Ultimate
1 Oct	The Gaylords + The Style
8 Oct	Yes 'n' No + Challengers
15 Oct	Tribe + New Generation
22 Oct	Fortunes + Ultimate
29 Oct	Neil Christian & the Crusaders + Roosters
5 Nov	Embers West + The Style
12 Nov	Stormsville Shakers + Challengers
16 Nov (Wed)	Fab Links Discotheque opening night
19 Nov	David Bowie & the Buz + New Generation
26 Nov	MI5 + Ultimate
3 Dec	Bo Street Runners + Eyes of Blond
10 Dec	Jimmie Brown Sound + Trends
17 Dec	Rosco Brown Combo + Soul Concern *(formerly The Style)*
24 Dec	The Gamblers + Plus Four *(now Candy Choir)* + New Generation
31 Dec	Sonny Childe & the TNTs + The Knack + Eyes of Blond

1967

7 Jan	The Syn + Ultimate
11 Jan (Wed)	Alex Wilson Set + Fab Links disco
14 Jan	Soul Reasons + Feel for Soul
21 Jan	Motivation + Soul Concern
28 Jan	Sonny Childe & the TNTs + New Generation
4 Feb	Fancy Bred + Ultimate

11 Feb	The Who + The Money Spiders + Alex Wilson Set
18 Feb	Long John Baldry & Bluesology + Soul Concern
25 Feb	Gates of Eden + New Generation
4 Mar	Tiffany Show + Feel for Soul
11 Mar	Soul Reasons + Eyes of Blond
18 Mar	Quiet Five + Soul Concern
25 Mar	Candy Choir + New Generation
1 Apr	Nite People *(British backing group for Martha & the Vandellas)* + Alex Wilson Set
8 Apr	Fancy Bred + Eyes of Blond
15 Apr	Sonny Childe & the TNTs + Soul Concern
22 Apr	The Coloured Raisins + New Generation
29 Apr	Jeff Beck Group + Marmalade + Feel for Soul
6 May	Chicago Line *(featuring Mike Patto)* + Tribe + New Generation
13 May	Denny Laine String Band + 1, 2, 3 + New Generation
20 May	Sonny Childe & the TNTs + New Generation
27 May	Graham Bond Organisation + Riot Squad + Southern Trust
3 Jun	Sugar Simone & the Programme + Human Instinct + Eyes of Blond
10 Jun	Monopoly + Feel for Soul
17 Jun	Long John Baldry & Bluesology + Soul Concern
24 Jun	Cock-a-Hoop + New Generation
1 Jul	Candy Choir + Johnny Lofty Sounds
8 Jul	Philip Goodhand Tait & the Stormsville Shakers + Soul Concern
15 Jul	The Maze *(was MI5)* + The Y Division
22 Jul	Ray King Soul Band + Alex Wilson Set
29 Jul	Jimmy Powell & the Five Dimensions + Mel Scott Feeling
5 Aug	Graham Bond Organisation + Eyes of Blond
12 Aug	Coloured Raisins + Original Ultimate
19 Aug	Sugar Simone & the Programme + New Generation
26 Aug	Syn + Soul Concern *(Special appearance of EA Regiment's Mascots)*
2 Sep	Human Instinct + Eyes of Blond
9 Sep	Bees + Alex Wilson Set
16 Sep	Studio Six + Ian & Danny Eaves with the Reformation
23 Sep	JE Young & the Tonics + Soul Concern
30 Sep	Ivan St Clair & the System Soul Band + New Generation
7 Oct	Love Affair + Trayne of Thought
14 Oct	Ten Years After + Alex Wilson Set
21 Oct	Philip Goodhand Tait & the Stormsville Shakers *(now Circus)* +

Soul Concern
28 Oct	Syrian Blues + Ian & Danny Eaves with the Reformation
4 Nov	Candy Choir + New Generation
11 Nov	Rick 'n' Beckers + Alex Wilson Set
18 Nov	Marmalade + Soul Concern
25 Nov	Studio Six + Trayne of Thought
2 Dec	Electric Prunes + Mel Scott Feeling + Out of Sight Blues Band
9 Dec	Tremeloes + Soul Concern
16 Dec	JE Young & the Tonics + Rubber Band
23 Dec	John Mayall & his Bluesbreakers + Hucklebucks
30 Dec	Candy Choir + Soul Kings + Soul Concern

1968

6 Jan	Ebony Keys + Alex Wilson Set
13 Jan	Alan Bown Set + Hi Jacks
20 Jan	Desmond Dekker & the Aces + Soul Concern
27 Jan	The Go-Go Show + Hucklebucks
3 Feb	The Tramline + Alex Wilson Set
10 Feb	Edwin Starr with J J Sounds + Ian & Danny Eaves with the Reformation + Django's Castle
17 Feb	Little John & the Shad Rocks + Trayne of Thought
24 Feb	Studio Six + Toby Jug Band *(was Soul Concern)*
2 Mar	St Valentines Day Massacre + Rubber Band *(Dress up as Bonnie & Clyde)*
9 Mar	Phoenix City Soul + Alex Wilson Set
16 Mar	Human Instinct + The Bohemians
23 Mar	Go-Go Show + Barries Magazine
30 Mar	Bees *(known as the Pyramids)* + Toby Jug Band
6 Apr	Wranglers + The Mel Scott Feeling
13 Apr	The Circus + Hi Jacks
20 Apr	Neat Change + Toby Jug Band
27 Apr	John Mayall & his Bluesbreakers + Bohemians
4 May	Firestones & the Go Go Show + Django's Castle
11 May	Humming Birds + Boz & the Ray West Set
18 May	Precious Few + Shade of Pale
25 May	Edwin Starr with State Express + Kiss
1 Jun	The Caste + The Rubber Band
8 Jun	Dobson's Choice + Soul Reaction
15 Jun	Studio Six + Blue Street Soul

22 Jun	Noel & The Fireballs + Kiss
29 Jun	The Sweet Shop + The Fabulous Bohemians
6 Jul	The Pyramids + Django's Castle
13 Jul	Opal Butterfly + The Traction
20 Jul	Candy Choir + Eyes of Blond
27 Jul	Precious Few + Kiss
3 Aug	Noel & The Fireballs + Django's Castle
10 Aug	The Young Blood + The Reformation
17 Aug	The House of Lords + Rubber Band
24 Aug	Chris McClure + Kiss
31 Aug	Max Baer + The Amalgamation
7 Sep	Watson T Brown + Shade of Pale
14 Sep	The Sharrons + The Mood
21 Sep	The J B Roadshow + Kiss
28 Sep	The Pyramids + Barries Magazine
5 Oct	Edwin Starr & The Nashville Hothouse + Music Hath Charms + Django's Castle
12 Oct	The Montanas + The Reformation
19 Oct	All Night Walkers + Impi
26 Oct	The Pearlettes + Jay Lane
2 Nov	The Pyramids + Kiss
9 Nov	The Epics + Reformation
16 Nov	The Paper Dolls & Bluesology + Music Hath Charms + Barries Magazine
23 Nov	Jo-Jo Gunn + Kiss
30 Nov	Pure Medicine + The Mood
7 Dec	Marmalade + Little John & the Shadrocks + The Reformation
14 Dec	The Foundations + The Precious Few + Bohemians
21 Dec	Root 'n' Jenny Jackson & the Hightimers + Chris McClure Section + Bumbly Hum
24 Dec (Tues)	The Pyramids + The Sweet + Kiss
28 Dec	The Gass + Impi
31 Dec (Tues)	Candy Choir + The Flares + Kiss

1969

4 Jan	All Night Workers + Sleepy Talk
11 Jan	Jenny & the Heart Beats + Bramble's Army
18 Jan	Skatelites + Impi
25 Jan	The Inter-State Road Show + Kiss
1 Feb	Noel & The Fireballs + Barries Magazine

8 Feb	Californians + Bumbly Hum
15 Feb	Chris McClure Section + Impi
22 Feb	The Procession + Kiss
1 Mar	The Epics + Sleepy Talk
8 Mar	Johnny Carr & the Cadillacs + Bumbly Hum
15 Mar	Marmalade + Kiss + Barries Magazine
22 Mar	Duffy Taylor + Lemon Honey Introduction
29 Mar	The Flirtations + Blue Ulysses + Sleepy Talk
5 Apr	Root 'n' Jenny Jackson & the Hightimers + Kiss
12 Apr	Village Green Road Show + Barries Magazine
19 Apr	Mooche + Impi
26 Apr	Sonic Invaders + Lemon Honey Introduction
3 May	Candy Choir + Uncle Rufus Band
10 May	Ferris Wheel + Kiss
17 May	The Right of Way + Barries Magazine
24 May	The Move + Eyes of Blond + Uncle Rufus Band
31 May	Raymond Froggatt + Impi
7 Jun	Jason Crest + Kiss
14 Jun	The Pavement + Rusty Spoon
21 Jun	Easybeats + Village Green Road Show
28 Jun	The Pyramids + Stock Pot
5 Jul	Raymond Froggatt + Barries Magazine
12 Jul	Dream Police + Blue Ulysses
19 Jul	Chris McClure Section + Kiss
26 Jul	Dictionary of Soul + Blue Ulysses
2 Aug	Oakley's Oracles + Impi
9 Aug	Sasparella + Stock Pot
16 Aug	Eyes of Blond + Kiss
23 Aug	Bumbly Hum + Barries Magazine
30 Aug	Magic Roundabout + Uncle Rufus Band
6 Sep	The Epics + Impi
13 Sep	Dave Amboy Big Band + Stock Pot
20 Sep	Ruby James & the Sound Trekkers + Village Green Road Show
27 Sep	The King Size Keen Show + Lemon Meringue
4 Oct	Trifle + Impi
11 Oct	Raymond Froggatt + Village Green Road Show
18 Oct	Slade + Stock Pot
25 Oct	Skinn + Kiss
1 Nov	Clearwater + Impi
8 Nov	Jimmy James & the Vagabonds + Village Green Road Show
15 Nov	The Epics + The Lloyd

22 Nov	Paradox + Eyes of Blond
29 Nov	The Equals + Kiss + Mel Scott Feelin'
6 Dec	Raymond Froggatt + Stock Pot
13 Dec	Sight 'n' Sound + Eyes of Blond
20 Dec	Bitter Suite + Barries Magazine
24 Dec (Wed)	Ruby James & the Sound Trekkers + Kiss
27 Dec	Matthew + Impi
31 Dec (Wed)	Candy Choir + The Epics + Kiss

1970

3 Jan	The Californians + Stock Pot
10 Jan	Trifle + Carnival
17 Jan	Liberty Pavilion + Barries Magazine
24 Jan	Rumble + Spencer's People
31 Jan	Raymond Froggatt + Apricot Brande
7 Feb	Memphis Index + Stock Pot
14 Feb	The Bandwagon + Barries Magazine
21 Feb	Badfinger + Kiss + Spencer's People
28 Feb	Hightimers + Root 'n' Jenny Jackson + The Lloyd
7 Mar	Marmalade + Impi + Richmond Green
14 Mar	Eyes of Blond + Barries Magazine + Spencer's People
21 Mar	Tikki, Takki, Suzy & Lies + Black Stump
28 Mar	Raymond Froggatt + Kiss
4 Apr	Sasparella + Impi
11 Apr	Rare Bird + Nimbus + Spencer's People
18 Apr	Sweet Water Canal + Barries Magazine
25 Apr	Clearwater + Kiss
2 May	Pickettywitch + Mister Toad + Richmond Green
9 May	Candy Choir + Acorns
16 May	Trifle + Animal Farm
23 May	McArthur Park + Black Stump
30 May	Raymond Froggatt + Barries Magazine
6 Jun	Rainbow Cottage + Zebedees
13 Jun	Tristam Shandy + Acorns
20 Jun	Wages of Sin + Sweet Ginger
27 Jun	Whisky Martin + Spencer's People
4 Jul	Salamander + Remedy
11 Jul	Nite People + Dear Mr Time
18 Jul	Siege Band + Barries Magazine
25 Jul	Locomotive + Spencer's People

1 Aug	Raymond Froggatt + Helios
8 Aug	Dream Police + Skinn
15 Aug	The State Express + Barries Magazine
22 Aug	Manfred Mann Chapter Three + Spencer's People
29 Aug	Siege Band + Mister Toad
5 Sep	Nite People + Helios
12 Sep	Love Affair + Barries Magazine
19 Sep	Blond on Blond + Skinn
26 Sep	David + Spencer's People
3 Oct	Kiss + Helios
10 Oct	Raymond Froggatt + Barries Magazine
17 Oct	Medicine Bow + Mister Toad
24 Oct	Trapeze + Spencer's People
31 Oct	Custers Track + Zebedees
7 Nov	Ginger + Helios
14 Nov	Axe + Barries Magazine
21 Nov	St Cecelia + Julias Pam
28 Nov	Nite People + Spencer's People
5 Dec	Trifle + Helios
12 Dec	Eyes of Blond + Wildfire
19 Dec	Siege Band + Barries Magazine
24 Dec (Thurs)	Candy Choir + Spencer's People
26 Dec	Raymond Froggatt + Julias Pam
31 Dec (Thurs)	Mamma Bear + Wildfire

1971

2 Jan	Orange Air + Helios
9 Jan	Merlin 'Q' + Barries Magazine
16 Jan	Status Quo + Spencer's People
23 Jan	Candy Choir + Wildfire
30 Jan	Chancery Lane + Murphy
6 Feb	John McFlare Band + Julias Pam
13 Feb	Clusters Track + Spencer's People
20 Feb	Ginger Bread + Wildfire
27 Feb	The Mixtures + Murphy
6 Mar	Voice + Helios
13 Mar	Raymond Froggatt + Barries Magazine
20 Mar	Elton Chess + Spencer's People
27 Mar	Status Quo + Murphy
3 Apr	Seige + Wildfire

10 Apr	The Equals + Magazine
17 Apr	Kiss + Helios
24 Apr	The Sweet + Julias Pam
1 May	Thin Lizzy + Murphy
8 May	Raymond Froggatt + Wildfire
15 May	Worth + Spencer's People
22 May	Generation + Magazine
29 May	Grass + Jeep
5 Jun	Seige + Wildfire
12 Jun	Christie + Kilroy
19 Jun	Thin Lizzy + Spencer's People
26 Jun	Fair Weather + Murphy
3 Jul	Van de Graaf Generator
10 Jul	Station + Reflections
17 Jul	Raymond Froggatt + Crow
24 Jul	Ginger + Barabas
31 Jul	Felix + Murphy
7 Aug	Danta + Wood Butcher
14 Aug	Jumbo + Phoenix
21 Aug	Slade + Barabas
28 Aug	Sam Apple Pie + Crow
4 Sep	Elton Chess + Magazine
11 Sep	Paddy Green Set + Murphy
18 Sep	Status Quo + The Hot
25 Sep	Orange + Magazine
2 Oct	Gnidrolog + Murphy
9 Oct	Raymond Froggatt + Wood Butcher
16 Oct	Writing on the Wall + The Hot
23 Oct	Matthew's Southern Comfort + Magazine
30 Oct	Hot Chocolate + Phoenix
6 Nov	Cochise + Barabas
13 Nov	Raymond Froggatt + Mister Toad
20 Nov	Brindsley Schwartz + Murphy
27 Nov	Crocodile + Magazine
4 Dec	Elton Chess + Murphy
11 Dec	Wild Turkey + Crow
18 Dec	Chicken Shack + Barabas
24 Dec (Fri)	Raymond Froggatt + Murphy
31 Dec (Fri)	Wild Turkey + Creed

1972

1 Jan	Crow + Natural Gas
8 Jan	Slade + Mister Toad
15 Jan	Kiss + Phoenix
22 Jan	Black Widow + Crow
29 Jan	Chicken Shack + Murphy
5 Feb	Stone the Crows + Mister Toad
12 Feb	Nazareth + Phoenix
19 Feb	Gentle Giant + Crow
26 Feb	Raymond Froggatt + Murphy
4 Mar	Crocodile + Raw
11 Mar	Status Quo + Mister Toad
18 Mar	Khan + Scapa Flow
25 Mar	Mick Abrahams Band + Murphy
1 Apr	Crow + Zoe
8 Apr	Super Tramp + The Hot
15 Apr	UFO + Mister Toad
22 Apr	Medicine Head + Murphy
29 Apr	Juicy Lucy + Scapa Flow
6 May	Mongrel + Raw
13 May	Quiver + The Hot
20 May	Raymond Froggatt + Mister Toad
27 May	Crow + Murphy
2 Jun (Fri)	Neil Martell
3 Jun	Atomic Rooster + Zoe
10 Jun	Sarah Gordon & Bondage + Graphite
17 Jun	Thin Lizzy + Annapurna
23 Jun (Fri)	Personal appearance of Norwich City football team
24 Jun	Danta + Scapa Flow
30 Jun (Fri)	The Nortones
1 Jul	Gnidrolog + Zoe
7 Jul (Fri)	The Geoff Stinton Band
8 Jul	UFO + Shaft
14 Jul (Fri)	The Trevor Copeman Band *(now resident every Friday)*
15 Jul	Quiver + Murphy
22 Jul	Crow + Raw
29 Jul	Status Quo *(did not appear – replaced by Christie)* + Scapa Flow
5 Aug	Pretty Things *(did not appear)* + Shaft
12 Aug	Gypsy + Murphy
19 Aug	Raymond Froggatt + Scapa Flow

26 Aug	Status Quo + Raw
2 Sep	Pretty Things + Animal Farm
8 Sep (Fri)	Disco *(every Friday)*
9 Sep	Quiver + Shy Fly
16 Sep	Holy Mackeral + Murphy
23 Sep	Crow + Annapurna
30 Sep	Screaming Lord Sutch & the New Savages + Scapa Flow
7 Oct	UFO + Raw
14 Oct	Ellis + Shy Fly
21 Oct	Juicy Lucy + P.O.D
28 Oct	Nazareth + Scapa Flow
4 Nov	Pink Fairies + Raw
11 Nov	Blackfoot Sue + Graphite
18 Nov	Brush + Scapa Flow
25 Nov	Gary Glitter + Murphy
2 Dec	Screaming Lord Sutch & the Rock Revolution + Shy Fly
9 Dec	Rory Gallagher + Raw
16 Dec	Danta + Ribs
23 Dec	The Paddy Green Set + Shy Fly + Scapa Flow
30 Dec	Crow + Murphy + Ribs

1973

6 Jan	Nazareth + Plod
13 Jan	Biggles + Raw
20 Jan	Jonessy + Shy Fly
27 Jan	Brush + Scapa Flow
3 Feb	Badger + Ribs
10 Feb	Raymond Froggatt + Murphy
17 Feb	Hook Foot + Scapa Flow
24 Feb	Thin Lizzy + Shy Fly
3 Mar	Brush + Graphite
10 Mar	Screaming Lord Sutch & the Rock Rebellion + Raw
17 Mar	Quiver + Ribs
24 Mar	Stealer's Wheel + Scapa Flow
31 Mar	Raymond Froggatt + Scapa Flow
7 Apr	Sam Apple Pie + Shy Fly
14 Apr	Skin Alley *(replaced Nazareth who were ill)* + Moonshine
21 Apr	Savoy Brown + Ribs
28 Apr	Crow + Raw
5 May	UFO + Murphy

12 May	Gary Moore Band *(Patto advertised first, but they broke up)* + Shy Fly
19 May	Chicken Shack + Scapa Flow
26 May	Golden Earring + Shark
2 Jun	Back Door + Ribs
9 Jun	Darryl Way's Wolf + Raw
16 Jun	Raymond Froggatt + Shy Fly
23 Jun	Gary Moore Band + Scapa Flow
30 Jun	Sam Apple Pie + Murphy
7 Jul	Pink Fairies + Shark
14 Jul	Thin Lizzy + Raw
21 Jul	Trapeze + Shy Fly
28 Jul	Chicken Shack + Scapa Flow
4 Aug	Screaming Lord Sutch & the Rock Rebellion + Vineyard
11 Aug	Darryl Way's Wolf + Chilli Willi & the Red Hot Peppers
18 Aug	Jack the Lad + Shy Fly
25 Aug	Edgar Broughton Band + Murphy
1 Sep	Raymond Froggatt + Hieronymus Bosch
8 Sep	Bitch + Coast Road Drive
15 Sep	The Average White Band + Judas Priest
22 Sep	Babe Ruth + Bronx Cheer
29 Sep	Geordie + Hieronymus Bosch
6 Oct	Sassafras + All Things New
13 Oct	Hummingbird + Murphy
20 Oct	Jonathan Kelly & Friends + Shark
27 Oct	Sam Apple Pie + Shy Fly
3 Nov	Duster Bennett + Million People
10 Nov	Crow + Moonshine
17 Nov	Bedlam + Graphite
24 Nov	Capability Brown + The Flying Hat Band
1 Dec	Sensational Alex Harvey Band + Iguana
8 Dec	Golden Earring + Shark
15 Dec	Wild Turkey + Hieronymus Bosch
22 Dec	Jack the Lad + Shy Fly
24 Dec (Mon)	Raymond Froggatt + Shy Fly
29 Dec	Chilli Willi & the Red Hot Peppers + Shark
31 Dec (Mon)	Screaming Lord Sutch & his band Yakketty Yak + Shark

1974

5 Jan	Bronx Cheer + Global Village Trucking Co
12 Jan	Judas Priest + Narnia
19 Jan	UFO + Cousin David *(ex Scapa Flow)*
26 Jan	Chicory Tip *(Budgie cancelled)* + The Flying Hat Band
2 Feb	Bees Make Honey + Graphite
9 Feb	Vinegar Joe + Stag
16 Feb	Bronx Cheer + Shark
23 Feb	SNAFU + Murphy
2 Mar	Kilburn & the High Roads + Shy Fly
9 Mar	Crow + Carnival
16 Mar	Budgie + Murphy
23 Mar	Queen + Nutz
30 Mar	Thin Lizzy + Cousin David
6 Apr	Medicine Head + The Flying Hat Band
13 Apr	SNAFU + Shy Fly
15 Apr (Mon)	Raymond Froggatt + Fantastic Shark Light Show
20 Apr	Stray + Spencer's People
27 Apr	Greenslade + Warlock
4 May	Hot Chocolate + Wedgwood
6 May (Mon)	Gypp + Spencer's People
11 May	Crunch + Moonshine
18 May	Merlin + Be Bop Deluxe
25 May	Nutz + Oxo Witney
1 Jun	Cockney Rebel + Be Bop Deluxe
8 Jun	Refugee + Carnival
15 Jun	The Butts Band
22 Jun	Blackfoot Sue + Zoe
29 Jun	Blue + Graphite
4 Jul (Wed)	Mid-week discos start with Howard Platt
6 Jul	UFO + Cousin David
13 Jul	The Groundhogs + King Arthurs Disco & Five by Four Lightshow
20 Jul	Raymond Froggatt + Disco
27 Jul	Cozy Powell + Disco
2 Aug (Fri)	Will Reynolds *(Free admission)*
3 Aug	Sarah Gordon & the Little Free Rock + Disco
8 Aug (Thurs)	Howard Platt Disco Show
9 Aug (Fri)	Will Reynolds
10 Aug	Hot Chocolate + King Aruthur's Disco with the Four by Five

	Light Show
15 Aug (Thurs)	Howard Platt Disco Show
16 Aug (Fri)	Will Reynolds
17 Aug	Bilbo Baggins + Disco
22 Aug (Thurs)	Howard Platt Disco Show
23 Aug (Fri)	Will Reynolds
24 Aug	Nutz
29 Aug (Thurs)	Howard Platt Disco Show
30 Aug (Fri)	Will Reynolds
31 Aug	Rubettes + Disco
7 Sep	Cousin David
14 Sep	Spencer's People
21 Sep	Hoss featuring Bob Walker
28 Sep	Gypp
5 Oct	Plod
12 Oct	Thunder *(Frank Lea's Super Group)*
19 Oct	Cheeks with ex members of Mott the Hoople
26 Oct	Judas Priest
2 Nov	Mister Big + Wedgwood
9 Nov	Buster James + Finger
16 Nov	Screaming Lord Sutch
23 Nov	Rare Bird + Train + DJ Gerry
30 Nov	Sarah Gordon
7 Dec	Heavy Metal Kids
14 Dec	Gay Perez & Anna + Spencer's People
21 Dec	Nutz + Wedgwood
28 Dec	Judas Priest + Memphis Index

1975

4 Jan	UFO + All Things New
22 Feb	Raymond Froggatt + Memphis Index
1 Mar	Mungo Jerry + Wedgwood
8 Mar	Budgie + Chaser
15 Mar	Rock Island Line + Terry Starr & the Planets
22 Mar	Marmalade *(replaced Hot Chocolate who were ill)* + Watch
29 Mar	Budgie + Train
5 Apr	Buster James + Sable
12 Apr	Geordie + Memphis Index
19 Apr	Raymond Froggatt Band + Emily
26 Apr	Horslips + All Things New

3 May	SNAFU + Nutz
10 May	Screaming Lord Sutch & the Savages + Train
17 May	Sweet Sensation
24 May	Mungo Jerry + Sable
31 May	Heavy Metal Kids + Chaser
7 Jun	Judas Priest + Gypp
14 Jun	Thin Lizzy + Black Jack
21 Jun	Jimmy James & the Vagabonds + Wedgwood
28 Jun	Shanghai featuring Cliff Bennett & Nick Green + Spencer's People
5 Jul	Desmond Dekker + Emily
12 Jul	Savoy Brown + Train
19 Jul	The Kursaal Flyers + Memphis Index
26 Jul	Hot Chocolate
2 Aug	Sam Apple Pie
9 Aug	Kenny + Spencer's People
16 Aug	Heavy Metal Kids + Teezer
23 Aug	Raymond Froggatt Band + Wedgwood
30 Aug	Thin Lizzy
6 Sep	Judas Priest + Buster James
13 Sep	Mungo Jerry + Tangent
20 Sep	Screaming Lord Sutch & the Savages + Bliss
27 Sep	Budgie
4 Oct	Horslips + All Things New + 3 Dimensional Sounds
11 Oct	Junior High & the Rockets + Bliss
18 Oct	Sailor
25 Oct	Heavy Metal Kids + Teezer
1 Nov	Biggest continuous live rock night ever and late bars
8 Nov	Slack Alice + Teezer
29 Nov	Be Bop Deluxe + Bliss
6 Dec	UFO + Train
13 Dec	Hustler + Wedgwood
20 Dec	Curved Air + Climax Blues Band
24 Dec (Wed)	Sam Apple Pie + The Hunter
27 Dec	S T R ET C H + Train

1976

3 Jan	Starry Eyed and Laughing + Palm Beach Express
7 Feb	SNAFU + Salt
14 Feb	Stray + Possessed

21 Feb	String-Driven Thing + The Zippa Kids
28 Feb	Nutz + Strife
6 Mar	SNAFU + Sorohan
13 Mar	Boxer + Casino
20 Mar	Sassafras + Train
27 Mar	Judas Priest + Cav
3 Apr	Edgar Broughton Band + Poacher
10 Apr	Charlie + The City Boy
17 Apr	Woman + The Second Hand Band
24 Apr	Fruup + Lion

1977

| 24 Dec | Sex Pistols |

Appendix B

Bands Advertised to appear at West Runton Pavilion 1973-1983

Headline band shown first, support band indicated by '+'
Thanks to Alan Hooker for verifying many of the dates.

1973

Sat 4 Aug	Carnival + Social Status
Sat 11 Aug	General Stream + Butch
Sat 18 Aug	Tony Charles Showband with the Downbeats
Sat 25 Aug	Train + Triangle
Mon 27 Aug	Berry & the Treetops
Sat 1 Sep	Last Wheel Showband
Sat 8 Sep	Zenith Showband + Berry & the Treetops
Sat 15 Sep	Emily's Cake Shop + Two Plus Two
Sat 22 Sep	Mebo + Storm
Sat 29 Sep	Nelson's Column + Second Opinion
Sat 6 Oct	Memphis Index + Storm
Sat 13 Oct	The Singing Gnomes
Sat 20 Oct	Fascinatin' Rythym
Sat 27 Oct	Train + Second Opinion
Sat 3 Nov	Berry & the Treetops + Tramp
Sat 10 Nov	Memphis Index + Storm
Sat 17 Nov	Memphis Index + Storm
Sat 24 Nov	Tremeloes + Second Opinion
Sat 1 Dec	Berry & the Treetops + Triangle
Sat 8 Dec	Train
Sat 15 Dec	Fascinatin' Rythym + Two Plus Two
Sat 22 Dec	Memphis Index
Mon 24 Dec	Fascinatin' Rythym
Wed 26 Dec	Berry & the Treetops
Sat 29 Dec	Social Status
Mon 31 Dec	Fascinatin' Rythym + Berry & the Treetops

1974

Sat 5 Jan	Norma & the Shade of Pale + Sable
Sat 12 Jan	Memphis Index + Social Status
Sat 19 Jan	Train + Fairy
Sat 26 Jan	Satin and Silk
Sat 2 Feb	Fascinatin' Rythym + Sable
Sat 9 Feb	Jackie Lynn Showband + Roger Cooke Trio & Elizabeth
Thu 14 Feb	Train + Berry & the Treetops
Sat 16 Feb	Hot Chocolate + Berry & the Treetops
Sat 23 Feb	Train + Sounds Natural
Sat 2 Mar	KC Smith Band
Sat 9 Mar	Fascinatin' Rythym + Triangle
Sat 16 Mar	Pete Douglas Combo
Sat 23 Mar	Memphis Index + Ice
Sat 30 Mar	The Berries + Dave Anthony
Sat 6 Apr	Tramp + Social Status
Sat 13 Apr	Fascinatin' Rythym + Triangle
Mon 15 Apr	Fascinatin' Rythym + The Berries
Sat 20 Apr	The Equals + Fascinatin' Rythym
Sat 27 Apr	KC Smith Band + Second Opinion
Sat 4 May	Memphis Index + Fastback
Fri 10 May	Fascinatin' Rythym + Social Status
Sat 11 May	The Berries
Sat 18 May	Blackwood
Fri 24 May	The Berries + Train
Sat 25 May	KC Smith Band + Ice
Mon 27 May	Wedgwood + McDivitt
Sat 1 Jun	Watch + Sable
Fri 7 Jun	The Reason Why + Social Status *(Cox & Wyman Sports Club Dance. The Hillsiders were originally advertised, then cancelled)*
Sat 8 Jun	Social Status
Sat 15 Jun	Shay + Memphis Index
Sat 22 Jun	Tramp + Social Status
Sat 29 Jun	Second Opinion + Accent
Sat 6 Jul	Pepperbox + Accent
Sat 13 Jul	Gesse & the Gang + Social Status
Sat 20 Jul	Vanity Fare
Wed 24 Jul	Charlie & the Wide Boys + Super Disco
Sat 27 Jul	Second Opinion + Wild Honey *(Champagne & valuable spot prizes)*

Wed 31 Jul	Tony Charles Showband *(Sheringham Carnival Dance)*
Thu 1 Aug	Trax + Super Mike Fancy Disco
Sat 3 Aug	Social Status + Train
Sat 10 Aug	Pepperbox + Two Plus One
Fri 16 Aug	New Silver Ace
Sat 17 Aug	Memphis Index
Sat 24 Aug	Sassafras + The Art Lewis Sound
Mon 26 Aug	The Berries + The Art Lewis Sound
Fri 30 Aug	The Sidewinders
Sat 31 Aug	Triangle + First Impression
Fri 6 Sep	Train + Second Opinion *(Sheringham Football Club Dance)*
Sat 7 Sep	Social Status + Exodus
Sat 14 Sep	Chris Stainton's Tundra
Fri 20 Sep	Geoff Stinton Musicmen
Sat 21 Sep	Second Opinion
Sat 28 Sep	Memphis Index + First Impression
Sat 5 Oct	Star featuring Peter Collins + First Impression
Fri 11 Oct	Roy Haig Trio *(Ballroom Dance)*
Sat 12 Oct	The Berries + Nocturne
Sat 19 Oct	Second Opinion + Exodus
Sat 26 Oct	First Impression + Finger
Sat 2 Nov	The Reason Why + Chaser
Fri 8 Nov	Geoff Stinton Musicmen *(Fabulous star prize – ladies and gents matching wrist watches)*
Sat 9 Nov	Memphis Index + Nocturne
Sat 16 Nov	The Berries
Fri 22 Nov	Jackie Lynn Showband + Tijuana Funtime with Cliffords Brass Barrel. Caberet night featuring comic Phil Grey.
Sat 23 Nov	Second Opinion + Exodus
Sat 30 Nov	Jackie Lynn Showband + First Impression
Fri 6 Dec	The Diversion Danceband *(Ballroom dance – 45 mins Jive tuition)*
Sat 7 Dec	Exodus
Sat 14 Dec	First Impression + Train
Sat 21 Dec	The Berries + Triangle
Tue 24 Dec	Star featuring Peter Collins + Social Status
Thu 26 Dec	Star featuring Peter Collins + New Silver Ace
Sat 28 Dec	Beano *(formerly The Reason Why)* + Second Opinion
Tue 31 Dec	Star featuring Peter Collins + Exodus

1975

Sat 4 Jan	Glass Wheel Showband
Sat 11 Jan	The Berries + This and That
Fri 17 Jan	The Dance Quartet *(Ballroom dance – 45 mins Cha Cha Cha tuition)*
Sat 18 Jan	Bedrock Showband + Social Status
Fri 24 Jan	Emily's Cake Shop
Sat 25 Jan	The Drifter's Showband
Fri 31 Jan	The Dance Quartet *(Ballroom dance – 45 mins Samba tuition)*
Sat 1 Feb	The Berries + Geoff Stinton
Fri 7 Feb	The Dance Quartet *(Ballroom dance – 45 mins Foxtrot tuition)*
Sat 8 Feb	McDivitt + Exodus
Fri 14 Feb	Geoff Stinton
Sat 15 Feb	Glass Wheel + Sable
Fri 21 Feb	Hal Dizney Danceband *(Ballroom dance – 45 mins Foxtrot tuition)*
Sat 22 Feb	Bedrock + Willie & the Poor Boys
Sat 1 Mar	Second Opinion + Tanglewood
Fri 7 Mar	The Dance Quartet *(Ballroom dance – 45 mins Cha Cha Cha tuition)*
Sat 8 Mar	Staggerlees + Exodus
Fri 14 Mar	Memphis Index + King Arthur's Disco
Sat 15 Mar	Sweet'Art + The Berries
Fri 21 Mar	The Dance Quartet *(Ballroom dance – 45 mins Tango tuition)*
Sat 22 Mar	Peter Oliver + Crunch
Sat 29 Mar	Cuff Links + Blue Velvet
Mon 31 Mar	Terry Starr & the Planets + First Impression
Fri 4 Apr	Second Opinion + International Disco
Sat 5 Apr	Easy Virtue + Memphis Index
Sat 12 Apr	New Pickettywitch + Blue Velvet
Sat 19 Apr	Marmalade + Blue Velvet
Sat 26 Apr	Beano
Sat 3 May	Leapy Lee + Memphis Index
Sat 10 May	Mr Superbad & His Mighty Power Band
Sat 17 May	Rubettes + Plastic Penny
Sat 24 May	Swinging Blue Jeans
Mon 26 May	Albatross + How It Works
Fri 30 May	Exodus
Sat 31 May	Nashville Teens
Sat 14 Jun	Kenny
Sat 21 Jun	The Applejacks + Guinevere

Sat 28 Jun	Mandarin Craze + Blue Velvet
Fri 4 Jul	Duane Eddy + Exodus + Girlie GaGa Dancers
Sat 5 Jul	Nosmo King & the Javels + Zipper
Fri 11 Jul	The Dance Quartet
Sat 12 Jul	Detroit Soul Machine + Together
Sat 19 Jul	The Foundations
Sat 26 Jul	Sweet Sensation + Quest
Sat 2 Aug	Wigan's Ovation + Crocodile
Wed 6 Aug	Treble Nine *(Carnival Dance)*
Sat 9 Aug	Merseybeats + Buzz
Tue 12 Aug	The Glitter Band + Fresh
Sat 16 Aug	Eclipse + Easy Virtue
Fri 22 Aug	The Emily + Geoff Stinton & his Musicmen *(Cromer Carnival Dance)*
Sat 23 Aug	The Overlanders + Crackers
Mon 25 Aug	Kid Jenson + Junior High & the Rockets + Walrus Disco
Fri 29 Aug	Brett Marvin & the Thunderbolts + Hellraisers
Sat 30 Aug	Mac and Katie Kissoon + First Impression
Fri 5 Sep	Geoff Stinton Band *(every Friday)*
Sat 6 Sep	Northern Soul Road Show
Sat 13 Sep	Linda Carr & the Love Squad + Lucky
Sat 20 Sep	Hot Chocolate
Sat 27 Sep	Beano + Dusk
Sat 4 Oct	Sheer Elegance + Plastic Penny
Fri 10 Oct	The Dance Quartet
Sat 11 Oct	Marmalade
Sat 18 Oct	Pan's People + Roadrunner + Malcolm May Disco
Sat 25 Oct	Showaddywaddy *(Did not play)*
Fri 31 Oct	Doctors of Madness + Applejacks
Sat 1 Nov	Swinging Blue Jeans + Quest
Sat 8 Nov	Mac and Katie Kissoon
Fri 14 Nov	Police Ball
Sat 15 Nov	Troggs + New Arrival
Sun 16 Nov	Fox + Tim Moore
Fri 21 Nov	Ballroom
Sat 22 Nov	Kenny + Spice
Fri 28 Nov	The Edgar Broughton Band + Jailbait
Sat 29 Nov	Chris Farlowe *(inc Madelin Bell and Albert Lee)* + Jailbait
Sat 6 Dec	Smokey + Crackers
Fri 12 Dec	Cadillac + Disco
Sat 13 Dec	Detroit Soul Machine + Butterscotch

Sun 14 Dec	Spiders from Mars *(informal concert, free admission)*
Sat 20 Dec	Shabby Tiger + Cisco
Wed 24 Dec	Junior High & the Rockets + Blue Velvet
Sat 27 Dec	Beano + Quest
Wed 31 Dec	Slack Alice + Blue Velvet

1976

Sat 3 Jan	Federation + Bethnal
Fri 9 Jan	Heavy Metal Kids + Kav *(HMKs did not play)*
Sun 11 Jan	Real Thing + Boy Bastin *(formerly Cadillac)*
Fri 16 Jan	Charlie *(free concert for members)*
Sat 17 Jan	Judge Dread
Sat 24 Jan	Hello + System
Fri 30 Jan	Crackers + The Hat Band
Sat 31 Jan	Sarah Gordon Show + Freedom
Sat 7 Feb	Charlie + Glyder + The Hat Band
Wed 11 Feb	Showaddywaddy
Fri 13 Feb	Ballroom
Sat 14 Feb	Gonzales
Fri 20 Feb	Jack the Lad
Sat 21 Feb	Soho Jets + Hasleden Band
Sat 28 Feb	Kursaal Flyers + Eddie & the Hot Rods
Fri 5 Mar	Smokey + City Boy
Sat 6 Mar	Stretch + Arbre
Fri 12 Mar	Al Collins Band *(Ballroom)*
Sat 13 Mar	Raymond Froggatt Band + Teezer
Fri 19 Mar	Doctors of Madness + Spiny Norman
Sat 20 Mar	Alvin Stardust + Memphis Index
Fri 26 Mar	Cissy Stone + Quest
Sat 27 Mar	Sadista Sisters
Fri 2 Apr	John Miles Band + Stevenson's Rocket
Sat 3 Apr	Shag Connors & the Carrot Crunchers + Moving Finger
Thu 8 Apr	Heavy Metal Kids + Lalla Hanson
Fri 9 Apr	Mike Batt's Mad Hatters + Bilbo Baggins
Sat 10 Apr	FBI + Dusk
Thu 15 Apr	Bavarian 'Oompah' Night
Sat 17 Apr	Radio Luxembourg/Daily Mirror Road Show + Crackers
Mon 19 Apr	Linda Leyton Unlimited + Fandango + Vertigo Disco
Fri 23 Apr	Brother Lees + Poacher
Sat 24 Apr	Jimmy James & the Vagabonds + Mad Lad Disco

Fri 30 Apr	Mother Superior + Fogg
Sat 1 May	Raymond Froggatt Band + Fast Buck
Sat 8 May	JALN + Clancy
Sat 15 May	Arrows + Fumble
Fri 21 May	Sam Apple Pie + Arbre
Sat 22 May	Boombaya + The 20th Century Steel Band
Fri 28 May	Country and Western Night
Sat 29 May	Yakety Yak + Memphis Index
Sat 5 Jun	The Glitter Band + Disco
Fri 11 Jun	Mott
Sat 12 Jun	The Troggs + Bethnal
Fri 18 Jun	Crazy Cavan + Mike Berry & the Original Outlaws
Sat 19 Jun	Al Matthews + Freedom
Sat 26 Jun	Jigsaw
Fri 2 Jul	Curved Air + Druid
Sat 3 Jul	O'Hara's Playboys + Train
Fri 9 Jul	Sassafras + Sad Café
Sat 10 Jul	Max Merritt & the Meteors + Emily
Fri 16 Jul	Tony Blackburn's Road Show + Giggles
Sat 17 Jul	Beano + Bumper Disco
Thu 22 Jul	The Strawbs + Grendel
Fri 23 Jul	Sheringham Carnival Dance
Sat 24 Jul	Raymond Froggatt Band + Burlesque
Fri 30 Jul	Summer Variety Show for all the family
Sat 31 Jul	Madame + Clud in the Boot
Sat 7 Aug	Sweet Sensation + Loco
Fri 13 Aug	Jimmy James & the Vagabonds + Fandango
Sat 14 Aug	Caledonia + Voice
Thu 19 Aug	Sex Pistols + Grendel
Fri 20 Aug	Cromer Carnival Dance
Sat 21 Aug	Johnny Wakelin + Zorro
Thu 26 Aug	Phil Manzanera Band featuring Brian Eno
Fri 27 Aug	Manfred Mann's Earth Band + Grendel
Sat 28 Aug	Mac Kissoon + Stress
Mon 30 Aug	The Count Bishops + Fresh + Disco
Fri 3 Sep	Paul Burnett Road Show
Sat 4 Sep	Shag Connors & the Carrot Crunchers
Fri 10 Sep	Crazy Cavan & the Rhythm Rockers + Flying Saucers
Sat 11 Sep	Swinging Blue Jeans
Fri 17 Sep	The Real Thing + Disco
Sat 18 Sep	Andy Fairweather-Low + Andy Desmond

Fri 24 Sep	Moon + Blue Angels
Sat 25 Sep	Sam Apple Pie + Urchin
Fri 1 Oct	Alberto y Los Trios Paranoias + Spiny Norman
Sat 2 Oct	Tavares + Disco
Thu 7 Oct	Mott + Lone Star or Zorro *(Both supports advertised, neither played)*
Fri 8 Oct	City Boy + Peaches
Sat 9 Oct	JALN + Soul Direction
Thu 14 Oct	Graham Parker & the Rumour *(replaced Can)* + Zorro
Fri 15 Oct	Max Merritt & the Meteors + DJ Tony Way
Sat 16 Oct	Boombaya + Roogaletor
Fri 22 Oct	Peter Powell + Giggles + Doug Read Disco
Sat 23 Oct	Slik + DJ Tony Way
Fri 29 Oct	Groundhogs + Unicorn
Sat 30 Oct	Tina Charles + DJ Chris Harris
Thu 4 Nov	Doctors of Madness + Spiny Norman
Fri 5 Nov	Pat Travers Band + Blue Angels
Sat 6 Nov	20th Century Steel Band
Fri 12 Nov	Kursaal Flyers + Burlesque
Sat 13 Nov	Sherbert + Trax
Wed 17 Nov	Andy Fairweather-Low
Thu 18 Nov	Flaming Groovies + The Damned
Sat 20 Nov	Beano + DJ Dougie Read
Fri 26 Nov	Deaf School + Choko
Sat 27 Nov	Geno Washington & the Ram Jam Band + The Emerald Orchestra
Thu 2 Dec	Can + Spiny Norman *(Spiny Norman did not play)*
Sat 4 Dec	The Drifters *(2 performances 7.30pm & 10.30pm)*
Sat 11 Dec	Charlie + Urchin
Sat 18 Dec	Fumble + Yakety Yak
Wed 22 Dec	John Miles + Spiny Norman
Fri 24 Dec	Sam Apple Pie + Ram
Mon 27 Dec	Syd Lawrence *(Ballroom Dance)*
Fri 31 Dec	Raymond Froggatt Band + Blueberry Hill

1977

Sat 1 Jan	Jimmy James & the Vagabonds + Hungry Horse
Fri 7 Jan	John Otway & Wild Willy Barrett
Sat 8 Jan	Carol Grimes & the London Boogie Band + Bumper Disco
Fri 14 Jan	Memphis Index + Second Opinion

Sat 15 Jan	Sparrow + Ram
Sat 22 Jan	Barry Biggs + DJ Dougie Read
Fri 28 Jan	John Otway & Wild Willy Barrett *(at the Village Inn)*
Sat 29 Jan	JALN + DJ Dougie Read
Fri 4 Feb	Smokie + Spiny Norman *(Fly By Night Removals originally advertised as support)*
Sat 5 Feb	Meal Ticket + Lee Kosmin Band + DJ Barry Whittle
Sat 12 Feb	Slik + Screamer
Fri 18 Feb	Widowmaker *(unable to appear)* + Remus Down Boulevard
Sat 19 Feb	Soul Direction *(Ex Freedom)* + Caledonia
Fri 25 Feb	Al Matthews Show + Fresh + DJ Chris Harris
Sat 26 Feb	Jimmy Helms + DJ Dougie Read
Fri 4 Mar	Cado Belle + Spiny Norman
Sat 5 Mar	Liverpool Express
Fri 11 Mar	Charlie + Nasty Pop
Sat 12 Mar	Mungo Jerry + Ram
Thu 17 Mar	Cherry Vanilla + The Police
Fri 18 Mar	Doctors of Madness + Pat Travers
Sat 19 Mar	Marc Bolan & T Rex + The Damned
Thu 24 Mar	The Commodores + Muscles
Fri 25 Mar	Michael Chapman + John Otway & Wild Willy Barrett
Sat 26 Mar	Showaddywaddy + John Otway & Wild Willy Barrett
Fri 1 Apr	Widowmaker + Quartz
Sat 2 Apr	Osibisa
Thu 7 Apr	John Cale + The Count Bishops + The Boys
Sat 9 Apr	Beano
Mon 11 Apr	Fresh
Fri 15 Apr	Flying Saucers + Second Opinion
Sat 16 Apr	Chi-lites
Fri 22 Apr	Nutz + Remus Down Boulevard
Sat 23 Apr	Fumble + Ram
Fri 29 Apr	Judas Priest + Spiny Norman
Sat 30 Apr	Mr Big + Spiny Norman
Thu 5 May	Ian Gillan Band + Spiny Norman *(Straps originally advertised as support)*
Fri 6 May	Jack the Lad + Zorro
Sat 7 May	Rokotto + Bandito
Fri 13 May	Burlesque + Grind
Sat 14 May	The Drifters + Ram
Fri 20 May	Sam Apple Pie + Warren Harry
Sat 21 May	Heatwave + Rokotto + DJ Tony Way

Fri 27 May	The Clash + The Buzzcocks + The Subway Sect + The Slits
	(*The Jam were also advertised but did not appear*)
Sat 28 May	David Parton + Lips
Fri 3 Jun	Heavy Metal Kids + The Motors
Sat 4 Jun	Kenny + Kite
Mon 6 Jun	Caravan + The Count Bishops + Spiny Norman
Fri 10 Jun	Raymond Froggatt Band + Spiny Norman
Sat 11 Jun	The Real Thing
Fri 17 Jun	George Hatcher Band + Babylon
Sat 18 Jun	Sweet Sensation + Cruiser
Fri 24 Jun	Jenny Haan's Lion + Spiny Norman
Sat 25 Jun	Darts + Pinto
Fri 1 Jul	The Damned + The Adverts
Sat 2 Jul	Light Fantastic + Exodus
Fri 8 Jul	The Vibrators + Wire
Sat 9 Jul	Billy Ocean + Muscles
Fri 15 Jul	Sheringham Carnival Dance
Sat 16 Jul	Dead End Kids + Zorro
Fri 22 Jul	The Jam + The Boys + The Advertisers (*or possibly New Hearts*)
Sat 23 Jul	Judge Dread + Skybirds Disco
Wed 27 Jul	Cromer Football Club Dance
Fri 29 Jul	Racing Cars + Warren Harry
Sat 30 Jul	Smokie + Lips + The Pleasers
Sat 30 Jul	Shakin' Stevens & the Sunsets (*at the Village Inn*)
Wed 3 Aug	Sheringham Carnival Dance
Fri 5 Aug	Kursaal Flyers + Rikki & The Last Days on Earth + Sidewinder
Sat 6 Aug	Raymond Froggatt + Kangeroo Alley
Fri 12 Aug	The 'O' Band + Quartz + Wilder
Sat 13 Aug	Souled Out (*ex JALN*) + Body Heat
Thu 18 Aug	Motorhead + The Count Bishops
Fri 19 Aug	Cromer Carnival Dance
Sat 20 Aug	Beano + Parchman Farm
Thu 25 Aug	John Miles + Krazy Kat or Trixter
Fri 26 Aug	Crazy Cavan & the Rhythm Rockers + Flight 56
Sat 27 Aug	Honky + Quasar
Mon 29 Aug	Camel + Andy Desmond
Fri 2 Sep	Trapeze + Remus Down Boulevard
Sat 3 Sep	Simon Bates + Soul Direction
Wed 7 Sep	Strife + Spiny Norman + Ruby Joe
Fri 9 Sep	Heavy Metal Kids + Trixter
Sat 10 Sep	Rokotto + World Champion Steel Band

Fri 16 Sep	Sam Apple Pie + No Dice
Sat 17 Sep	Sutherland Brothers & Quiver + City Boy
Fri 23 Sep	Steve Gibbons Band + American Train
Sat 24 Sep	Black Gorillas + Disco
Fri 30 Sep	Chris Spedding
Sat 1 Oct	Judge Dread
Fri 7 Oct	Hawkwind + Bethnal
Sat 8 Oct	Renaissance
Fri 14 Oct	Stray + Sidewinder
Sat 15 Oct	The Four Tops + Souled Out
Fri 21 Oct	Motorhead + The Winders
Sat 22 Oct	Roy Harpers Black Sheep + The Spriggans
Fri 28 Oct	Pat Travers
Sat 29 Oct	Foster Brothers + Whisper
Fri 4 Nov	Flying Saucers + Cruisers + Dynamite
Sat 5 Nov	Fabulous Poodles + Warren Harry
Fri 11 Nov	British Lions + Remus Down Boulevard
Sat 12 Nov	Screaming Lord Sutch + Dimitri
Fri 18 Nov	Shakin' Stevens & the Sunsets + Route 66
Sat 19 Nov	David Hamilton + Window
Fri 25 Nov	Split Enz + Rumblestrips
Sat 26 Nov	Linda Lewis + Alf Alpha
Fri 2 Dec	Motorhead *(Ian Dury originally advertised)* + Buster James Band. *(John Otway advertised as second support, but did not play.)*
Sat 3 Dec	Heavy Metal Kids + Pinto
Fri 9 Dec	Heatwave + Sex O Tech Disco
Sat 10 Dec	Jimmy James with his large new band + Dimitri *(tickets were printed for Hot Chocolate on this date)*
Sat 17 Dec	Mud + Memphis Index
Fri 23 Dec	Doctors of Madness + Prince Philip + Ian Mac Disco
Sat 24 Dec	Rockotto + Quasar + Ian Mac Disco
Fri 30 Dec	Buddy & the Dimes + Graham Fenton's Matchbox + Whirlwind + Ian Mac Disco
Sat 31 Dec	Raymond Froggatt + Kangaroo Alley + Ian Mac Disco

1978

Fri 6 Jan	Crazy Cavan + Route 66
Sat 7 Jan	All Stars Steel Band + Emily
Fri 13 Jan	Nutz + Buster James Band + Band With No Name
Sat 14 Jan	Carvells + Ian Mac Disco

Wed 18 Jan	Caravan + Meals
Thu 19 Jan	Judas Priest
Fri 20 Jan	Freddie 'Fingers' Lee + Second Opinion
Sat 21 Jan	City Boy
Thu 26 Jan	The Saints + Barry St James Album Show
Fri 27 Jan	Mike Berry + Route 66
Sat 28 Jan	Mac Kissoon + Ian Mac Disco
Fri 3 Feb	Split Enz + Johnny G
Sat 4 Feb	Osibisa + Spartacus
Fri 10 Feb	Heavy Metal Kids + Rumblestrips
Sat 11 Feb	Souled Out + Dimitri
Fri 17 Feb	Wire + Meals
Sat 18 Feb	Souled Out + Ian Mac Disco
Fri 24 Feb	XTC + The Secret
Sat 25 Feb	Alvin Stardust + Pin-Ups
Fri 3 Mar	Rich Kids
Sat 4 Mar	Supremes
Wed 8 Mar	Darts + Route 66
Thu 9 Mar	Renaissance
Fri 10 Mar	Barry St James Disco – Snake Pit Special
Sat 11 Mar	Rokotto + Ian Mac Disco
Wed 15 Mar	Snake Pit – in business as usual
Fri 17 Mar	Roy Wood
Sat 18 Mar	Gonzales + Warren Harry
Wed 22 Mar	Tom Robinson Band + 90 degrees inclusive
Thu 23 Mar	Slade
Sat 25 Mar	Geno Washington + Dimitri
Mon 27 Mar	Beano
Fri 31 Mar	Top Toaster + Tapper Zukie
Sat 1 Apr	Boomtown Rats + Black Slate
Fri 7 Apr	Wilko Johnson Band
Sat 8 Apr	Sweet Sensation
Fri 14 Apr	Dead Fingers Talk + Remould
Sat 15 Apr	Honky + Dimitri
Thu 20 Apr	Rory Gallagher + Joe O'Donnell
Fri 21 Apr	Freddie 'Fingers' Lee + The Flying Saucers
Sat 22 Apr	Ozo + Delegation
Fri 28 Apr	The Gladiators + Reggae Regulator + Explosion Disco
Sat 29 Apr	Suzi Quatro + Zorro
Fri 5 May	Heavy Metal Kids + The Star Jets
Sat 6 May	Memphis Index + Ram

Fri 12 May	Climax Blues Band + Dire Straits *(postponed)*
Sat 13 May	AC/DC + British Lions *(postponed)*
Fri 19 May	The Motors + Marseilles + The Jolt
Sat 20 May	Brass Construction + Rokotto
Mon 22 May	Slaughter and the Dogs
Fri 26 May	The Pirates + Route 66
Sat 27 May	Souled Out
Fri 2 Jun	Lindisfarne
Sat 3 Jun	Heatwave
Mon 5 Jun	AC/DC + British Lions
Wed 7 Jun	Snake Pit Disco – every Wed
Fri 9 Jun	Penetration + Kangaroo Alley
Sat 10 Jun	Johnny Cougar + Disco
Fri 16 Jun	Sailor
Sat 17 Jun	Osibisa
Fri 23 Jun	Trapeze + Kamakazee
Sat 24 Jun	Emperor Roscoe + Champion
Fri 30 Jun	Nashville Teens + Disco
Sat 1 Jul	Marty Wilde & the Wild Cats *(postponed)*
Sat 8 Jul	Marty Wilde & the Wild Cats
Thu 13 Jul	The Runaways *(did not play)*
Sat 15 Jul	The Searchers
Mon 17 Jul	Family Discos start
Tue 18 Jul	Family dance night with Magnus Swing Band + Disco
Sat 22 Jul	Rokotto + Spectrum Road Show
Sat 29 Jul	Love Affair + Ian Mac Disco
Mon 31 Jul	Family Disco weekdays
Sat 5 Aug	Dozy, Beaky, Mick and Titch + Missing Link Disco
Wed 9 Aug	Sheringham Carnival Dance
Sat 12 Aug	Swinging Blue Jeans + Ian Mac Disco
Wed 16 Aug	Rupert *(Tribute to Elvis)* + Disco
Fri 18 Aug	Cromer Carnival Dance
Sat 19 Aug	Marianne Faithfull + Ian Mac Disco
Sat 26 Aug	Slade + Disco
Mon 28 Aug	Paul Gambaccini + Liquid
Fri 1 Sep	Mac Curtis Rockabilly Show and Carl Simmons + Matchbox
Sat 2 Sep	Mojo's + Disco
Sat 9 Sep	The Realistics + Disco
Sat 16 Sep	Wildlife + English Rogues
Sat 23 Sep	Hi Tension + Spring Offensive
Fri 29 Sep	Rock Island Line + Memphis Index

Sat 30 Sep	Marshall Hain + Missing Link Disco
Wed 4 Oct	Snake Pit Disco every Wed & Fri unless group advertised
Sat 7 Oct	Reggae Regular + Ian Mac Disco
Fri 13 Oct	Split Enz *(cancelled)*
Sat 14 Oct	999 + Disco
Fri 20 Oct	Motorhead + Lightning Raiders
Sat 21 Oct	Raymond Froggatt + Kangaroo Alley
Fri 27 Oct	Third World
Sat 28 Oct	Billy J Kramer + Explosion Disco
Fri 3 Nov	Ma Tumbi
Sat 4 Nov	Dozy, Beaky, Mick and Titch
Sat 11 Nov	Budgie + Strife
Sat 18 Nov	The Bishops + Kangaroo Alley
Fri 24 Nov	The Rich Kids + TNT
Sat 25 Nov	Light of the World
Sat 2 Dec	Generation X + The Cure
Fri 8 Dec	Magazine + Neo
Sat 9 Dec	Beano + Disco
Fri 15 Dec	Tapper Zukie + Cygnus
Sat 16 Dec	Frankie Miller's Full House *(postponed)*
Fri 22 Dec	Wild Horses + Boy Bastin
Sat 23 Dec	Rokotto + Disco
Sat 30 Dec	Raymond Froggatt + Kangaroo Alley
Sun 31 Dec	New Year's Eve Party with DJ David Hamilton *(cancelled)*

1979

Sat 6 Jan	Sweet Sensation + Disco
Sat 13 Jan	David Hamilton + Dimitri
Sat 20 Jan	Simon Bates + Disco
Fri 26 Jan	Stiff Little Fingers *(cancelled)*
Sat 27 Jan	Frankie Miller
Tue 30 Jan	Suzi Quatro + Billy Robinson Disco
Fri 2 Feb	Wreckless Eric + The Softies
Sat 3 Feb	Crown Heights Affair
Sat 10 Feb	Gary Holton's Gems + Ian Mac Disco
Sat 17 Feb	Street Band + Trimmer and Jenkins *(ex Burlesque)*
Sat 24 Feb	Chairman of the Board
Fri 2 Mar	The Pretenders + Ian Mac's cult Disco
Sat 3 Mar	Brown Sugar
Tue 6 Mar	Robert Rental and the Normal

Fri 9 Mar	The Only Ones + Running Dogs
Sat 10 Mar	90 degrees inclusive
Fri 16 Mar	Pierre Moerlen's Gong + David Sancious
Sat 17 Mar	Culture and the Revolutionaires
Tue 20 Mar	Rock Against Racialism
Fri 23 Mar	Motorhead + Girlschool
Sat 24 Mar	The Movies + Bruce Woollie
Fri 30 Mar	The Cure + Bitch
Sat 31 Mar	Bram Tchaikovsky
Fri 6 Apr	Leargo + Disco
Sat 7 Apr	Dave Lee Travis + Trimmer and Jenkins + Missing Link Disco
Sat 14 Apr	Sore Throat + Dimitri
Mon 16 Apr	Simon Bates
Fri 20 Apr	Toyah Willcox + Zorro
Sat 21 Apr	Raymond Froggatt + Disco
Fri 27 Apr	Iggy Pop
Sat 28 Apr	Rokotto + Disco
Fri 4 May	XTC + NW10 + Bruce Woolley
Sat 5 May	Disco
Mon 7 May	John Otway & his band + Disco
Fri 11 May	The Doll + Disco
Sat 12 May	Light of the World + Disco
Fri 18 May	Violinski *(did not play)* + Bliss
Sat 19 May	Clint Eastwood + Disco
Thu 24 May	The Members + Pinpoint
Fri 25 May	Steel Pulse + Disco
Sat 26 May	Bumper Disco
Mon 28 May	Kid Jenson + Disco
Fri 1 Jun	The Records
Sat 2 Jun	Slade + Nick Van Eede
Fri 8 Jun	The Damned + The Ruts
Sat 9 Jun	Mud + Spitfire
Fri 15 Jun	No Dice
Sat 16 Jun	Beano
Fri 22 Jun	Gordon Giltrap
Sat 23 Jun	90 degrees inclusive
Fri 29 Jun	Ian Mac's Disco
Sat 30 Jun	Wilko Johnson's Solid Senders
Fri 6 Jul	Tourists + Disco
Sat 7 Jul	Charity Rock and Roll Festival. Freddie 'Fingers' Lee + Crazy Cavan & the Rhythm Rockers + Wild Angels + The Riot

	Rockers + The Jets + Memphis Index + Oregon Rock Disco
Fri 13 Jul	Gary Holton's Gems + Disco
Sat 14 Jul	The Pretenders + Interview
Sun 15 Jul	Nightly Summer Discos start
Fri 20 Jul	Voyager + Wildlife
Sat 21 Jul	Radio Luxembourg Starlight Road Show + The Fabulous Poodles + Trimmer & Jenkins
Wed 25 Jul	Sheringham Carnival Dance
Sat 28 Jul	Tradition
Wed 1 Aug	Sheringham Carnival Dance *(Fancy dress grand final)*
Fri 3 Aug	Frank Jennings + Crystalwood
Sat 4 Aug	Merton Parkas + Disco
Fri 10 Aug	The Bombers + Honky
Sat 11 Aug	Tribesman + Disco
Fri 17 Aug	Cromer Carnival Dance
Sat 18 Aug	Simon Bates + Dafne + The Tender Spots
Fri 24 Aug	Secret Affair + Purple Hearts + Back to Zero
Sat 25 Aug	Star Jets + Spitfire
Mon 27 Aug	Straight Eight + Roy Sundholm + The Dazzlers
Fri 31 Aug	Angelic Upstarts + Honky
Sat 1 Sep	Rokotto
Sat 8 Sep	Andy Peebles + Def Leppard
Fri 14 Sep	Budgie
Sat 15 Sep	Chairman of the Board
Fri 21 Sep	UK Subs + Urge
Sat 22 Sep	Souled Out
Tue 25 Sep	Penetration
Sat 29 Sep	The Chords + One Eyed Jacks
Fri 5 Oct	Merton Parkas
Sat 6 Oct	Siouxsie & the Banshees + The Cure
Fri 12 Oct	Slaughter & the Dogs
Sat 13 Oct	Sore Throat
Thu 18 Oct	Judie Tzuke
Fri 19 Oct	Girlschool
Sat 20 Oct	Mike Read
Fri 26 Oct	Gillan + Randy California & Friends + Speedometers
Sat 27 Oct	Ruts + The Flies
Fri 2 Nov	Writz
Sat 3 Nov	Kandidate
Tue 6 Nov	Steve Hackett
Wed 7 Nov	Buzzcocks + Joy Division

Fri 9 Nov	Caravan
Sat 10 Nov	Bumper Disco with extra prizes
Fri 16 Nov	Richard and Linda Thompson + Bob Davenport
Sat 17 Nov	Bumper Disco evening
Fri 23 Nov	Bumper Disco evening
Sat 24 Nov	Tours + Paul Gambaccini
Fri 30 Nov	Screams
Sat 1 Dec	The Dickies + Chelsea
Sat 8 Dec	Purple Hearts
Fri 14 Dec	Secret Affair + Squire
Sat 15 Dec	Dr Feelgood + Philip Rambow
Fri 21 Dec	Matchbox
Sat 22 Dec	Super Bumper Disco + Beano
Mon 24 Dec	Super Bumper Disco
Fri 28 Dec	Super Bumper Disco
Mon 31 Dec	Raymond Froggatt

1980

Discos were advertised for most Fridays when no band shown

Sat 5 Jan	Marmalade
Sat 12 Jan	Disco
Sat 19 Jan	Crazy Cavan & the Rhythm Rockers + Beaky & the Bobcats
Sat 26 Jan	Ian Mac's Disco + Running Dogs
Fri 1 Feb	The Pretenders + UB40
Sat 2 Feb	Rockpile + Fabulous Thunderbirds
Fri 8 Feb	Def Leppard + Magnum
Sat 9 Feb	Bumper Disco
Sat 16 Feb	Saxon + Iron Maiden
Sat 23 Feb	Johnny Storm & Memphis + Rhythm Hawk + Bop Street
Fri 29 Feb	The Original Mirrors
Sat 1 Mar	Elvis Costello
Sat 8 Mar	The Psychedelic Furs + Propaganda
Fri 14 Mar	Rokotto
Sat 15 Mar	Motorhead + Subway
Fri 21 Mar	Magnum + Tygers of Pan Tang
Sat 22 Mar	The Lambrettas
Fri 28 Mar	Johnny Carroll + Judy Lindsey + The Dixie Phoenix
Sat 29 Mar	Headline + Disco
Wed 2 Apr	Tramps Ball, free supper
Sat 5 Apr	B A Robertson + Film Stars

Wed 9 Apr	Snake Pit Disco
Fri 11 Apr	Diamond Head
Sat 12 Apr	Kid Jenson
Fri 18 Apr	Secret Affair + The Step
Sat 19 Apr	Ian Mac's Disco, free supper for all
Wed 23 Apr	Noel Edmonds
Fri 25 Apr	The Cure
Wed 7 May	Suzi Quatro
Fri 9 May	Wild Horses + McKitty
Sat 10 May	Dave Lee Travis
Fri 16 May	Angel Witch + Radio Caroline Road Show
Sat 17 May	New Muzik
Fri 23 May	Vapors + Winner
Sat 24 May	Gary Glitter & the Glitter Band + Feet First
Mon 26 May	Girl
Fri 30 May	Tom Robinson & Sector 27 *(cancelled)*
Sat 31 May	Chuck Berry + Red Lightning Boogie Band
Fri 6 Jun	Iron Maiden + Praying Mantis + DJ Neal Kay
Sat 7 Jun	UB40 + Honey Bane + Fatal Microbes
Sat 14 Jun	Toyah Willcox + Disco
Thu 19 Jun	Steve Harley & Cockney Rebel
Sat 21 Jun	Budgie + Vardis
Sat 28 Jun	Slade + Taurus
Sat 5 Jul	Denny Laine *(postponed)*
Fri 11 Jul	Hawkwind + Alverna Gunn
Sat 12 Jul	Samson + Sledgehammer or Troubleshooter
Mon 14 Jul	Family Discos start Sun, Mon, Tue, Thu & Fri
Wed 16 Jul	Sheringham Carnival Dance
Thu 17 Jul	Wayne Kennedy's Flash Cats
Fri 18 Jul	Dark Star + Chevy + Thumper
Sat 19 Jul	Stiff Little Fingers + Weapon of Peace
Wed 23 Jul	Radio Luxembourg Road Show
Fri 25 Jul	Witchfynde + Gaskin
Sat 26 Jul	Trespass + Bastille
Fri 1 Aug	Krakan + Wildfire
Sat 2 Aug	Disco
Wed 6 Aug	Sheringham Carnival Dance
Fri 8 Aug	Denny Laine Band + Exit
Sat 9 Aug	The Q Tips + The Espressos + The Blades
Wed 13 Aug	Sheringham Carnival Fancy Dress
Fri 15 Aug	Angel Witch

Sat 16 Aug	Charity Rock and Roll Festival. Crazy Cavan & the Rhythm Rockers + The Jets + Dynamite + TNT + The Blue Cat Trio + Big K Disco
Thu 21 Aug	Iron Maiden + Praying Mantis + The Angels
Fri 22 Aug	Cromer Carnival Dance
Sat 23 Aug	Odyssey *(or Ded Ringers)*
Mon 25 Aug	Piranhas *(or Body Snatchers)* + The Cheaters + Capital 539 Road Show with Steve Parker
Sat 30 Aug	9 Below Zero + Zilch
Fri 5 Sep	Blizzard of Ozz *(advertised as 'Law')*
Sat 6 Sep	Rokotto
Sat 13 Sep	Heavy Metal Sound House Disco with DJ Neal Kay + Ethel the Frog + Gaskin
Fri 19 Sep	Michael Schenker Group *(cancelled)*
Sat 20 Sep	Atomic Rooster + Tutch + Paralex
Sat 27 Sep	The Revillos + Zilch + Red Letters + V-Disc
Fri 3 Oct	Tygers of Pan Tang + Shock Treatment
Sat 4 Oct	Beano + Disco
Sat 11 Oct	Dead Kennedys
Fri 17 Oct	Slade + Straight 8
Sat 18 Oct	Simple Minds + Music for Pleasure + Zilch
Fri 24 Oct	Nick Turner's Inner City Unit + Money
Sat 25 Oct	UK Subs + Citizens + The Adicts
Fri 31 Oct	The Four Tops
Sat 1 Nov	Splodgenessabounds
Wed 5 Nov	Uriah Heep + Samson + Spider
Sat 8 Nov	The Shades + The Cruisers
Sat 15 Nov	Adam & the Ants + God's Toys
Fri 21 Nov	Girlschool + Angel Witch + Tank
Sat 22 Nov	The Damned + The Adicts + The Straps
Fri 28 Nov	Needles + G Squad + Moscow Olympics + Exploding Hamsters
Fri 5 Dec	Wildlife + Alverna Gunn + Angels + Winner *(Winner did not play)*
Sat 6 Dec	Generation X
Sat 13 Dec	Bad Manners *(did not play)* + Shock
Thu 18 Dec	Bow Wow Wow
Fri 19 Dec	Steve Harley & Cockney Rebel + Straight 8
Sat 20 Dec	Budgie + Wildlife + Alverna Gunn
Wed 24 Dec	Standing Room Only
Sat 27 Dec	Snakepit Disco

Wed 31 Dec   Geno Washington

1981

Sat 3 Jan	Snakepit Disco
Sat 17 Jan	The Look
Fri 23 Jan	Freddie 'Fingers' Lee + White Lightning
Sat 24 Jan	Racey + Toys
Fri 30 Jan	Steel Pulse
Sat 31 Jan	Toyah Willcox + Huang Chung
Sat 7 Feb	Wilko Johnson
Sat 14 Feb	Matchbox + Quarter Moon
Sat 21 Feb	Gordon Giltrap
Fri 27 Feb	Weapon of Peace + Denizens
Sat 28 Feb	UK Decay + The Adicts + The Lines
Thu 5 Mar	The Stranglers + Modern Eon
Sat 7 Mar	UK Subs + The Stiffs + Anti Pasti
Fri 13 Mar	The Kinks
Sat 14 Mar	Chevy + Shock Treatment
Fri 20 Mar	Stray Cats + Barracudas *(cancelled)*
Sat 21 Mar	Pole Cats + Motovatin'
Wed 25 Mar	Odyssey + Billy Robinson Disco
Fri 27 Mar	Motorhead + Tank
Sat 28 Mar	Gang of Four + Pereubu + Delta 5
Sat 4 Apr	Osibisa
Fri 10 Apr	Girlschool *(cancelled)*
Sat 11 Apr	Culture + Far Image
Thu 16 Apr	The Spizzles + Department S
Sat 18 Apr	Flashcats + Oregon Rock Record Hop
Fri 24 Apr	Vardis + 720
Sat 25 Apr	Zilch + The Rapids
Sat 2 May	Lionheart + Alverna Gunn
Fri 8 May	Tygers of Pan Tang + Magnum + Alcatraz
Sat 9 May	Ruts DC
Fri 15 May	Girlschool + A II Z
Sat 16 May	Sam Apple Pie
Fri 22 May	The Members
Sat 23 May	Chevy + Shock Treatment + Remould
Mon 25 May	Paul Burnett + Zilch
Fri 29 May	Undertones + TV21
Sat 30 May	Crazy Cavan + Motovatin'

Sat 6 Jun	Budgie + Trespass
Fri 12 Jun	Praying Mantis + Export
Sat 13 Jun	Aerial FX
Fri 19 Jun	Classix Nouveaux + Wasted Youth + Our Daughter's Wedding
Sat 20 Jun	Diamond Head + Silverwing
Fri 26 Jun	Discharge + Exploited + Anti Pasti *(the Apocalypse Now tour)*
Sat 27 Jun	Aswad
Fri 3 Jul	George Melly in Concert *(Charity Dance)*
Sat 11 Jul	Sounds Atlantic Road Show featuring More
Sat 18 Jul	Freddie 'Fingers' Lee
Mon 20 Jul	Family Discos nightly except Snake Pit Disco Wed
Fri 24 Jul	Magnum + Dark Star
Sat 15 Aug	Flying Saucers + Big K's Disco
Tue 18 Aug	Blue Oyster Cult *(advertised as 'Soft White Underbelly')* + Quartz
Sat 22 Aug	Loch Ness Monster – ring for clues *(cancelled)*
Sat 5 Sep	Bow Wow Wow + The Higsons
Sat 12 Sep	720 + Street Fighter
Sat 19 Sep	Tobruck + Clientelle + Stranger Station
Fri 25 Sep	Echo & the Bunnymen
Sat 26 Sep	The Stargazers + Oregon Rock Record Hop
Wed 30 Sep	Nazareth + Vic Vergat
Sat 3 Oct	Renaissance
Fri 9 Oct	John Miles + Devetos
Sat 10 Oct	Clint Eastwood + General Saint
Fri 16 Oct	Theatre of Hate + King Pleasure
Sat 17 Oct	Gordon Giltrap
Fri 23 Oct	UK Subs + Long Tall Shortie
Sat 24 Oct	Stray *(did not turn up)* + Alverna Gunn + Grinder
Thu 29 Oct	Madness + Belle Stars
Fri 30 Oct	Flying Saucers
Sat 31 Oct	The Gladiators
Sat 7 Nov	Anti Pasti + Vice Squad + Chrongen
Sat 14 Nov	Rage and the Bailey Brothers
Fri 20 Nov	Samson + 720
Sat 21 Nov	Ten Pole Tudor + Zilch
Fri 27 Nov	The Adicts + Special Duties + Section A
Sat 28 Nov	Dr Feelgood
Thu 3 Dec	Slade + Spider
Sat 5 Dec	The Damned
Fri 11 Dec	9 Below Zero *(cancelled)*
Sat 12 Dec	Rose Tattoo + Lightning Raiders *(cancelled)*

Sat 19 Dec	Suzi Quatro
Thu 24 Dec	King Cole Disco
Thu 31 Dec	The Billy Robinson Disco

1982

Sat 9 Jan	Freddie 'Fingers' Lee
Thu 21 Jan	Sad Café
Fri 19 Feb	Tygers of Pan Tang + Inner Vision
Sat 27 Feb	Crazy Cavan
Fri 5 Mar	Theatre of Hate
Sat 6 Mar	Magnum + Trouble
Thu 11 Mar	The Four Tops
Fri 12 Mar	King Crimson
Sat 20 Mar	Secret Affair
Sat 3 Apr	Diamond Head + Airbridge
Sat 10 Apr	Freddie 'Fingers' Lee + Oregon Rock Disco
Fri 16 Apr	Classix Nouveaux + Cuddly Toys
Fri 23 Apr	Tank
Sat 1 May	Vardis + Scaramoosh
Sat 8 May	Angel Witch + Portland
Sat 15 May	Camel + Jon Benns
Sat 22 May	Wishbone Ash + Mama's Boys
Sun 23 May	Roller-skating starts every Tue and Sun
Sat 19 Jun	Talisman *('Last Concert')*
Wed 28 Jul	Denim *(Sheringham Carnival Dance)*
Sat 28 Aug	Marty Wilde & the Wild Cats + Fourmost *(Sheringham and Cromer Round Table fund raiser for the Spinal Research Trust)*

1983

Fri 20 May	Magnum + Santers
Fri 1 Jul	Motorhead + Anvil
Sat 10 Dec	Magnum *(cancelled due to illness)*
Sat 17 Dec	Hanoi Rocks + Saigon

1984

Sat 7 Jan	Last evening to skate
Wed 11 Jan	Last Disco